GOKKUN PUCHO™

Volume 1

by Ema Toyama

HAMBURG // LONDON // LOS ANGELES // TOKYO

Pixie Pop: Gokkun Pucho Volume 1
Created by Ema Toyama

Translation - Aska Yoshizu
Associate Editor - Hope Donovan
Retouch and Lettering - Michael Paolilli
Production Artist - Jennifer Carbajal
Graphic Designer - James Lee

Editor - Katherine Schilling
Digital Imaging Manager - Chris Buford
Pre-Production Supervisor - Erika Terriquez
Art Director - Anne Marie Horne
Production Manager - Elisabeth Brizzi
Managing Editor - Vy Nguyen
VP of Production - Ron Klamert
Editor-in-Chief - Rob Tokar
Publisher - Mike Kiley
President and C.O.O. - John Parker
C.E.O. and Chief Creative Officer - Stuart Levy

A  Manga

TOKYOPOP Inc.
5900 Wilshire Blvd. Suite 2000
Los Angeles, CA 90036

E-mail: info@TOKYOPOP.com
Come visit us online at www.TOKYOPOP.com

ISBN: 978-1-59816-813-6

First TOKYOPOP printing: February 2007
10 9 8 7 6 5 4 3 2
Printed in the USA

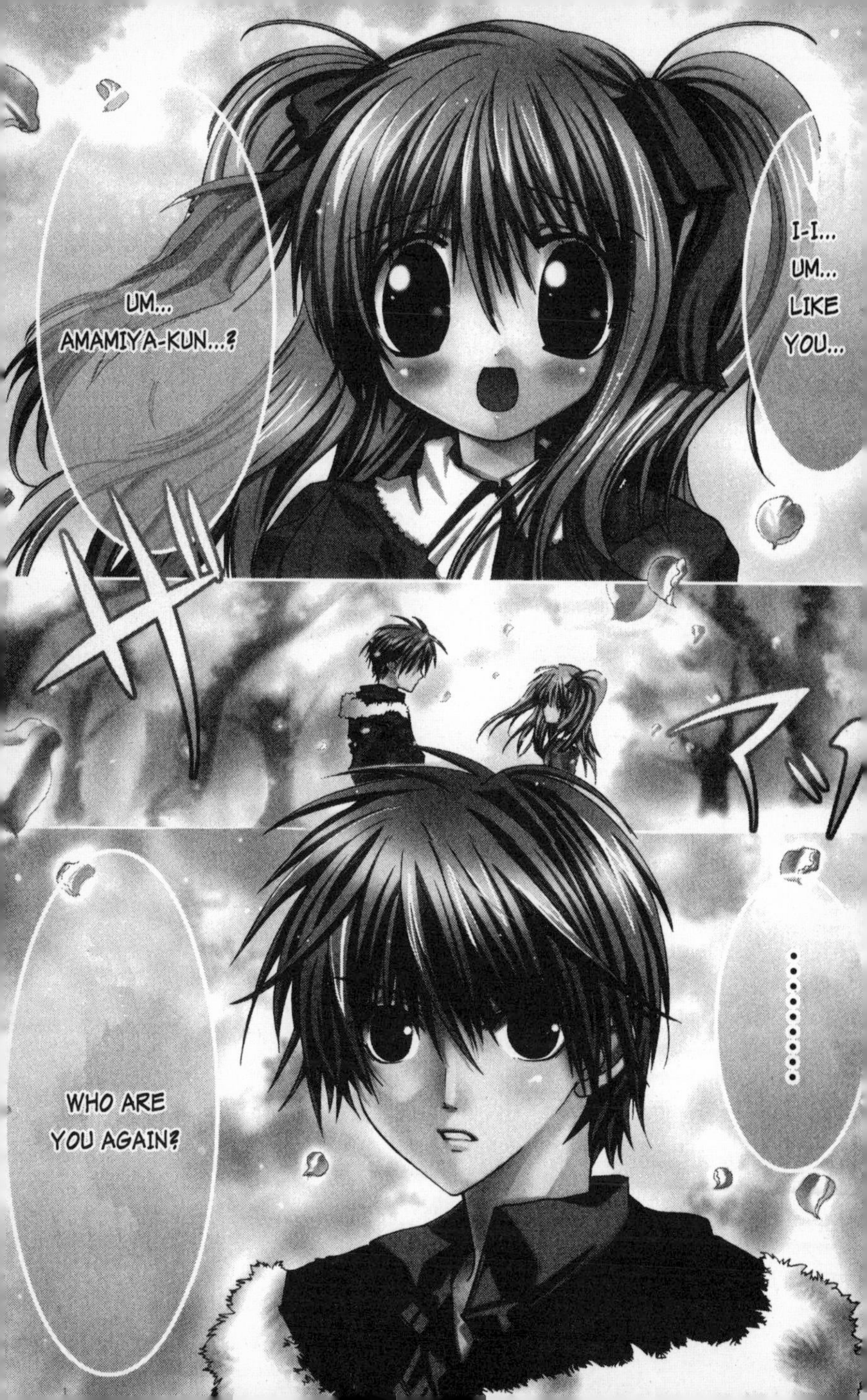
I-I... UM... LIKE YOU...
UM... AMAMIYA-KUN...?
....
WHO ARE YOU AGAIN?

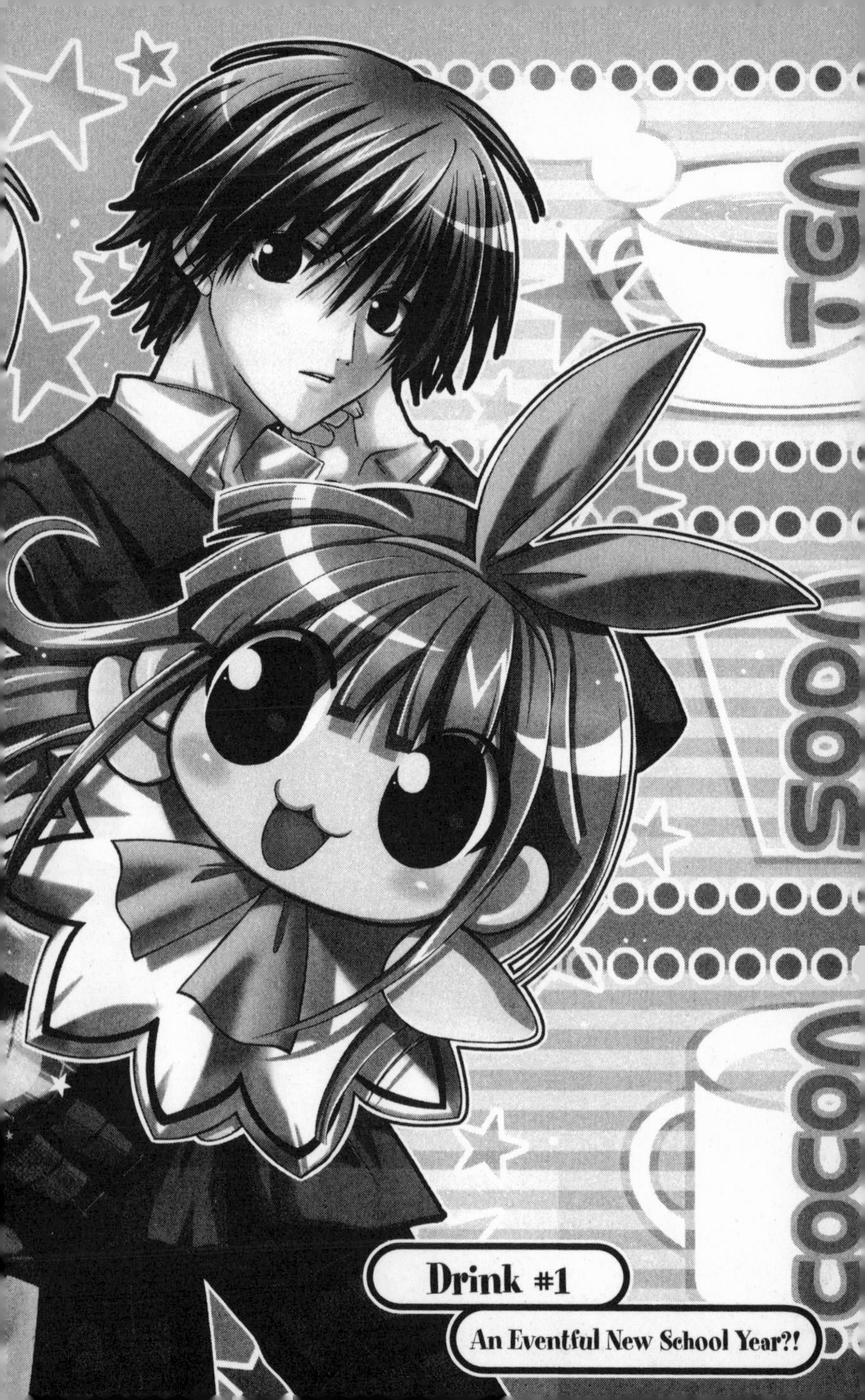
Drink #1
An Eventful New School Year?!

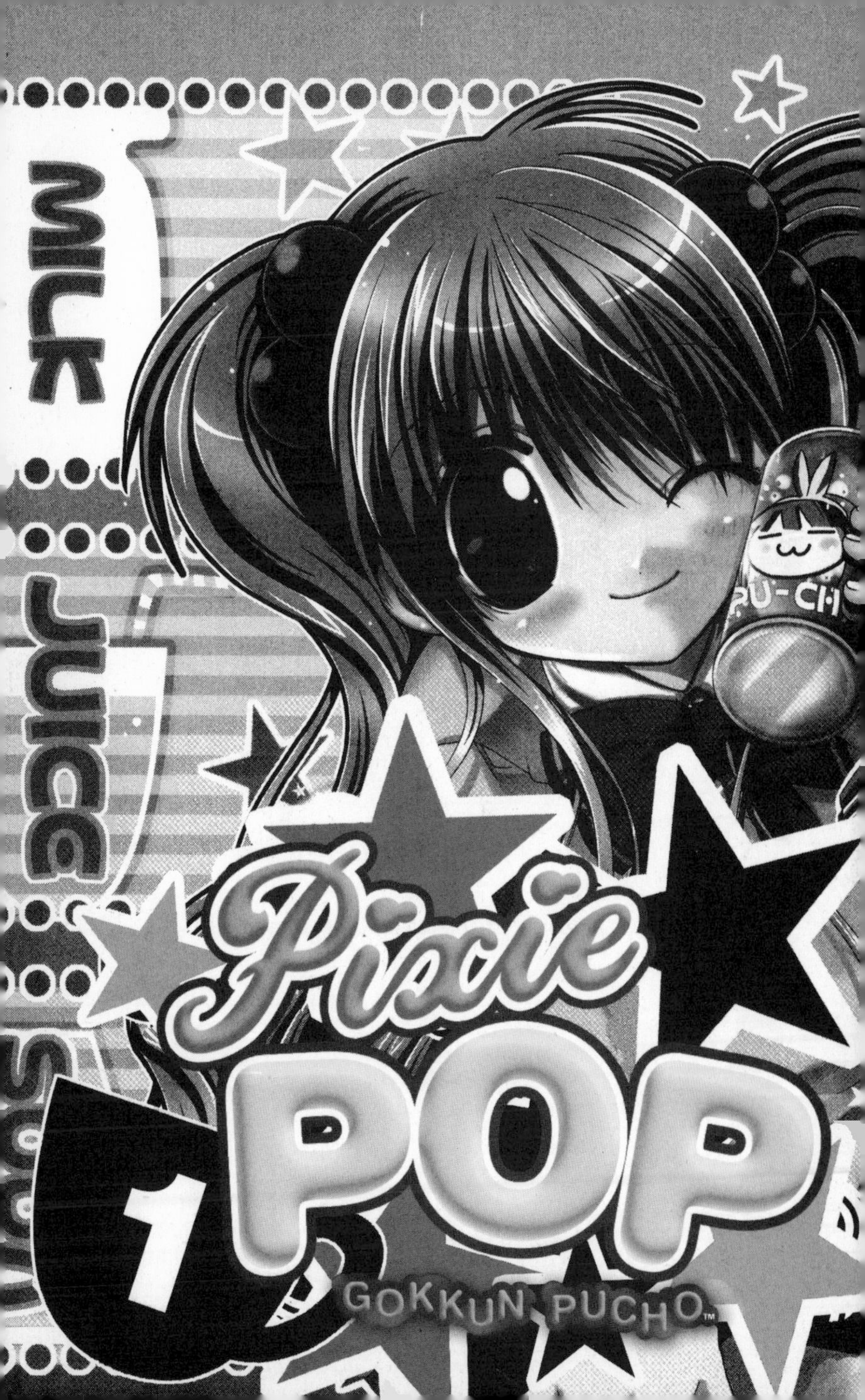
MILK JUICE
Pixie
POP
1
GOKKUN PUCHO™

Cafe Clover

Hi, nice to meet you! I'm Ema Toyama.
Thank you for picking up my first book!
Although I'm still new to drawing manga,
I work very hard drawing each story, and
I'd be tickled if you enjoy them! Please,
read all the way to the end! ♪

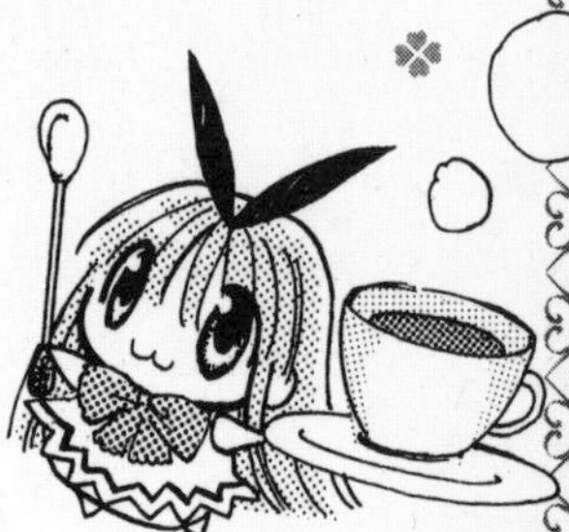

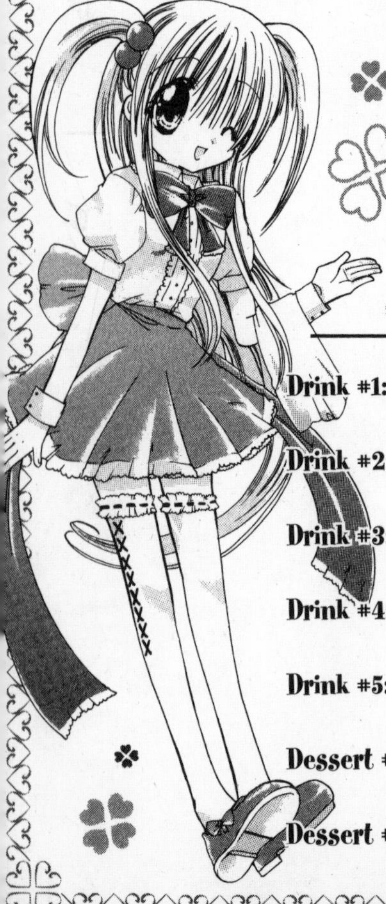

MENU

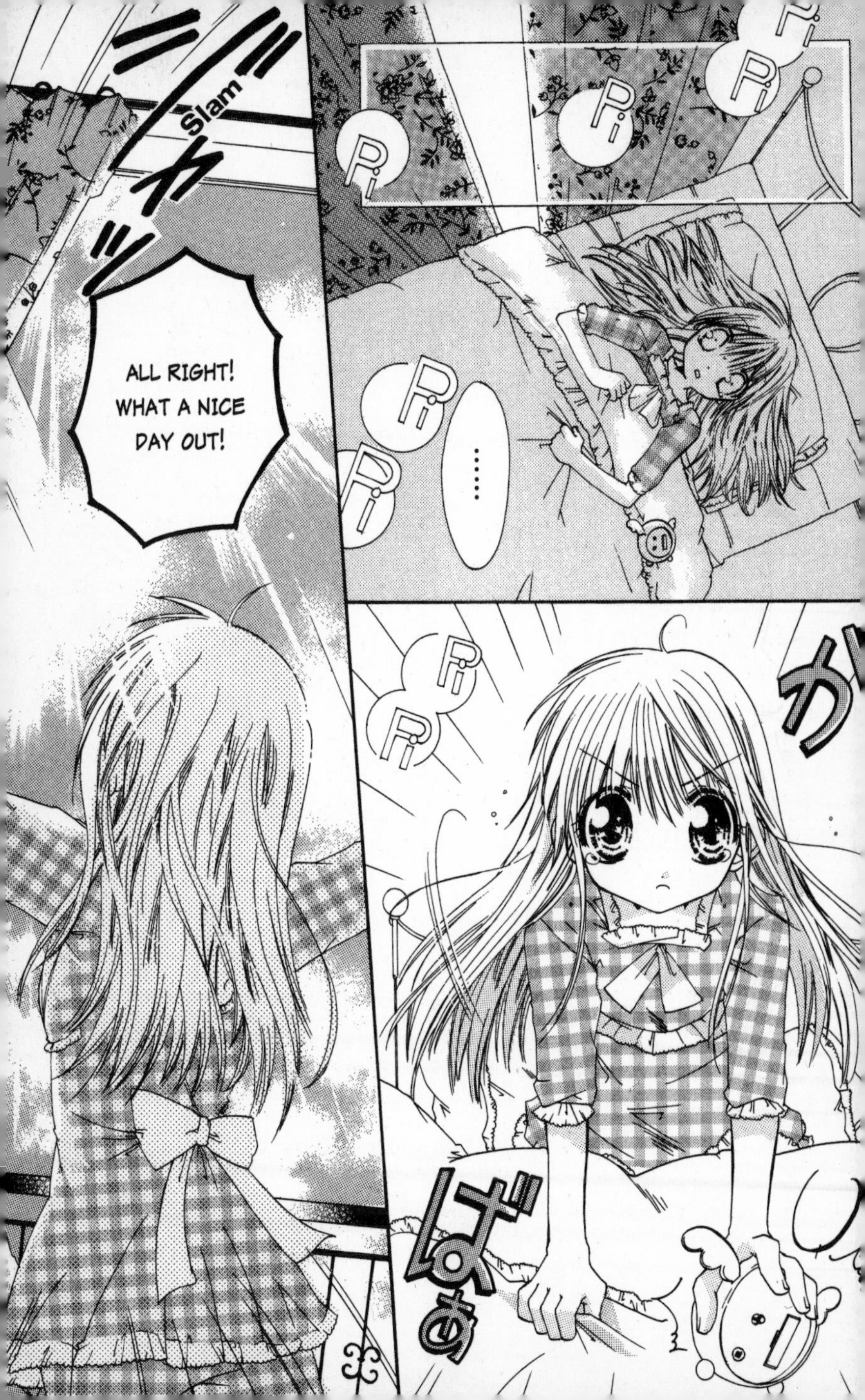

Pi
Pi
Pi
Pi
Pi
……
Pi
Pi
Pi
Pi
Slam
ALL RIGHT! WHAT A NICE DAY OUT!

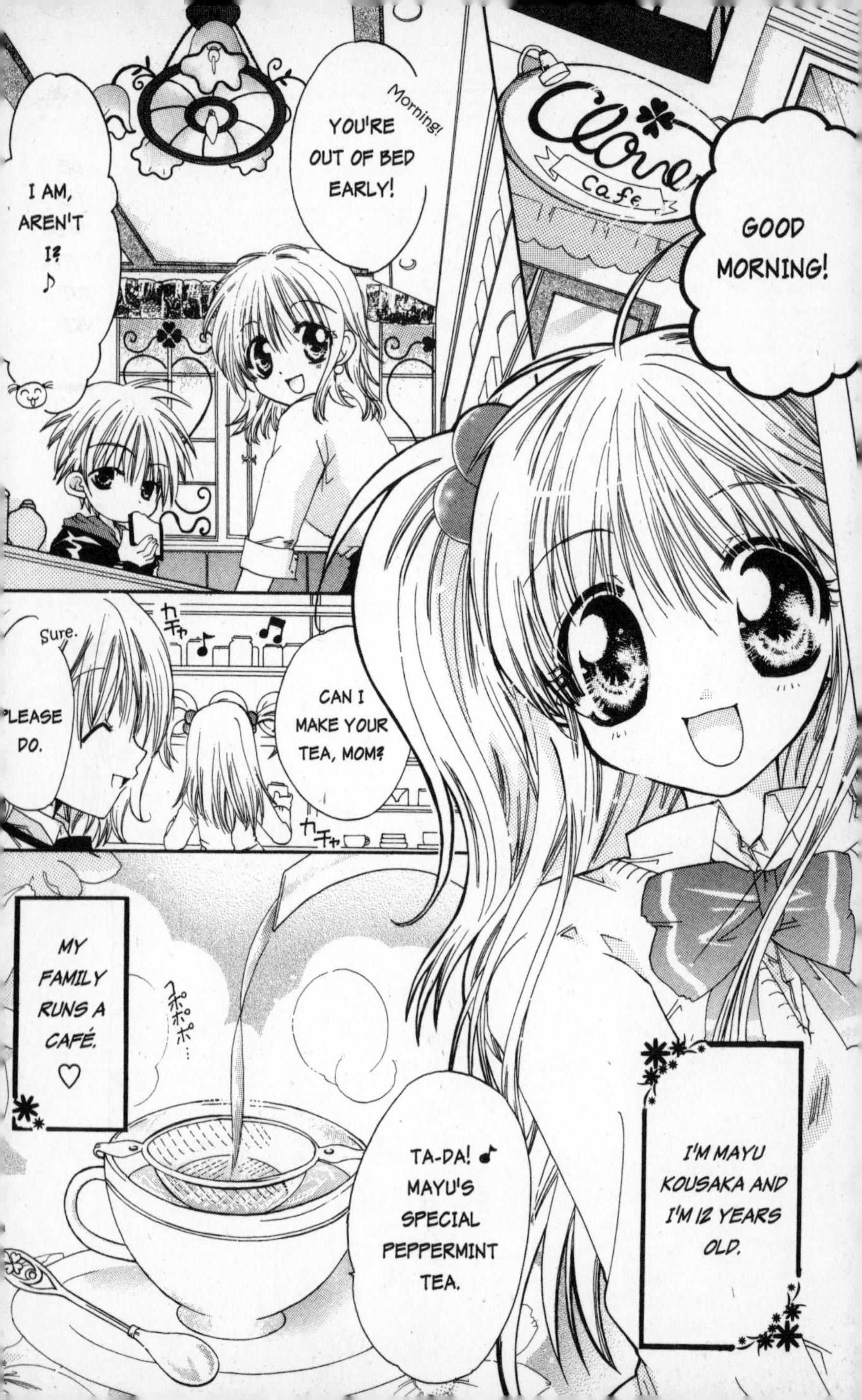
GOOD MORNING!
Morning!
YOU'RE OUT OF BED EARLY!
I AM, AREN'T I? ♪
カチャ
CAN I MAKE YOUR TEA, MOM?
カチャ
Sure.
PLEASE DO.
TA-DA! ♪ MAYU'S SPECIAL PEPPERMINT TEA.
ポポポ…
MY FAMILY RUNS A CAFÉ. ♡
I'M MAYU KOUSAKA AND I'M 12 YEARS OLD.

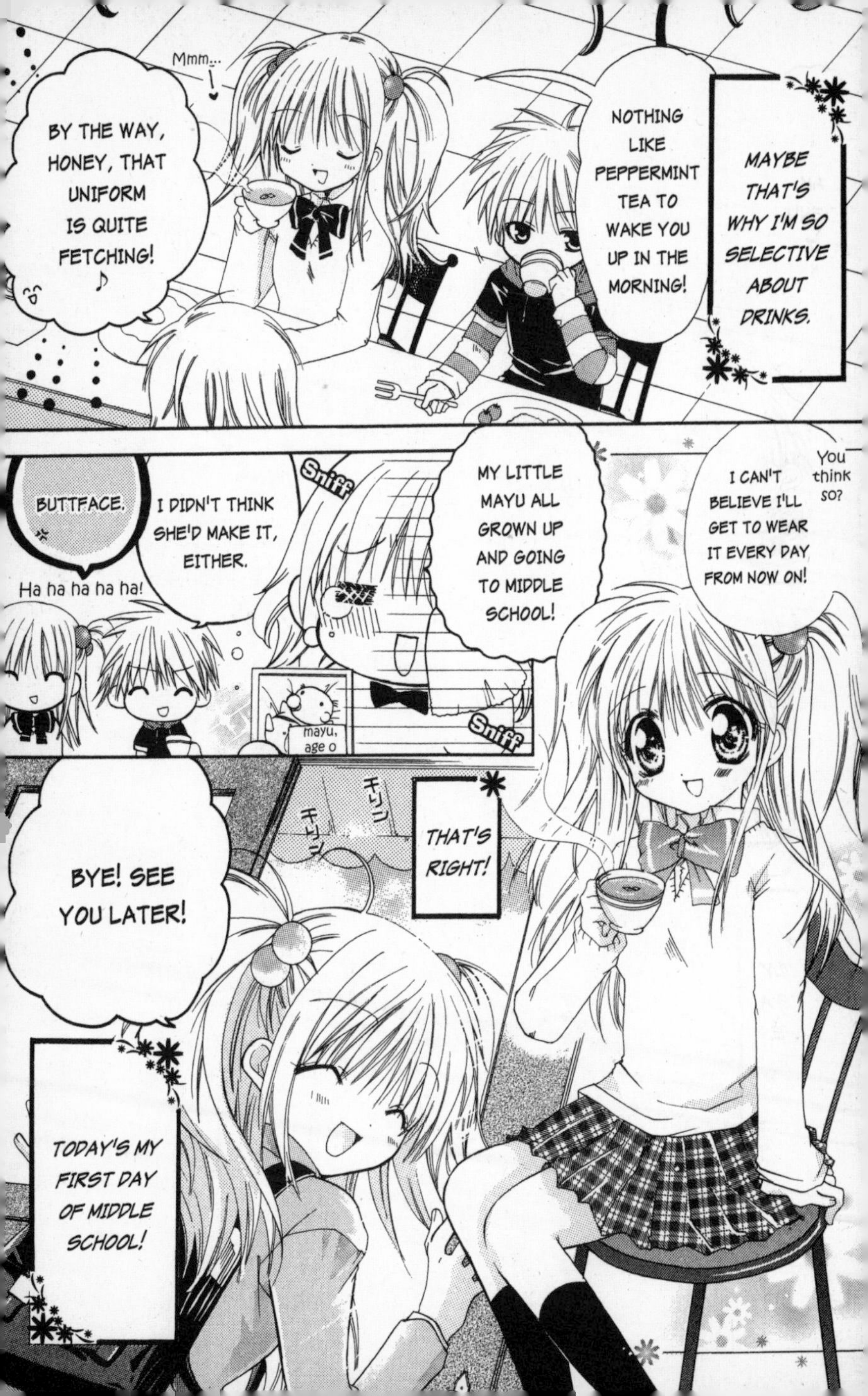
MAYBE THAT'S WHY I'M SO SELECTIVE ABOUT DRINKS.
NOTHING LIKE PEPPERMINT TEA TO WAKE YOU UP IN THE MORNING!
Mmm...
BY THE WAY, HONEY, THAT UNIFORM IS QUITE FETCHING! ♪
I CAN'T BELIEVE I'LL GET TO WEAR IT EVERY DAY FROM NOW ON!
You think so?
MY LITTLE MAYU ALL GROWN UP AND GOING TO MIDDLE SCHOOL!
Sniff
Sniff
mayu, age 0
I DIDN'T THINK SHE'D MAKE IT, EITHER.
BUTTFACE.
Ha ha ha ha ha!
THAT'S RIGHT!
TODAY'S MY FIRST DAY OF MIDDLE SCHOOL!
チリン
チリン
BYE! SEE YOU LATER!

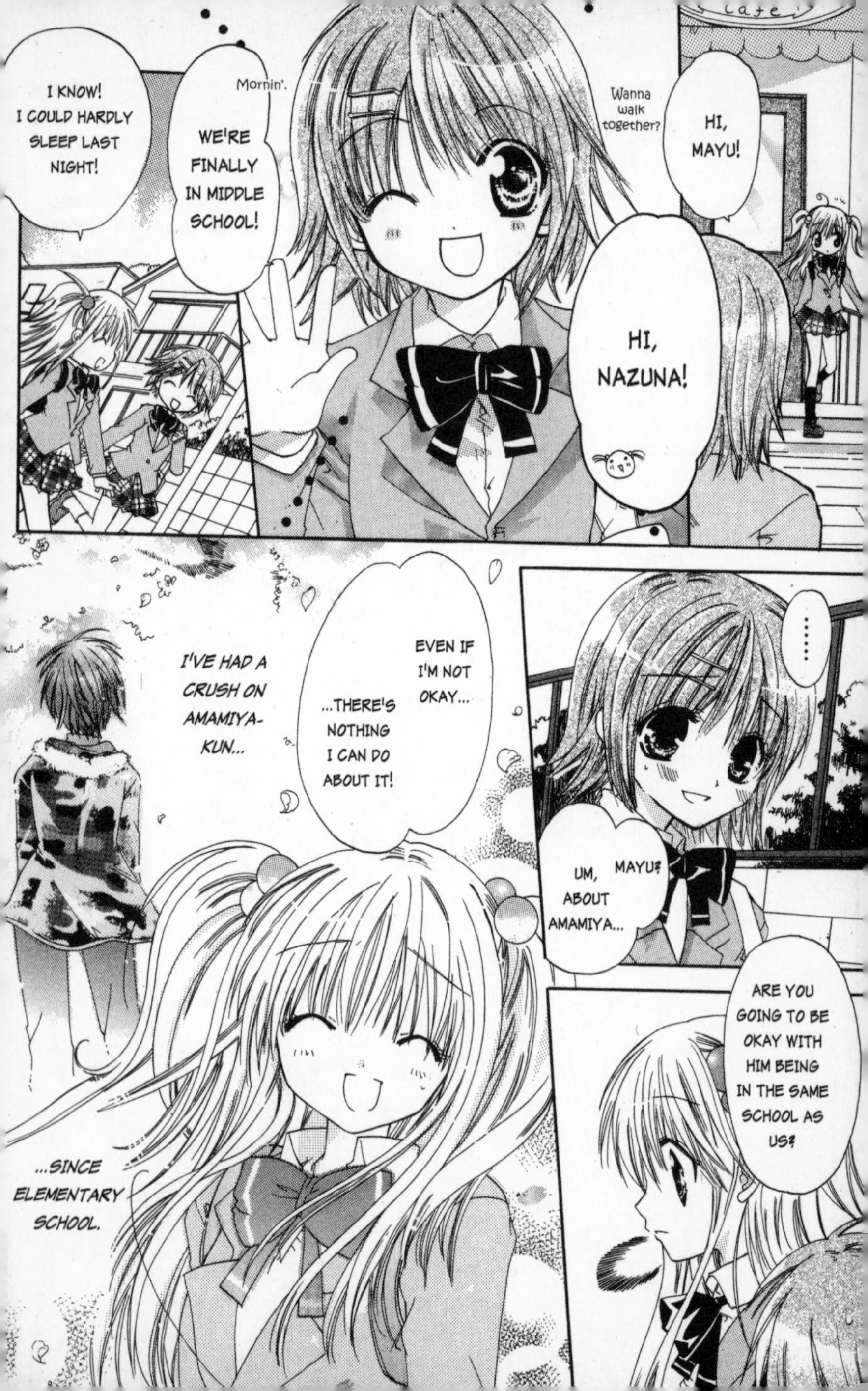
HI, MAYU!
Wanna walk together?
HI, NAZUNA!
WE'RE FINALLY IN MIDDLE SCHOOL!
Mornin'.
I KNOW! I COULD HARDLY SLEEP LAST NIGHT!
......
MAYU?
UM, ABOUT AMAMIYA...
ARE YOU GOING TO BE OKAY WITH HIM BEING IN THE SAME SCHOOL AS US?
EVEN IF I'M NOT OKAY...
...THERE'S NOTHING I CAN DO ABOUT IT!
I'VE HAD A CRUSH ON AMAMIYA-KUN...
...SINCE ELEMENTARY SCHOOL.

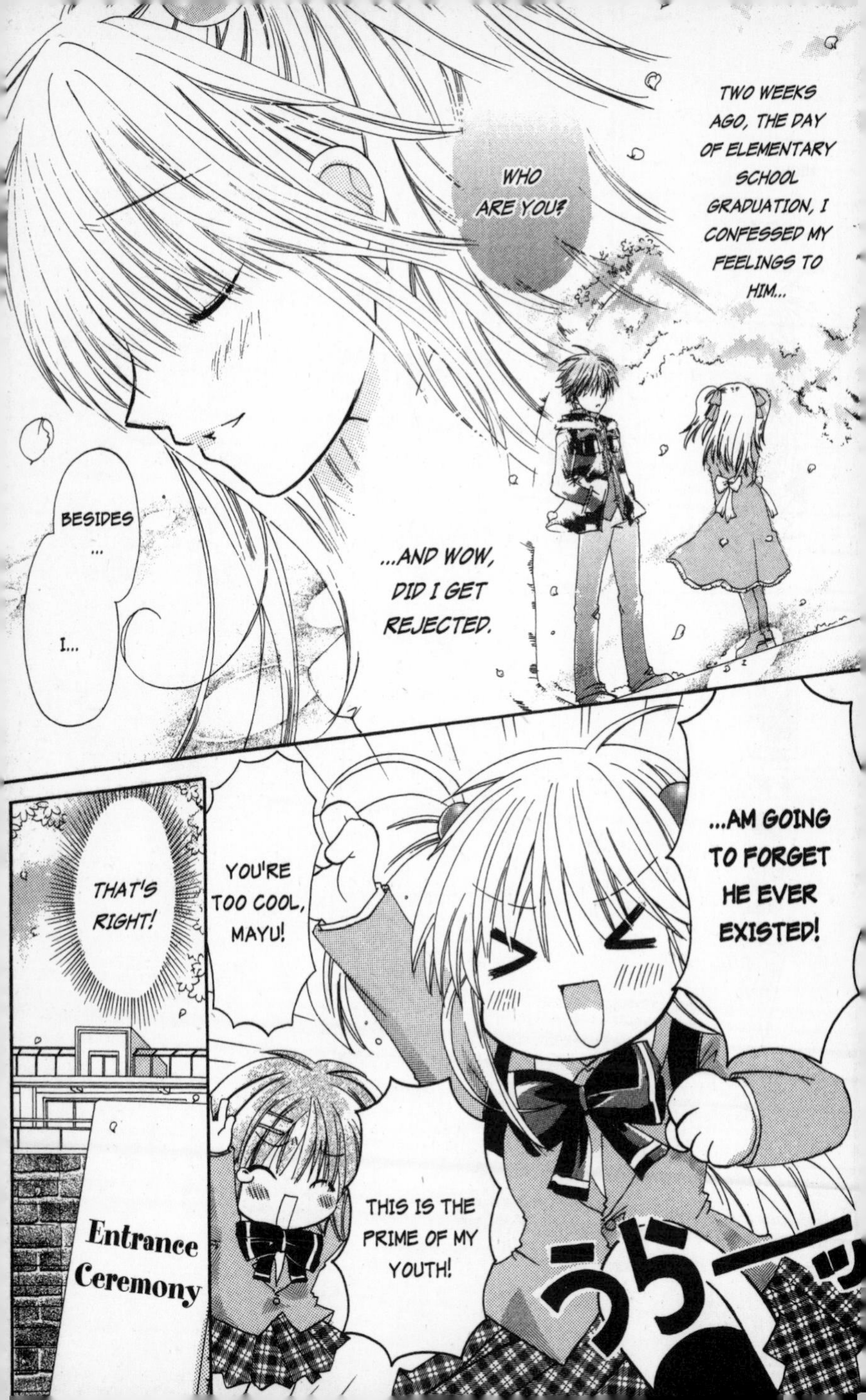
TWO WEEKS AGO, THE DAY OF ELEMENTARY SCHOOL GRADUATION, I CONFESSED MY FEELINGS TO HIM...
WHO ARE YOU?
...AND WOW, DID I GET REJECTED.
BESIDES ... I...
...AM GOING TO FORGET HE EVER EXISTED!
YOU'RE TOO COOL, MAYU!
THAT'S RIGHT!
うらーッ
THIS IS THE PRIME OF MY YOUTH!
Entrance Ceremony

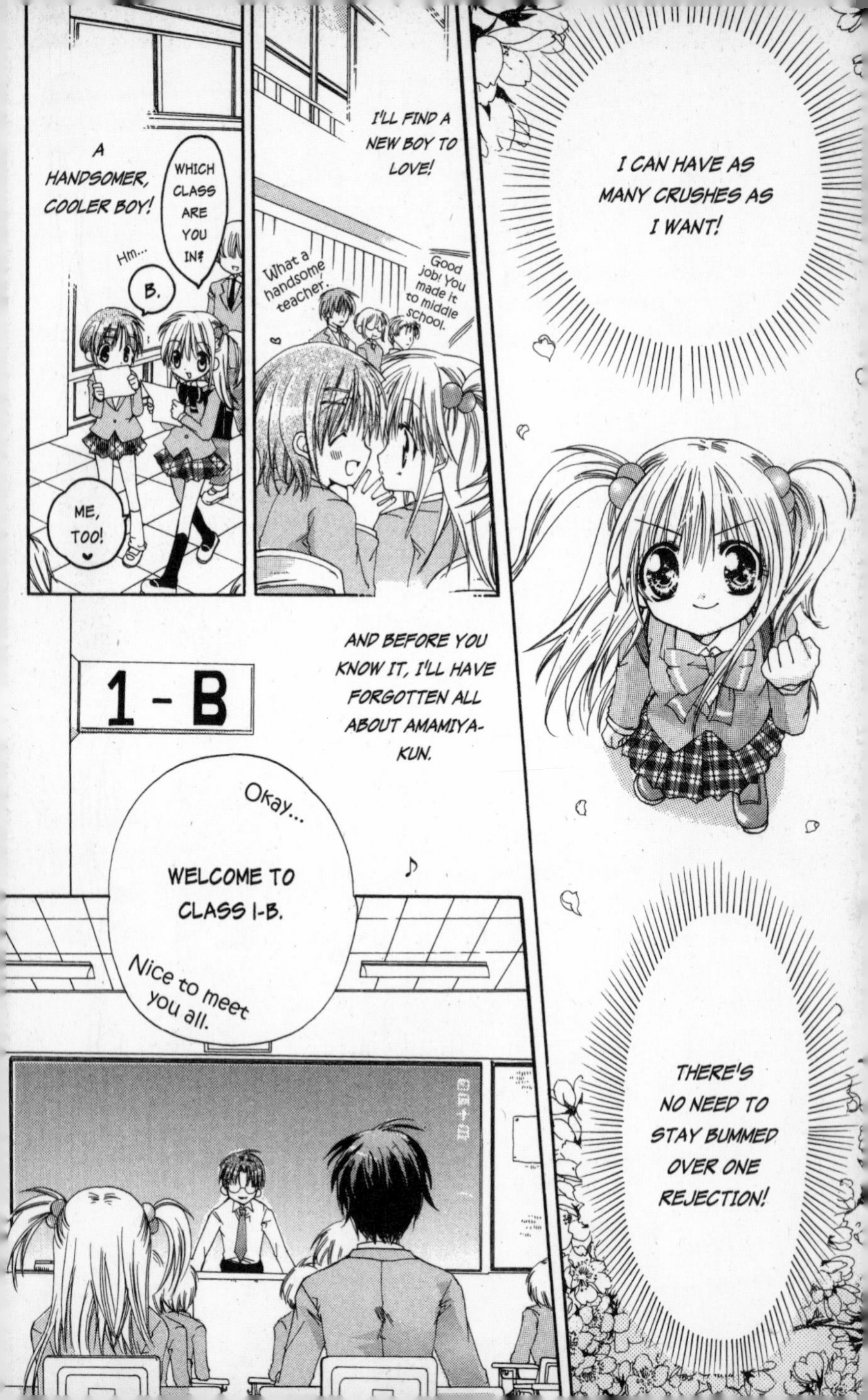
I CAN HAVE AS MANY CRUSHES AS I WANT!
THERE'S NO NEED TO STAY BUMMED OVER ONE REJECTION!
I'LL FIND A NEW BOY TO LOVE!
Good job! You made it to middle school.
What a handsome teacher.
A HANDSOMER, COOLER BOY!
WHICH CLASS ARE YOU IN?
Hm...
B.
ME, TOO!
1 - B
AND BEFORE YOU KNOW IT, I'LL HAVE FORGOTTEN ALL ABOUT AMAMIYA-KUN.
Okay...
WELCOME TO CLASS 1-B.
Nice to meet you all.
♪

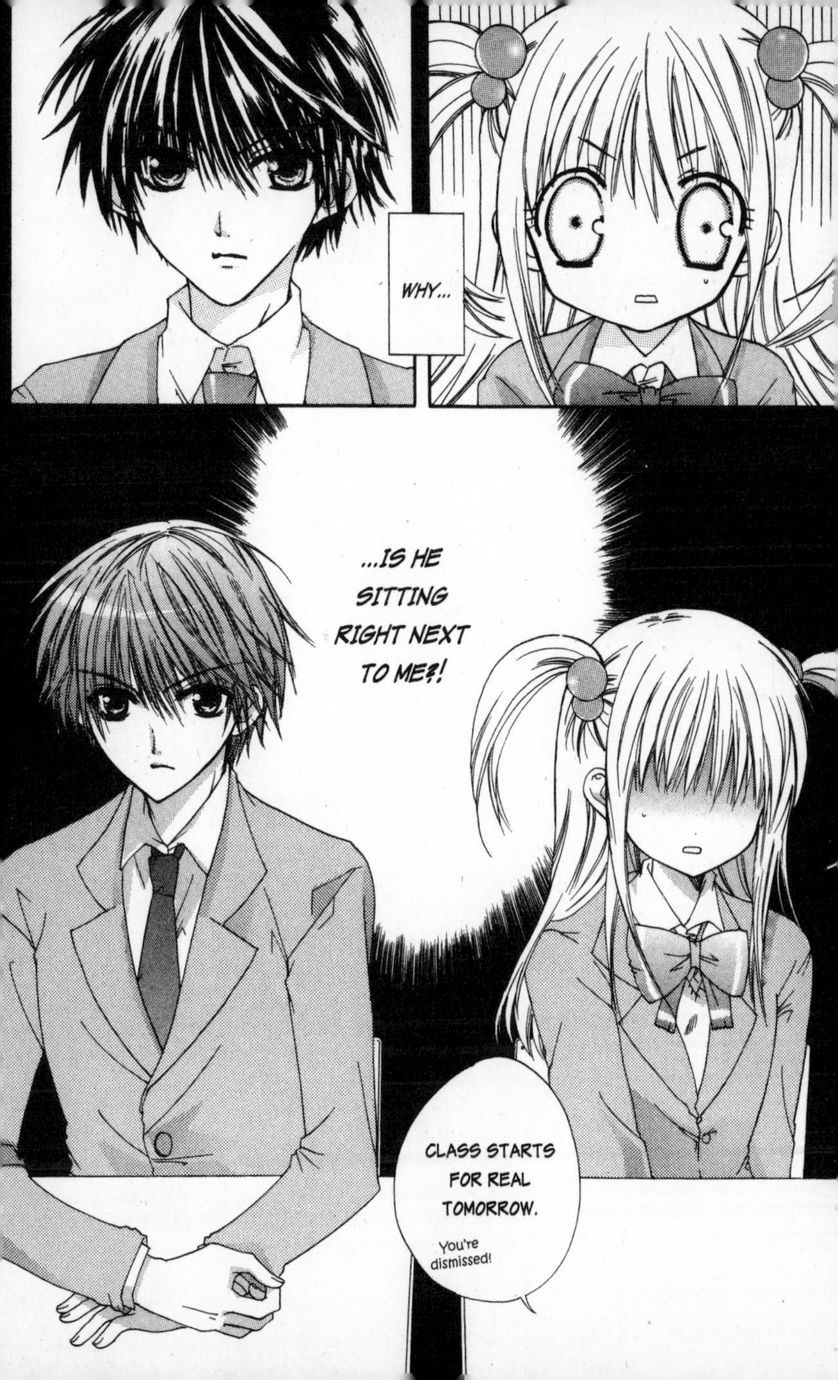
WHY...
...IS HE SITTING RIGHT NEXT TO ME?!
CLASS STARTS FOR REAL TOMORROW.
You're dismissed!

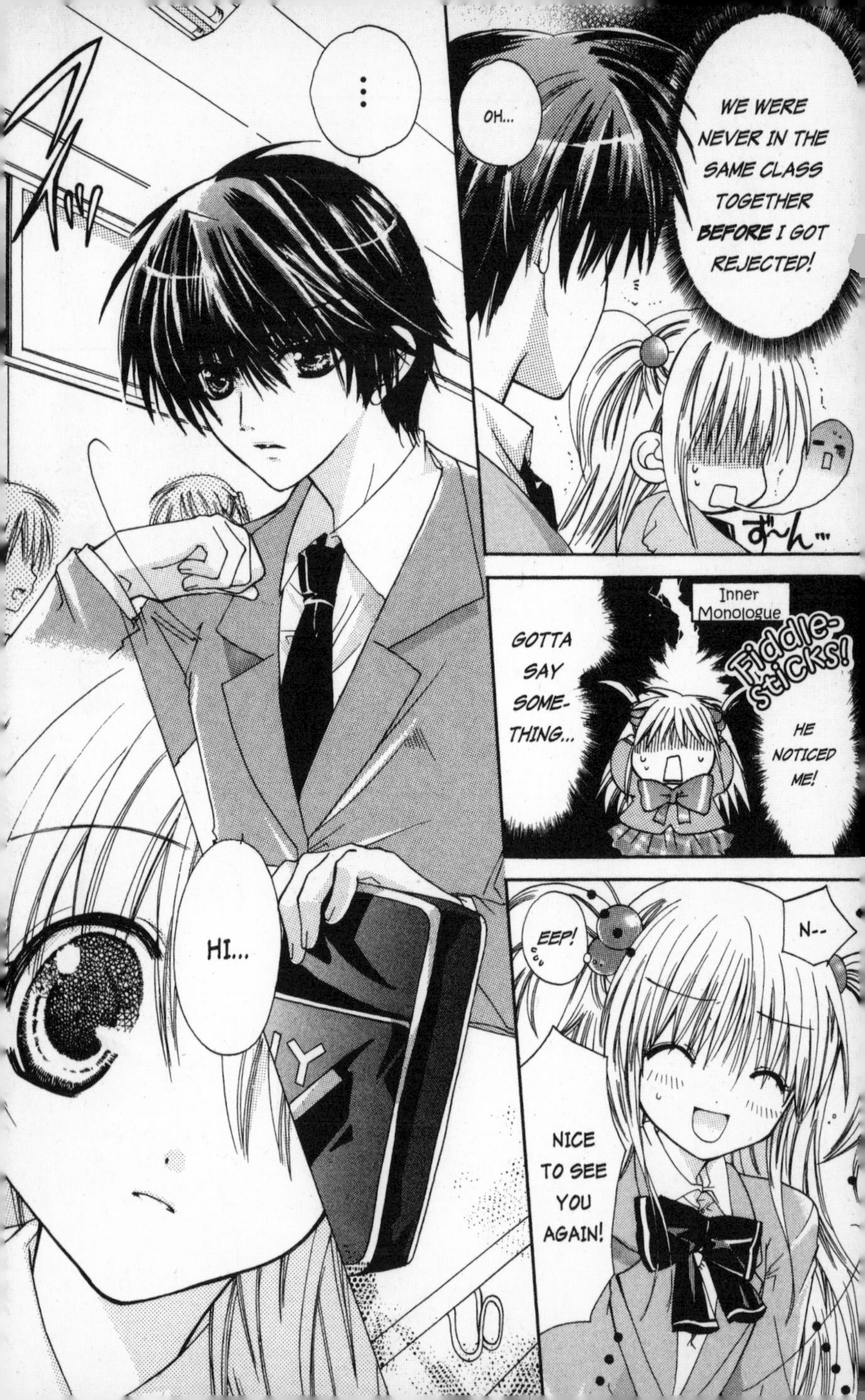

WE WERE NEVER IN THE SAME CLASS TOGETHER BEFORE I GOT REJECTED!
OH...
ず〜ん
Inner Monologue
Fiddle-sticks!
HE NOTICED ME!
GOTTA SAY SOME-THING...
N--
EEP!
NICE TO SEE YOU AGAIN!
...
HI...

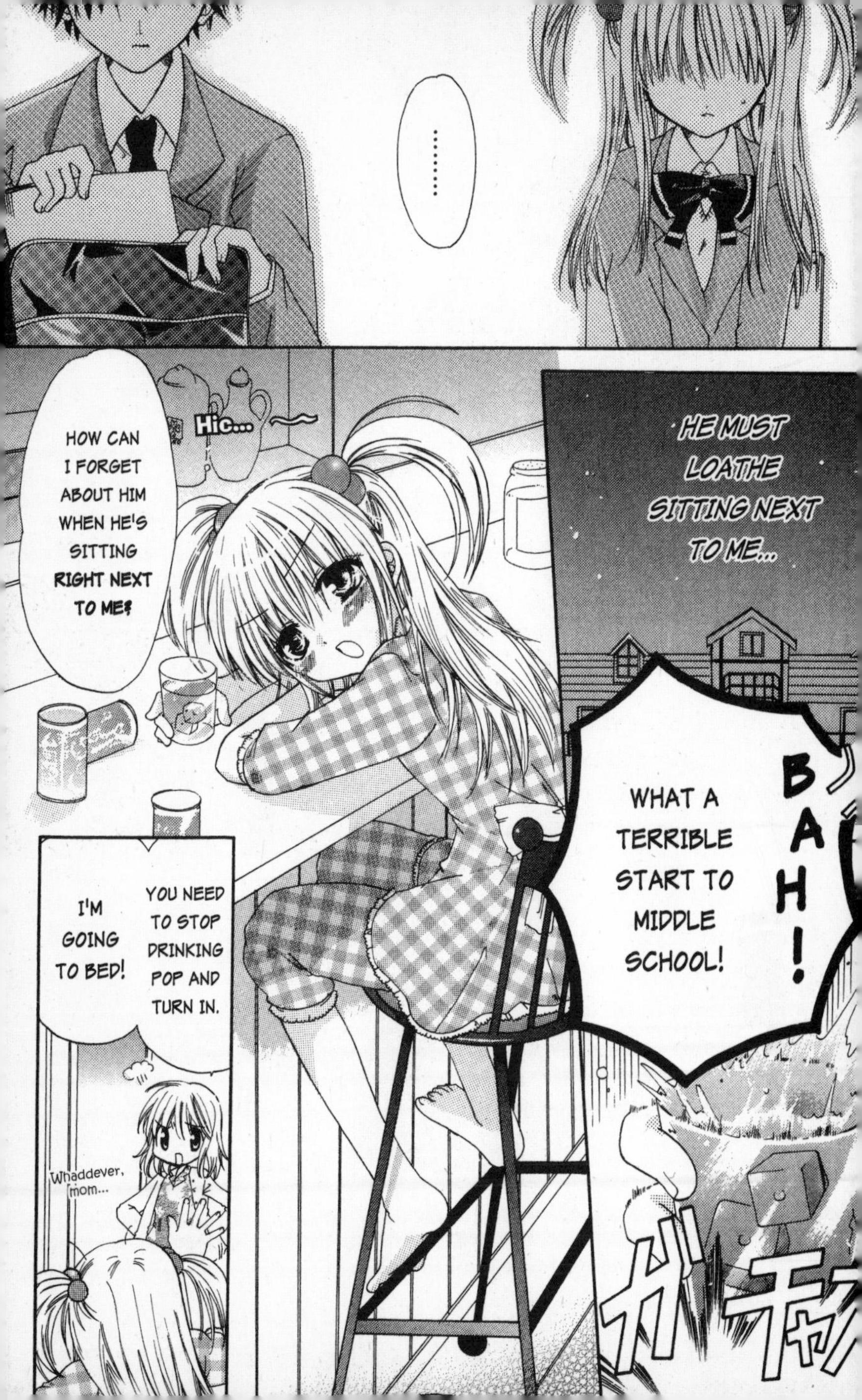
......
HE MUST LOATHE SITTING NEXT TO ME...
WHAT A TERRIBLE START TO MIDDLE SCHOOL!
BAH!
ガチャ
HOW CAN I FORGET ABOUT HIM WHEN HE'S SITTING RIGHT NEXT TO ME?
Hic...
YOU NEED TO STOP DRINKING POP AND TURN IN.
I'M GOING TO BED!
Whaddever, mom...

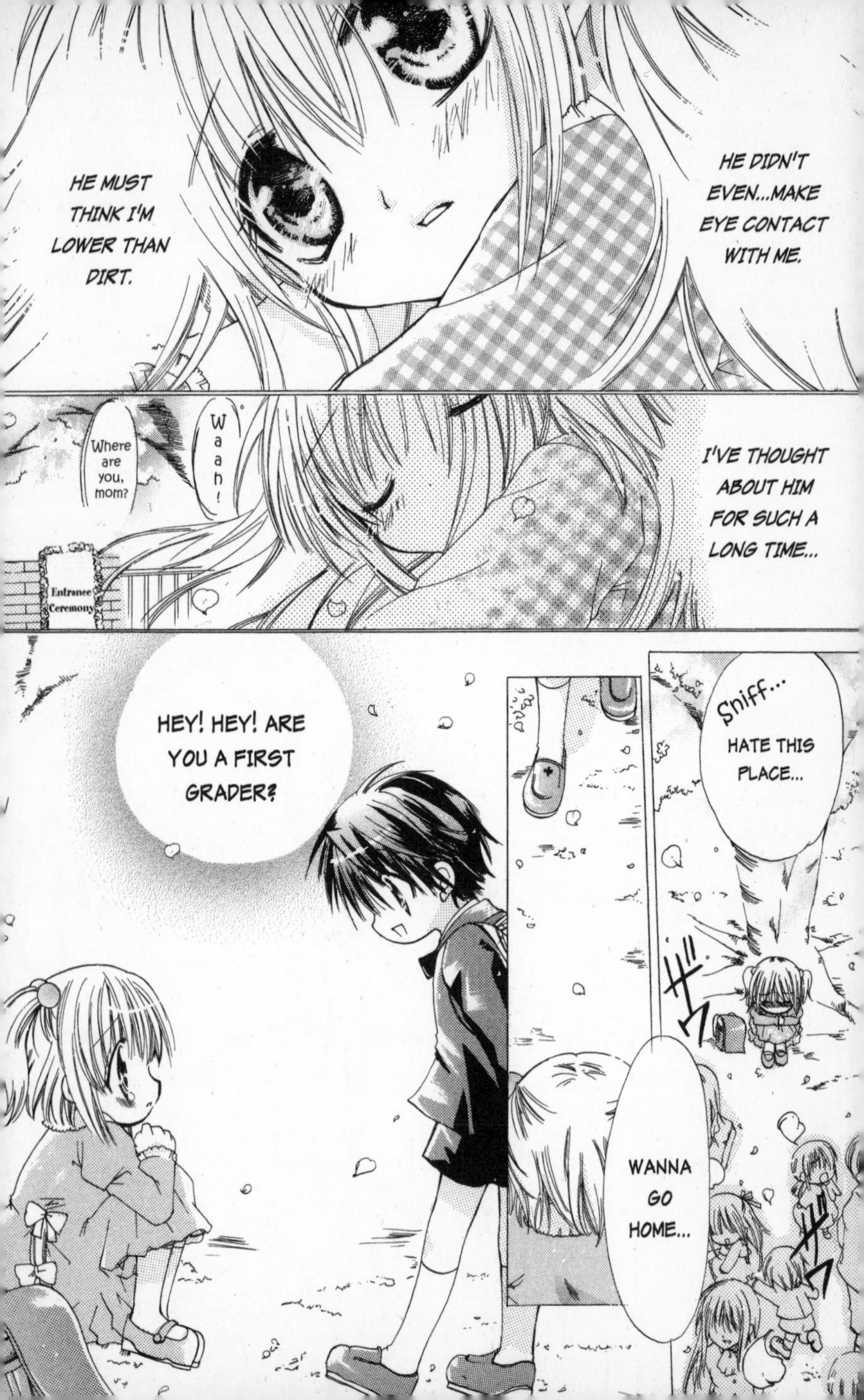
HE DIDN'T EVEN...MAKE EYE CONTACT WITH ME.
HE MUST THINK I'M LOWER THAN DIRT.
I'VE THOUGHT ABOUT HIM FOR SUCH A LONG TIME...
Waah!
Where are you, mom?
Entrance Ceremony
Sniff... HATE THIS PLACE...
WANNA GO HOME...
HEY! HEY! ARE YOU A FIRST GRADER?

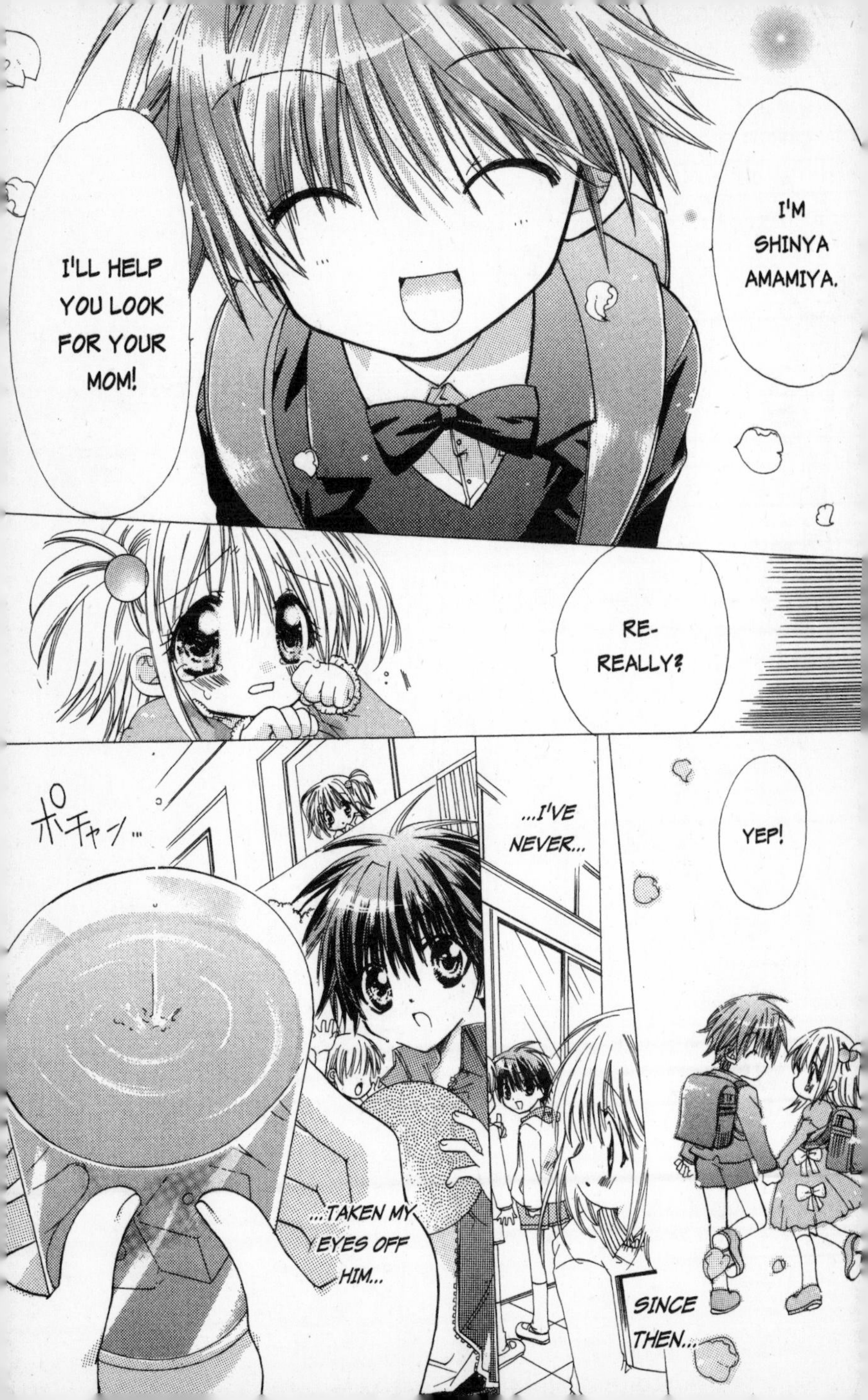
I'M SHINYA AMAMIYA.
I'LL HELP YOU LOOK FOR YOUR MOM!
RE- REALLY?
YEP!
SINCE THEN...
...I'VE NEVER...
ポチャン...
...TAKEN MY EYES OFF HIM...

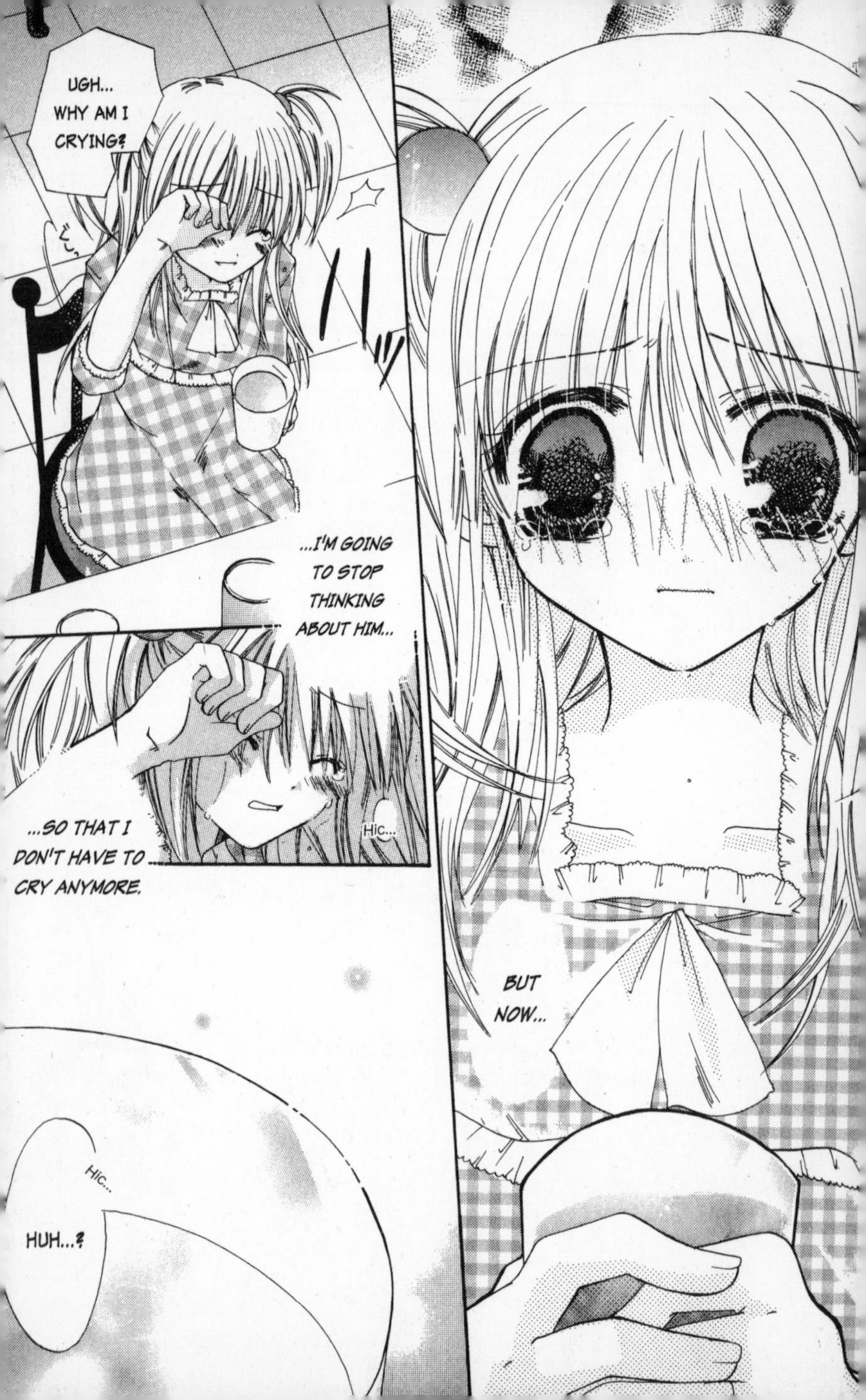
BUT NOW...
UGH... WHY AM I CRYING?
...I'M GOING TO STOP THINKING ABOUT HIM...
Hic...
...SO THAT I DON'T HAVE TO CRY ANYMORE.
Hic...
HUH...?

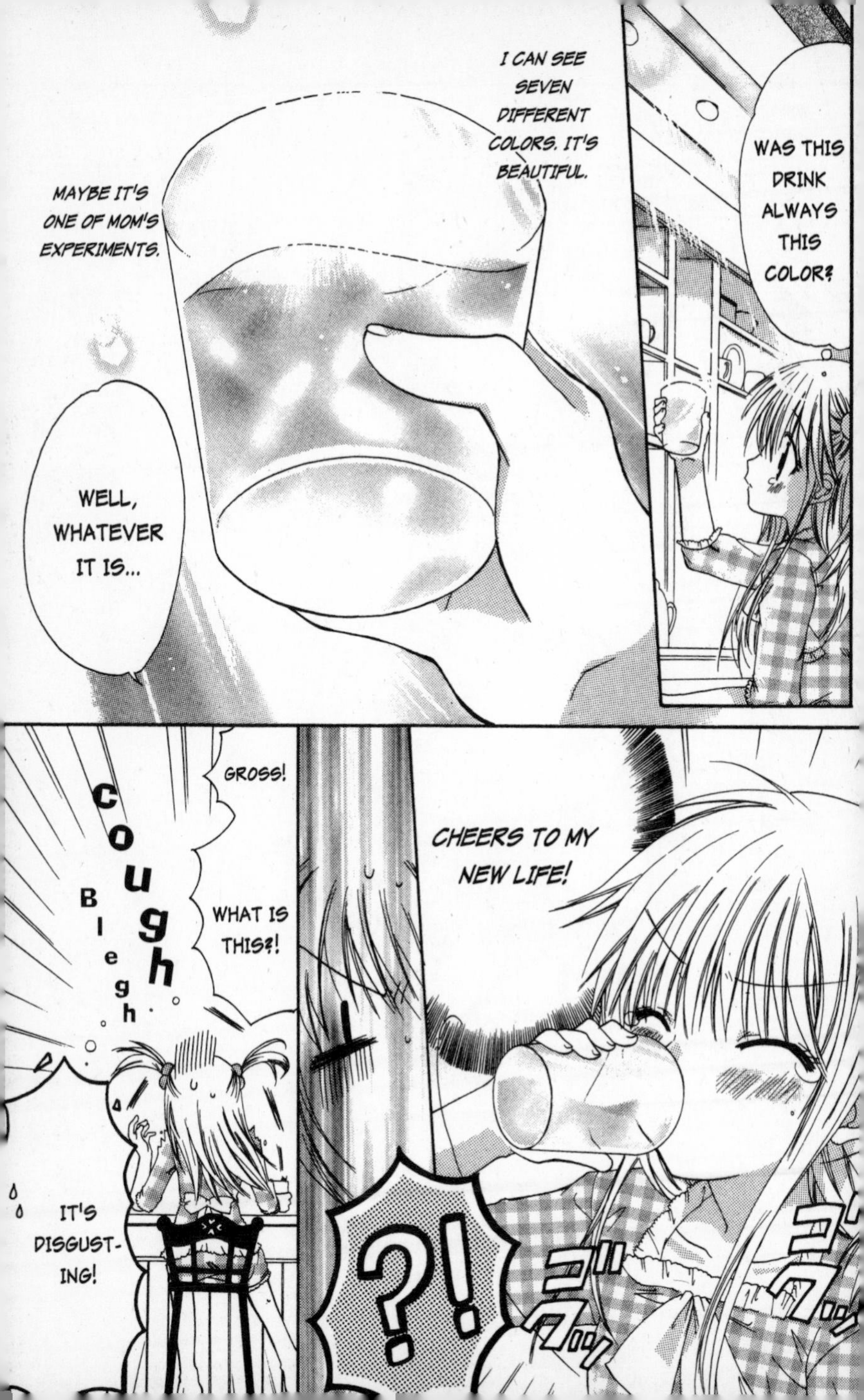
WAS THIS DRINK ALWAYS THIS COLOR?
I CAN SEE SEVEN DIFFERENT COLORS. IT'S BEAUTIFUL.
MAYBE IT'S ONE OF MOM'S EXPERIMENTS.
WELL, WHATEVER IT IS...
CHEERS TO MY NEW LIFE!
?!
GROSS!
Cough
Blegh
WHAT IS THIS?!
IT'S DISGUST-ING!

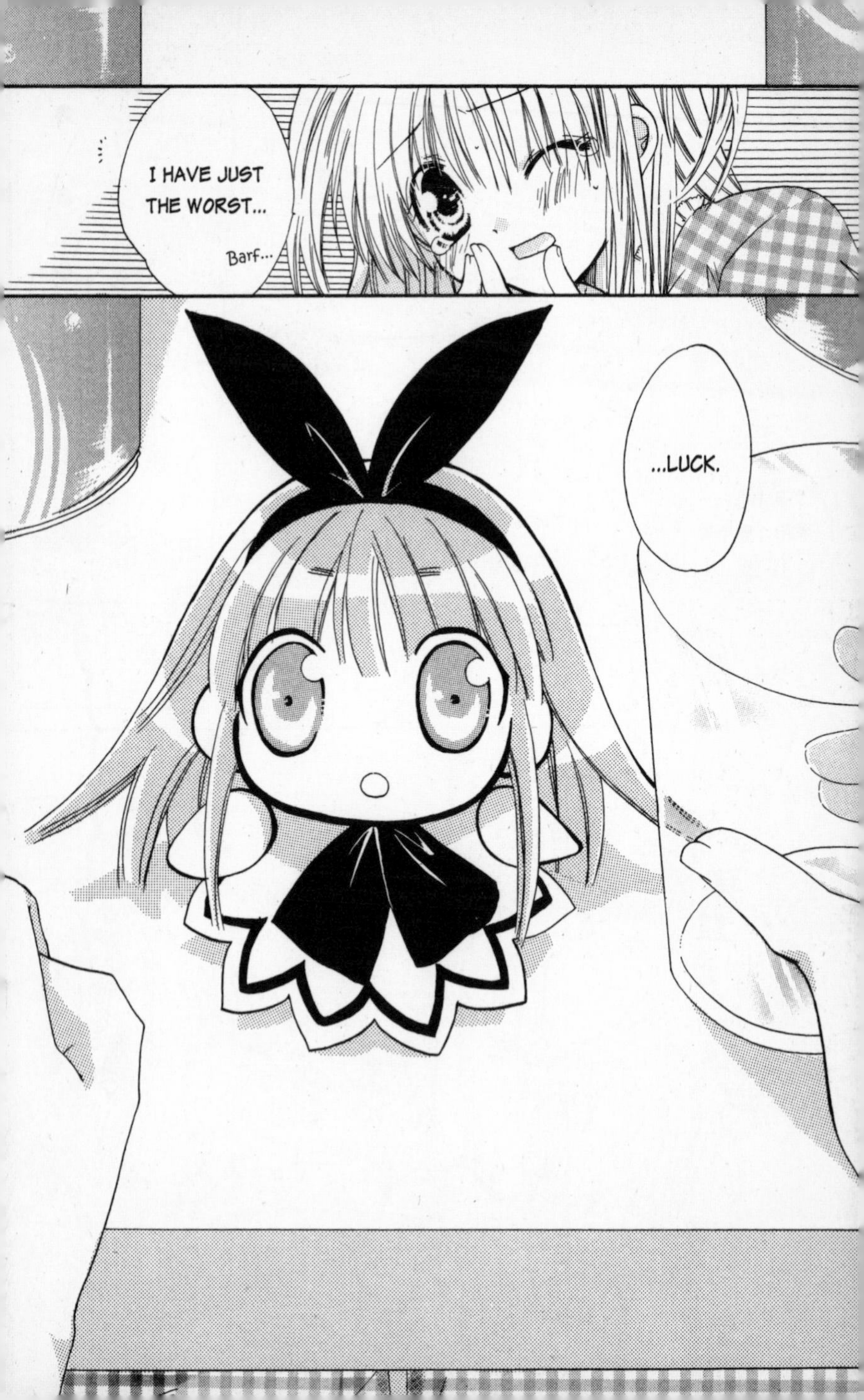
I HAVE JUST THE WORST...
Barf...
...LUCK.

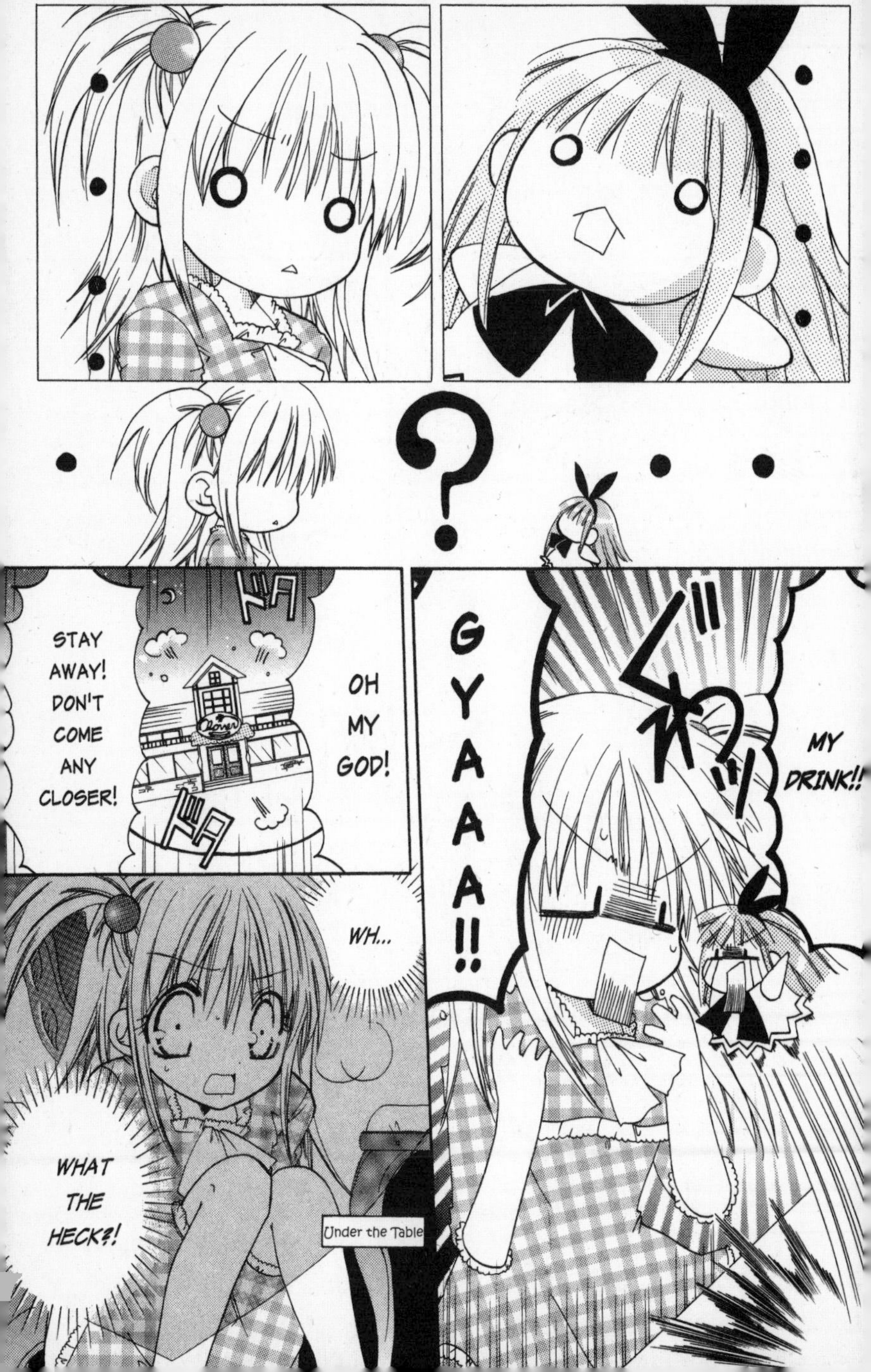
?
GYAAAA!!
MY DRINK!!
OH MY GOD!
STAY AWAY! DON'T COME ANY CLOSER!
WH...
WHAT THE HECK?!
Under the Table

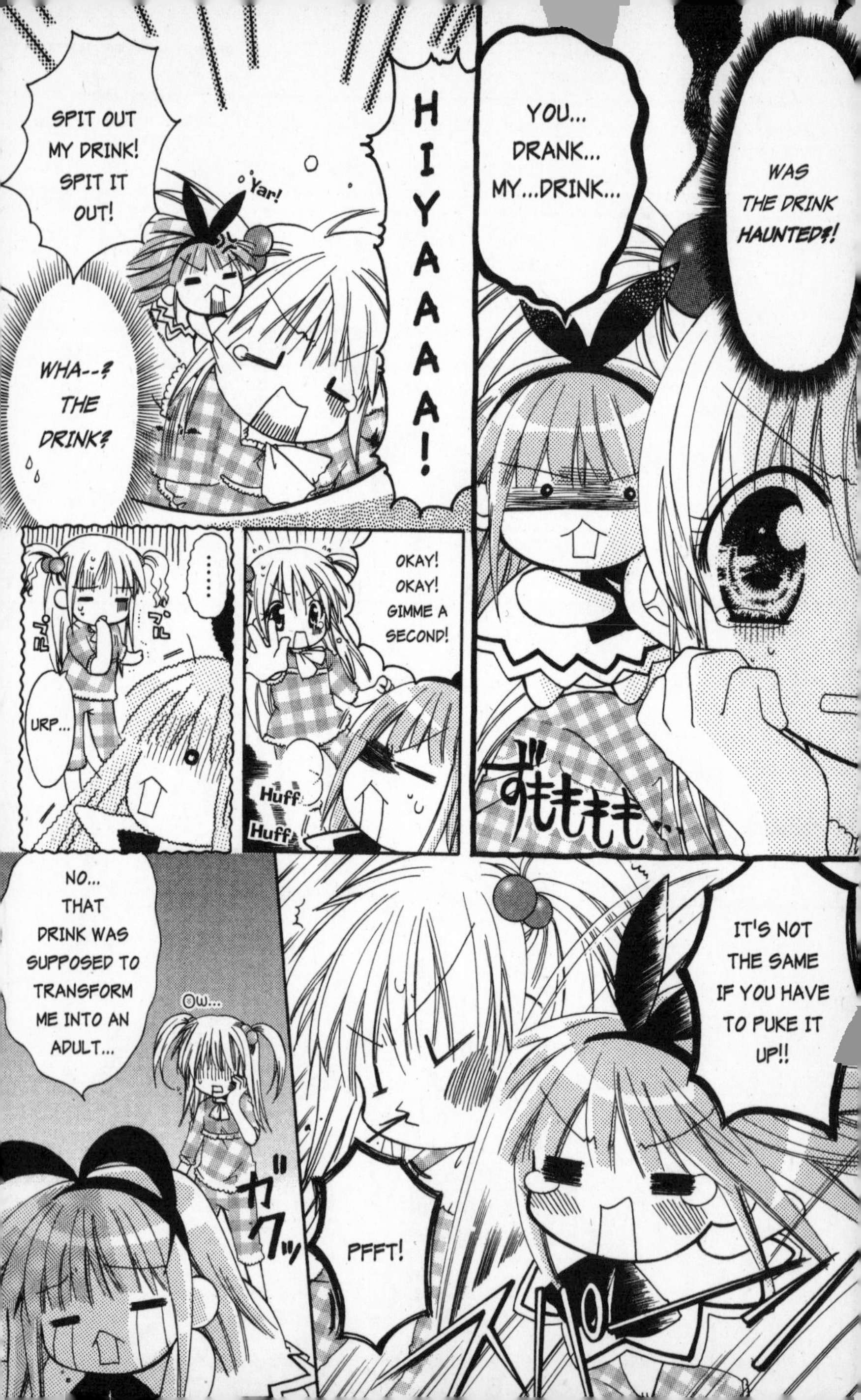
WAS THE DRINK HAUNTED?!
YOU... DRANK... MY...DRINK...
ずもももも
HIYAAAA!
Yar!
SPIT OUT MY DRINK! SPIT IT OUT!
WHA--? THE DRINK?
OKAY! OKAY! GIMME A SECOND!
Huff
Huff
......
プル
プル
URP...
IT'S NOT THE SAME IF YOU HAVE TO PUKE IT UP!!
PFFT!
NO... THAT DRINK WAS SUPPOSED TO TRANSFORM ME INTO AN ADULT...
OW...
ガクッ

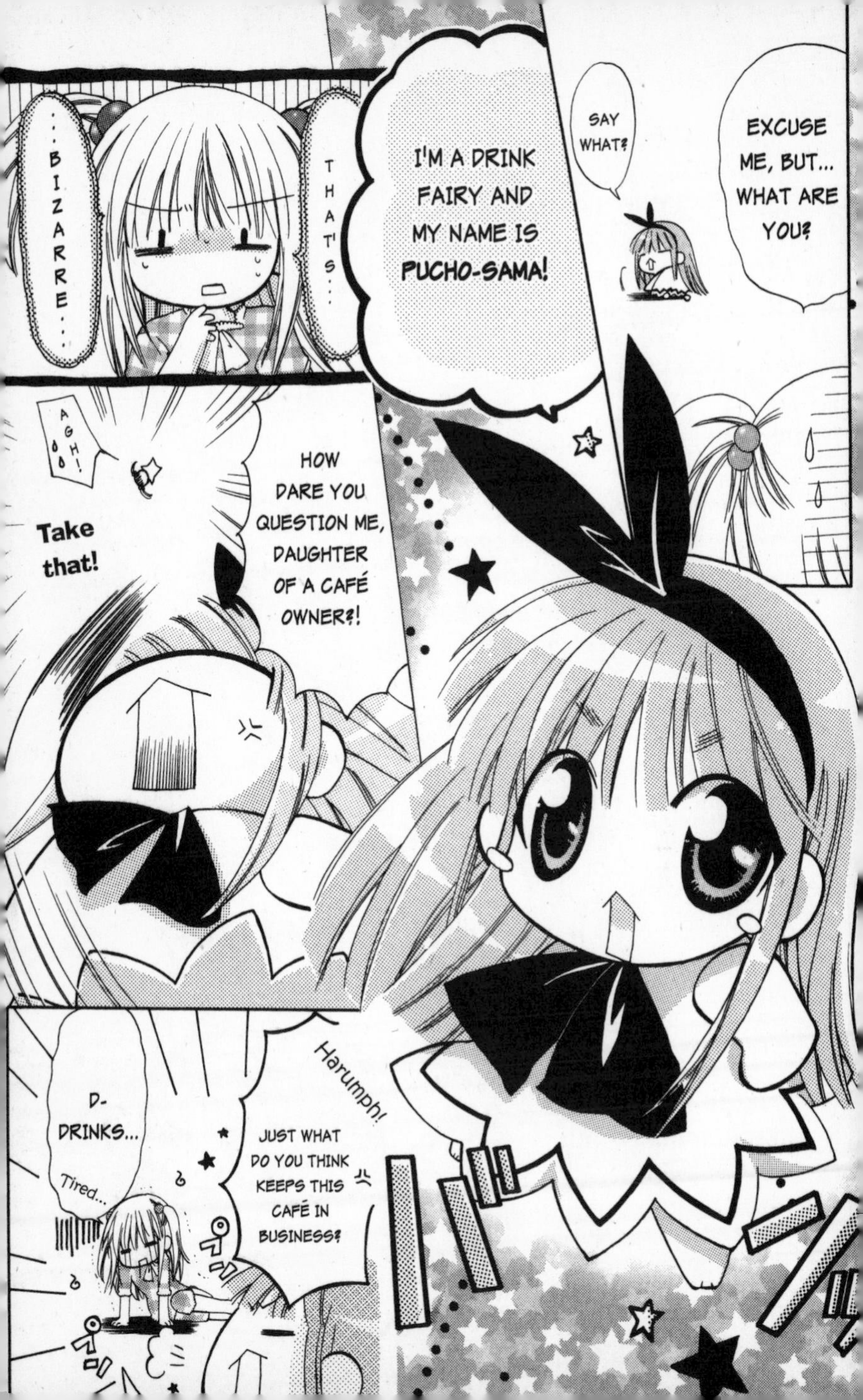
EXCUSE ME, BUT... WHAT ARE YOU?
SAY WHAT?
I'M A DRINK FAIRY AND MY NAME IS PUCHO-SAMA!
THAT'S...
...BIZARRE...
HOW DARE YOU QUESTION ME, DAUGHTER OF A CAFÉ OWNER?!
AGH!
Take that!
Harumph!
JUST WHAT DO YOU THINK KEEPS THIS CAFÉ IN BUSINESS?
D-DRINKS...
Tired...

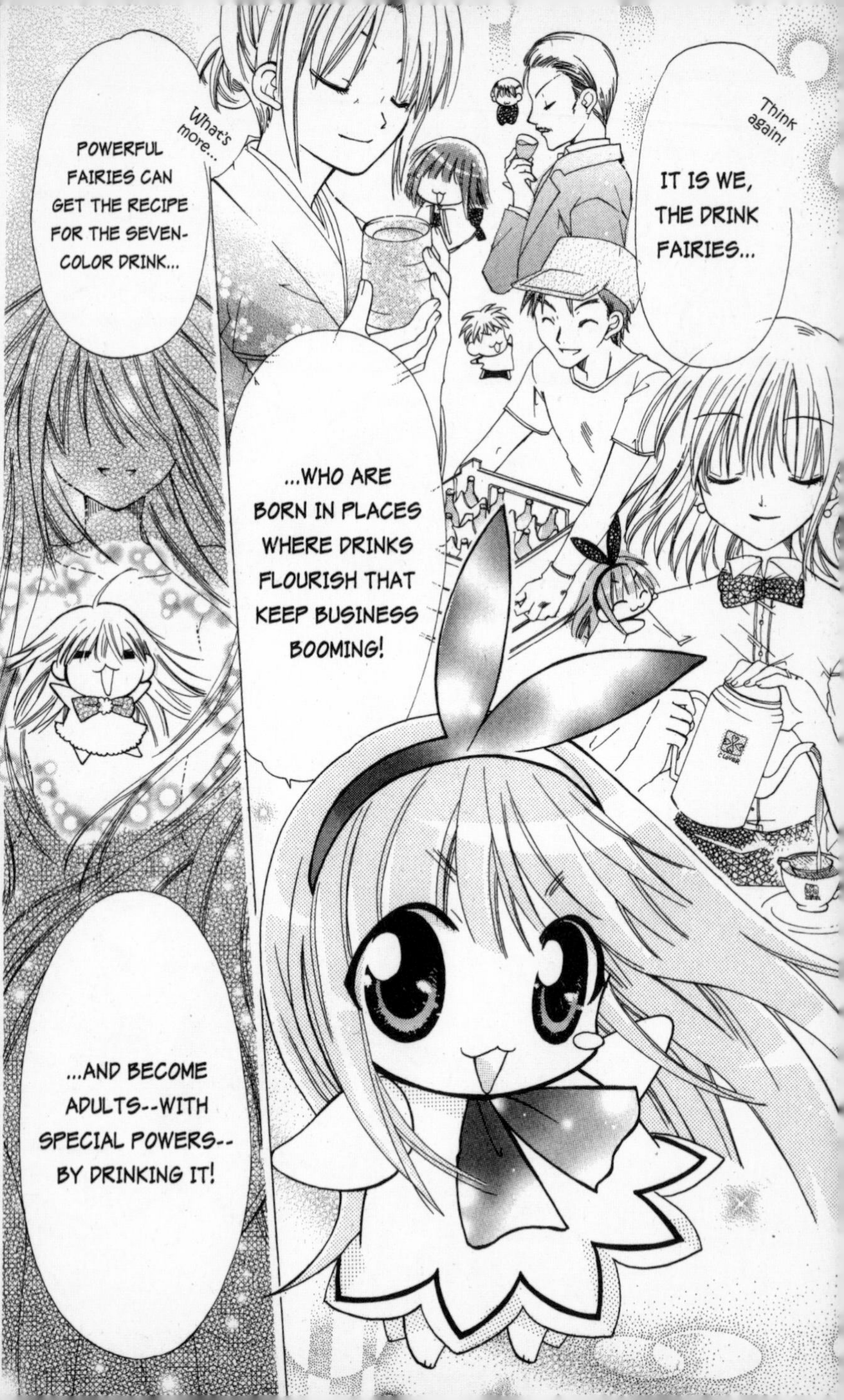
Think again!
IT IS WE, THE DRINK FAIRIES...
...WHO ARE BORN IN PLACES WHERE DRINKS FLOURISH THAT KEEP BUSINESS BOOMING!
What's more...
POWERFUL FAIRIES CAN GET THE RECIPE FOR THE SEVEN-COLOR DRINK...
...AND BECOME ADULTS--WITH SPECIAL POWERS--BY DRINKING IT!

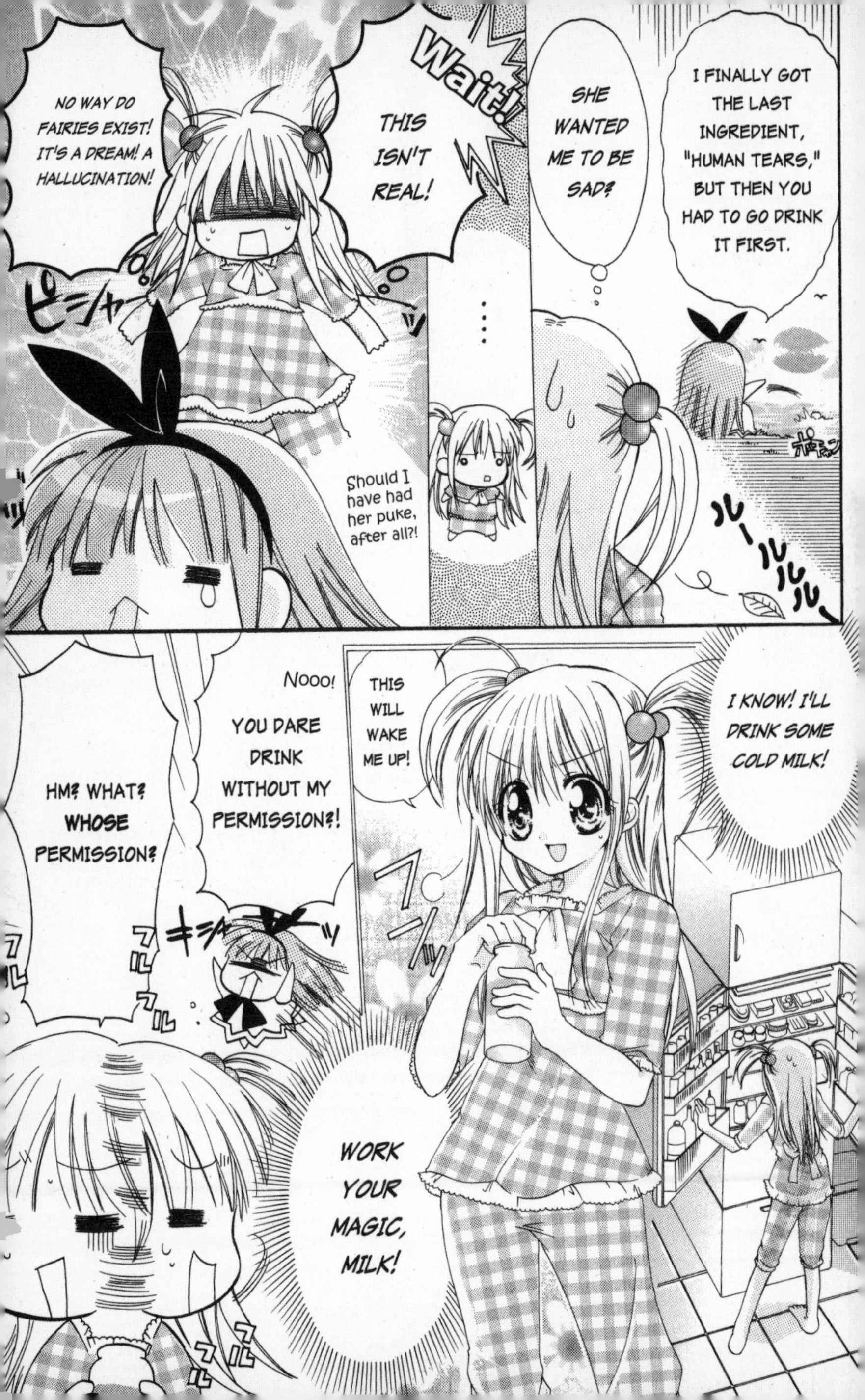
I FINALLY GOT THE LAST INGREDIENT, "HUMAN TEARS," BUT THEN YOU HAD TO GO DRINK IT FIRST.
SHE WANTED ME TO BE SAD?
....
Should I have had her puke, after all?!
Wait!!
THIS ISN'T REAL!
NO WAY DO FAIRIES EXIST! IT'S A DREAM! A HALLUCINATION!
I KNOW! I'LL DRINK SOME COLD MILK!
THIS WILL WAKE ME UP!
WORK YOUR MAGIC, MILK!
Nooo!
YOU DARE DRINK WITHOUT MY PERMISSION?!
HM? WHAT? WHOSE PERMISSION?

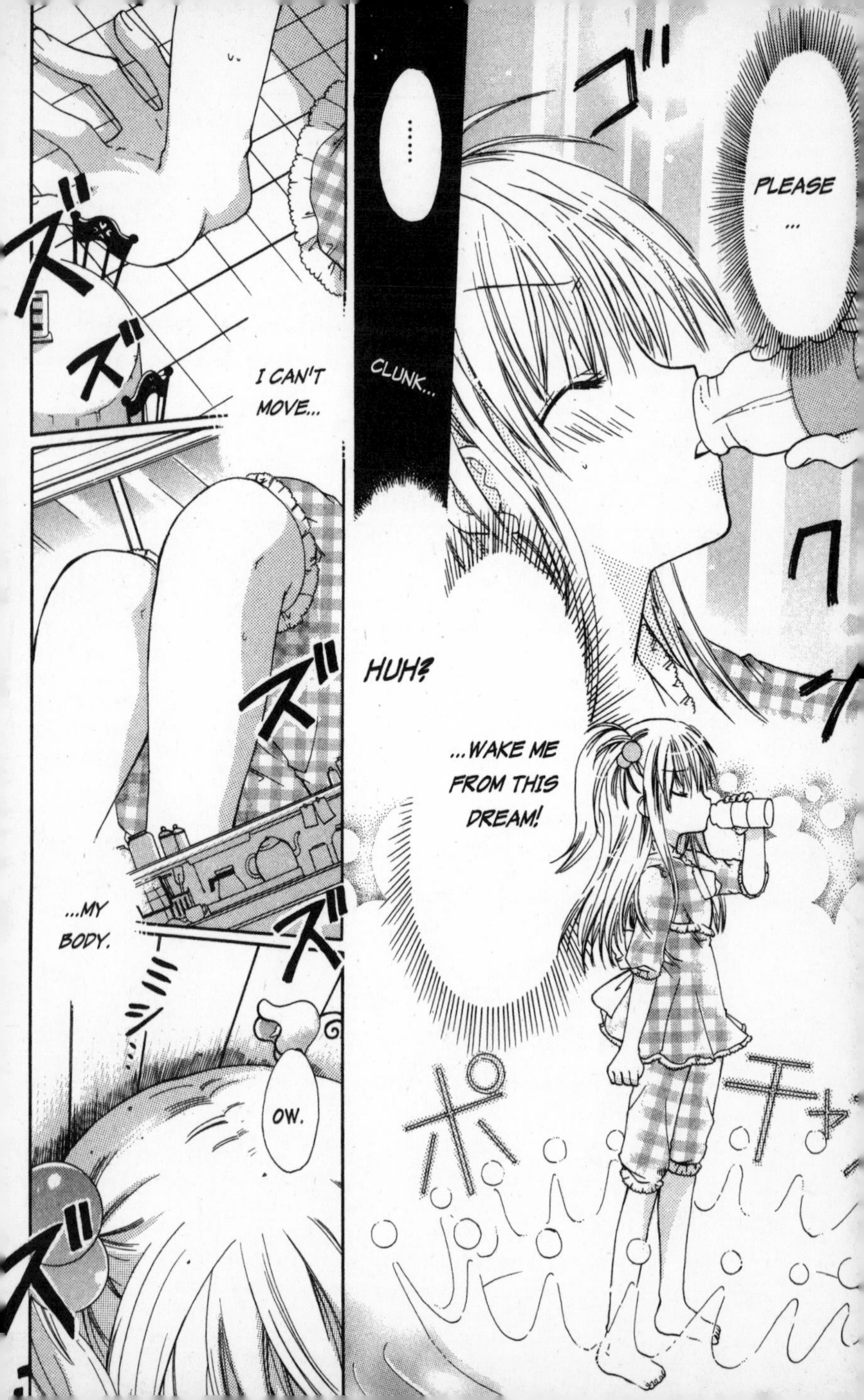
PLEASE ...
...WAKE ME FROM THIS DREAM!
......
CLUNK...
HUH?
I CAN'T MOVE...
...MY BODY.
OW.

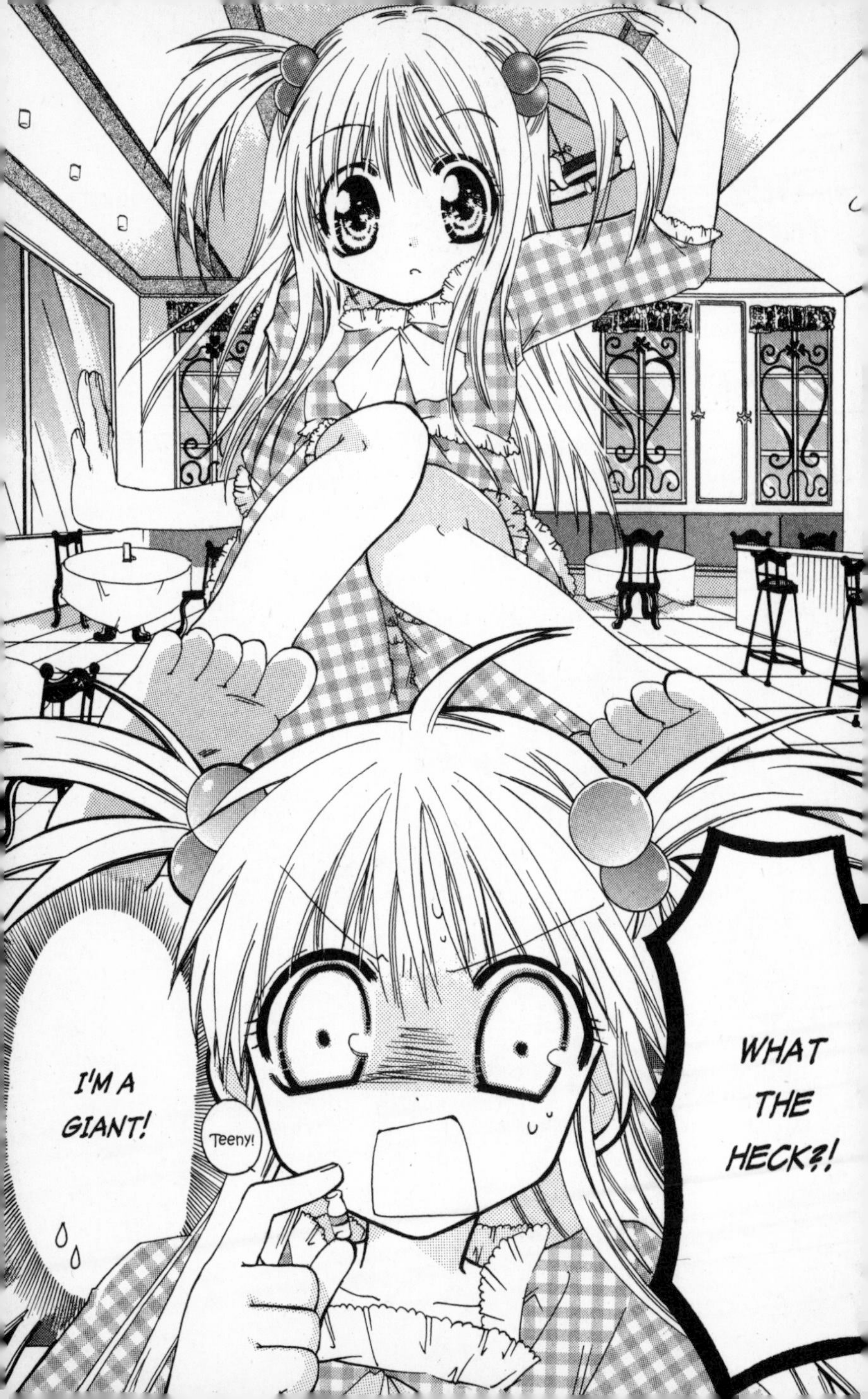
WHAT THE HECK?!
I'M A GIANT!
Teeny!

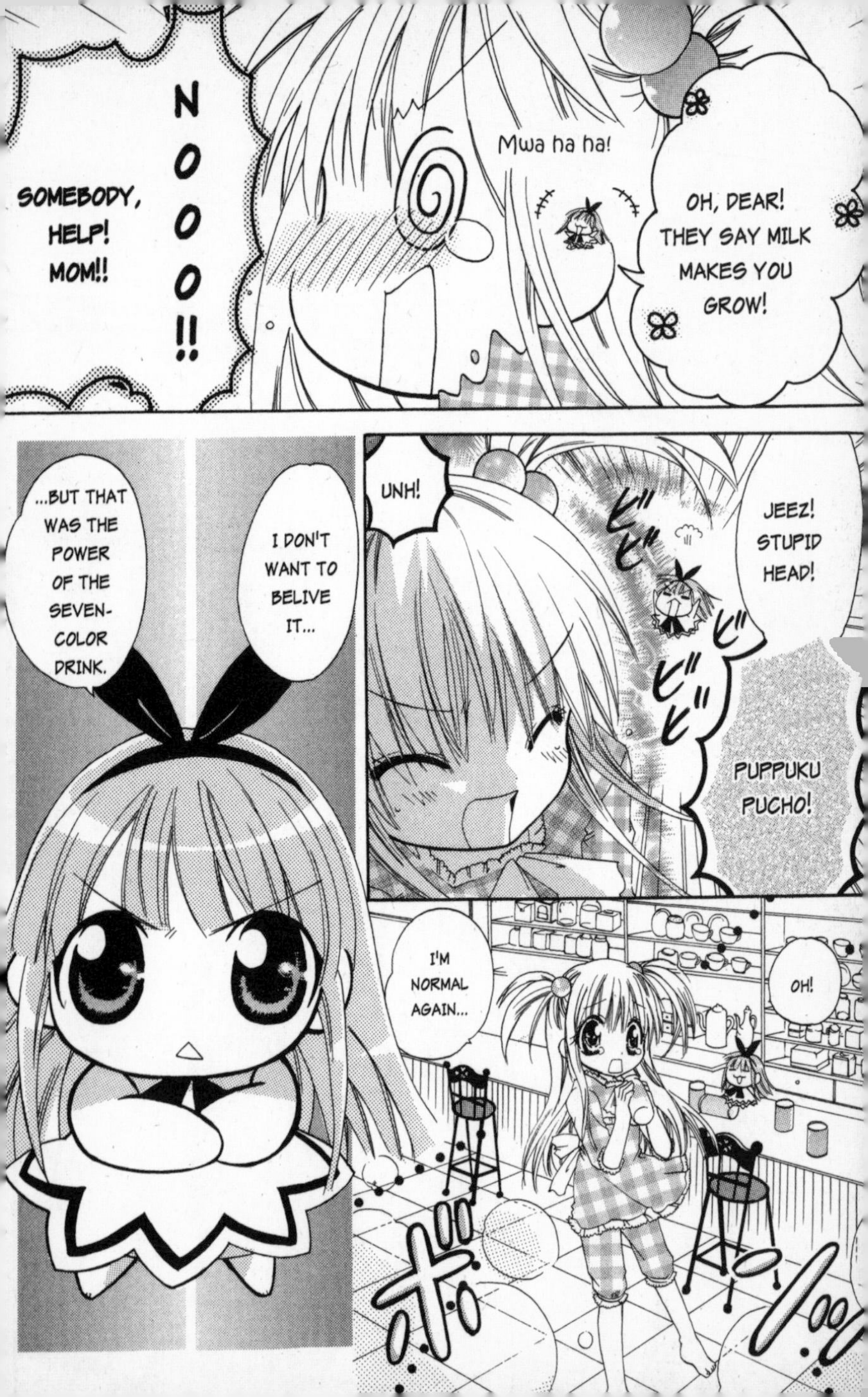
OH, DEAR! THEY SAY MILK MAKES YOU GROW!
Mwa ha ha!
NOOOO!!
SOMEBODY, HELP! MOM!!
JEEZ! STUPID HEAD!
UNH!
PUPPUKU PUCHO!
OH!
I'M NORMAL AGAIN...
I DON'T WANT TO BELIVE IT...
...BUT THAT WAS THE POWER OF THE SEVEN-COLOR DRINK.

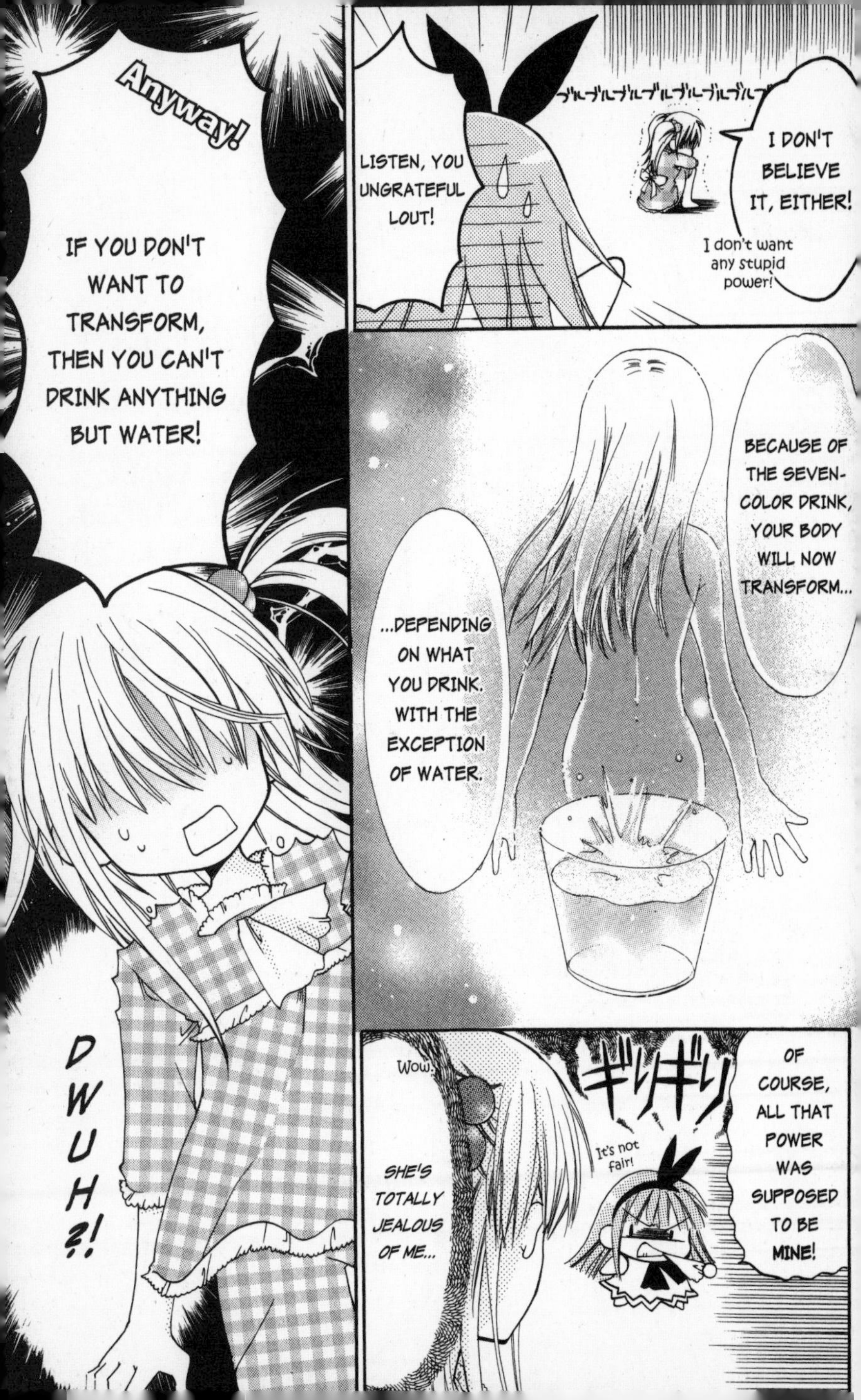
ブルブルブルブルブルブルブル
I DON'T BELIEVE IT, EITHER!
I don't want any stupid power!
LISTEN, YOU UNGRATEFUL LOUT!
BECAUSE OF THE SEVEN-COLOR DRINK, YOUR BODY WILL NOW TRANSFORM...
...DEPENDING ON WHAT YOU DRINK. WITH THE EXCEPTION OF WATER.
OF COURSE, ALL THAT POWER WAS SUPPOSED TO BE MINE!
ギリギリ
It's not fair!
Wow.
SHE'S TOTALLY JEALOUS OF ME...
Anyway!
IF YOU DON'T WANT TO TRANSFORM, THEN YOU CAN'T DRINK ANYTHING BUT WATER!
DWUH?!

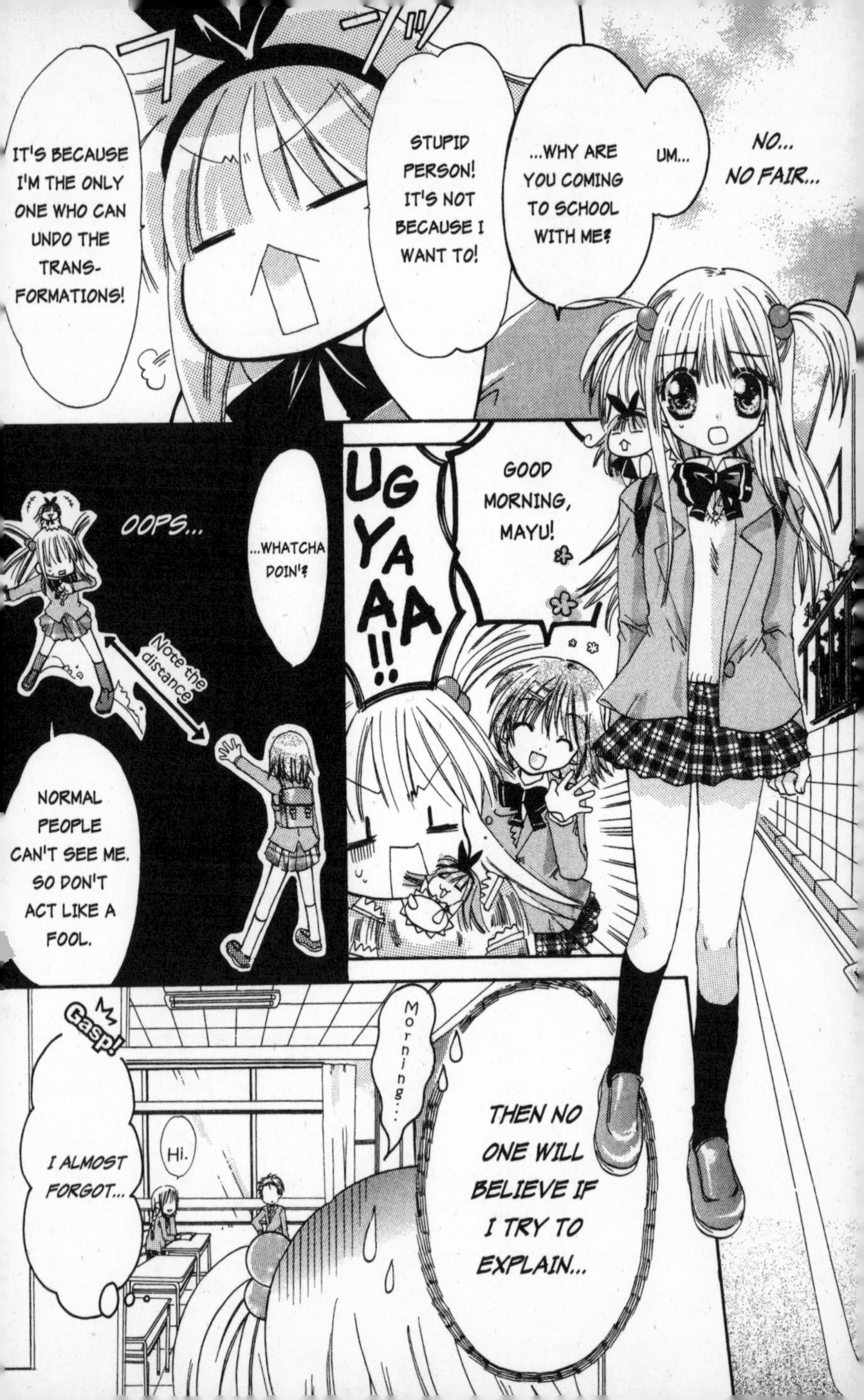
NO... NO FAIR...
UM...
...WHY ARE YOU COMING TO SCHOOL WITH ME?
STUPID PERSON! IT'S NOT BECAUSE I WANT TO!
IT'S BECAUSE I'M THE ONLY ONE WHO CAN UNDO THE TRANS-FORMATIONS!
GOOD MORNING, MAYU!
UGYAAA!!
...WHATCHA DOIN'?
OOPS...
Note the distance
NORMAL PEOPLE CAN'T SEE ME. SO DON'T ACT LIKE A FOOL.
THEN NO ONE WILL BELIEVE IF I TRY TO EXPLAIN...
Morning...
Hi.
Gasp!
I ALMOST FORGOT...

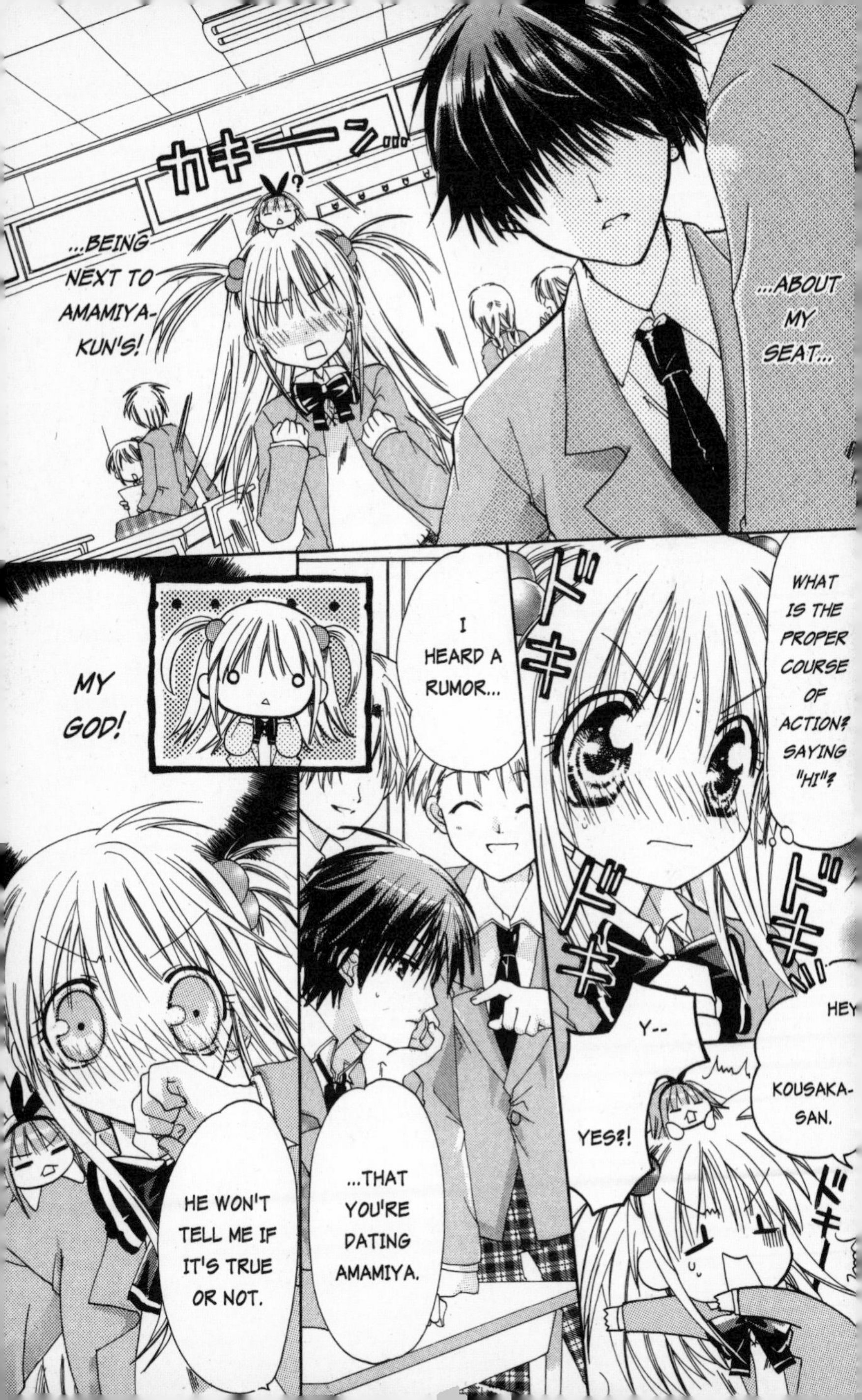
...ABOUT MY SEAT...
カキーーン
...BEING NEXT TO AMAMIYA-KUN'S!
WHAT IS THE PROPER COURSE OF ACTION? SAYING "HI"?
ドキ
ドキ
ドキ
HEY KOUSAKA-SAN.
Y--
YES?!
ドキー
I HEARD A RUMOR...
...THAT YOU'RE DATING AMAMIYA.
MY GOD!
HE WON'T TELL ME IF IT'S TRUE OR NOT.

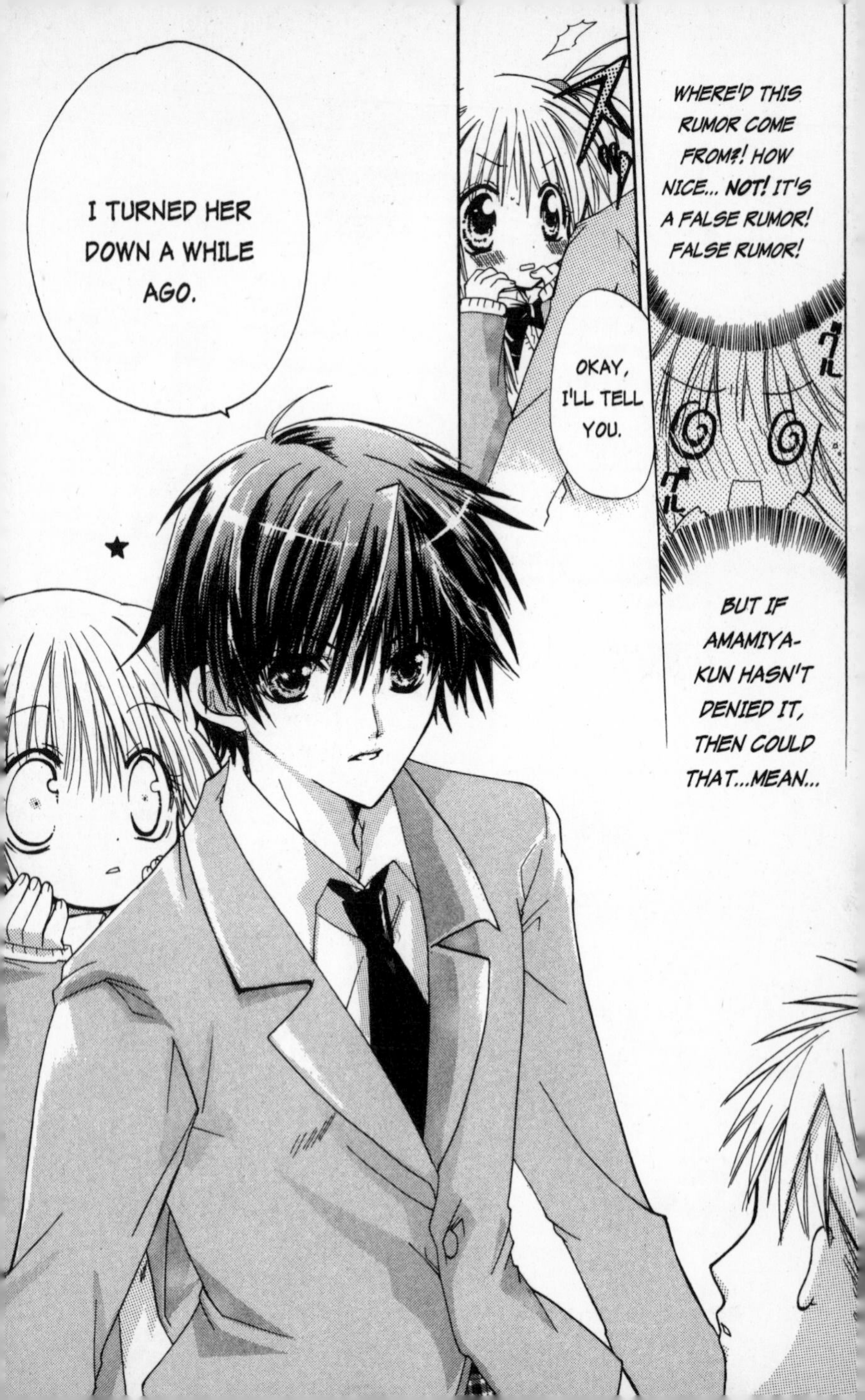

WHERE'D THIS RUMOR COME FROM?! HOW NICE... NOT! IT'S A FALSE RUMOR! FALSE RUMOR!
BUT IF AMAMIYA-KUN HASN'T DENIED IT, THEN COULD THAT...MEAN...
OKAY, I'LL TELL YOU.
I TURNED HER DOWN A WHILE AGO.

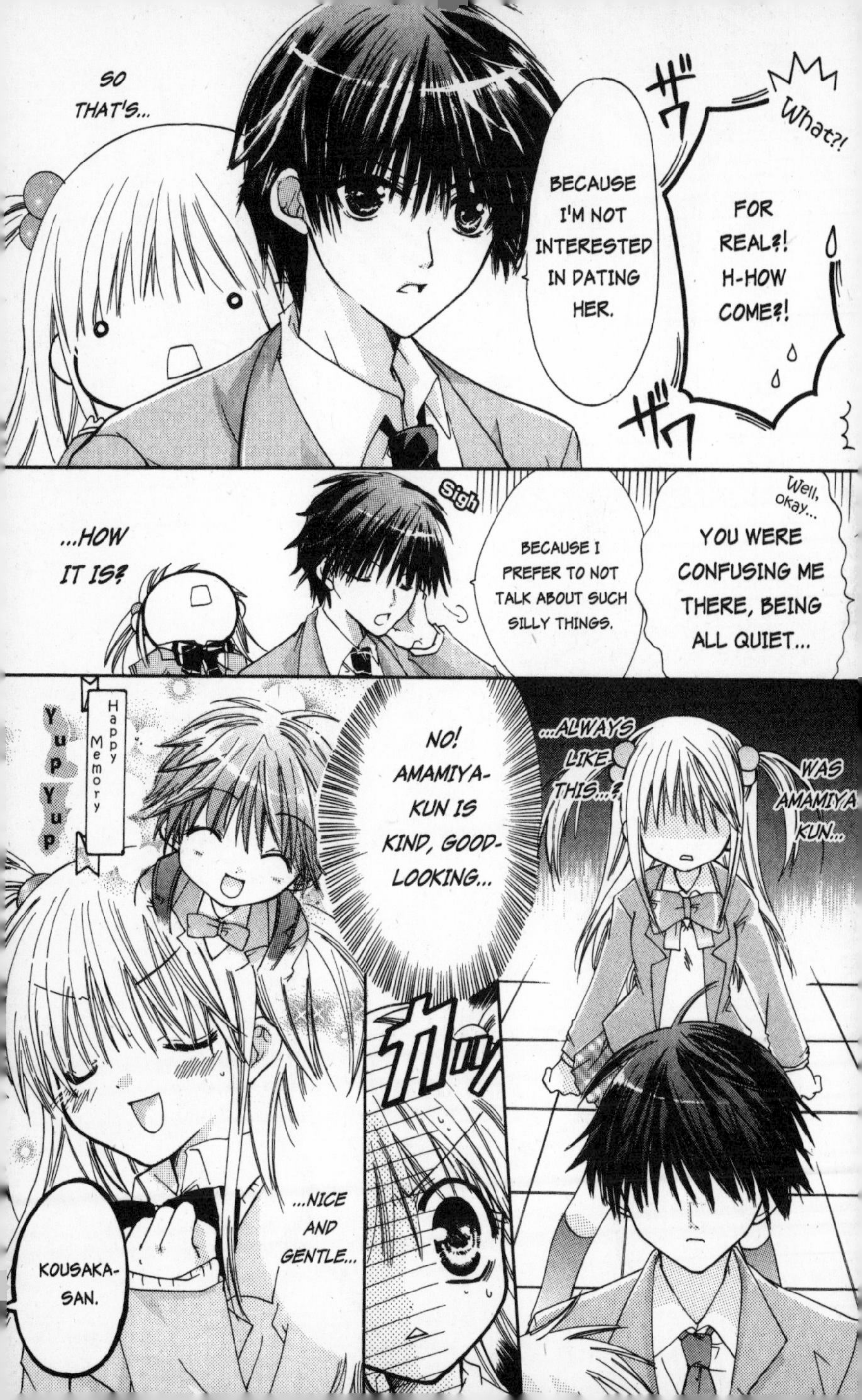
What?!
FOR REAL?! H-HOW COME?!
ザワ
ザワ
BECAUSE I'M NOT INTERESTED IN DATING HER.
SO THAT'S...
Well, okay...
YOU WERE CONFUSING ME THERE, BEING ALL QUIET...
BECAUSE I PREFER TO NOT TALK ABOUT SUCH SILLY THINGS.
Sigh
...HOW IT IS?
WAS AMAMIYA KUN...
...ALWAYS LIKE THIS...?
NO! AMAMIYA-KUN IS KIND, GOOD-LOOKING...
Happy Memory
Yup Yup
カッ
...NICE AND GENTLE...
KOUSAKA-SAN.

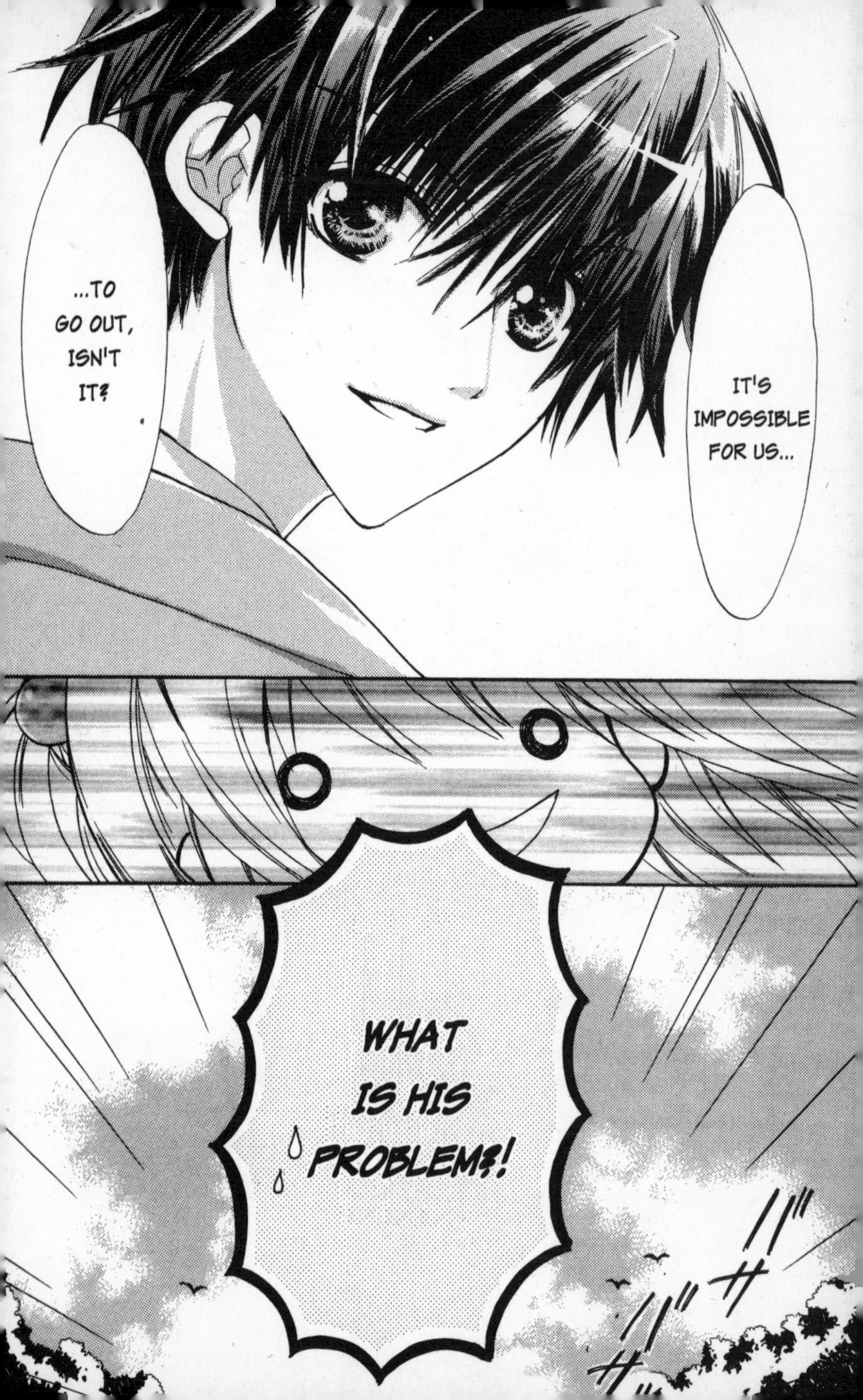
IT'S IMPOSSIBLE FOR US...
...TO GO OUT, ISN'T IT?
WHAT IS HIS PROBLEM?!

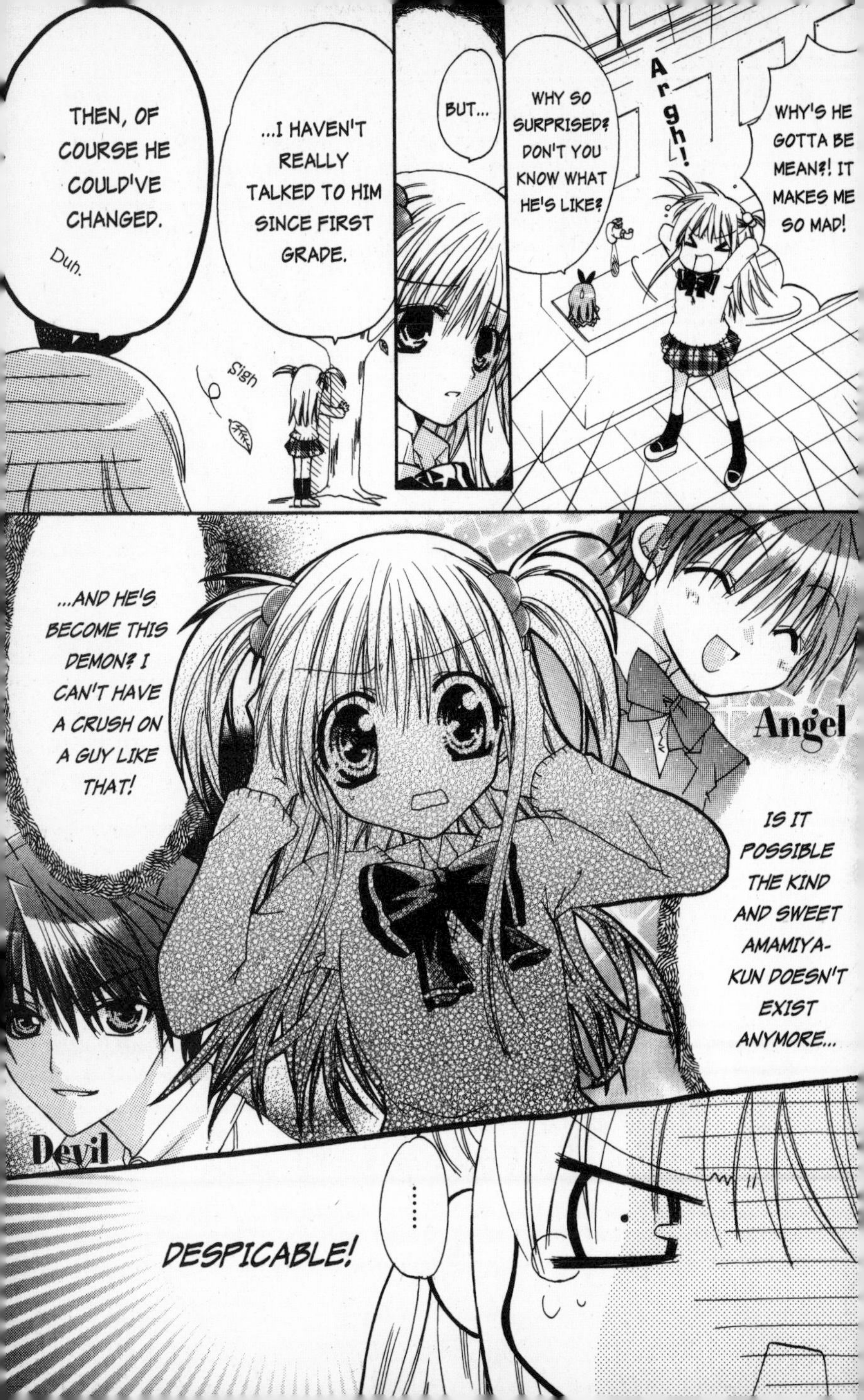
WHY'S HE GOTTA BE MEAN?! IT MAKES ME SO MAD!
Argh!
WHY SO SURPRISED? DON'T YOU KNOW WHAT HE'S LIKE?
BUT...
...I HAVEN'T REALLY TALKED TO HIM SINCE FIRST GRADE.
Sigh
THEN, OF COURSE HE COULD'VE CHANGED.
Duh.
Angel
IS IT POSSIBLE THE KIND AND SWEET AMAMIYA-KUN DOESN'T EXIST ANYMORE...
...AND HE'S BECOME THIS DEMON? I CAN'T HAVE A CRUSH ON A GUY LIKE THAT!
Devil
......
DESPICABLE!

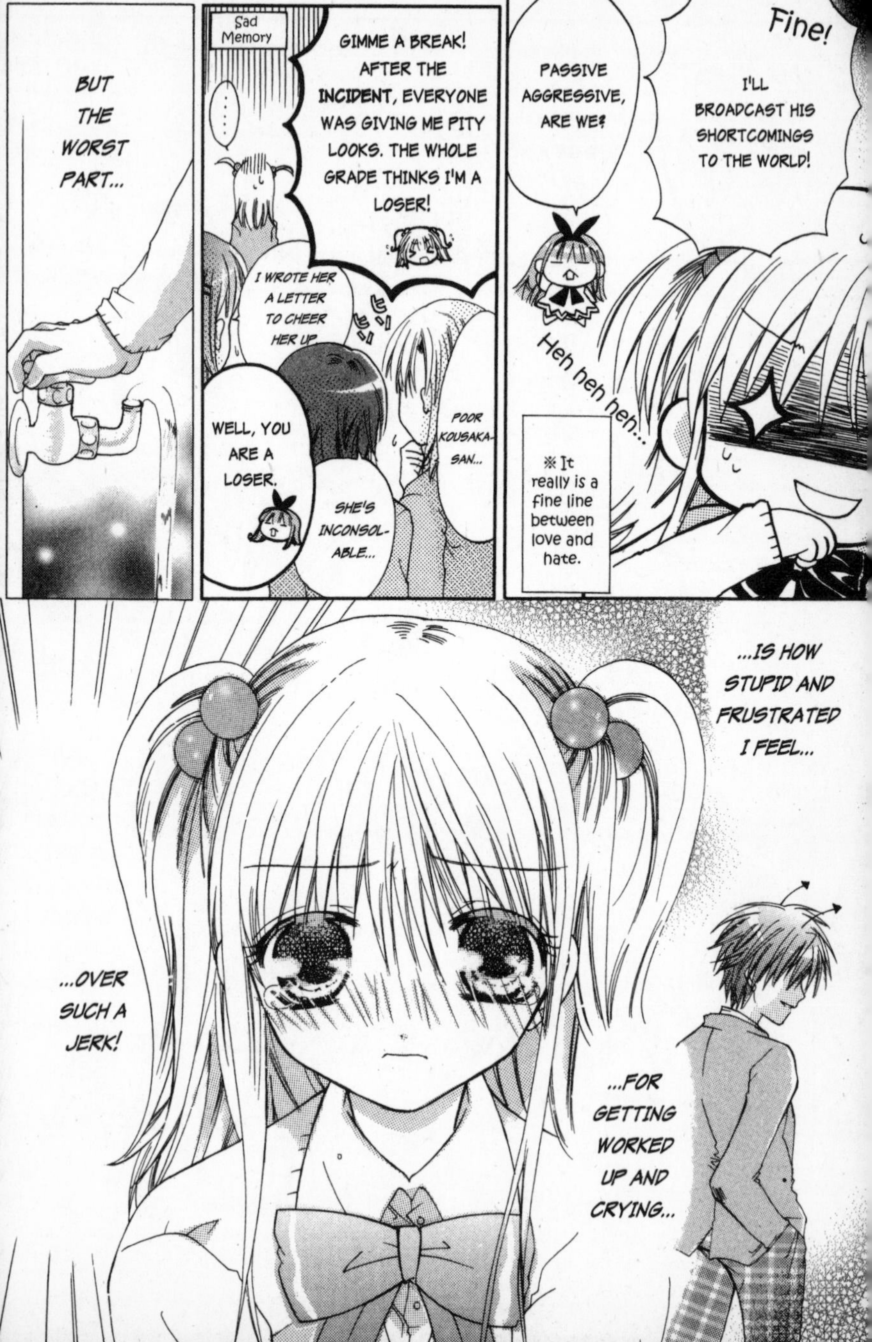

Fine!
I'LL BROADCAST HIS SHORTCOMINGS TO THE WORLD!
PASSIVE AGGRESSIVE, ARE WE?
Heh heh heh...
※It really is a fine line between love and hate.
Sad Memory
GIMME A BREAK! AFTER THE INCIDENT, EVERYONE WAS GIVING ME PITY LOOKS. THE WHOLE GRADE THINKS I'M A LOSER!
.....
I WROTE HER A LETTER TO CHEER HER UP.
POOR KOUSAKA-SAN...
WELL, YOU ARE A LOSER.
SHE'S INCONSOL-ABLE...
BUT THE WORST PART...
...IS HOW STUPID AND FRUSTRATED I FEEL...
...FOR GETTING WORKED UP AND CRYING...
...OVER SUCH A JERK!

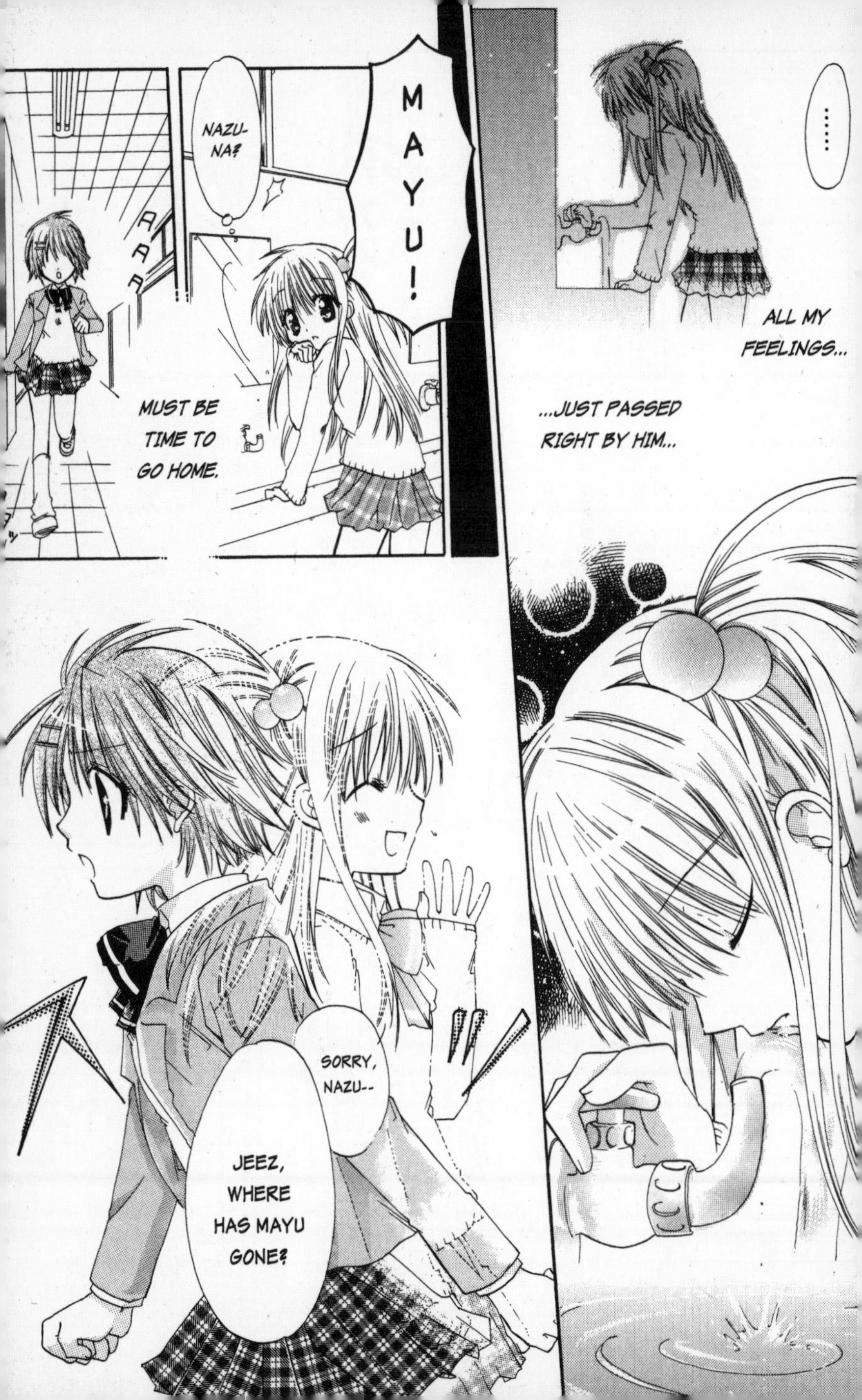
......
ALL MY FEELINGS...
...JUST PASSED RIGHT BY HIM...
MAYU!
NAZU-NA?
MUST BE TIME TO GO HOME.
SORRY, NAZU--
JEEZ, WHERE HAS MAYU GONE?

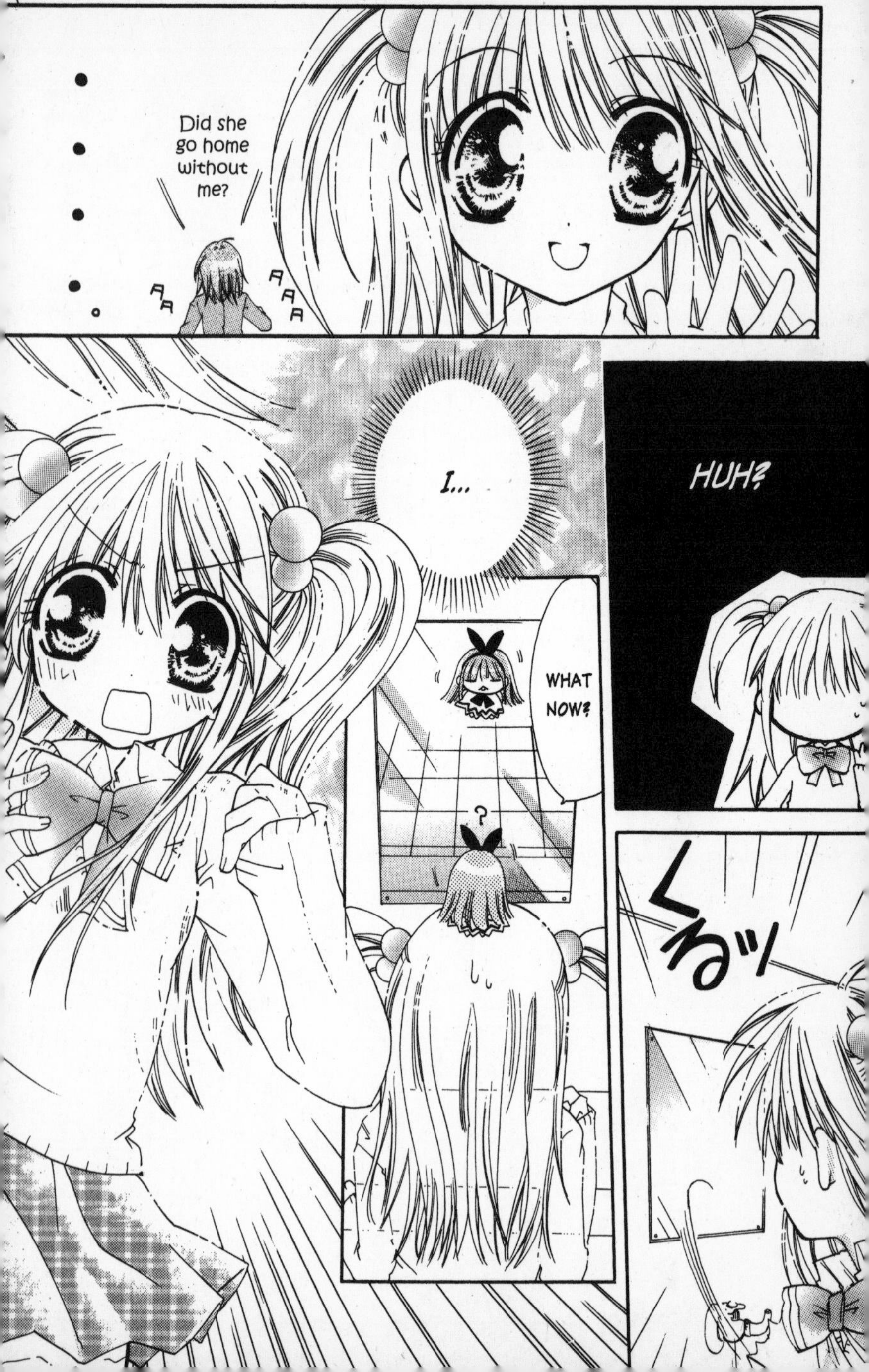
Did she go home without me?
HUH?
くるッ
WHAT NOW?
I...

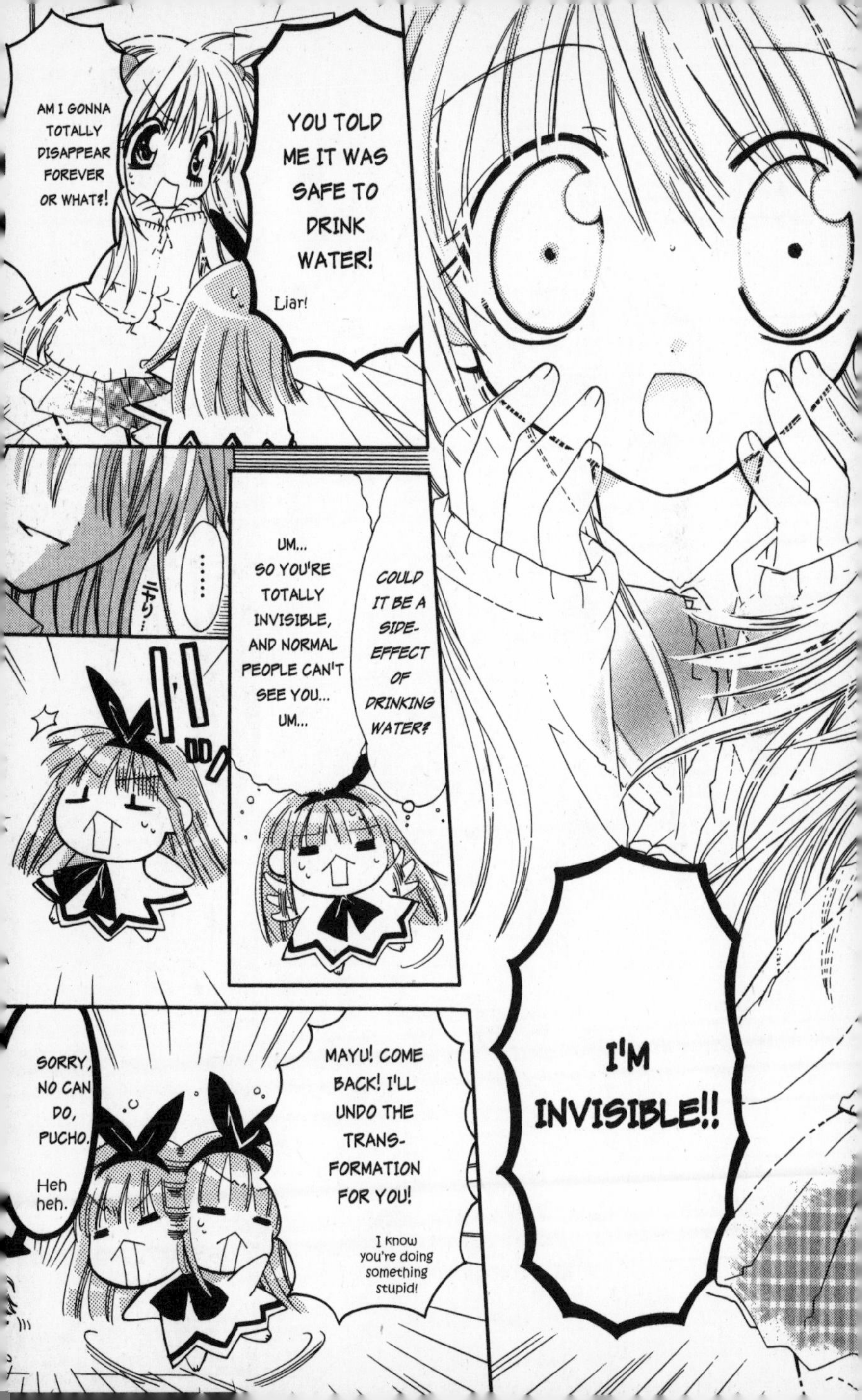
I'M INVISIBLE!!
YOU TOLD ME IT WAS SAFE TO DRINK WATER!
Liar!
AM I GONNA TOTALLY DISAPPEAR FOREVER OR WHAT?!
COULD IT BE A SIDE-EFFECT OF DRINKING WATER?
UM... SO YOU'RE TOTALLY INVISIBLE, AND NORMAL PEOPLE CAN'T SEE YOU... UM...
......
MAYU! COME BACK! I'LL UNDO THE TRANS-FORMATION FOR YOU!
I know you're doing something stupid!
SORRY, NO CAN DO, PUCHO.
Heh heh.

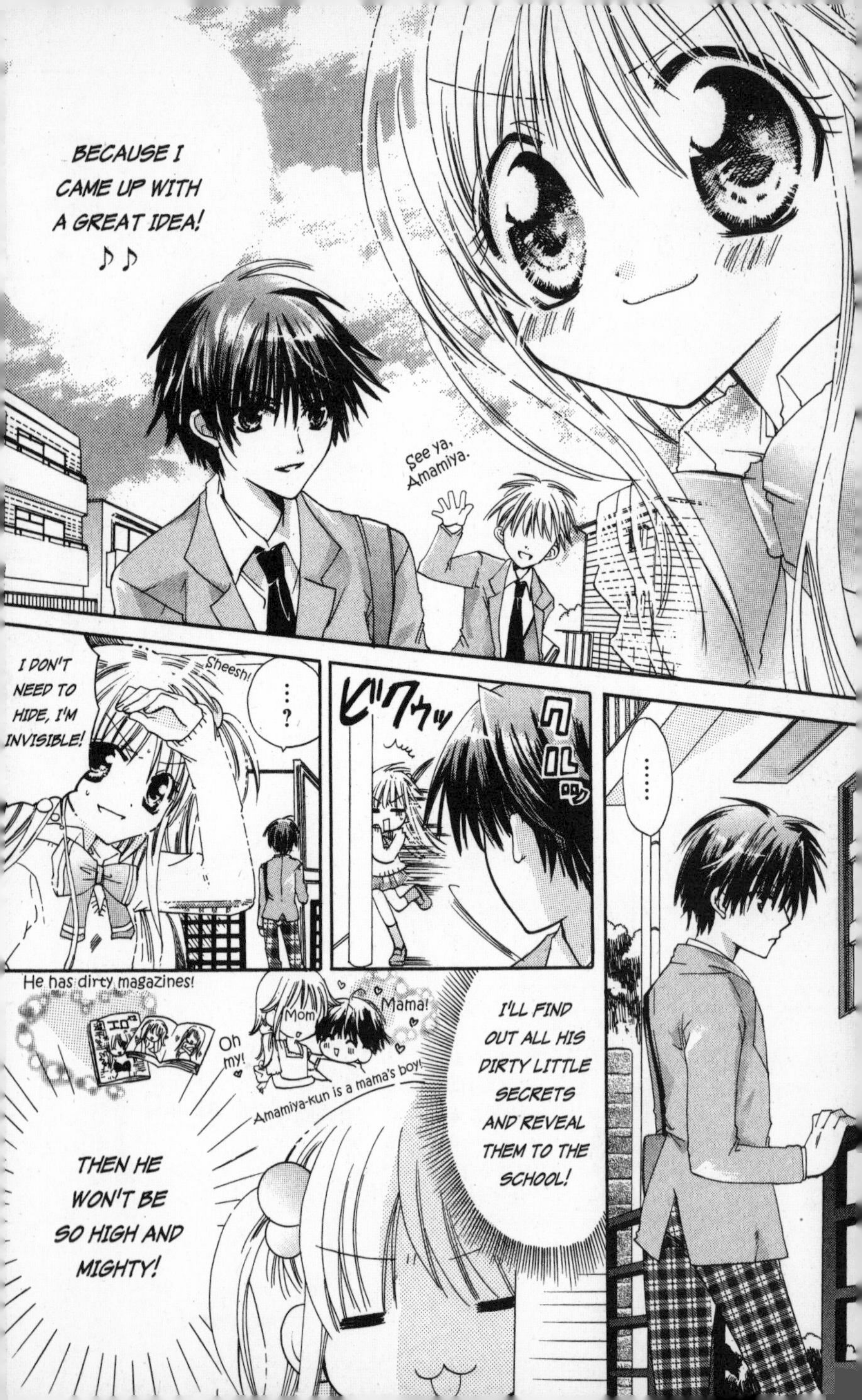
BECAUSE I CAME UP WITH A GREAT IDEA! ♪♪
See ya, Amamiya.
......
ビクゥッ
クルッ
I DON'T NEED TO HIDE, I'M INVISIBLE!
Sheesh!
...?
I'LL FIND OUT ALL HIS DIRTY LITTLE SECRETS AND REVEAL THEM TO THE SCHOOL!
Mama!
Mom
Oh my!
Amamiya-kun is a mama's boy!
He has dirty magazines!
THEN HE WON'T BE SO HIGH AND MIGHTY!

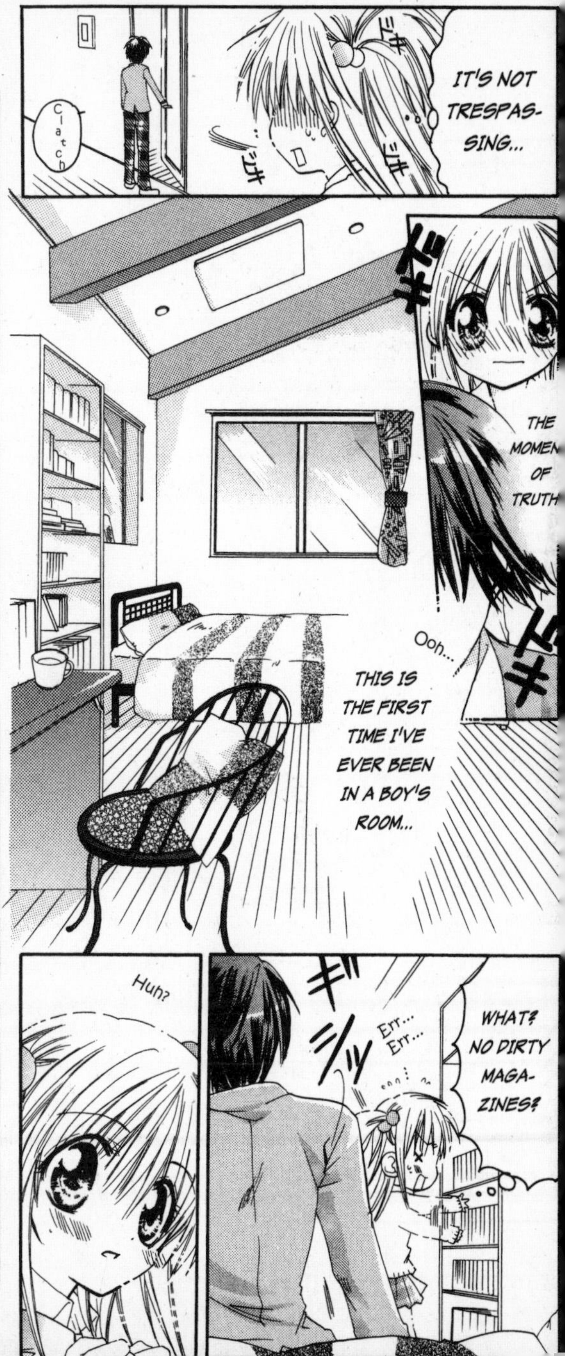
IT'S NOT TRESPAS-SING...
Clatch
THE MOMENT OF TRUTH
Ooh...
THIS IS THE FIRST TIME I'VE EVER BEEN IN A BOY'S ROOM...
WHAT? NO DIRTY MAGA-ZINES?
Err... Err...
Huh?

The Passion of the Amamiya-kun

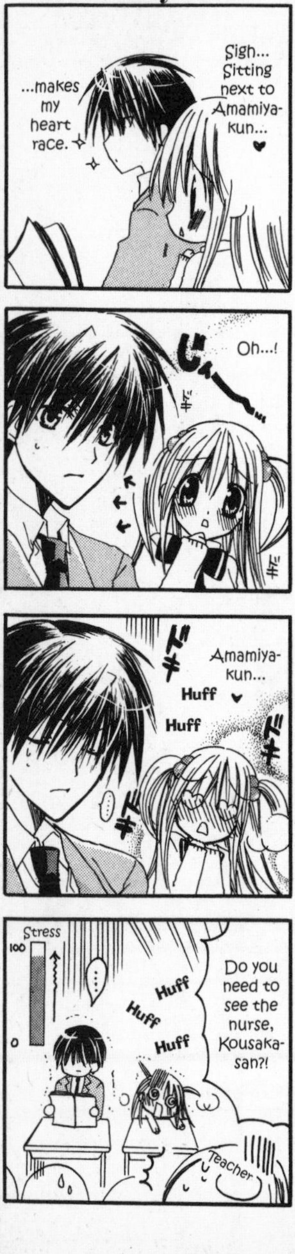
Sigh... Sitting next to Amamiya-kun...
...makes my heart race.
Oh...!
Amamiya-kun...
Huff
Huff
Do you need to see the nurse, Kousaka-san?!
Huff
Huff
Huff
Stress
100
0
Teacher

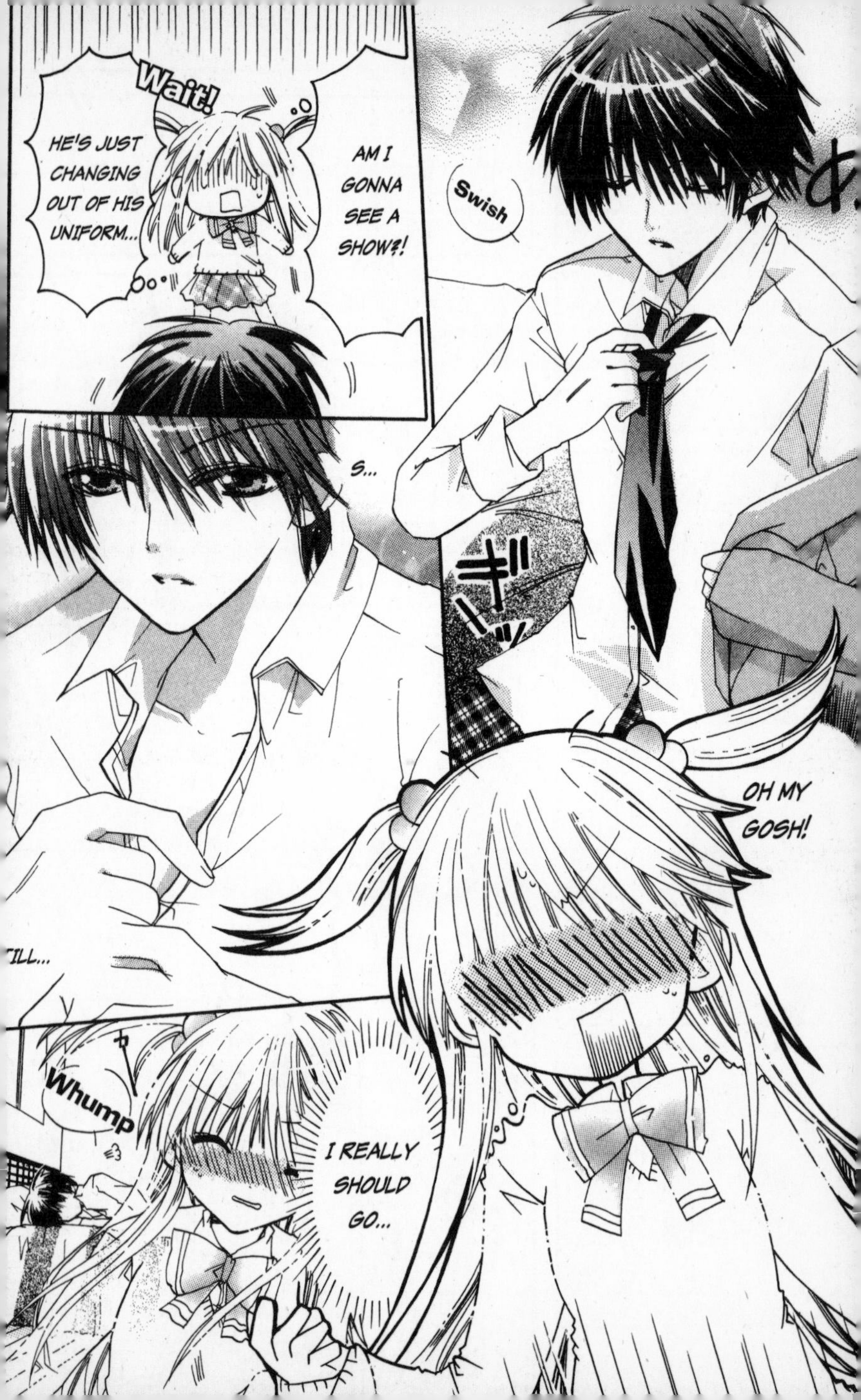
Swish
ギュッ
Wait!
HE'S JUST CHANGING OUT OF HIS UNIFORM...
AM I GONNA SEE A SHOW?!
S...
TILL...
OH MY GOSH!
Whump
I REALLY SHOULD GO...

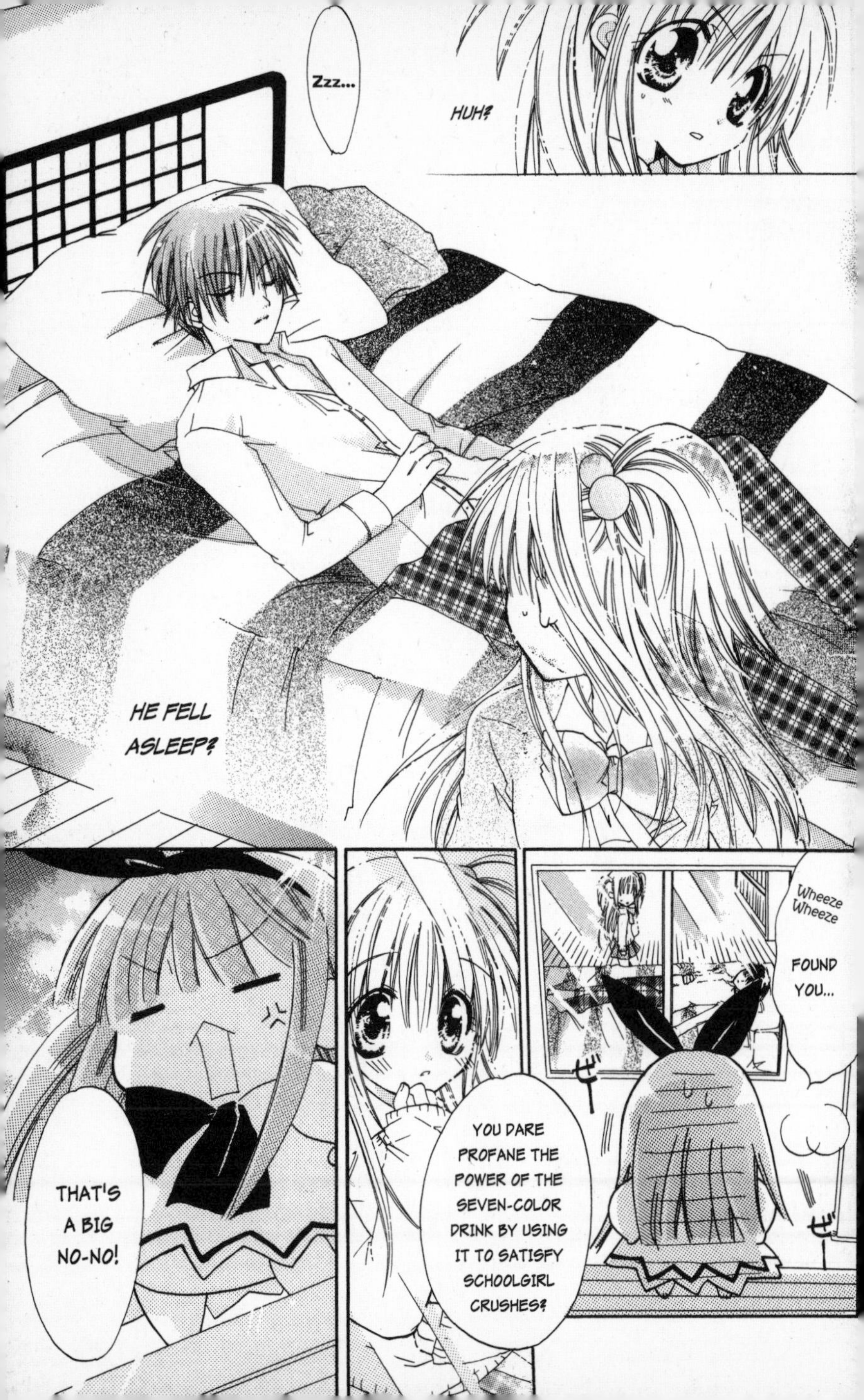
HUH?
Zzz...
HE FELL ASLEEP?
Wheeze Wheeze
FOUND YOU...
YOU DARE PROFANE THE POWER OF THE SEVEN-COLOR DRINK BY USING IT TO SATISFY SCHOOLGIRL CRUSHES?
THAT'S A BIG NO-NO!

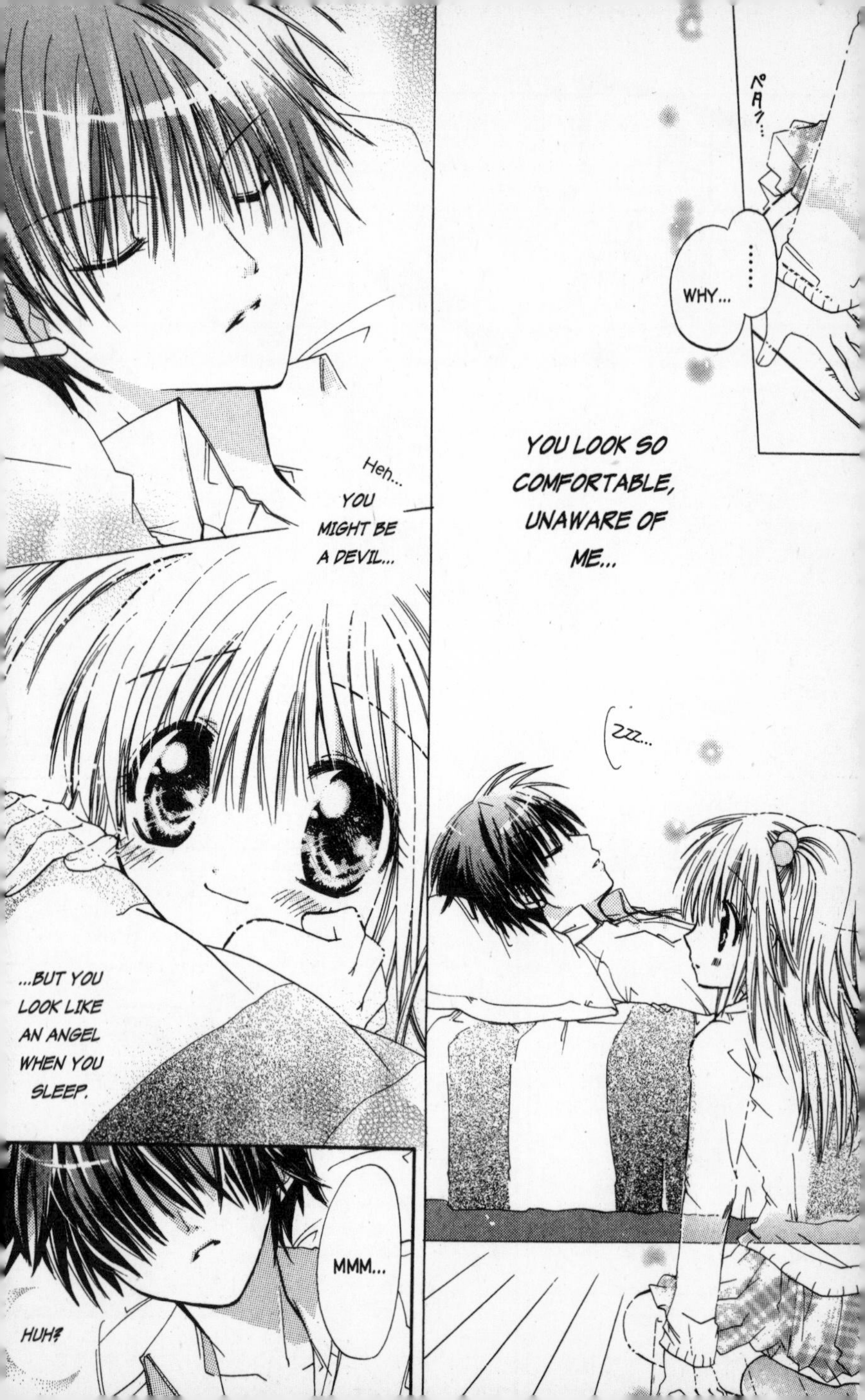
......
WHY...
YOU LOOK SO COMFORTABLE, UNAWARE OF ME...
ZZZ...
Heh...
YOU MIGHT BE A DEVIL...
...BUT YOU LOOK LIKE AN ANGEL WHEN YOU SLEEP.
MMM...
HUH?

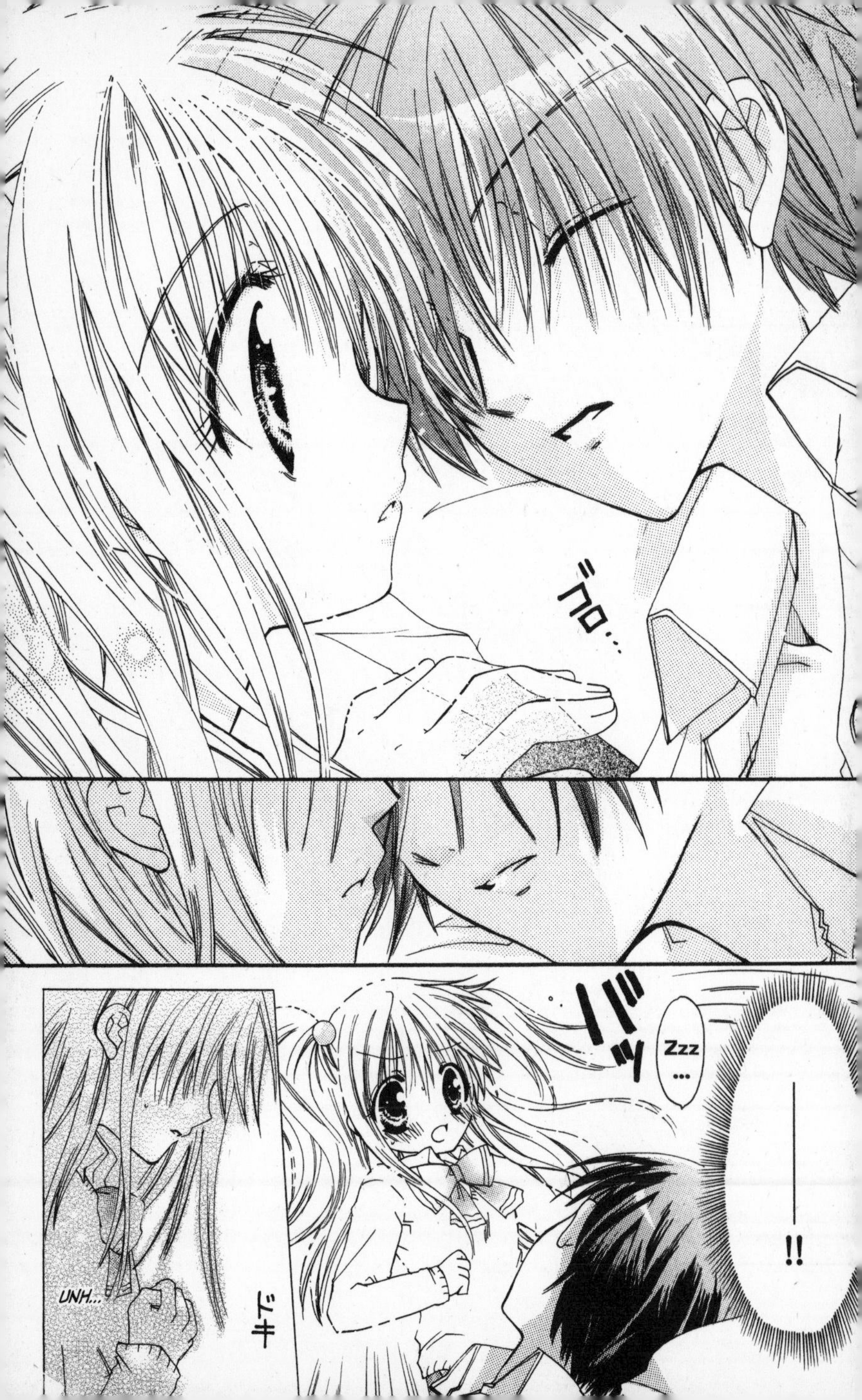
ゴロ…
――――!!
Zzz ...
バッ
ドキ
UNH...

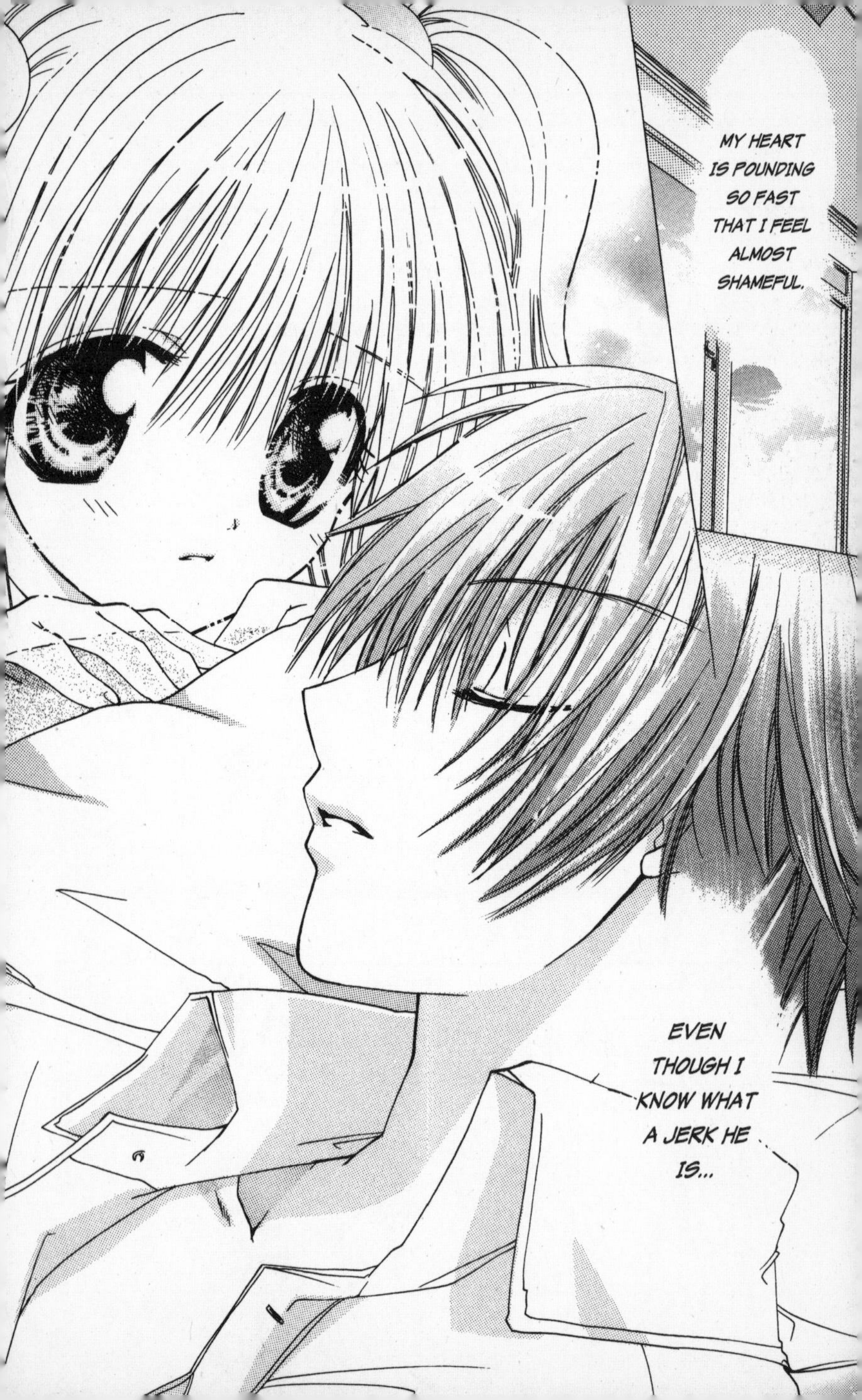
MY HEART IS POUNDING SO FAST THAT I FEEL ALMOST SHAMEFUL.
EVEN THOUGH I KNOW WHAT A JERK HE IS...

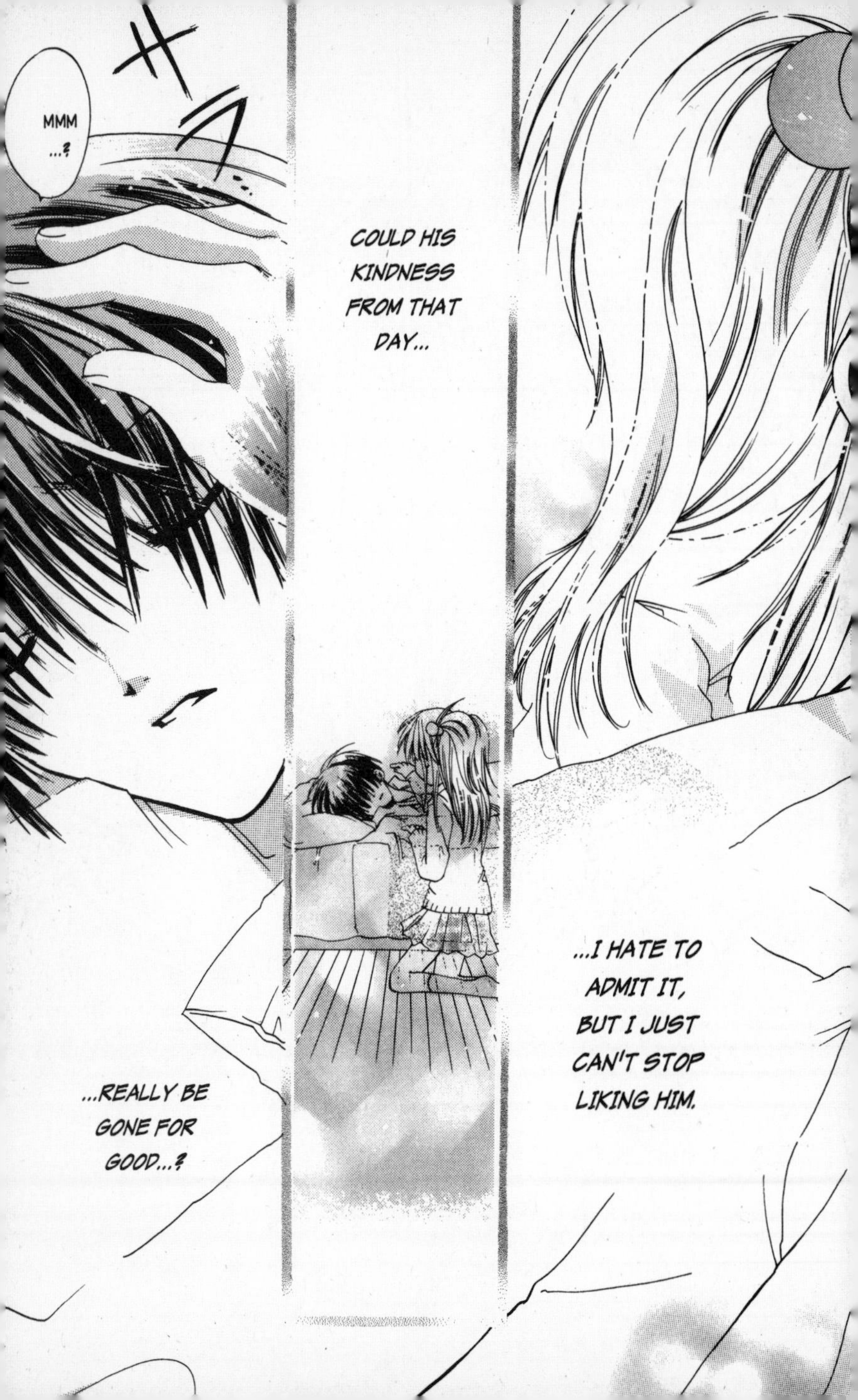

...I HATE TO ADMIT IT, BUT I JUST CAN'T STOP LIKING HIM.
COULD HIS KINDNESS FROM THAT DAY...
MMM ...?
...REALLY BE GONE FOR GOOD...?

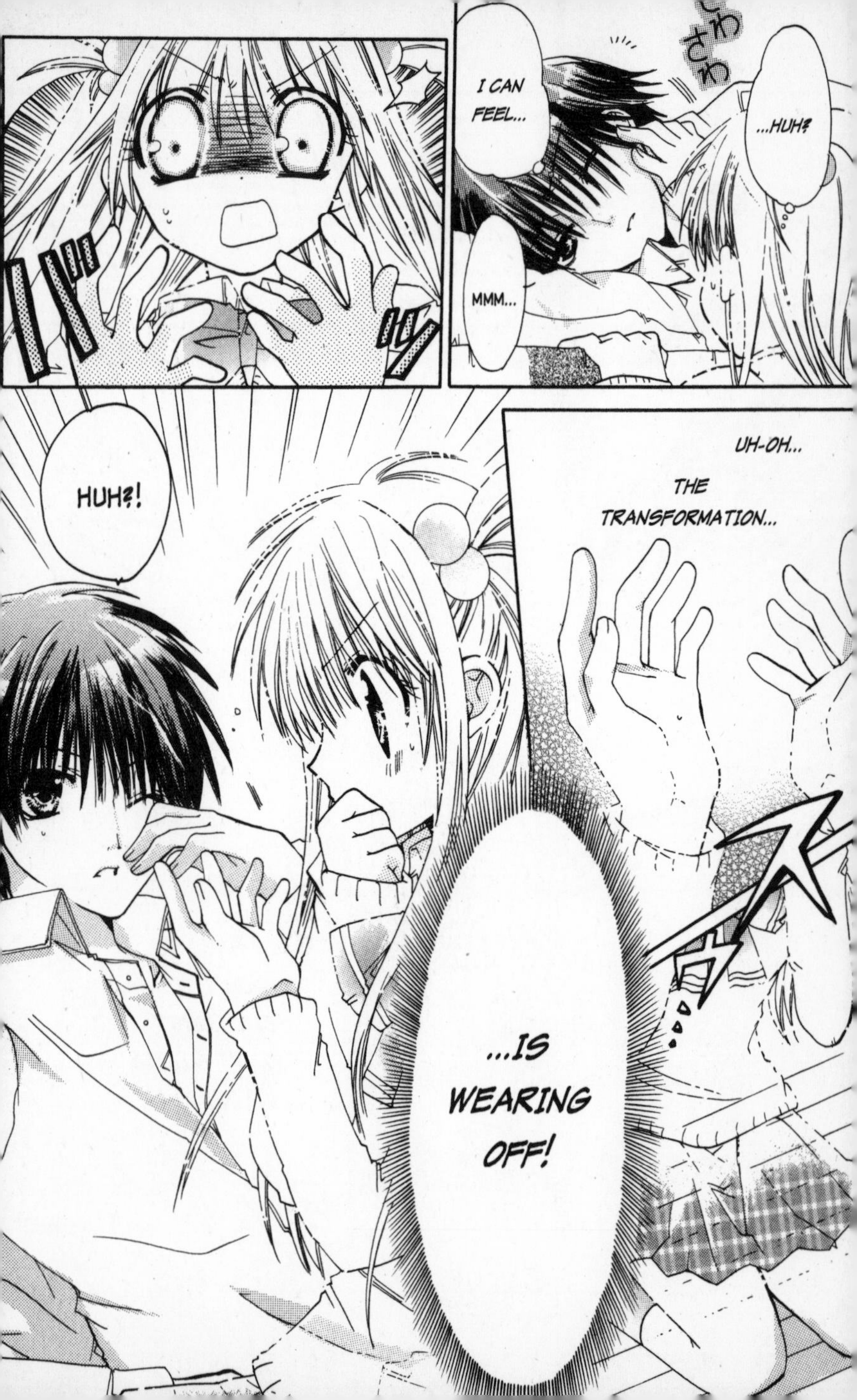
...HUH?
I CAN FEEL...
MMM...
HUH?!
UH-OH...
THE TRANSFORMATION...
...IS WEARING OFF!

GOKKUN!
PŪCHO

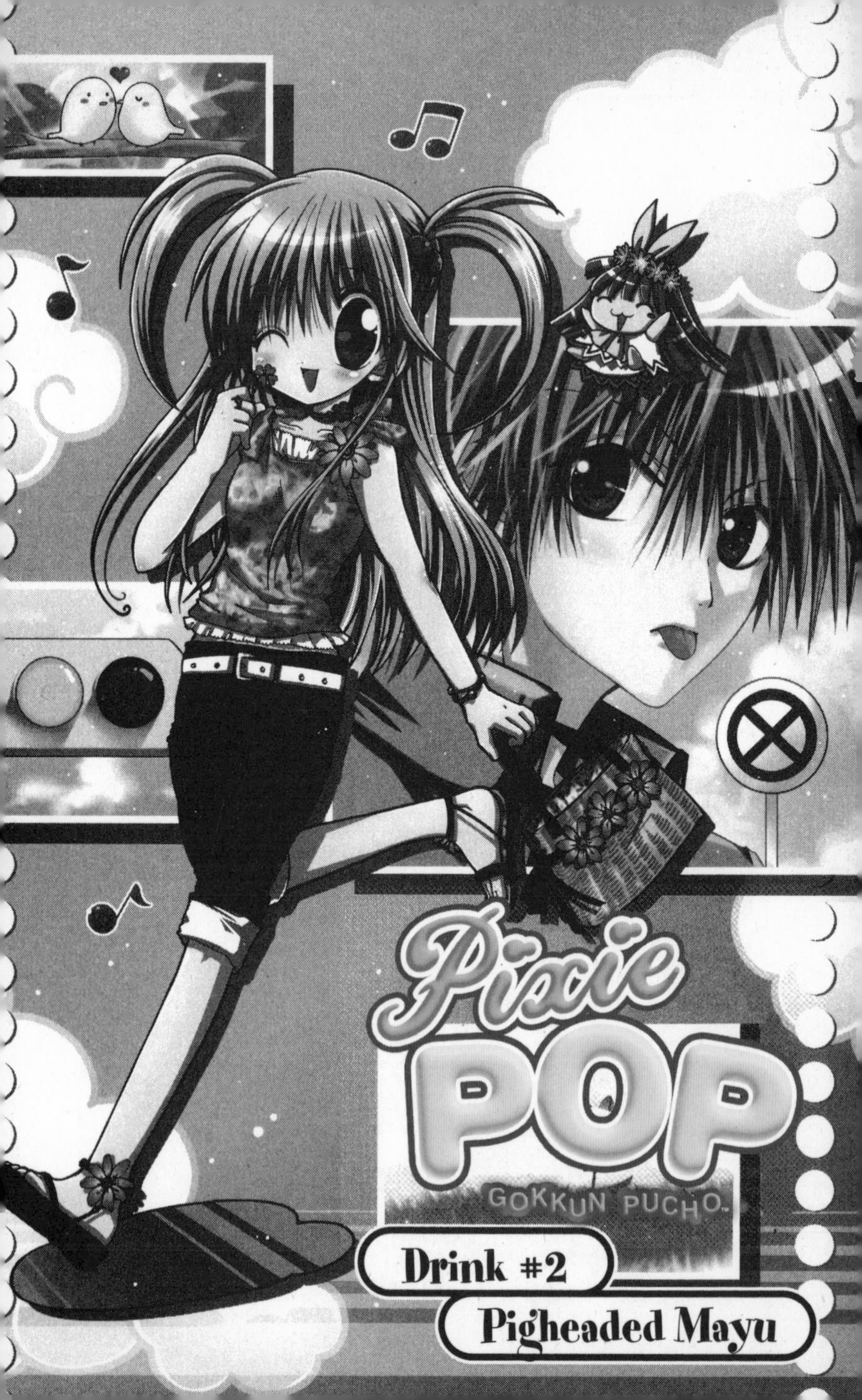
Pixie POP
GOKKUN PUCHO
Drink #2
Pigheaded Mayu

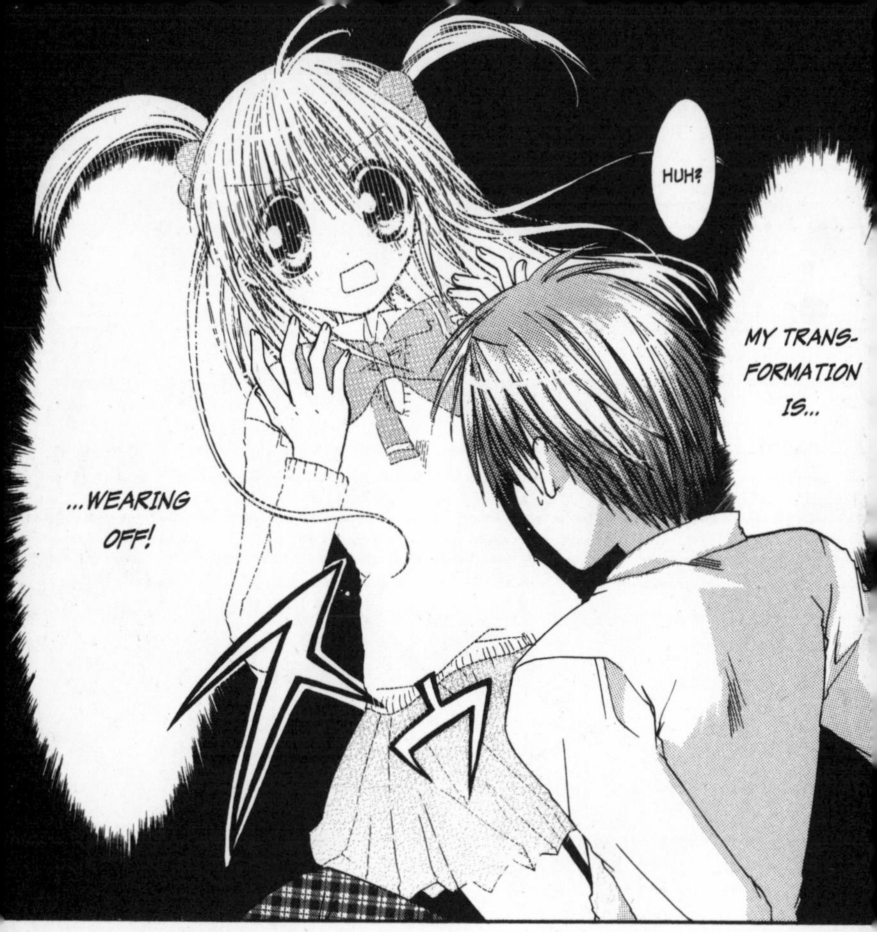
HUH?
MY TRANS-FORMATION IS...
...WEARING OFF!

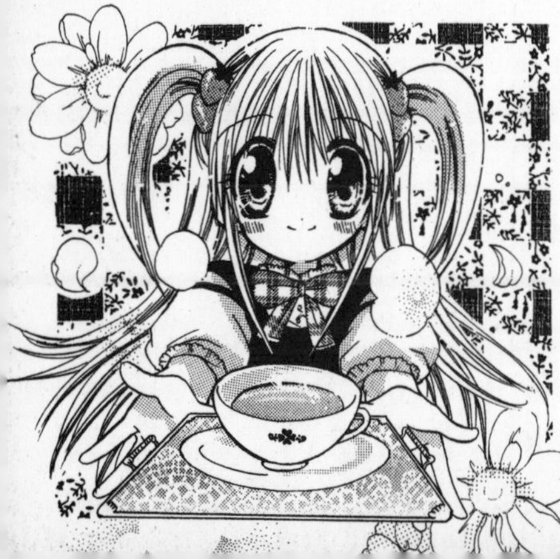

****

♥ Mayu Kousaka ♥

Birthday: November 17th
Sign: Scorpio Blood Type: A
Height: 148cm Weight: 40kg
Favorite Drink: Black Tea

****

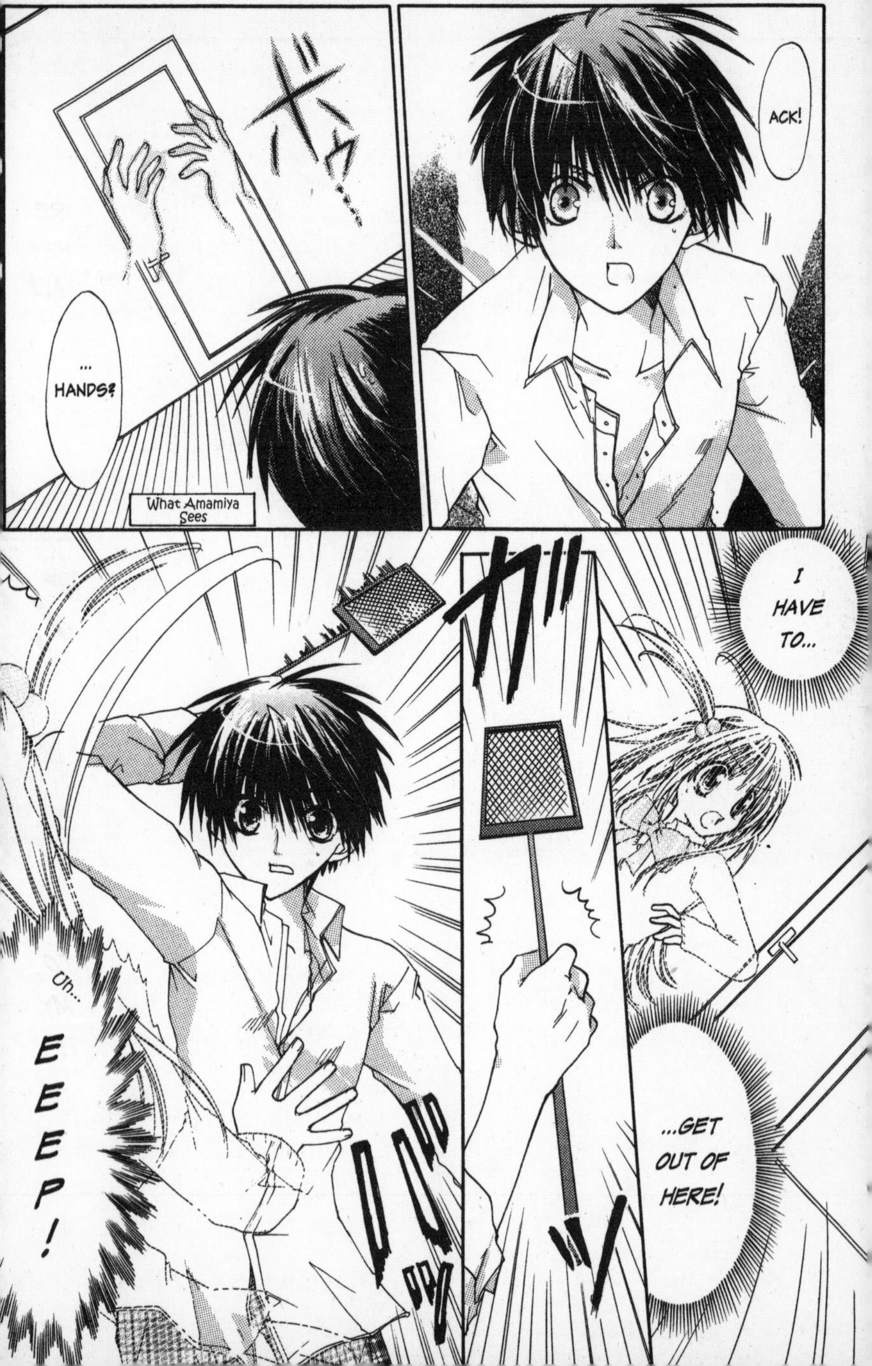
ACK!
... HANDS?
What Amamiya Sees
I HAVE TO...
...GET OUT OF HERE!
Uh...
EEEEP!

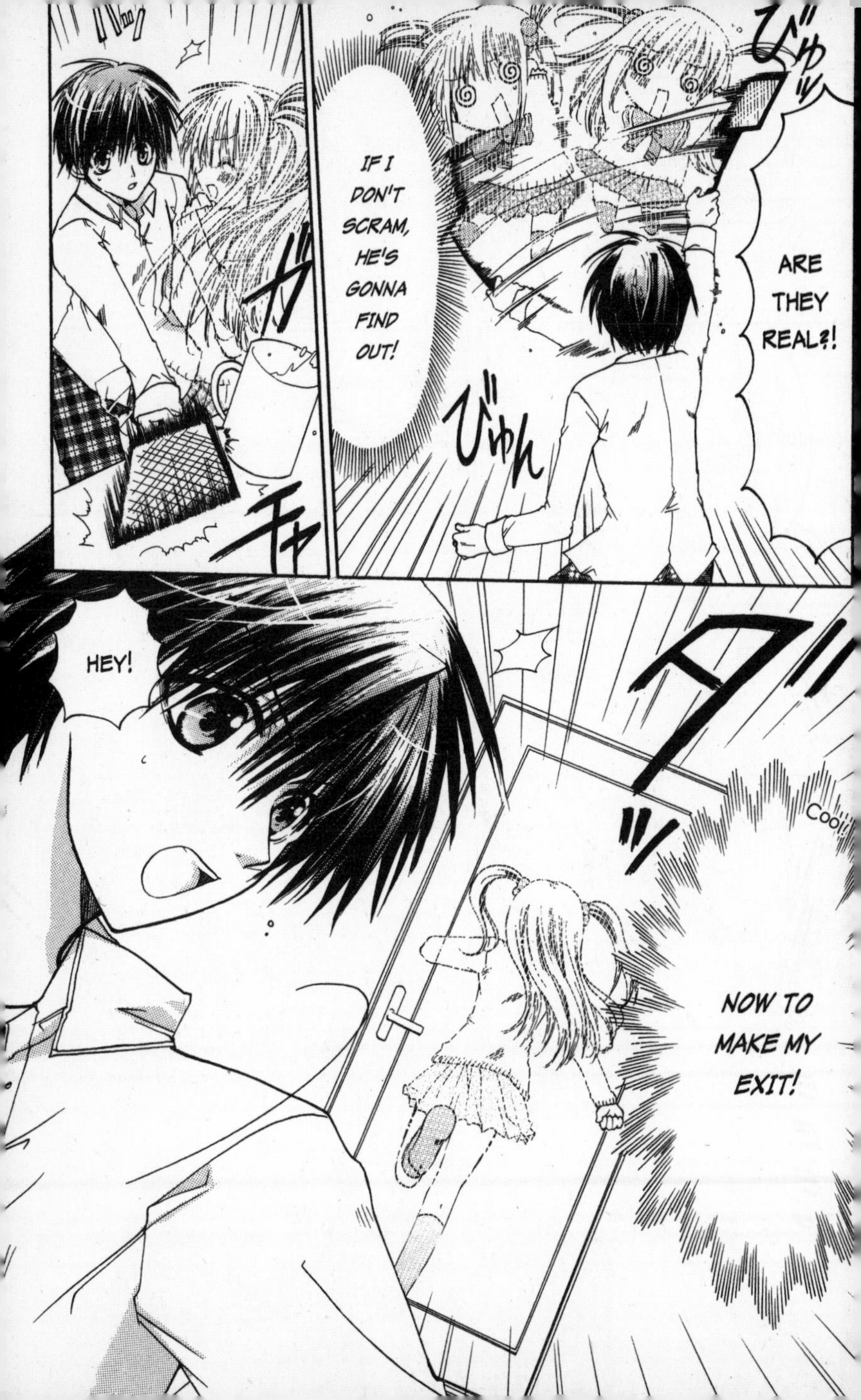
ARE THEY REAL?!
IF I DON'T SCRAM, HE'S GONNA FIND OUT!
びゅん
ガチャ
ダッ
Cool!
NOW TO MAKE MY EXIT!
HEY!

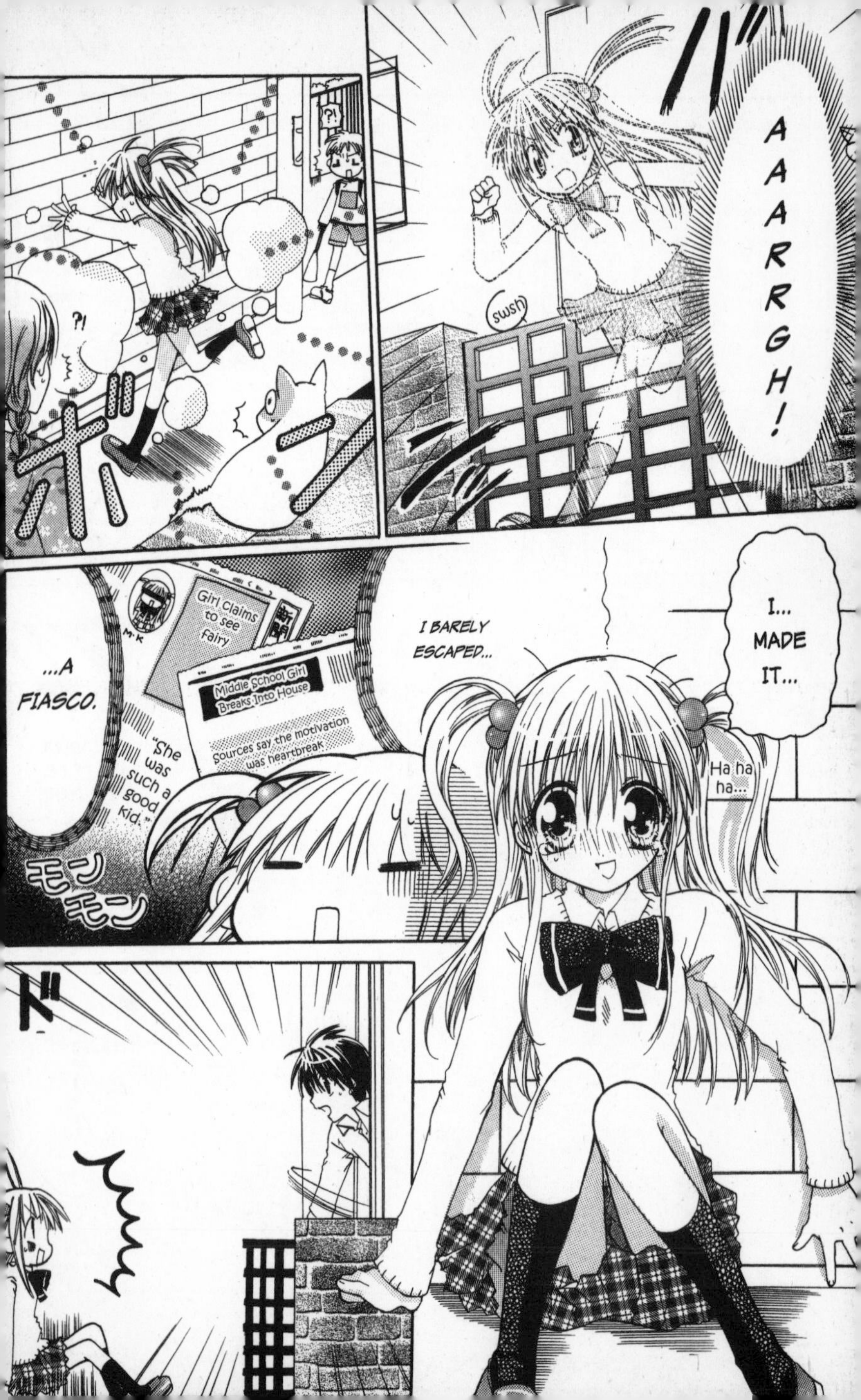
AAARRGH!
swsh
?!
?!
I... MADE IT...
Ha ha ha...
I BARELY ESCAPED...
Girl Claims to see fairy
Middle School Girl Breaks Into House
Sources say the motivation was heartbreak
"She was such a good kid."
...A FIASCO.

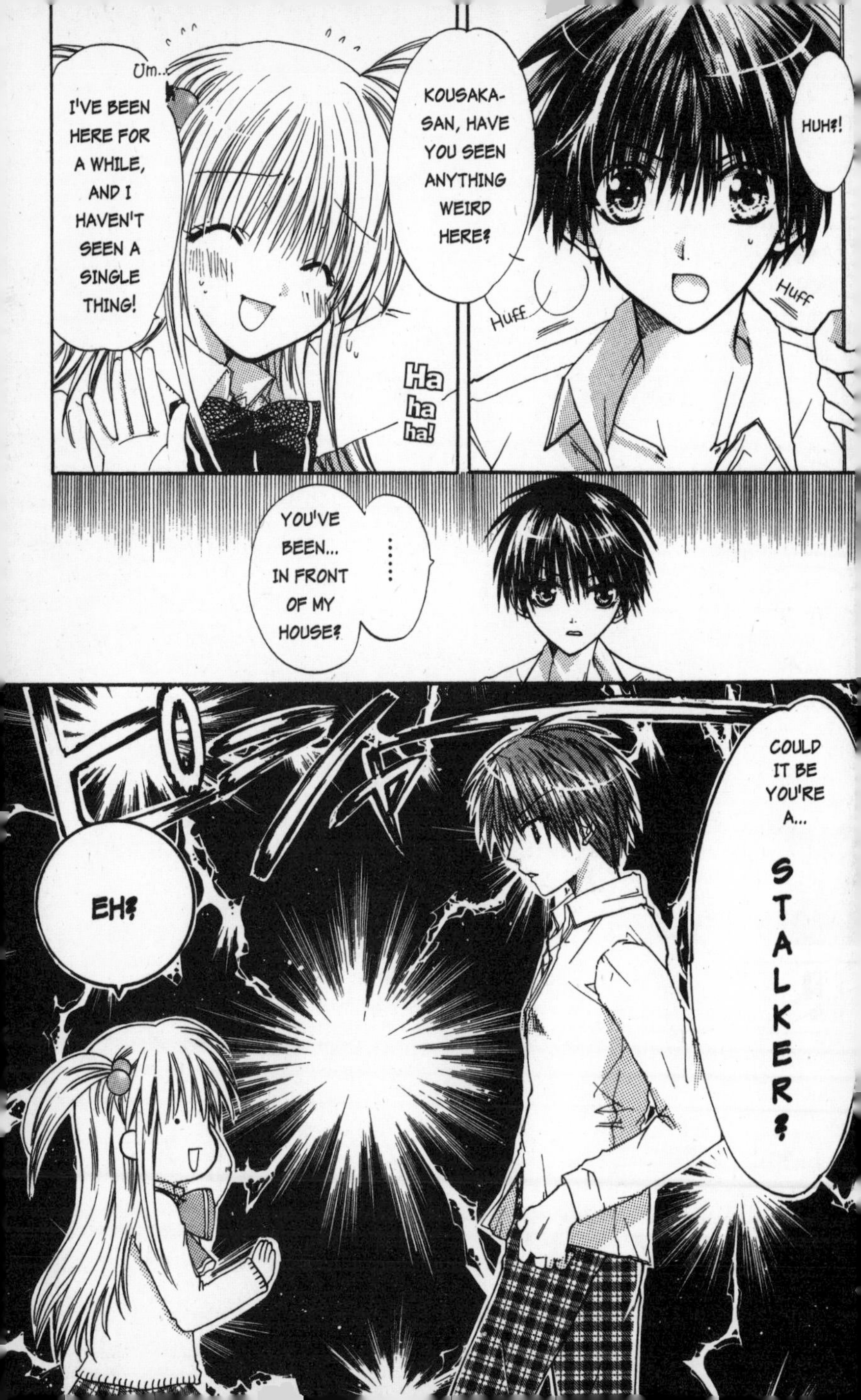
HUH?!
Huff
Huff
KOUSAKA-SAN, HAVE YOU SEEN ANYTHING WEIRD HERE?
Um...
I'VE BEEN HERE FOR A WHILE, AND I HAVEN'T SEEN A SINGLE THING!
Ha ha ha!
......
YOU'VE BEEN... IN FRONT OF MY HOUSE?
COULD IT BE YOU'RE A... STALKER?
EH?

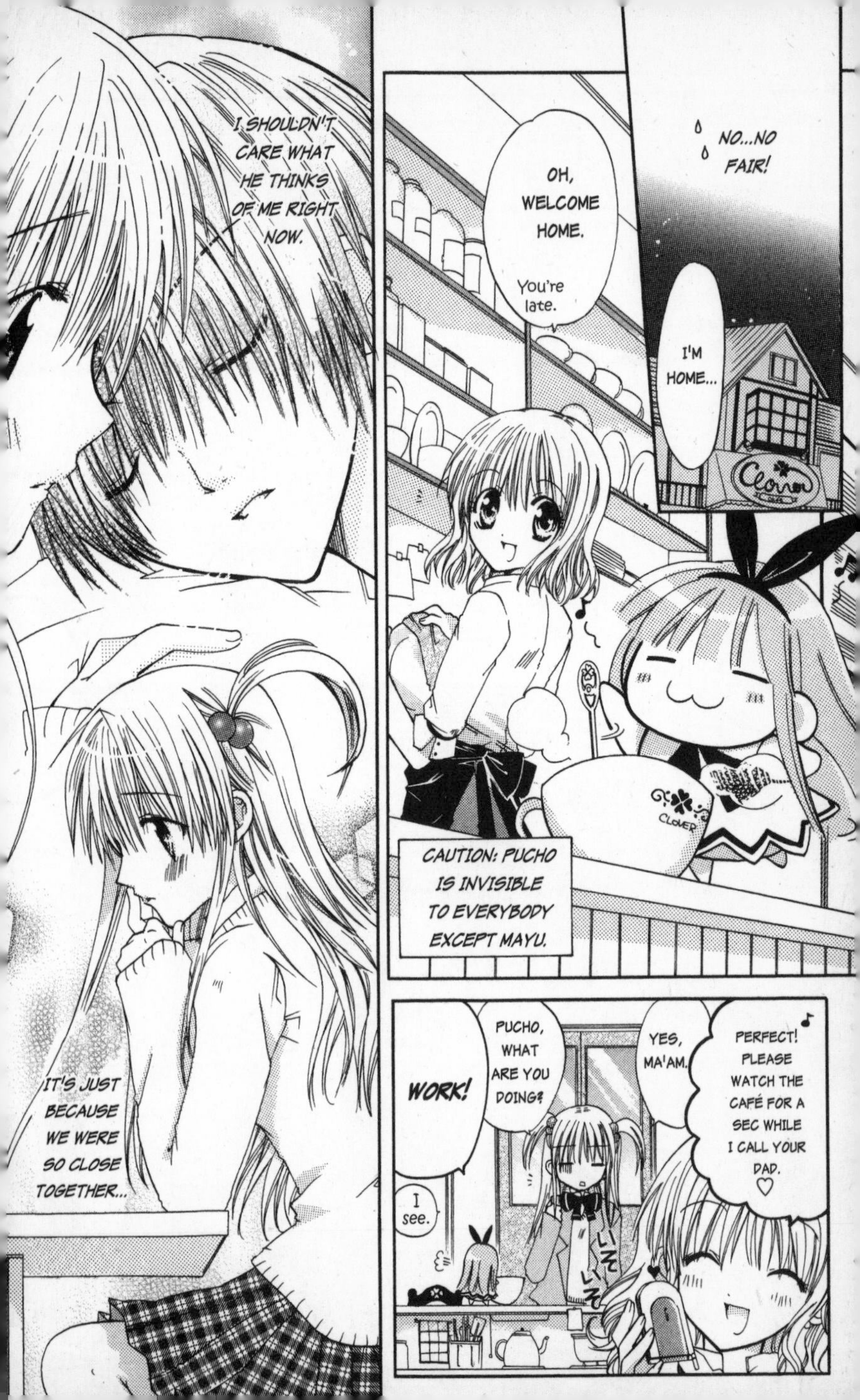
NO...NO FAIR!
I'M HOME...
OH, WELCOME HOME.
You're late.
CAUTION: PUCHO IS INVISIBLE TO EVERYBODY EXCEPT MAYU.
PERFECT! PLEASE WATCH THE CAFÉ FOR A SEC WHILE I CALL YOUR DAD. ♡
YES, MA'AM.
PUCHO, WHAT ARE YOU DOING?
WORK!
I see.
I SHOULDN'T CARE WHAT HE THINKS OF ME RIGHT NOW.
IT'S JUST BECAUSE WE WERE SO CLOSE TOGETHER...

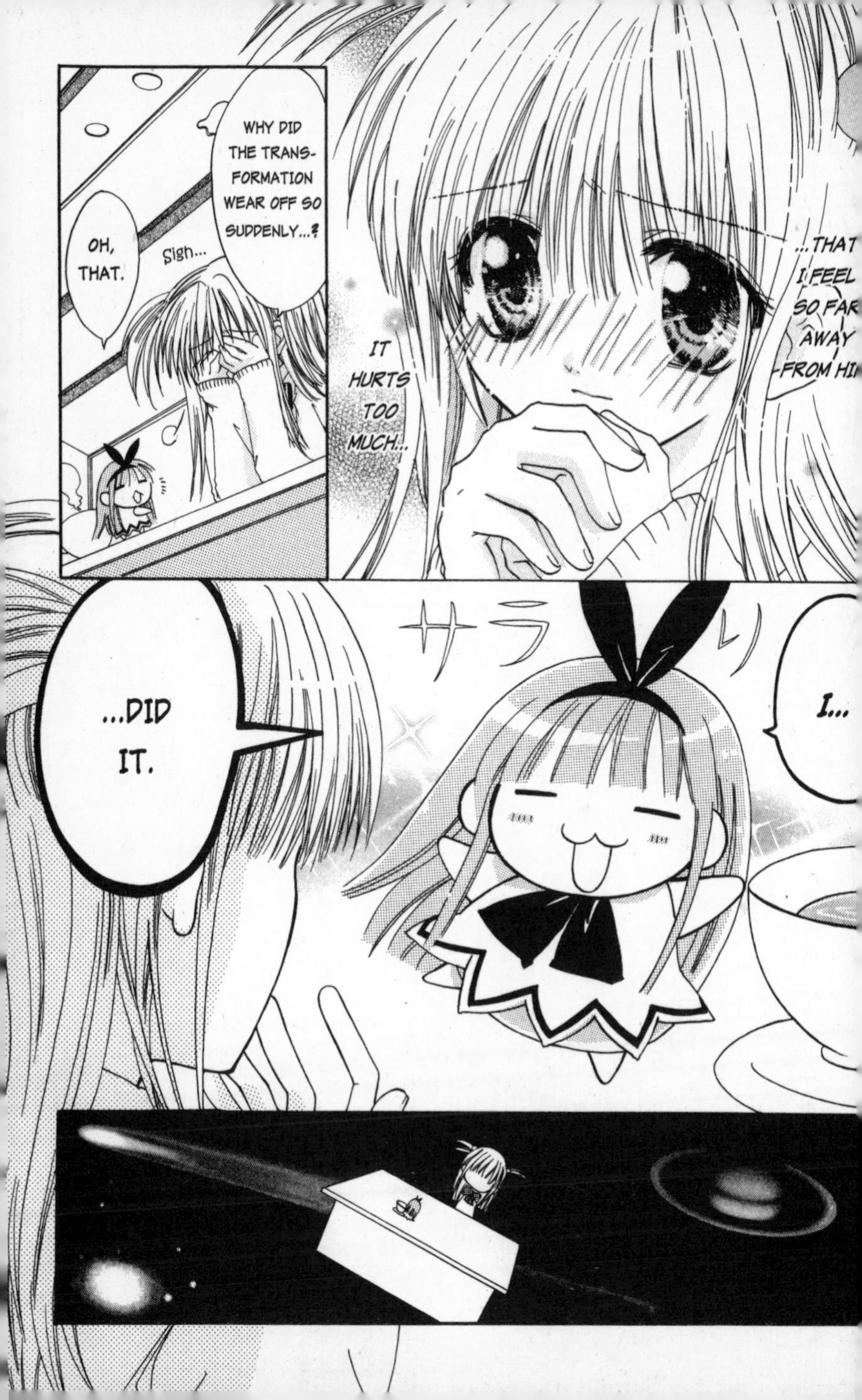
...THAT I FEEL SO FAR AWAY FROM HI
IT HURTS TOO MUCH...
WHY DID THE TRANS-FORMATION WEAR OFF SO SUDDENLY...?
Sigh...
OH, THAT.
I...
サラ
...DID IT.

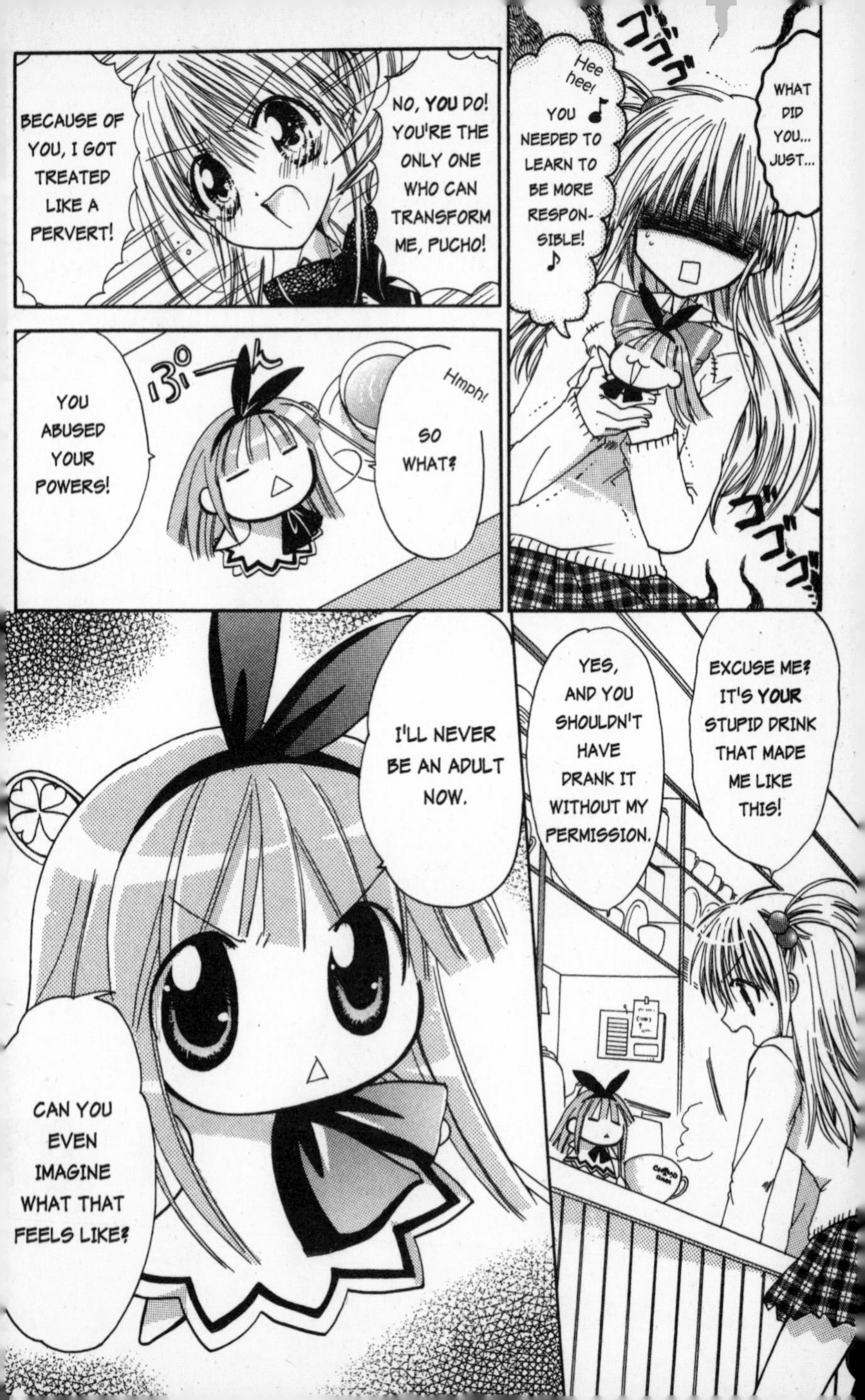

ゴゴゴ
WHAT DID YOU... JUST...
Hee hee!
YOU ♪ NEEDED TO LEARN TO BE MORE RESPON-SIBLE! ♪
ゴゴゴ
BECAUSE OF YOU, I GOT TREATED LIKE A PERVERT!
NO, YOU DO! YOU'RE THE ONLY ONE WHO CAN TRANSFORM ME, PUCHO!
YOU ABUSED YOUR POWERS!
Hmph!
SO WHAT?
EXCUSE ME? IT'S YOUR STUPID DRINK THAT MADE ME LIKE THIS!
YES, AND YOU SHOULDN'T HAVE DRANK IT WITHOUT MY PERMISSION.
I'LL NEVER BE AN ADULT NOW.
CAN YOU EVEN IMAGINE WHAT THAT FEELS LIKE?

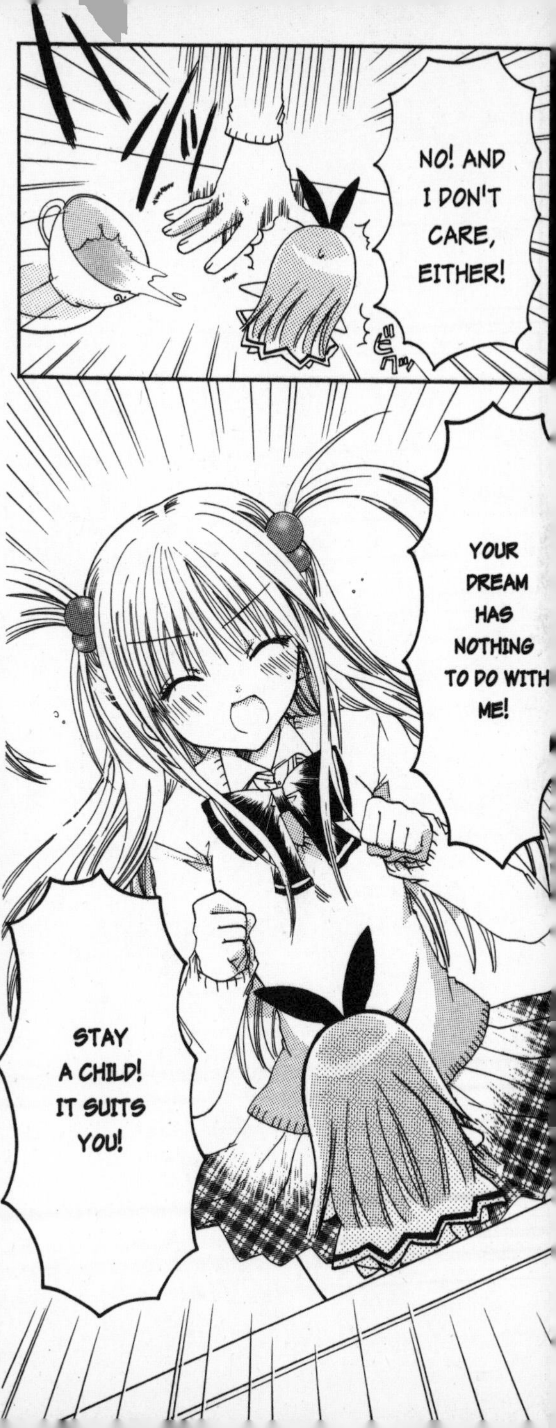
NO! AND I DON'T CARE, EITHER!
YOUR DREAM HAS NOTHING TO DO WITH ME!
STAY A CHILD! IT SUITS YOU!

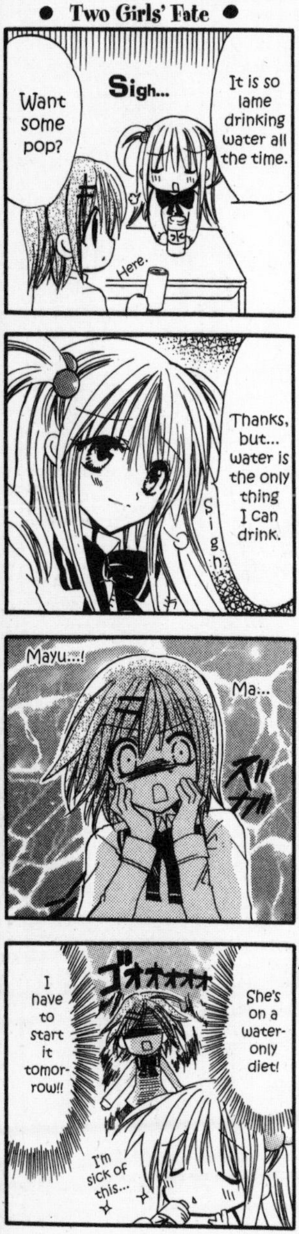
Two Girls' Fate
It is so lame drinking water all the time.
Sigh...
Want some pop?
Here.
Thanks, but... water is the only thing I can drink.
Sigh
Mayu...!
Ma...
ゴオオオオオ
She's on a water-only diet!
I have to start it tomorrow!!
I'm sick of this...

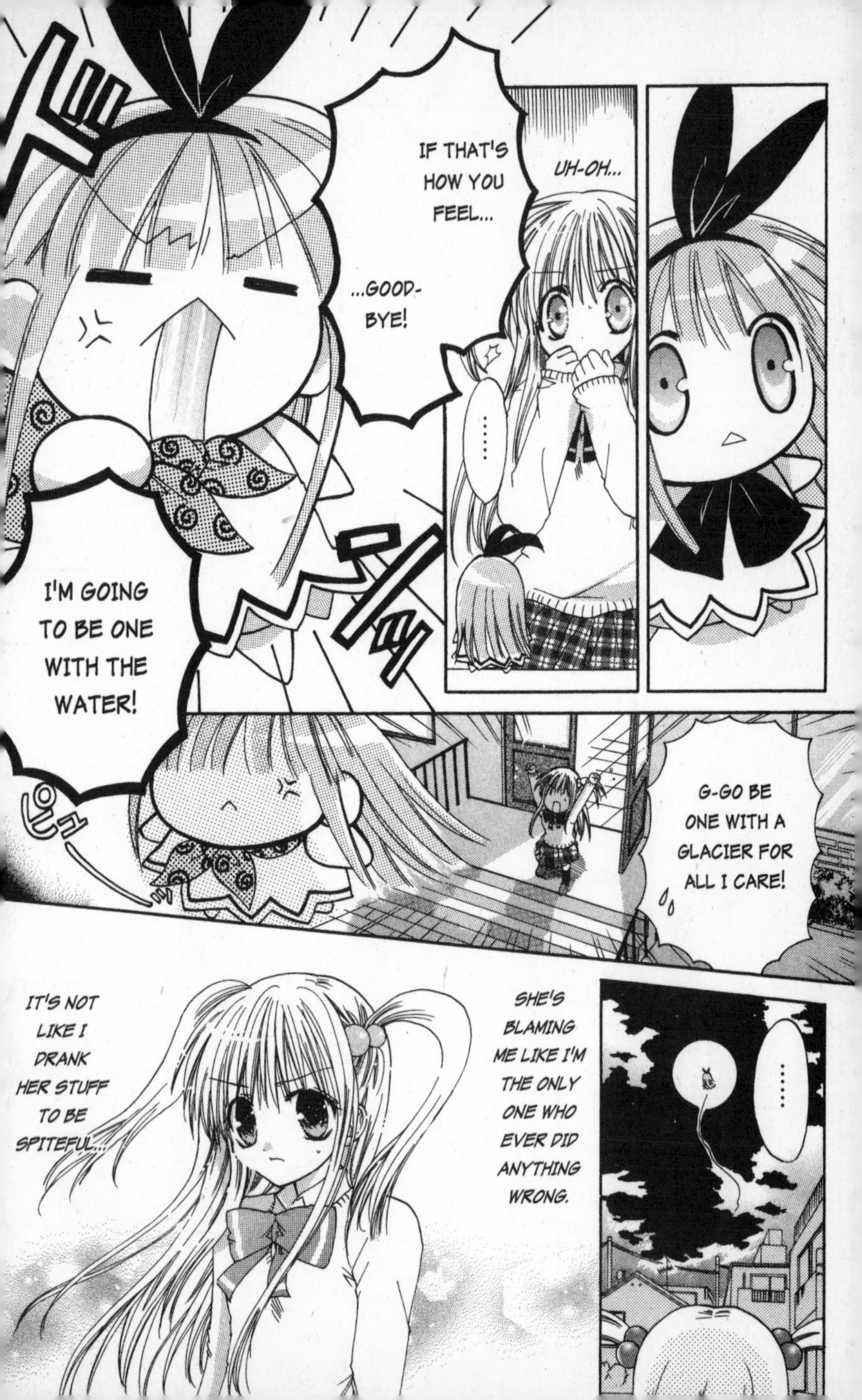
UH-OH...
......
IF THAT'S HOW YOU FEEL...
...GOOD-BYE!
I'M GOING TO BE ONE WITH THE WATER!
G-GO BE ONE WITH A GLACIER FOR ALL I CARE!
......
SHE'S BLAMING ME LIKE I'M THE ONLY ONE WHO EVER DID ANYTHING WRONG.
IT'S NOT LIKE I DRANK HER STUFF TO BE SPITEFUL...

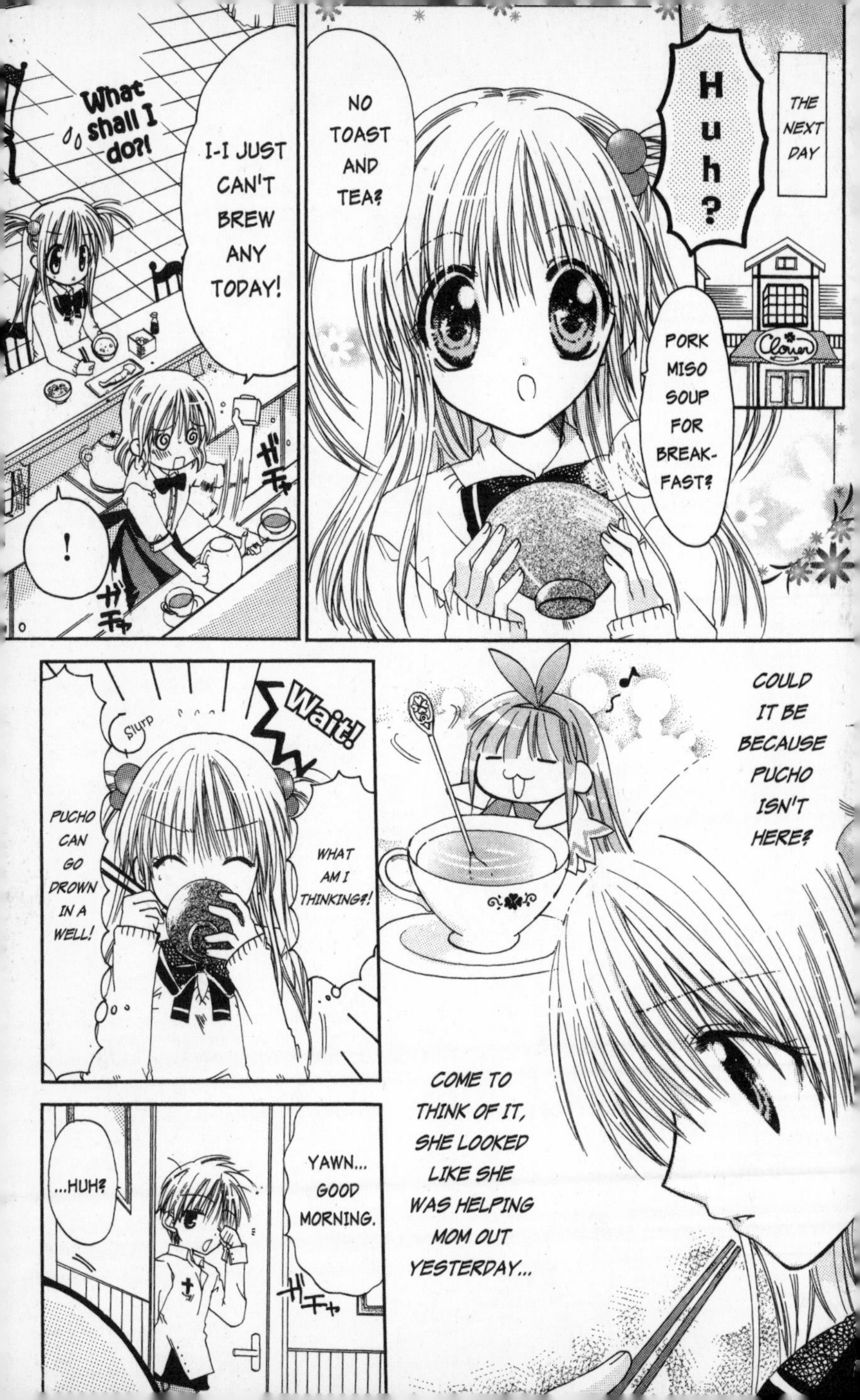
THE NEXT DAY
Huh?
PORK MISO SOUP FOR BREAK-FAST?
NO TOAST AND TEA?
I-I JUST CAN'T BREW ANY TODAY!
What shall I do?!
ガチャ
!
ガチャ
COULD IT BE BECAUSE PUCHO ISN'T HERE?
COME TO THINK OF IT, SHE LOOKED LIKE SHE WAS HELPING MOM OUT YESTERDAY...
Wait!
Slurp
WHAT AM I THINKING?!
PUCHO CAN GO DROWN IN A WELL!
YAWN... GOOD MORNING.
...HUH?
ガチャ

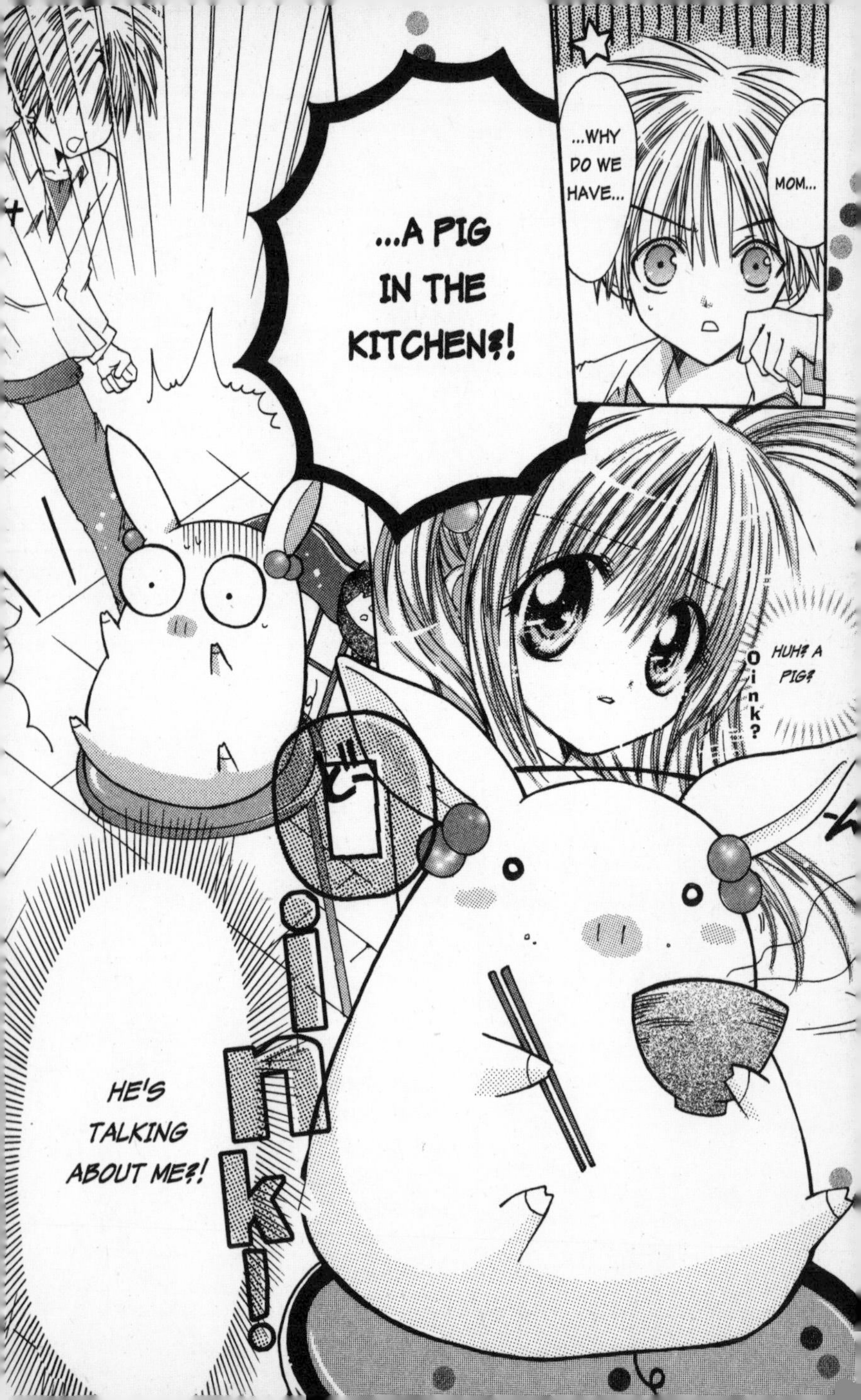
MOM...
...WHY DO WE HAVE...
...A PIG IN THE KITCHEN?!
HUH? A PIG?
Oink?
Oink!
HE'S TALKING ABOUT ME?!

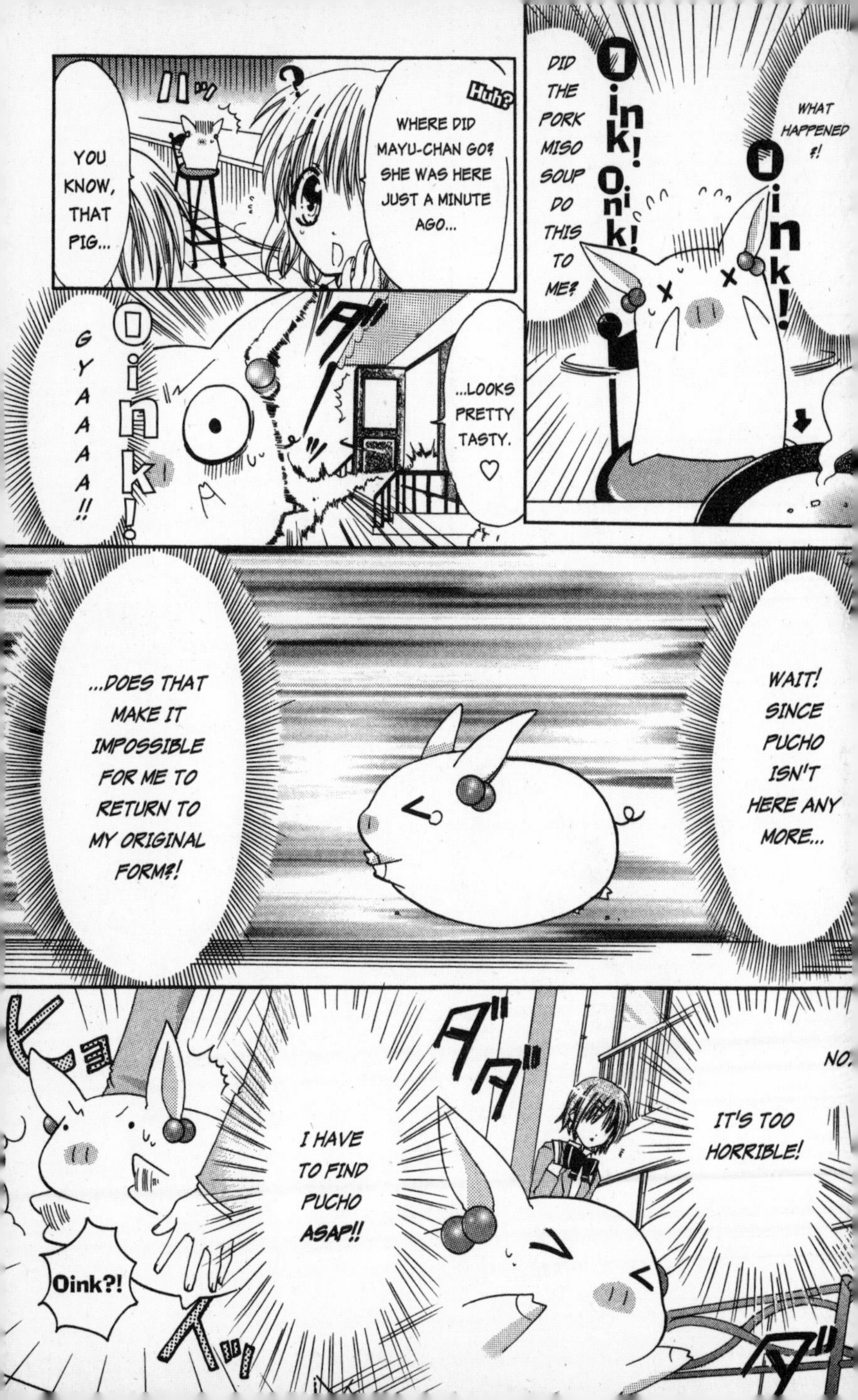
WHAT HAPPENED ?!
Oink!
Oink! Oink!
DID THE PORK MISO SOUP DO THIS TO ME?
Huh?
WHERE DID MAYU-CHAN GO? SHE WAS HERE JUST A MINUTE AGO...
YOU KNOW, THAT PIG...
...LOOKS PRETTY TASTY. ♡
Oink!
GYAAAAA!!
WAIT! SINCE PUCHO ISN'T HERE ANY MORE...
...DOES THAT MAKE IT IMPOSSIBLE FOR ME TO RETURN TO MY ORIGINAL FORM?!
NO.
IT'S TOO HORRIBLE!
I HAVE TO FIND PUCHO ASAP!!
Oink?!

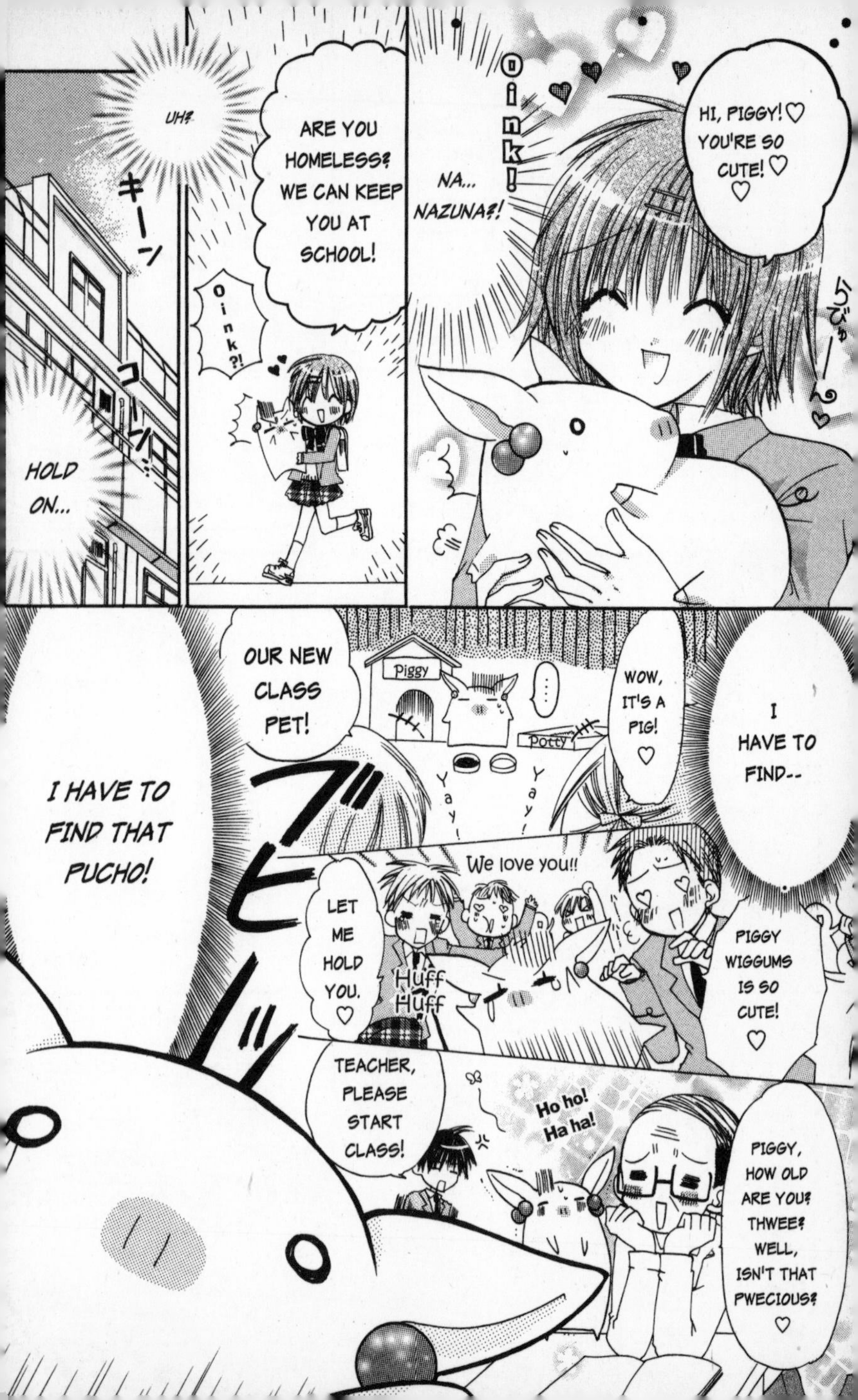
Oink!
NA... NAZUNA?!
HI, PIGGY! ♡ YOU'RE SO CUTE! ♡ ♡
ARE YOU HOMELESS? WE CAN KEEP YOU AT SCHOOL!
Oink?!
UH?
キーン
HOLD ON...
I HAVE TO FIND--
WOW, IT'S A PIG! ♡
...
OUR NEW CLASS PET!
Piggy
Potty
Yay!
Yay!
PIGGY WIGGUMS IS SO CUTE! ♡
We love you!!
LET ME HOLD YOU. ♡
Huff Huff
PIGGY, HOW OLD ARE YOU? THWEE? WELL, ISN'T THAT PWECIOUS? ♡
Ho ho! Ha ha!
TEACHER, PLEASE START CLASS!
I HAVE TO FIND THAT PUCHO!

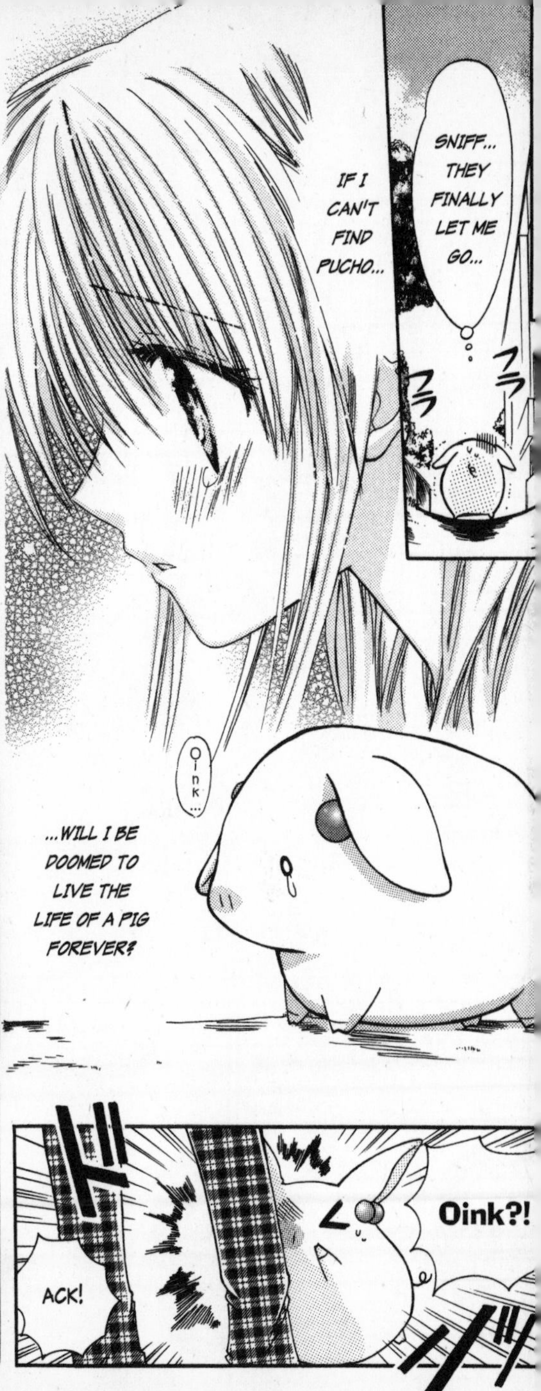
SNIFF... THEY FINALLY LET ME GO...
IF I CAN'T FIND PUCHO...
Oink...
...WILL I BE DOOMED TO LIVE THE LIFE OF A PIG FOREVER?
Oink?!
ACK!

● Trauma ●

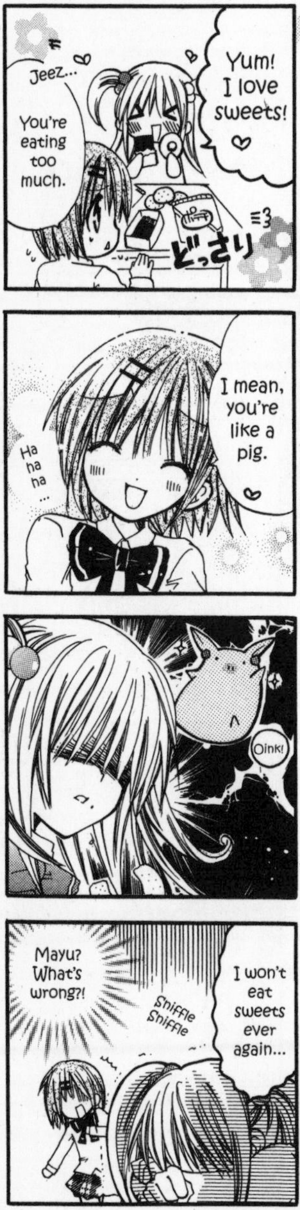
Yum! I love sweets!
Jeez...
You're eating too much.
どっさり
I mean, you're like a pig.
Ha ha ha ...
Oink!
I won't eat sweets ever again...
Sniffle Sniffle
Mayu? What's wrong?!

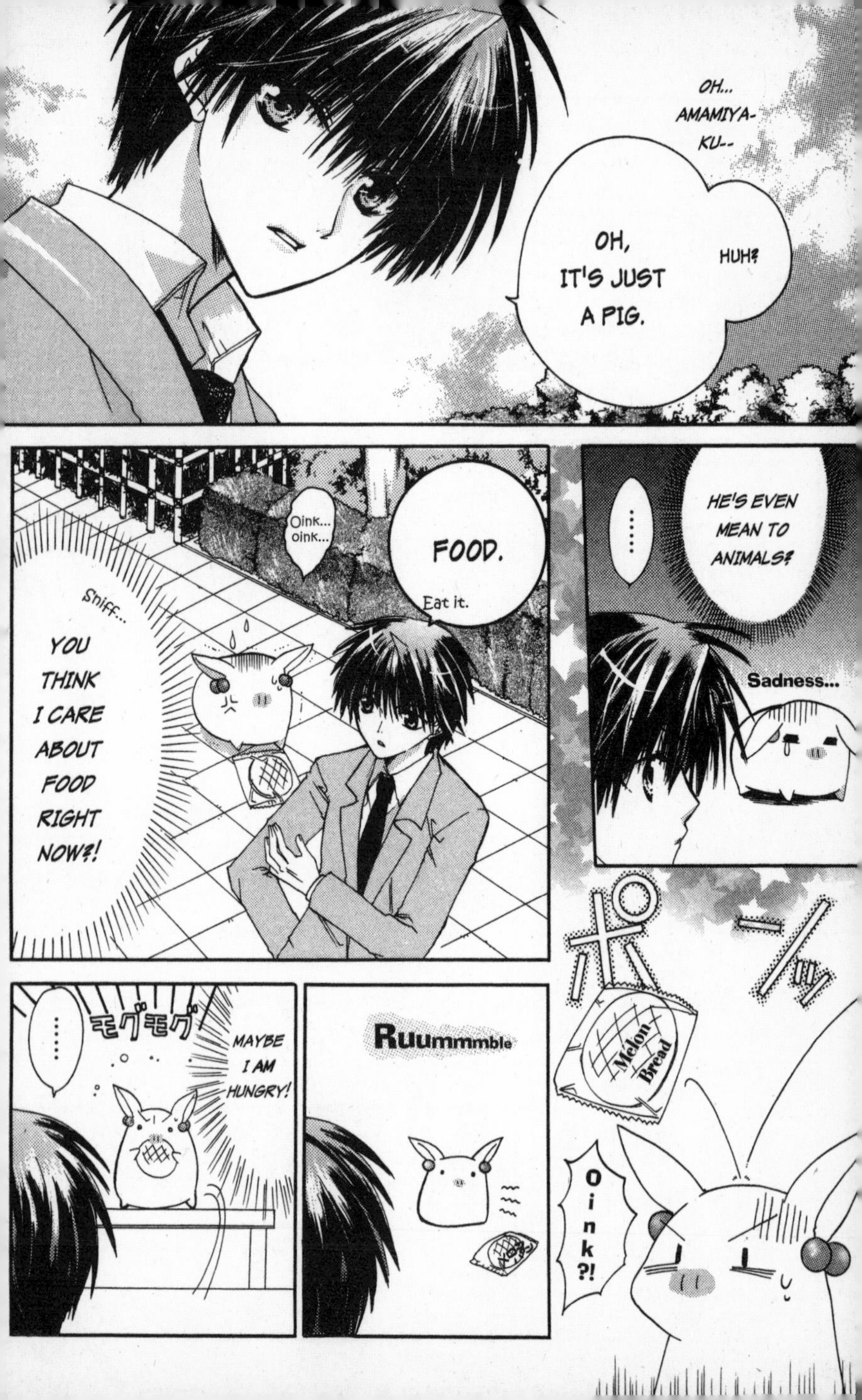
OH... AMAMIYA-KU--
HUH?
OH, IT'S JUST A PIG.
HE'S EVEN MEAN TO ANIMALS?
......
Sadness...
FOOD.
Eat it.
Oink... oink...
Sniff...
YOU THINK I CARE ABOUT FOOD RIGHT NOW?!
Melon Bread
Oink?!
Ruummmble
......
モグモグ
MAYBE I AM HUNGRY!

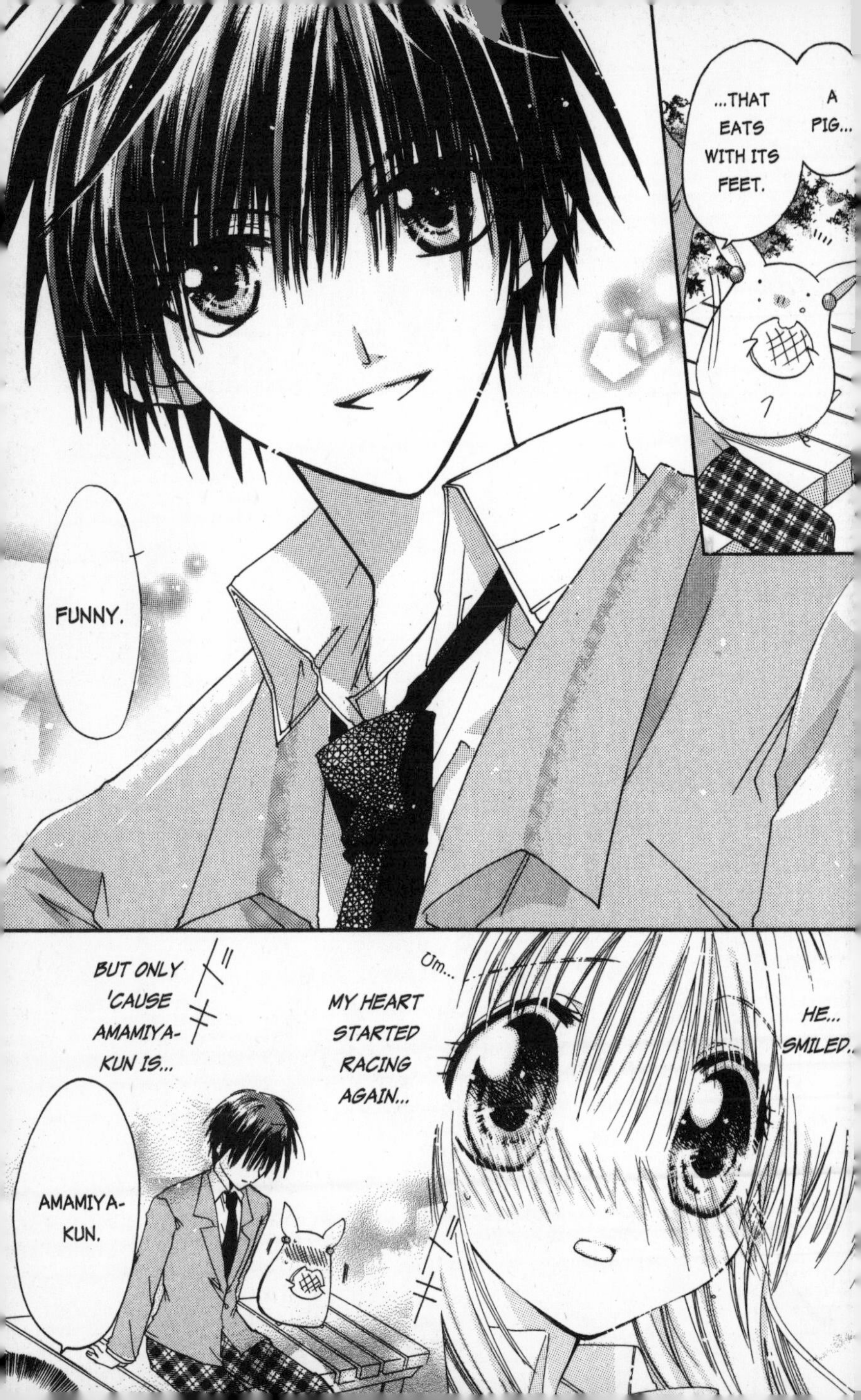
A PIG...
...THAT EATS WITH ITS FEET.
FUNNY.
HE... SMILED...
Um...
MY HEART STARTED RACING AGAIN...
BUT ONLY 'CAUSE AMAMIYA-KUN IS...
AMAMIYA-KUN.

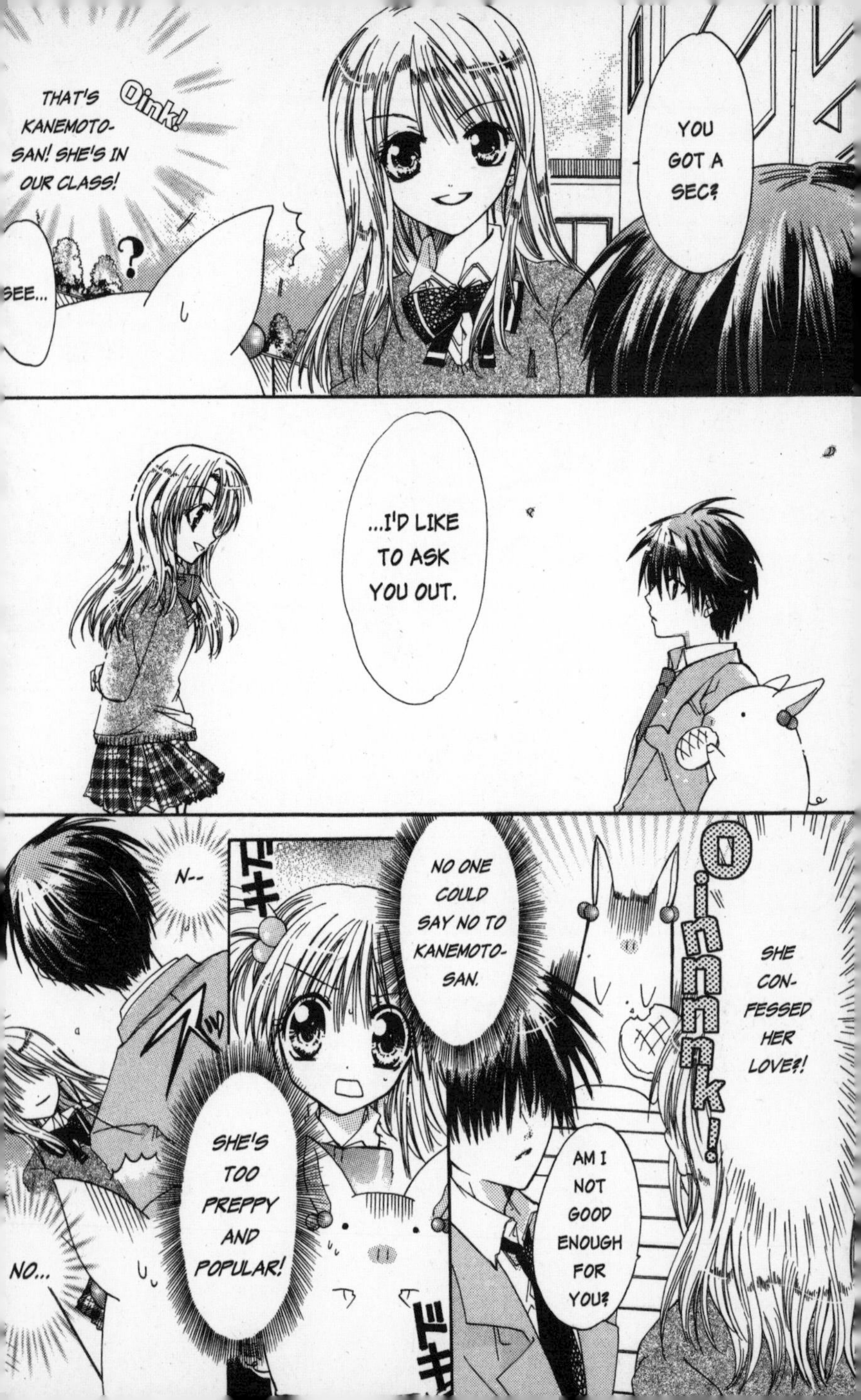
YOU GOT A SEC?
THAT'S KANEMOTO-SAN! SHE'S IN OUR CLASS!
Oink!
?
SEE...
...I'D LIKE TO ASK YOU OUT.
Oinnnk!
SHE CON-FESSED HER LOVE?!
NO ONE COULD SAY NO TO KANEMOTO-SAN.
ドキ
N--
AM I NOT GOOD ENOUGH FOR YOU?
SHE'S TOO PREPPY AND POPULAR!
ドキ
NO...

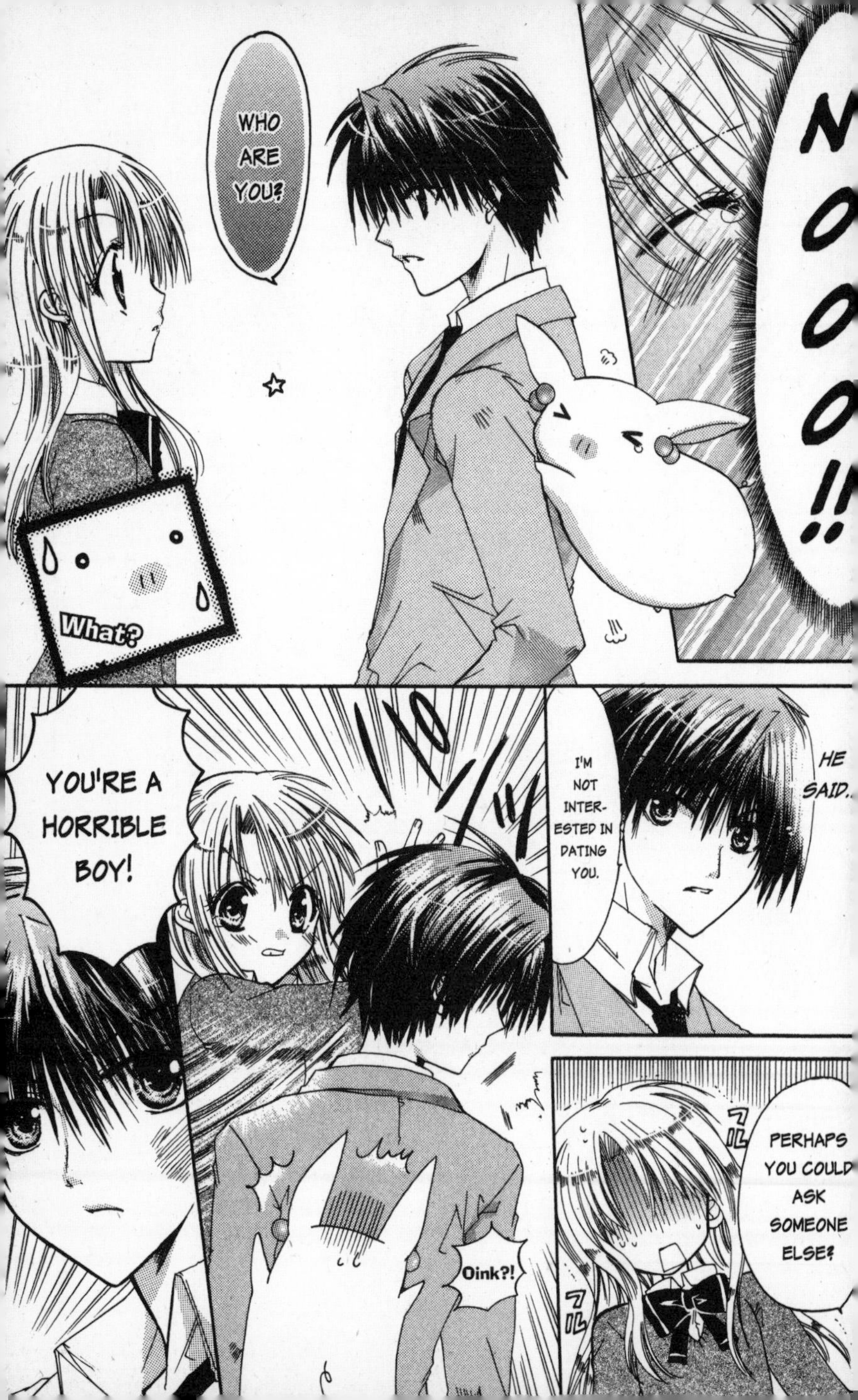
NOOO!!
WHO ARE YOU?
What?
I'M NOT INTERESTED IN DATING YOU.
HE SAID...
PERHAPS YOU COULD ASK SOMEONE ELSE?
YOU'RE A HORRIBLE BOY!
Oink?!

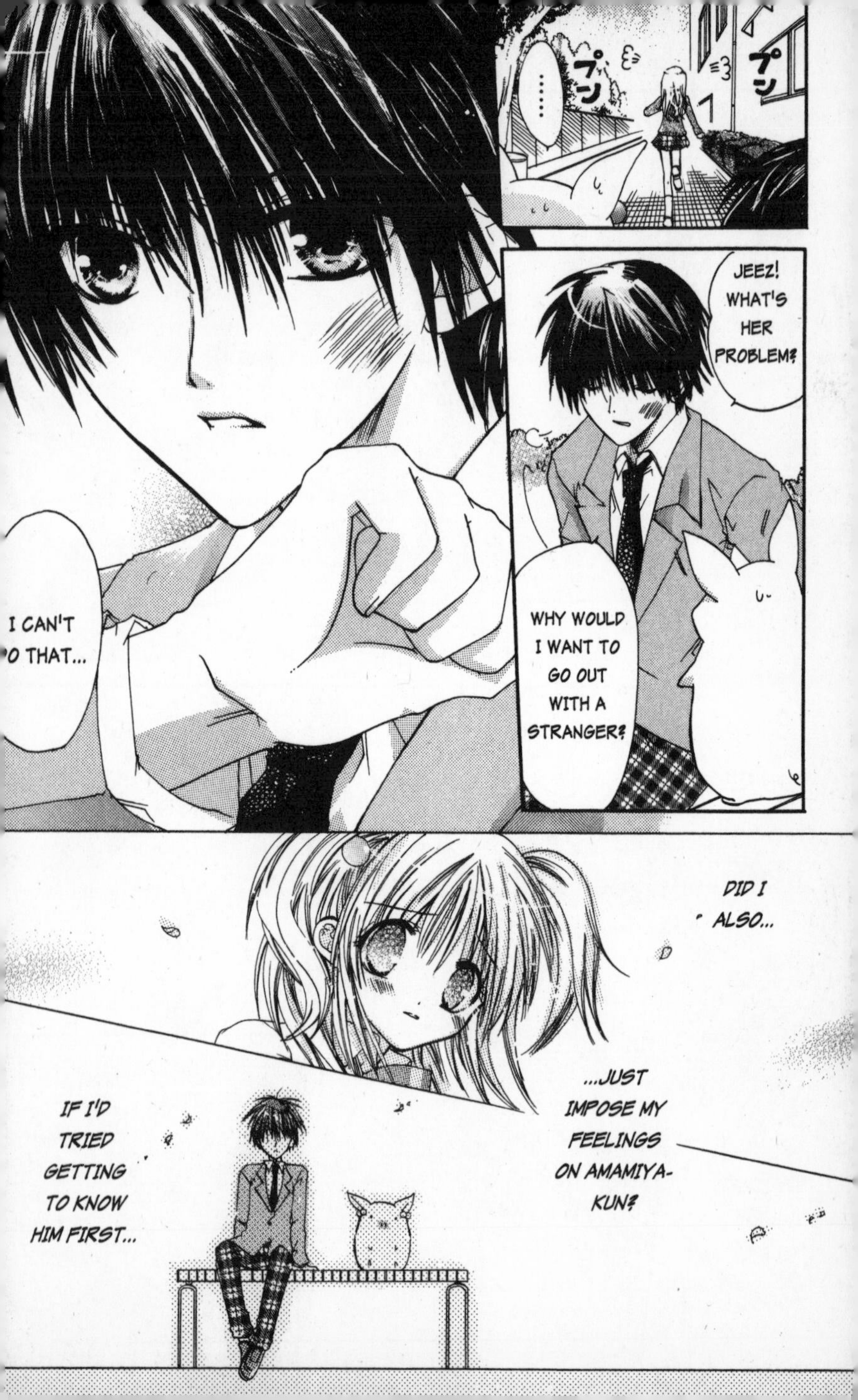

プン
プン
......
JEEZ! WHAT'S HER PROBLEM?
WHY WOULD I WANT TO GO OUT WITH A STRANGER?
I CAN'T
O THAT...
DID I ALSO...
...JUST IMPOSE MY FEELINGS ON AMAMIYA-KUN?
IF I'D TRIED GETTING TO KNOW HIM FIRST...

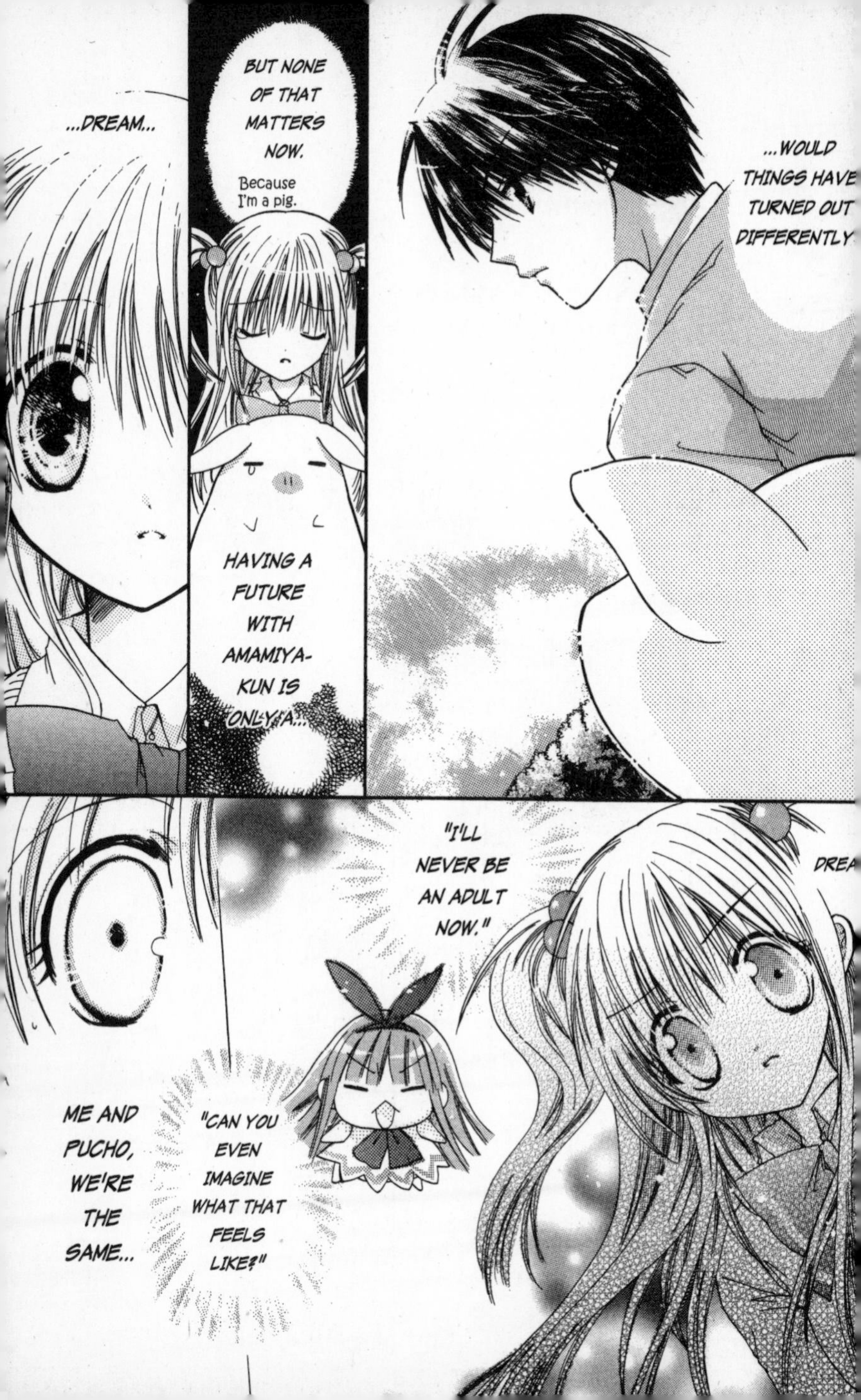
...WOULD THINGS HAVE TURNED OUT DIFFERENTLY
BUT NONE OF THAT MATTERS NOW.
Because I'm a pig.
HAVING A FUTURE WITH AMAMIYA-KUN IS ONLY A...
...DREAM...
DREA
"I'LL NEVER BE AN ADULT NOW."
"CAN YOU EVEN IMAGINE WHAT THAT FEELS LIKE?"
ME AND PUCHO, WE'RE THE SAME...

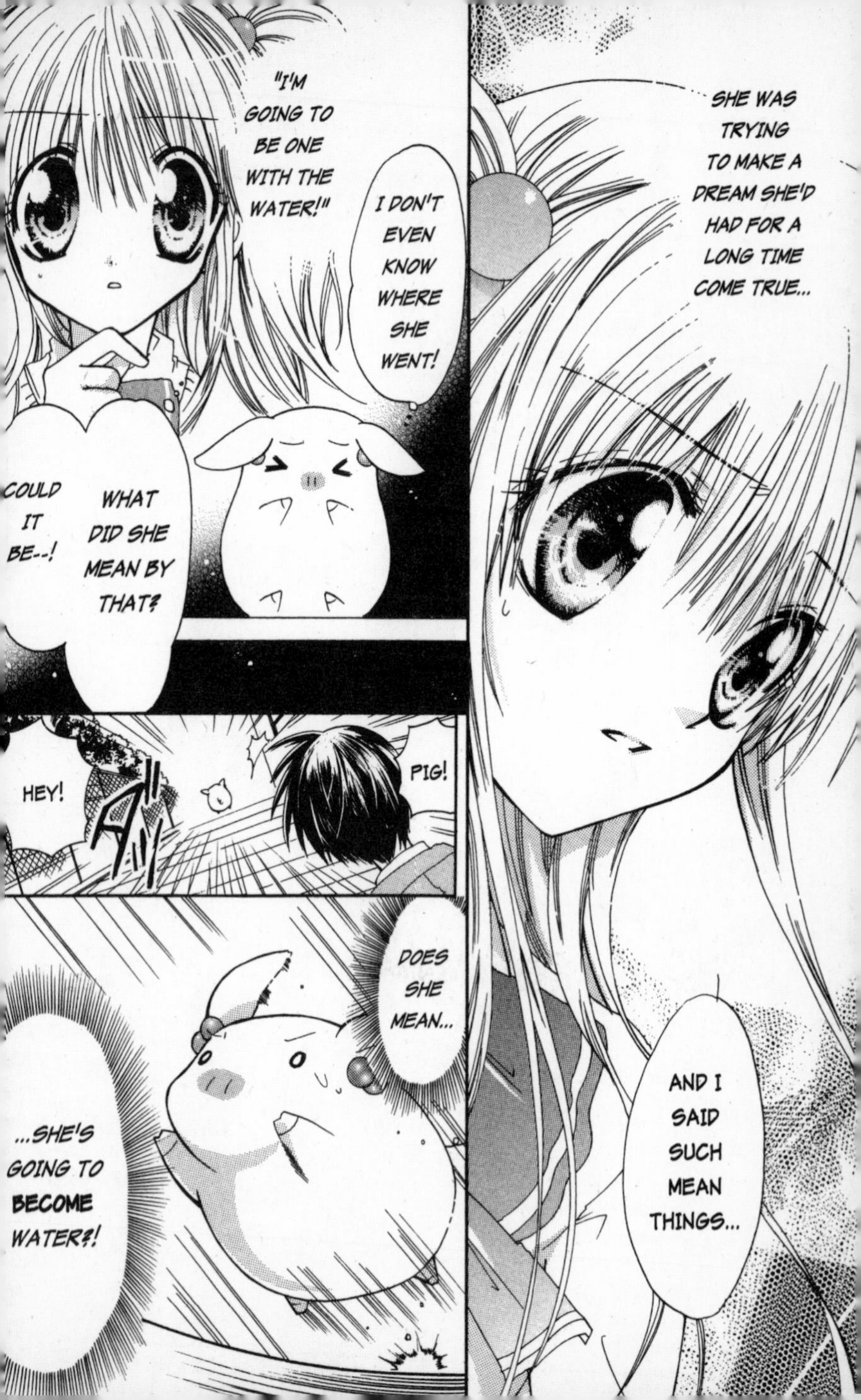

SHE WAS TRYING TO MAKE A DREAM SHE'D HAD FOR A LONG TIME COME TRUE...
AND I SAID SUCH MEAN THINGS...
"I'M GOING TO BE ONE WITH THE WATER!"
I DON'T EVEN KNOW WHERE SHE WENT!
WHAT DID SHE MEAN BY THAT?
COULD IT BE--!
PIG!
HEY!
DOES SHE MEAN...
...SHE'S GOING TO **BECOME** WATER?!

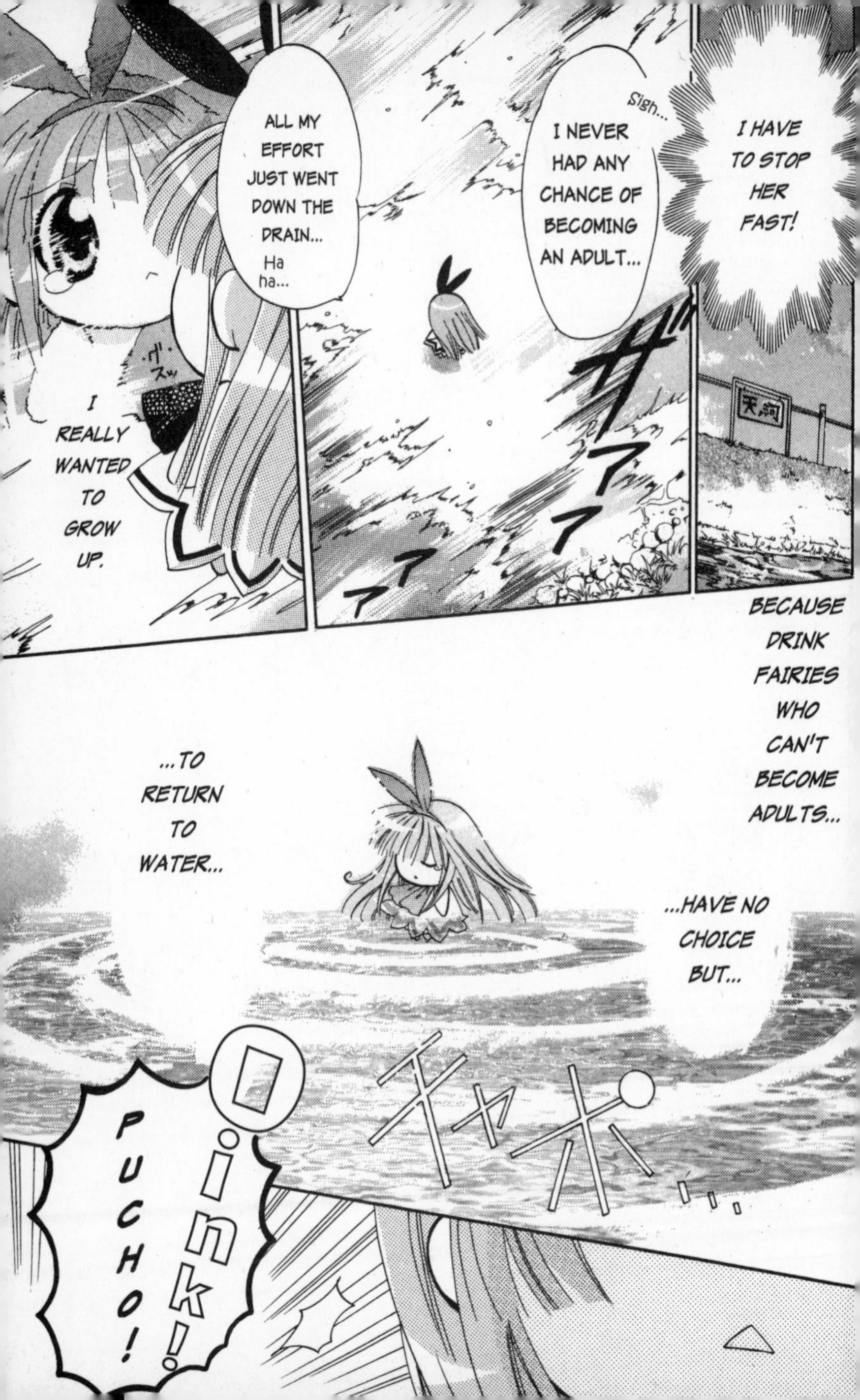
I HAVE TO STOP HER FAST!
Sigh...
I NEVER HAD ANY CHANCE OF BECOMING AN ADULT...
ALL MY EFFORT JUST WENT DOWN THE DRAIN...
Ha ha...
I REALLY WANTED TO GROW UP.
BECAUSE DRINK FAIRIES WHO CAN'T BECOME ADULTS...
...HAVE NO CHOICE BUT...
...TO RETURN TO WATER...
Oink!
PUCHO!

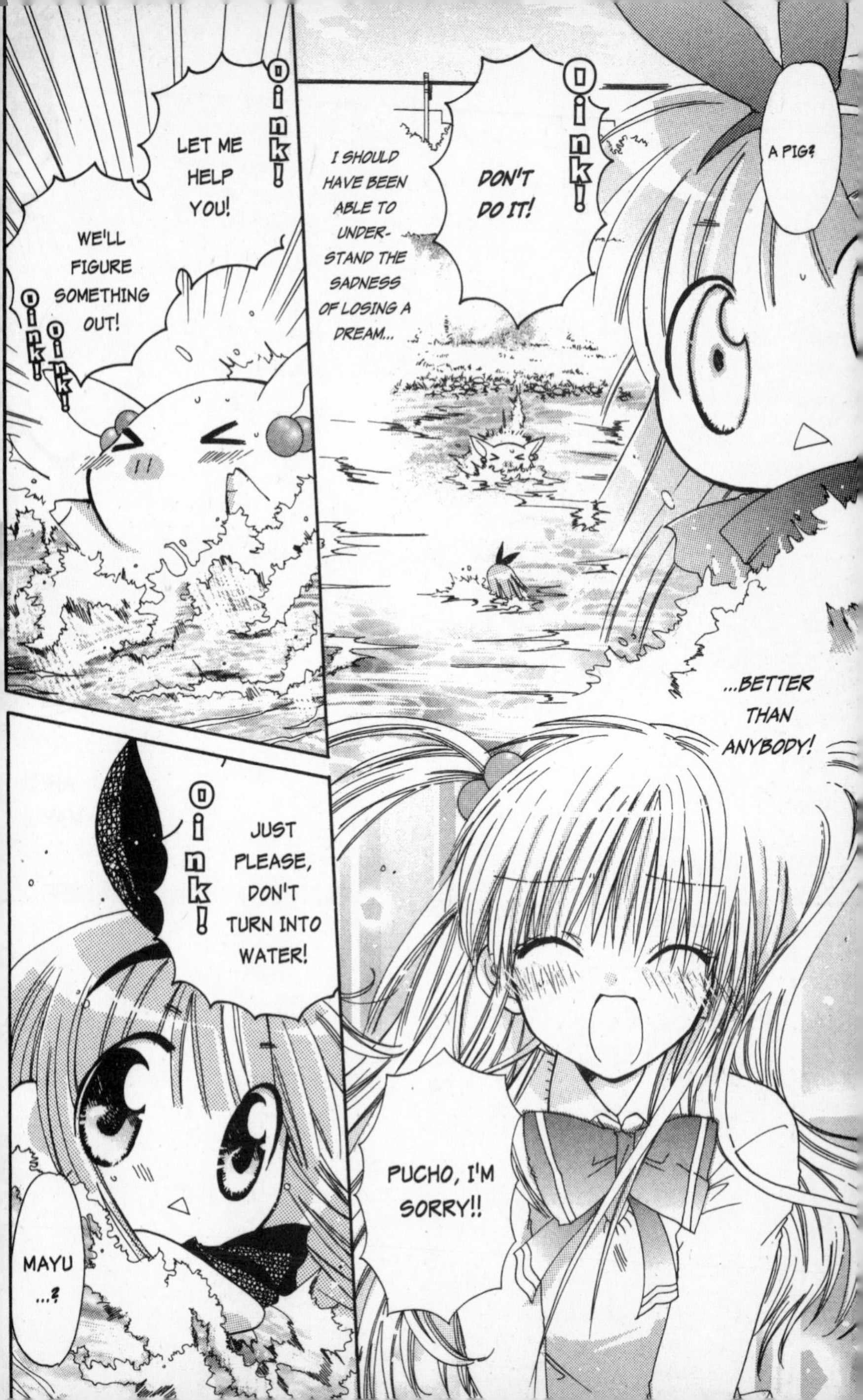
A PIG?
OINK!
DON'T DO IT!
I SHOULD HAVE BEEN ABLE TO UNDER-STAND THE SADNESS OF LOSING A DREAM...
...BETTER THAN ANYBODY!
OINK!
LET ME HELP YOU!
WE'LL FIGURE SOMETHING OUT!
OINK! OINK!
PUCHO, I'M SORRY!!
OINK!
JUST PLEASE, DON'T TURN INTO WATER!
MAYU ...?

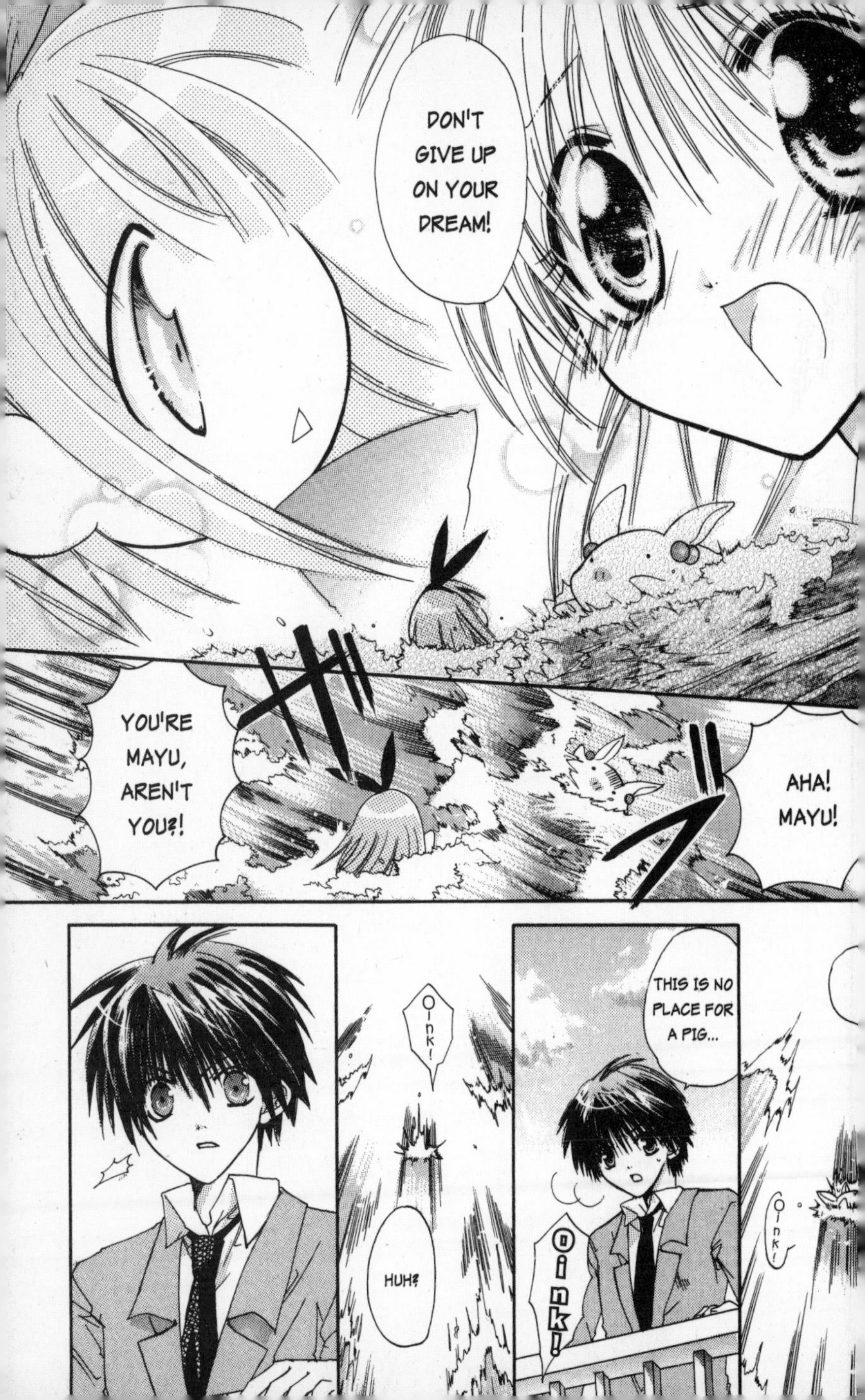
DON'T GIVE UP ON YOUR DREAM!
AHA! MAYU!
YOU'RE MAYU, AREN'T YOU?!
Oink!
THIS IS NO PLACE FOR A PIG...
Oink!
Oink!
HUH?

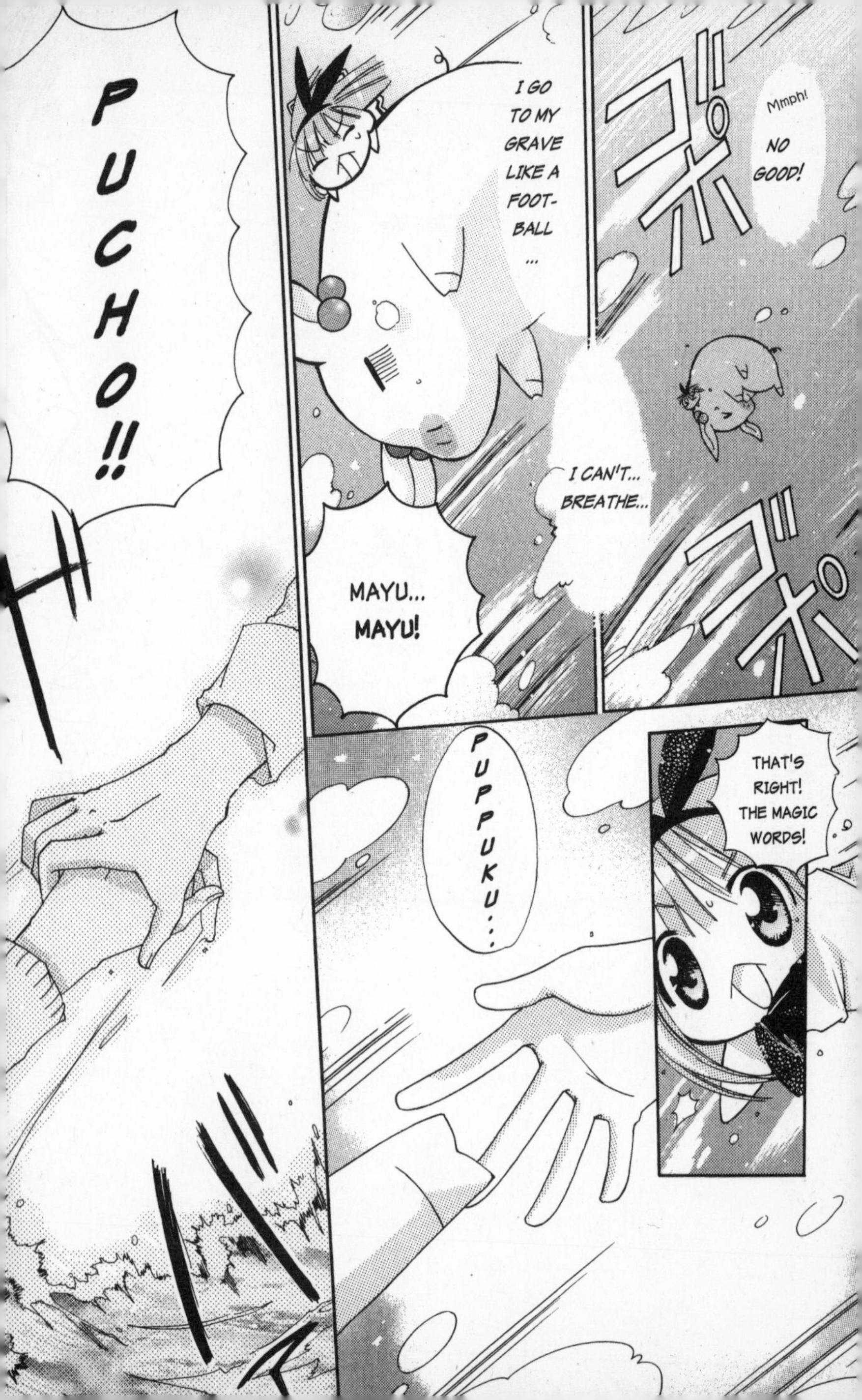
ゴポ
Mmph!
NO GOOD!
I CAN'T... BREATHE...
ゴポ
I GO TO MY GRAVE LIKE A FOOT-BALL ...
MAYU... MAYU!
THAT'S RIGHT! THE MAGIC WORDS!
PUPPUKU...
PUCHO!!

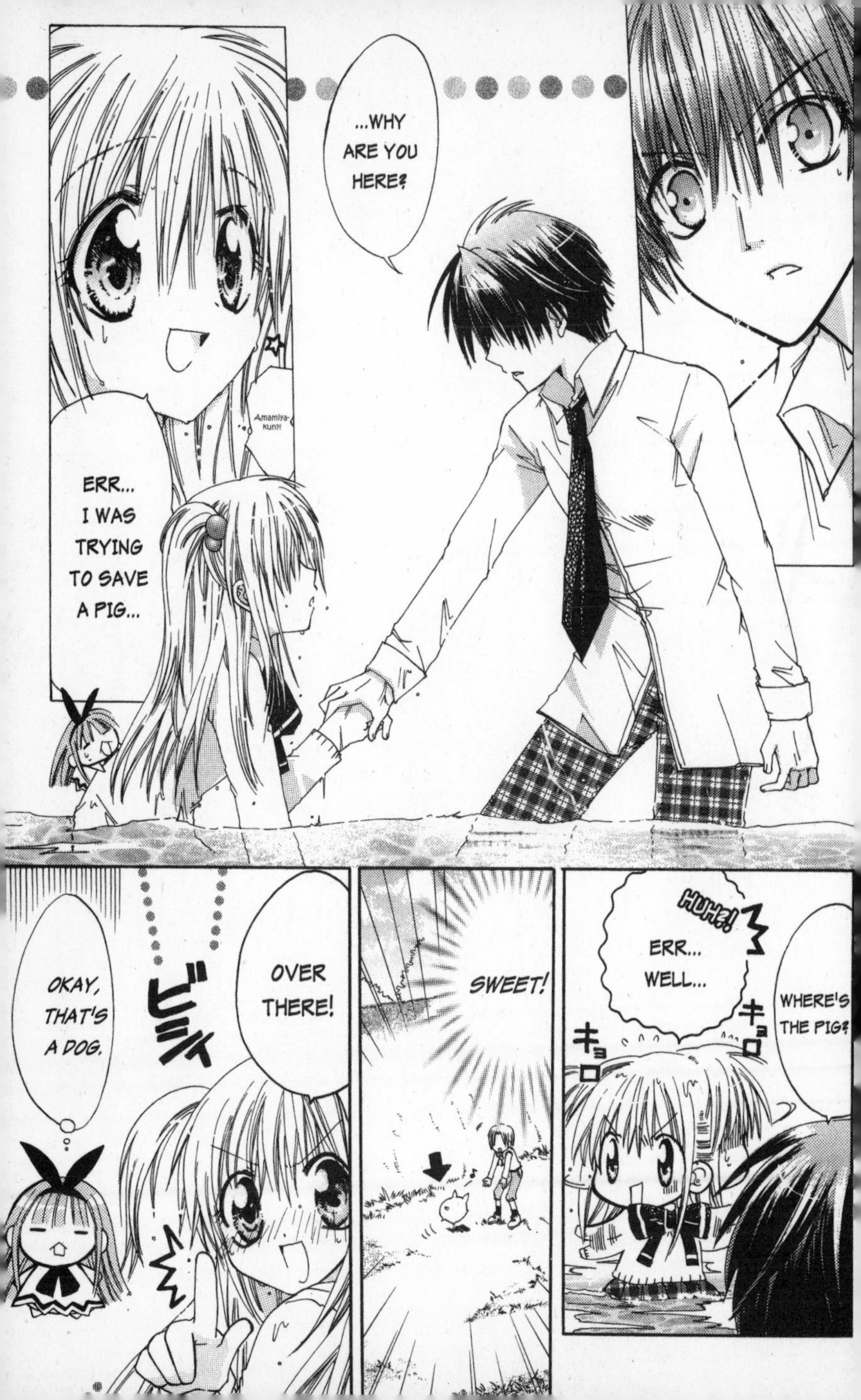
...WHY ARE YOU HERE?
Amamiya-kun?!
ERR... I WAS TRYING TO SAVE A PIG...
WHERE'S THE PIG?
HUH?!
ERR... WELL...
キョロ
キョロ
SWEET!
OVER THERE!
ビシィ
OKAY, THAT'S A DOG.

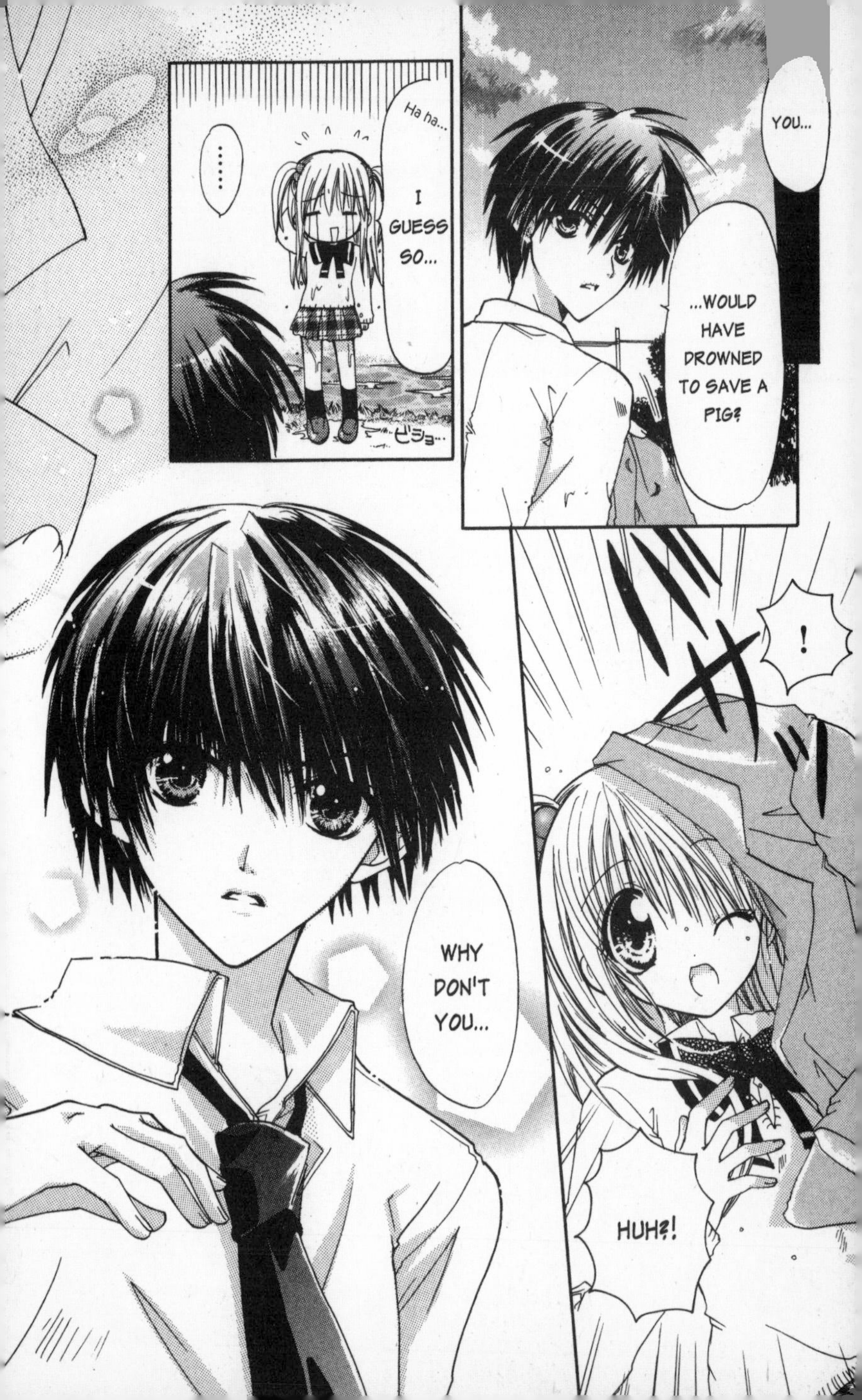
YOU...
...WOULD HAVE DROWNED TO SAVE A PIG?
Ha ha... I GUESS SO...
......
ビショ…
!
HUH?!
WHY DON'T YOU...

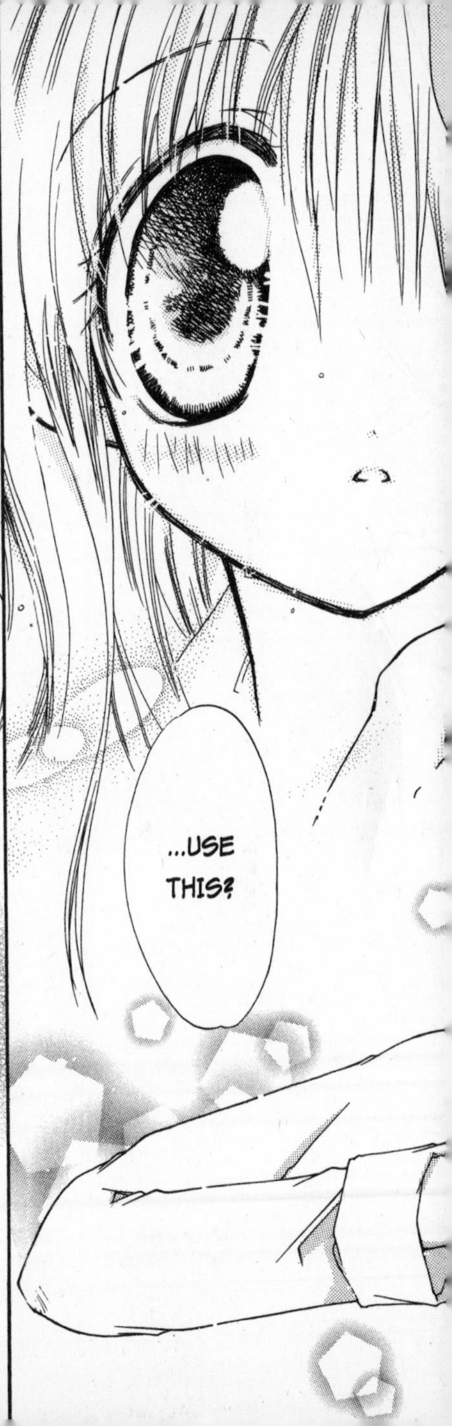
...USE THIS?
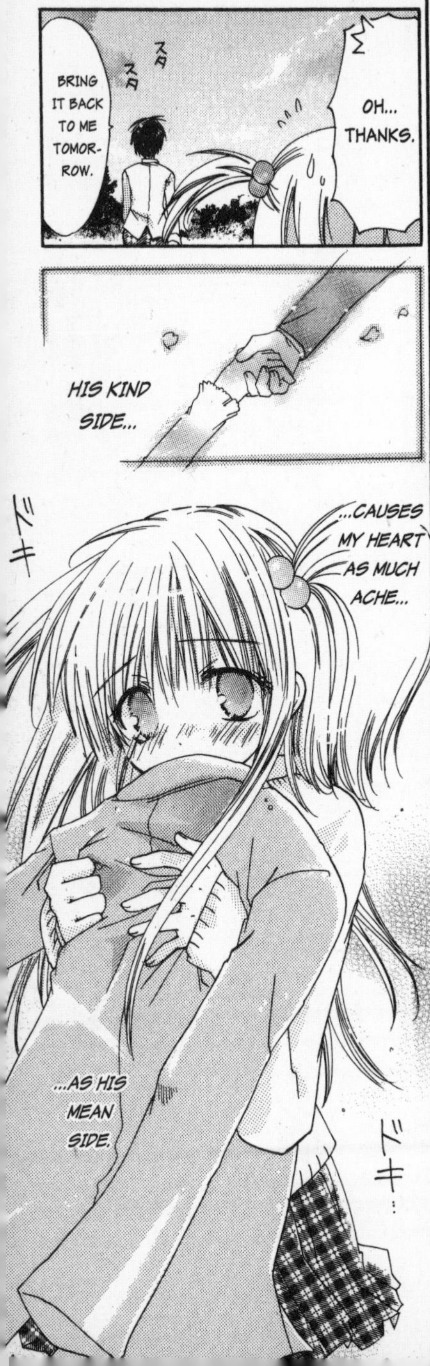
OH... THANKS.
スタ
スタ
BRING IT BACK TO ME TOMOR-ROW.
HIS KIND SIDE...
...CAUSES MY HEART AS MUCH ACHE...
ドキ
...AS HIS MEAN SIDE.
ドキ…

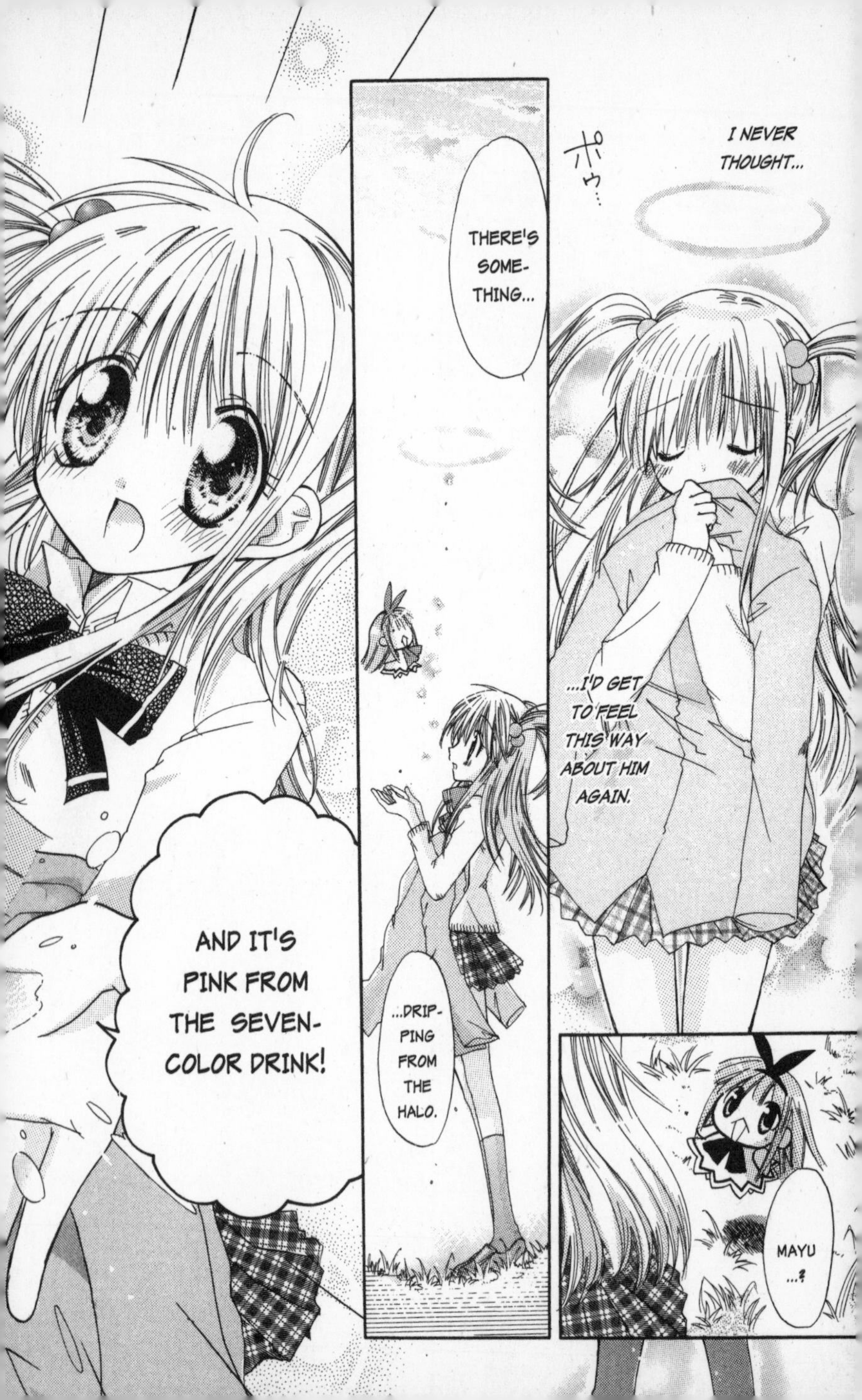
I NEVER THOUGHT...
ポゥ…
...I'D GET TO FEEL THIS WAY ABOUT HIM AGAIN.
MAYU ...?
THERE'S SOME-THING...
...DRIP-PING FROM THE HALO.
AND IT'S PINK FROM THE SEVEN-COLOR DRINK!

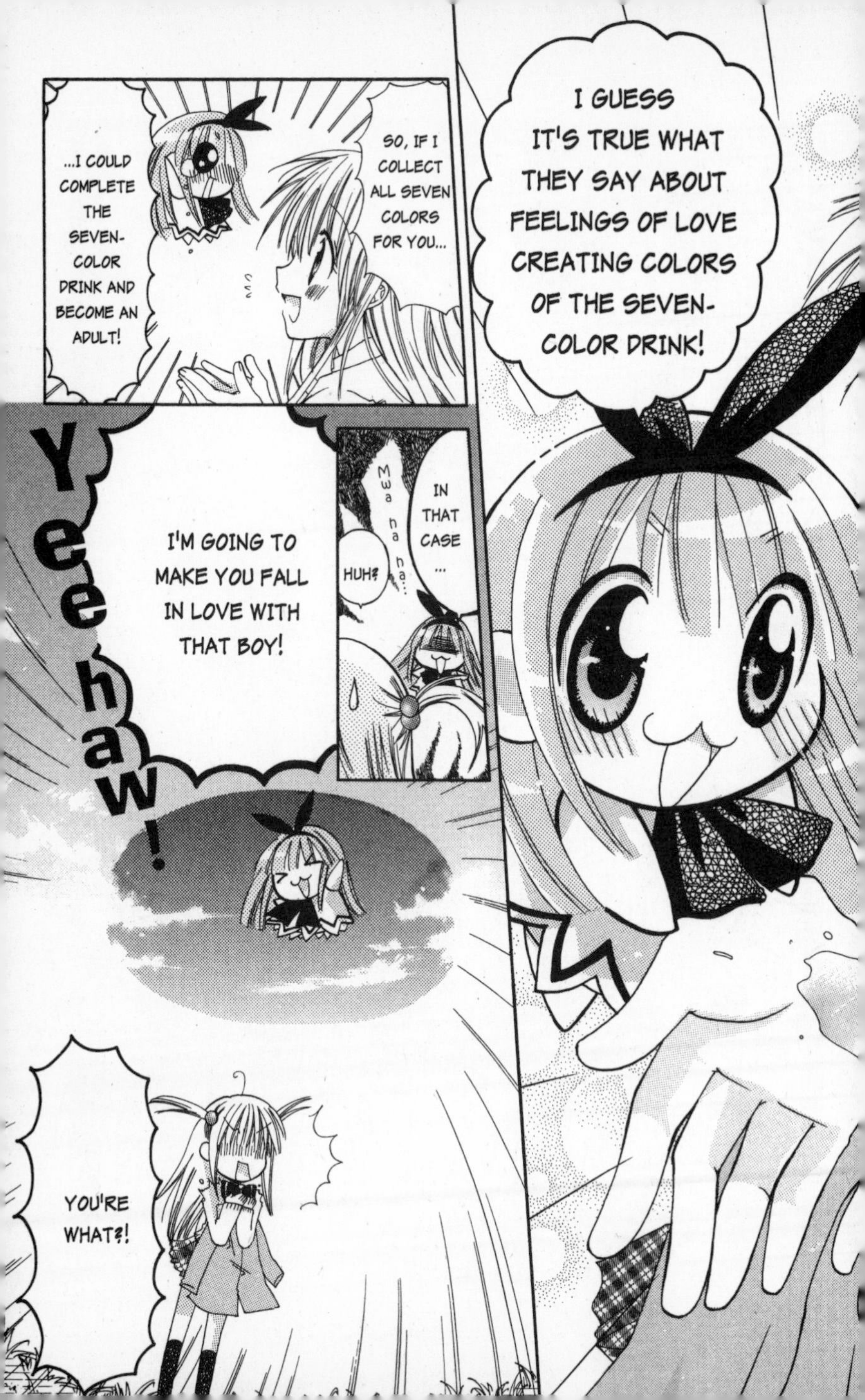
I GUESS IT'S TRUE WHAT THEY SAY ABOUT FEELINGS OF LOVE CREATING COLORS OF THE SEVEN-COLOR DRINK!
SO, IF I COLLECT ALL SEVEN COLORS FOR YOU...
...I COULD COMPLETE THE SEVEN-COLOR DRINK AND BECOME AN ADULT!
IN THAT CASE...
Mwa ha ha...
HUH?
I'M GOING TO MAKE YOU FALL IN LOVE WITH THAT BOY!
Yeehaw!
YOU'RE WHAT?!

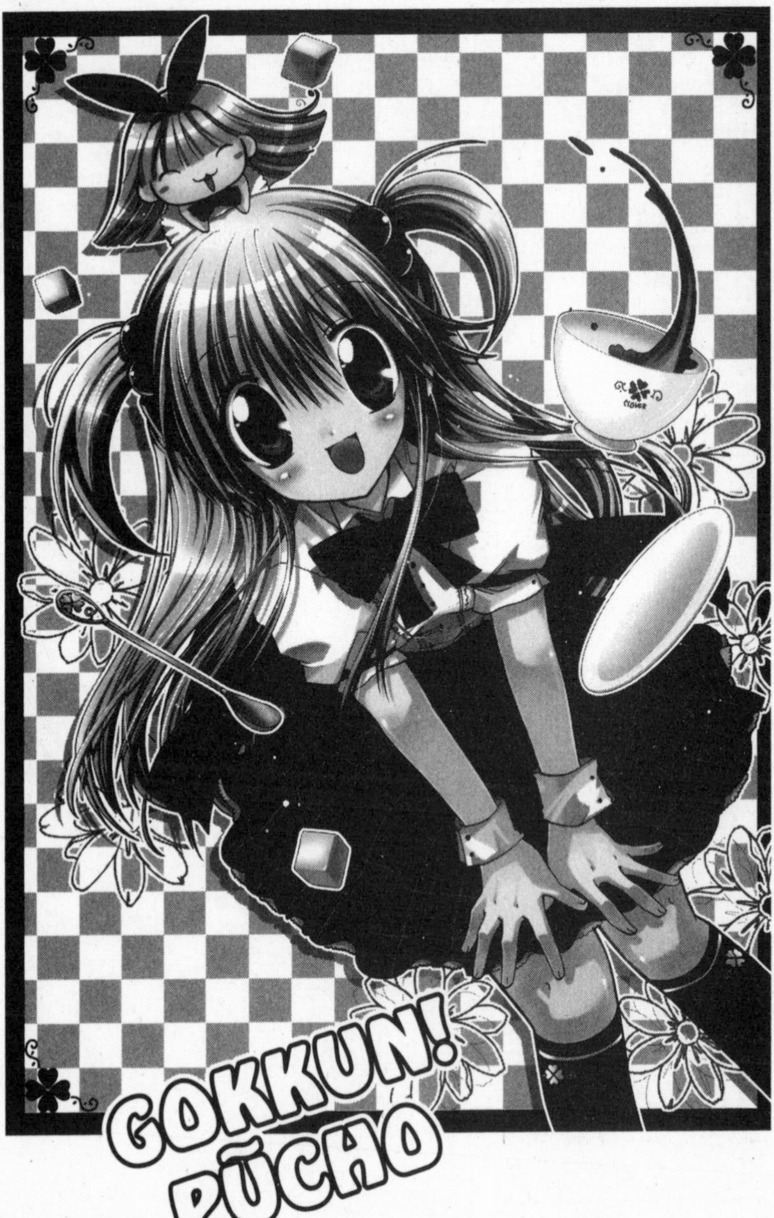
GOKKUN!
PŪCHO

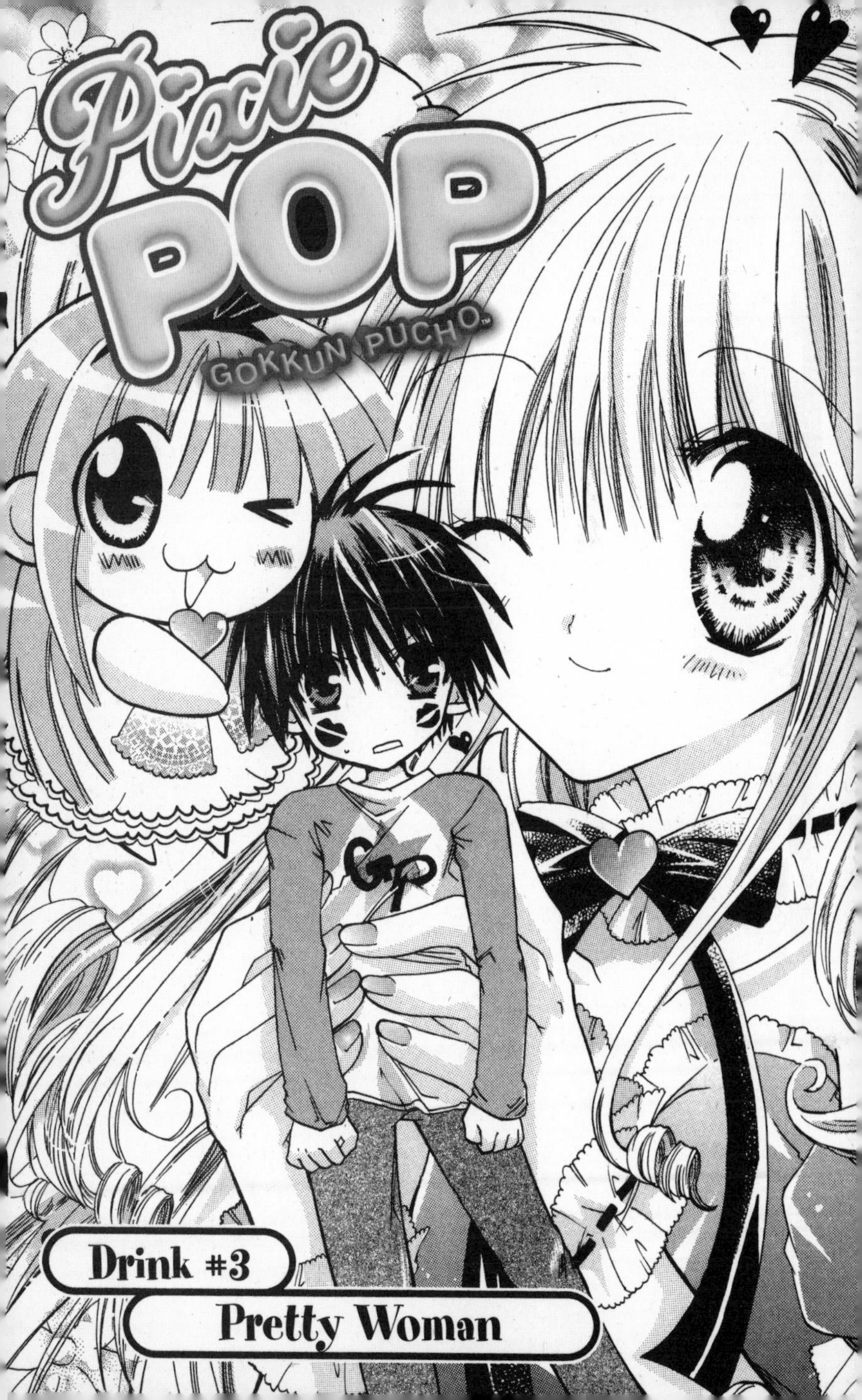
Pixie POP
GOKKUN PUCHO
Drink #3
Pretty Woman

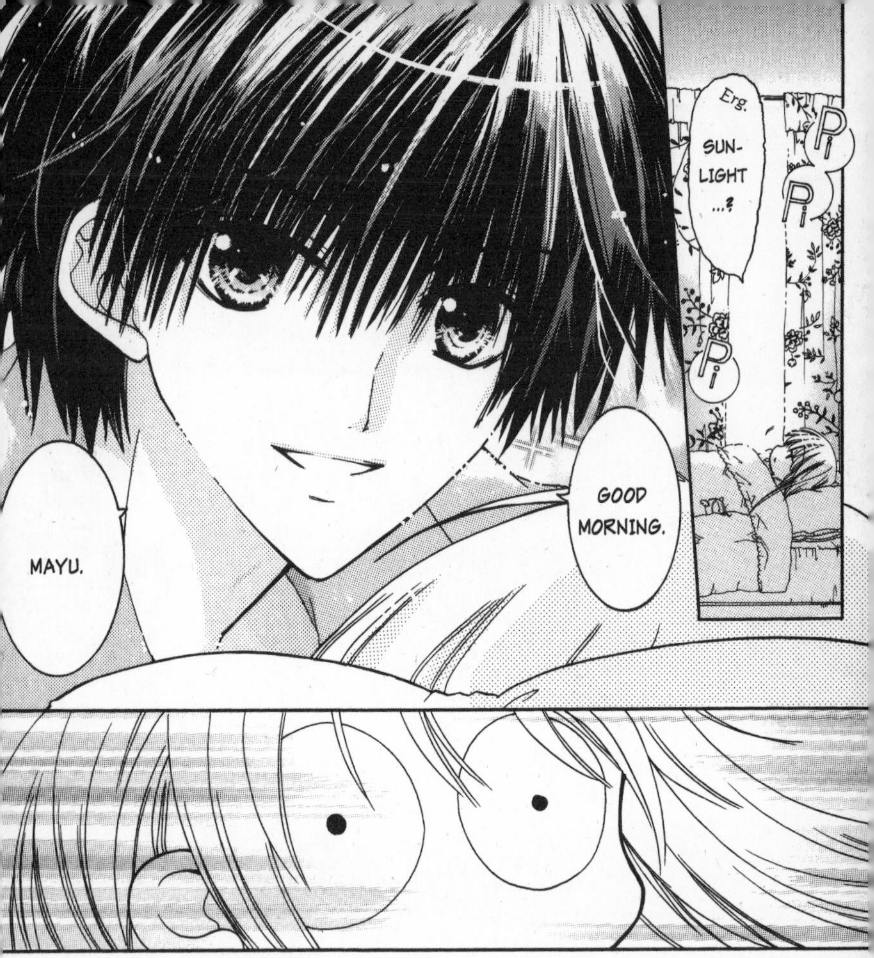
Pi
Pi
Pi
Erg.
SUN-LIGHT ...?
GOOD MORNING.
MAYU.

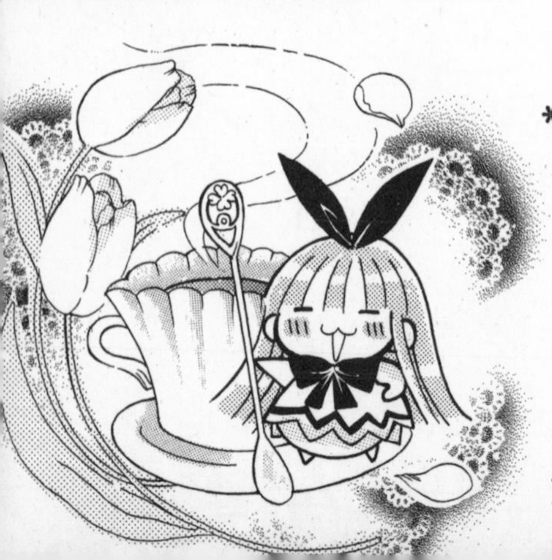

****

♥ Pucho ♥

Birthday: ??

Sign: ?? Bloodtype: ??

Height: 15cm Weight: 150g

Favorite Drink: Everything!

****

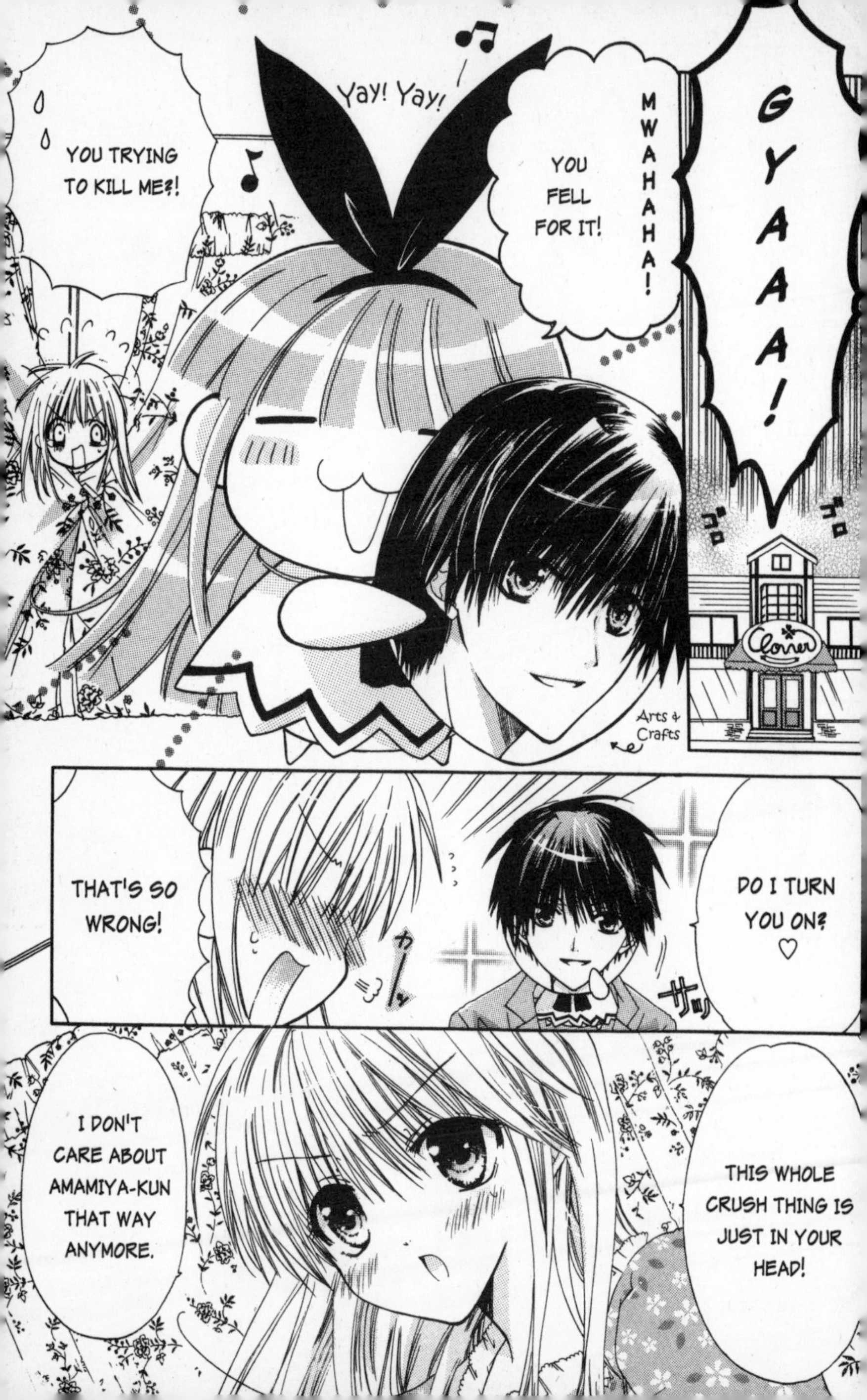
GYAAA!
ゴロ ゴロ
Clover
Arts & Crafts
MWAHAHA!
YOU FELL FOR IT!
Yay! Yay!
YOU TRYING TO KILL ME?!
DO I TURN YOU ON? ♡
THAT'S SO WRONG!
THIS WHOLE CRUSH THING IS JUST IN YOUR HEAD!
I DON'T CARE ABOUT AMAMIYA-KUN THAT WAY ANYMORE.

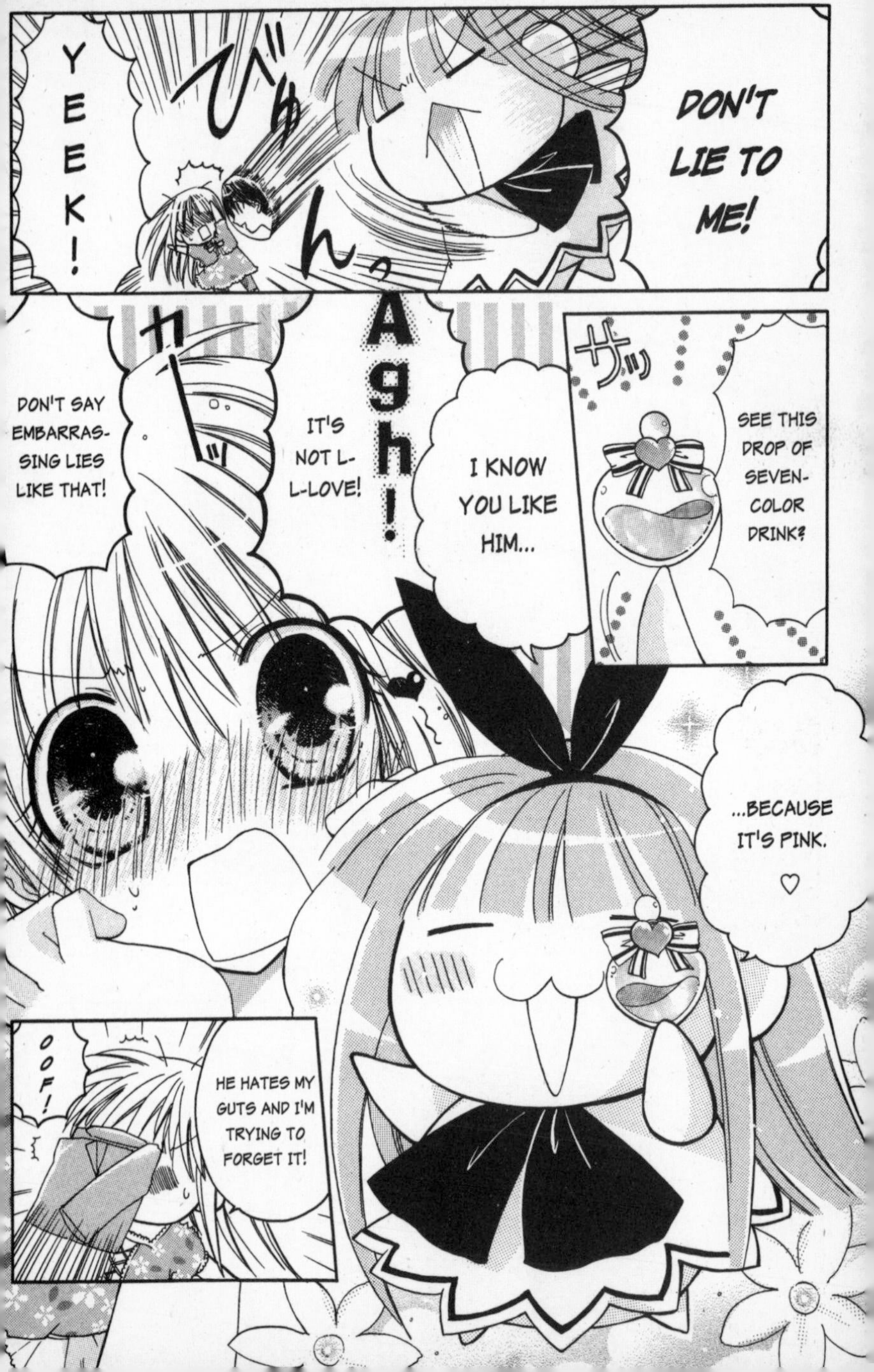
DON'T LIE TO ME!
びゅんっ
YEEK!
Agh!
ザッ
SEE THIS DROP OF SEVEN-COLOR DRINK?
I KNOW YOU LIKE HIM...
...BECAUSE IT'S PINK. ♡
IT'S NOT L-L-LOVE!
カーッ
DON'T SAY EMBARRASSING LIES LIKE THAT!
HE HATES MY GUTS AND I'M TRYING TO FORGET IT!
OOF!

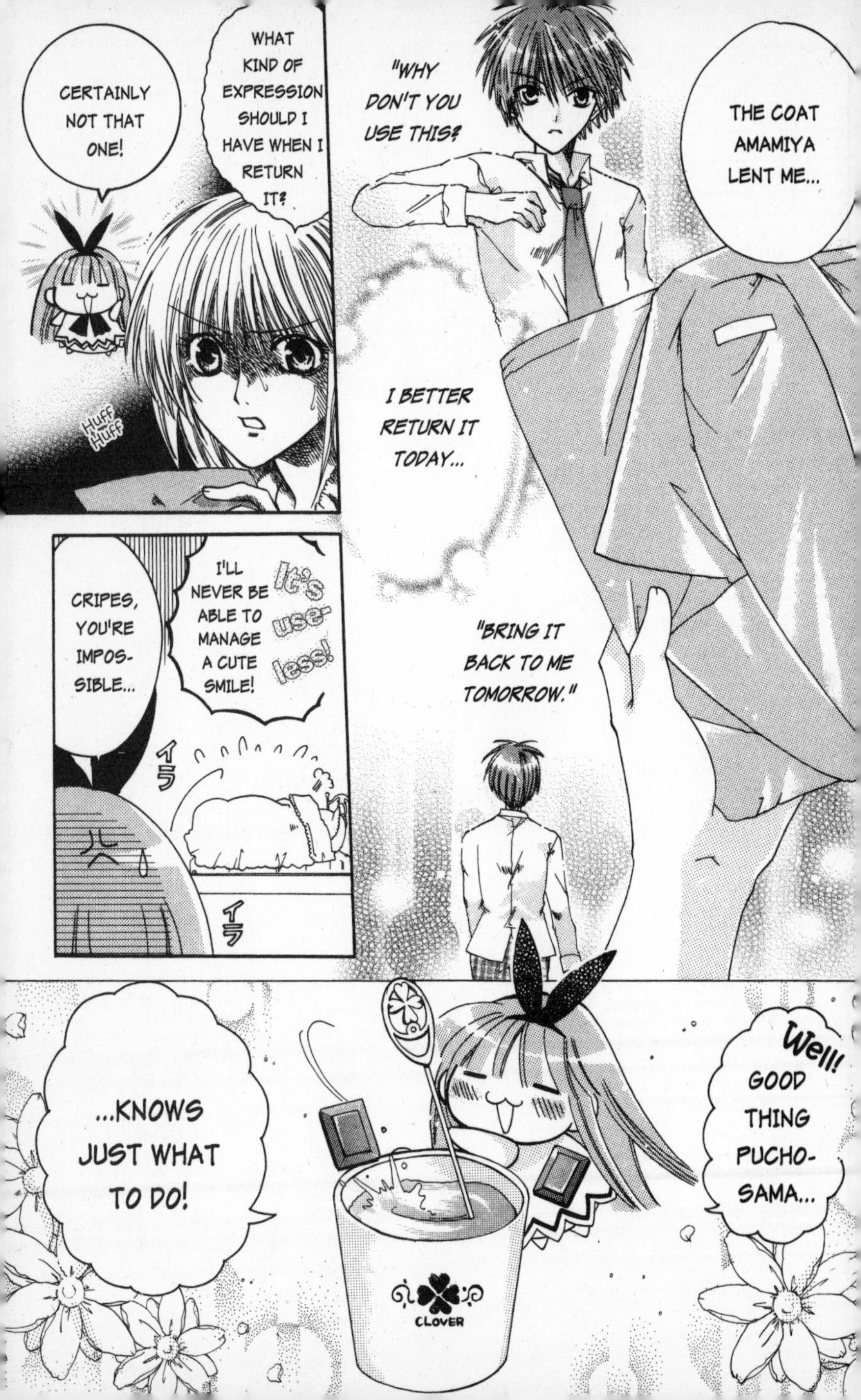
THE COAT AMAMIYA LENT ME...
"WHY DON'T YOU USE THIS?
I BETTER RETURN IT TODAY...
"BRING IT BACK TO ME TOMORROW."
WHAT KIND OF EXPRESSION SHOULD I HAVE WHEN I RETURN IT?
CERTAINLY NOT THAT ONE!
Huff Huff
I'LL NEVER BE ABLE TO MANAGE A CUTE SMILE!
It's use-less!
CRIPES, YOU'RE IMPOS-SIBLE...
イラ
イラ
Well!
GOOD THING PUCHO-SAMA...
...KNOWS JUST WHAT TO DO!
CLOVER

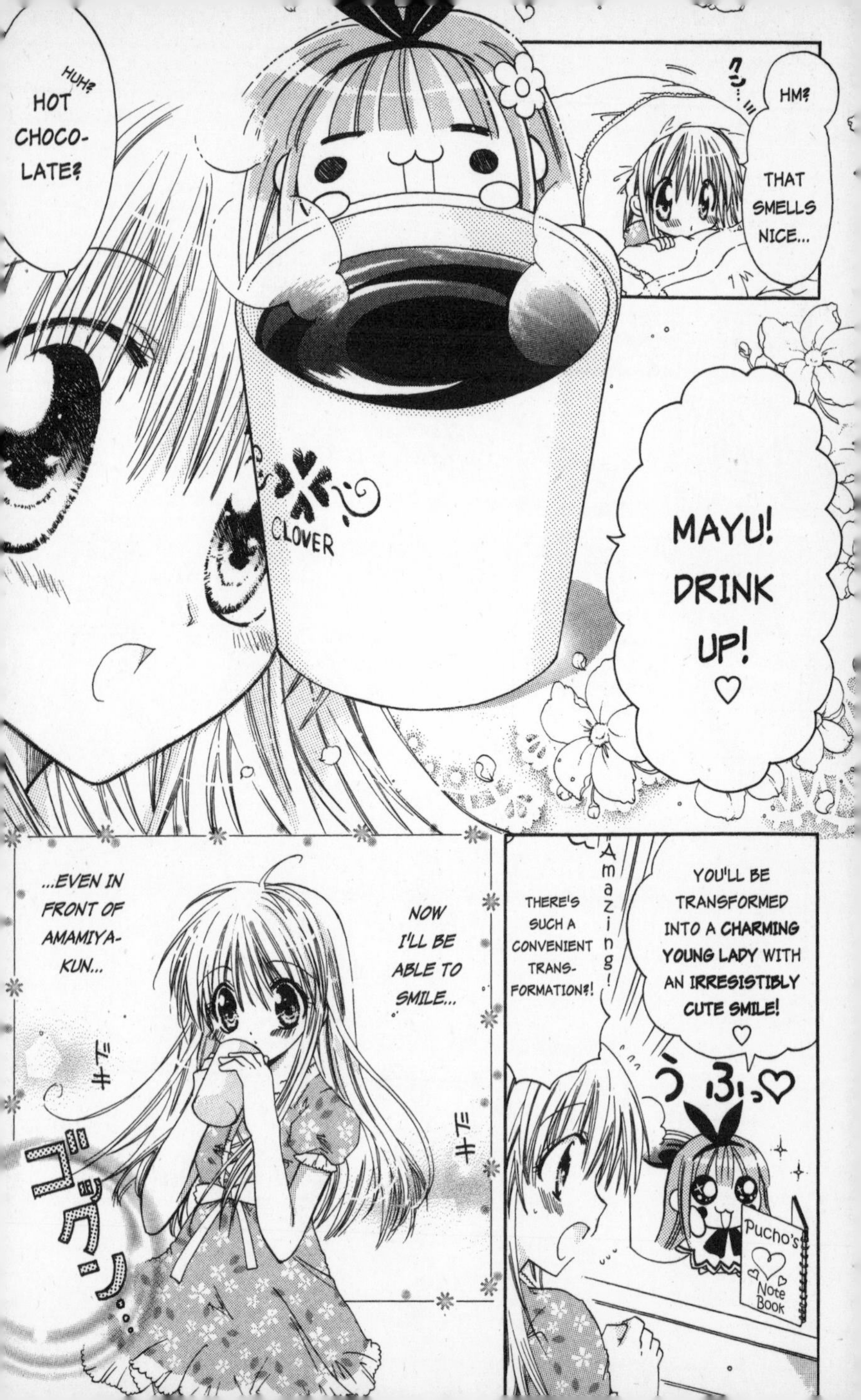
HM?
THAT SMELLS NICE...
HUH? HOT CHOCO-LATE?
MAYU! DRINK UP! ♡
CLOVER
YOU'LL BE TRANSFORMED INTO A CHARMING YOUNG LADY WITH AN IRRESISTIBLY CUTE SMILE! ♡
うふっ♡
Amazing!
THERE'S SUCH A CONVENIENT TRANS-FORMATION?!
Pucho's Note Book
NOW I'LL BE ABLE TO SMILE...
...EVEN IN FRONT OF AMAMIYA-KUN...
ドキ
ドキ
ゴクン…

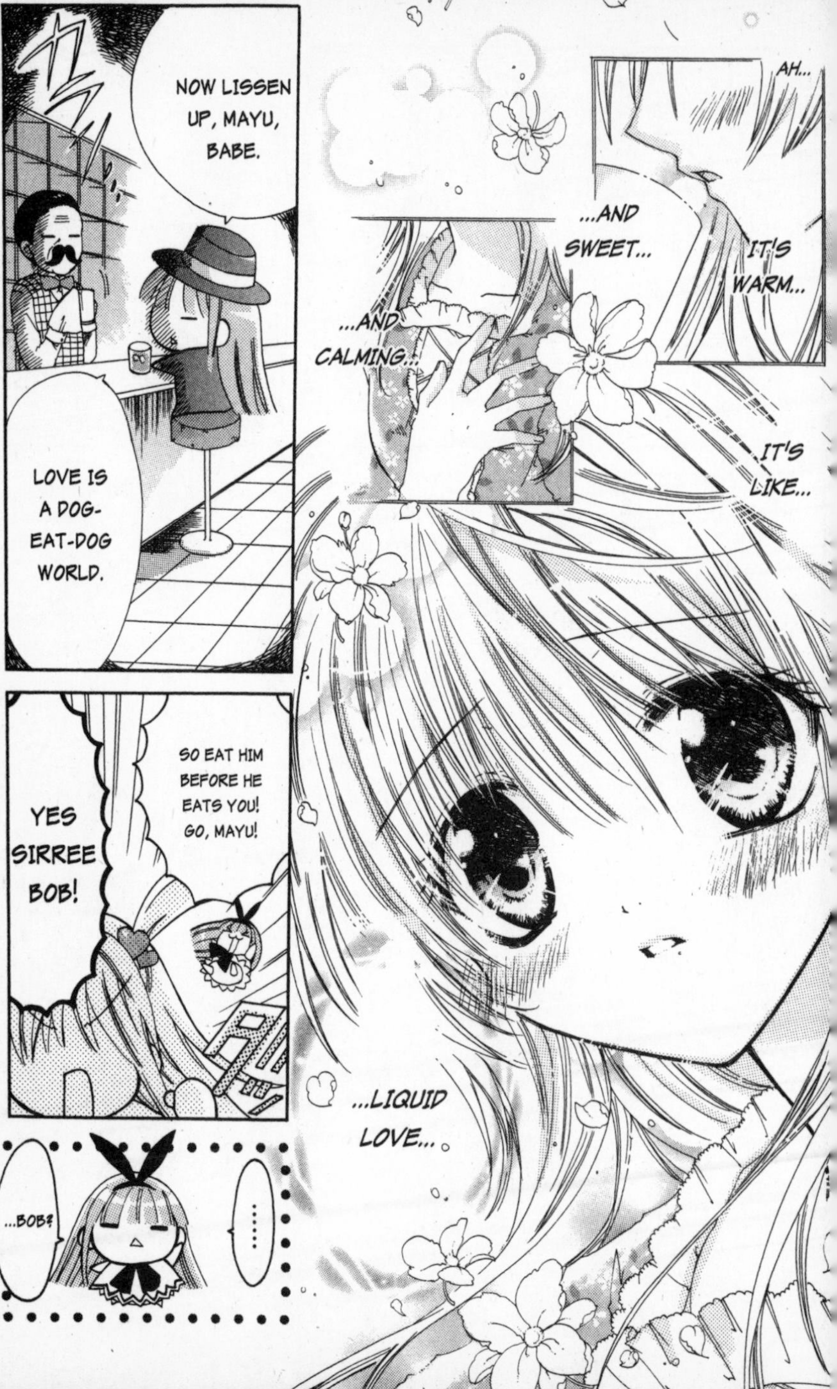
AH...
IT'S WARM...
...AND SWEET...
...AND CALMING...
IT'S LIKE...
...LIQUID LOVE...
NOW LISSEN UP, MAYU, BABE.
LOVE IS A DOG-EAT-DOG WORLD.
SO EAT HIM BEFORE HE EATS YOU! GO, MAYU!
YES SIRREE BOB!
......
...BOB?

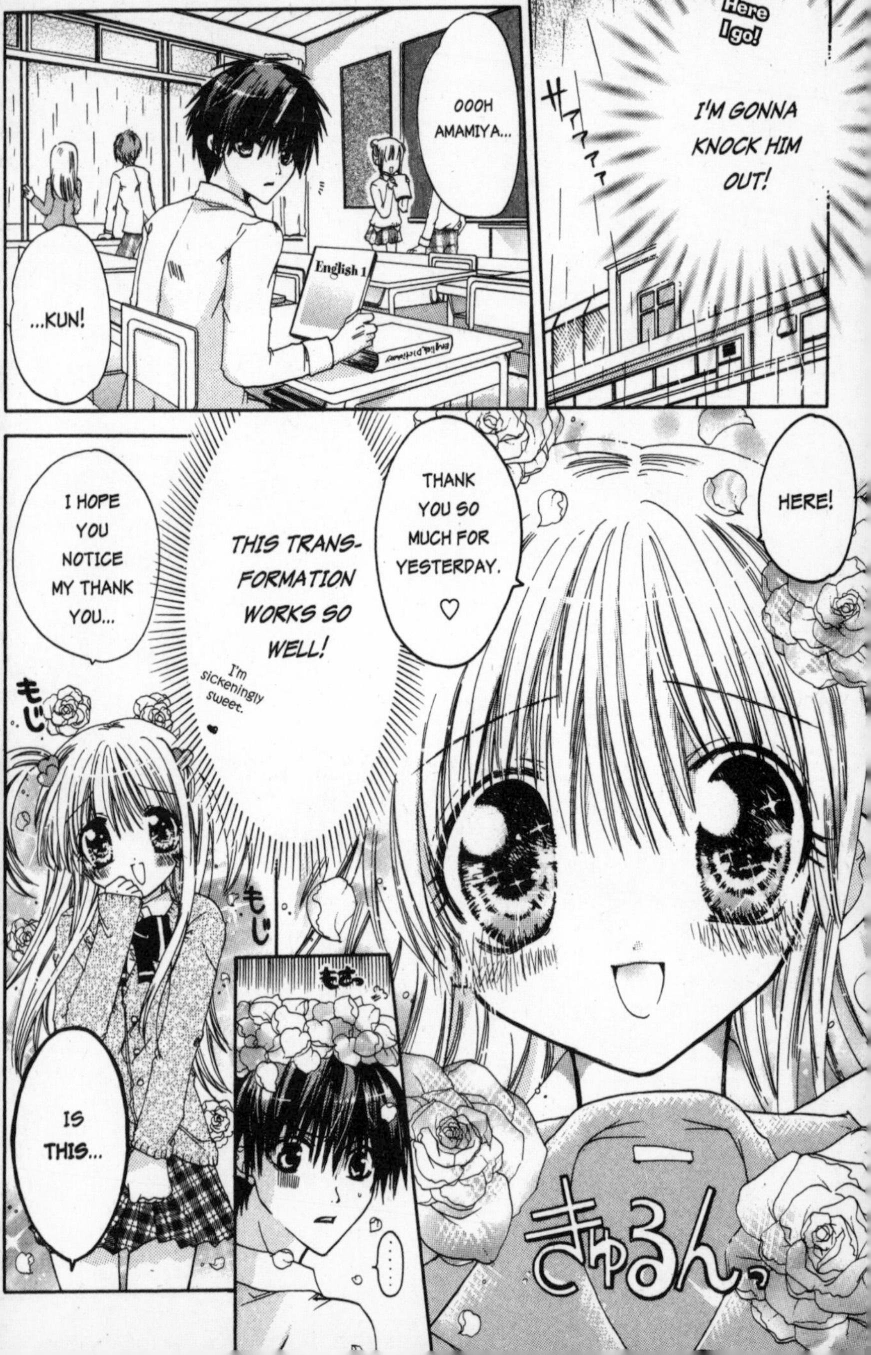
Here I go!
ザァァァァ
I'M GONNA KNOCK HIM OUT!
OOOH AMAMIYA...
English 1
...KUN!
HERE!
THANK YOU SO MUCH FOR YESTERDAY. ♡
THIS TRANS-FORMATION WORKS SO WELL!
I'm sickeningly sweet.
I HOPE YOU NOTICE MY THANK YOU...
もじ
もじ
きゅるん
もさっ
...
IS THIS...

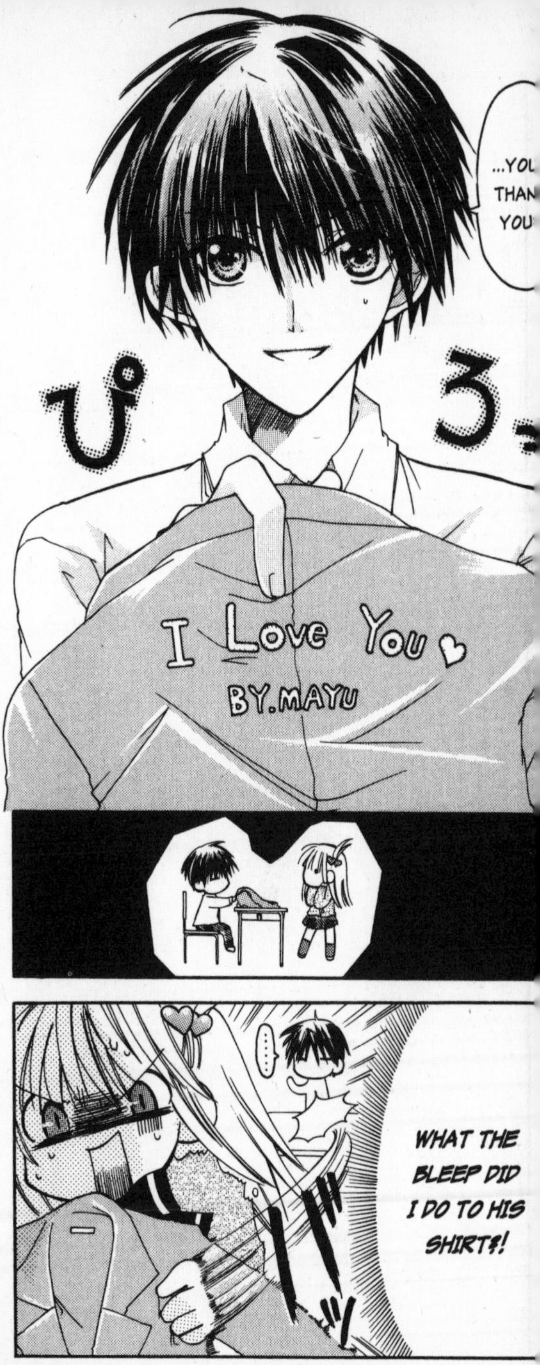

...YOU
THAN
YOU
ぴろっ
I Love You
BY.MAYU
WHAT THE BLEEP DID I DO TO HIS SHIRT?!

An Honest Mistake

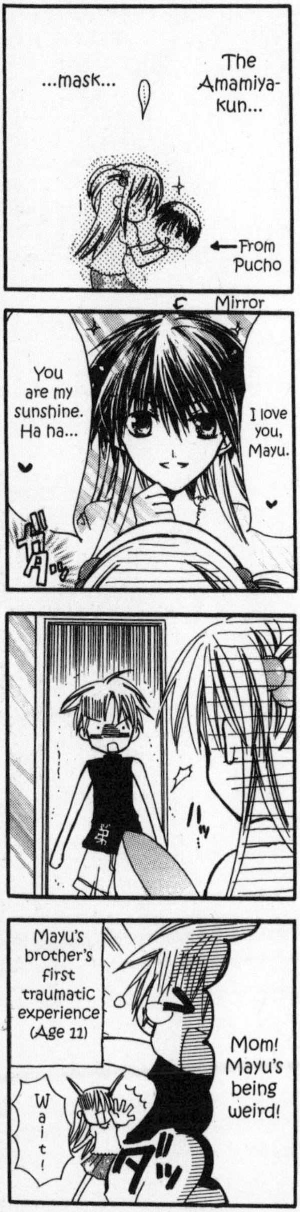

The Amamiya-kun...
...mask...
From Pucho
Mirror
I love you, Mayu.
You are my sunshine. Ha ha...
ガタッ
ハッ
Mayu's brother's first traumatic experience (Age 11)
Mom! Mayu's being weird!
Wait!
ダッ

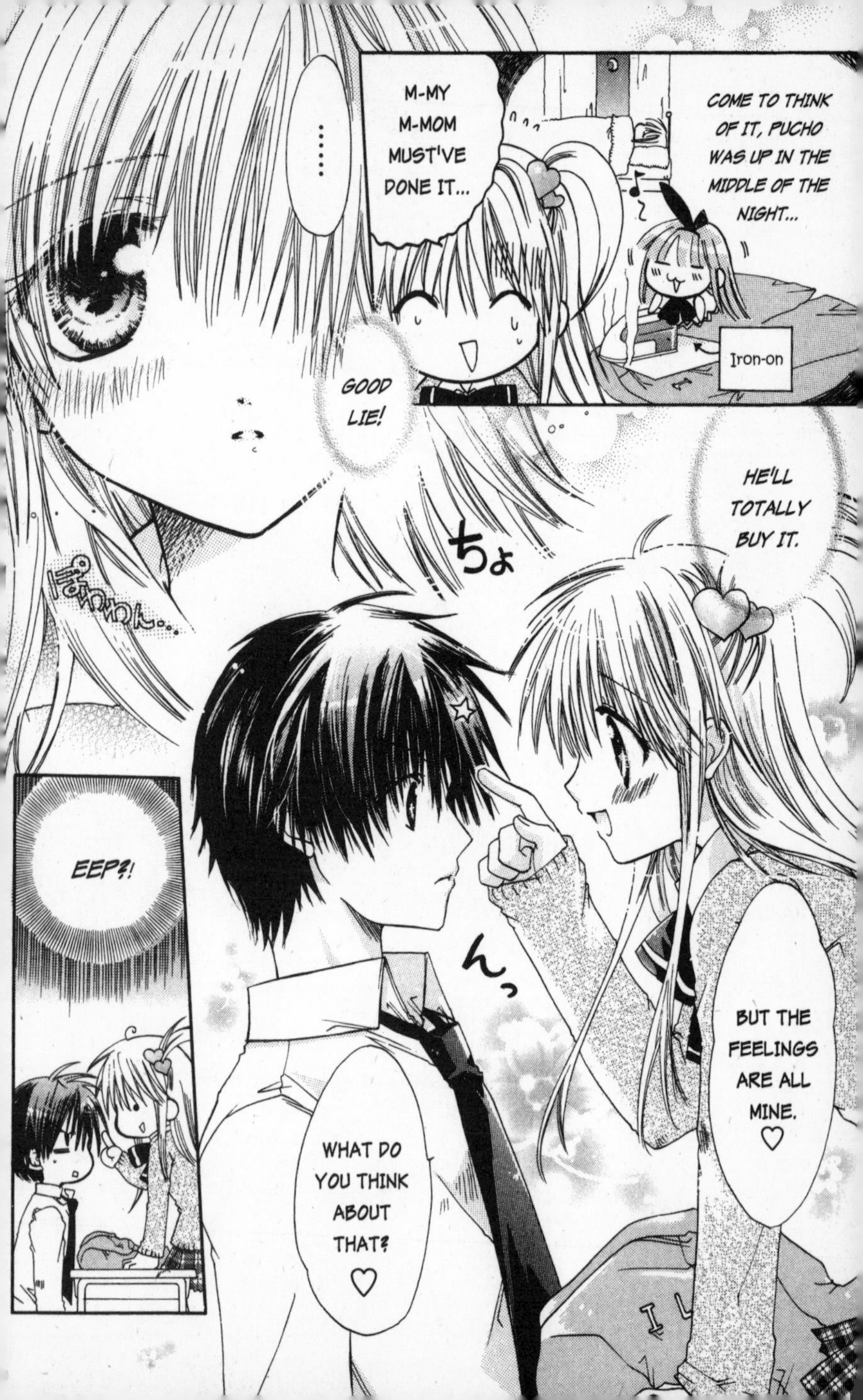
COME TO THINK OF IT, PUCHO WAS UP IN THE MIDDLE OF THE NIGHT...
Iron-on
M-MY M-MOM MUST'VE DONE IT...
......
GOOD LIE!
HE'LL TOTALLY BUY IT.
ちょ
ぽわわん...
んっ
BUT THE FEELINGS ARE ALL MINE. ♡
WHAT DO YOU THINK ABOUT THAT? ♡
EEP?!

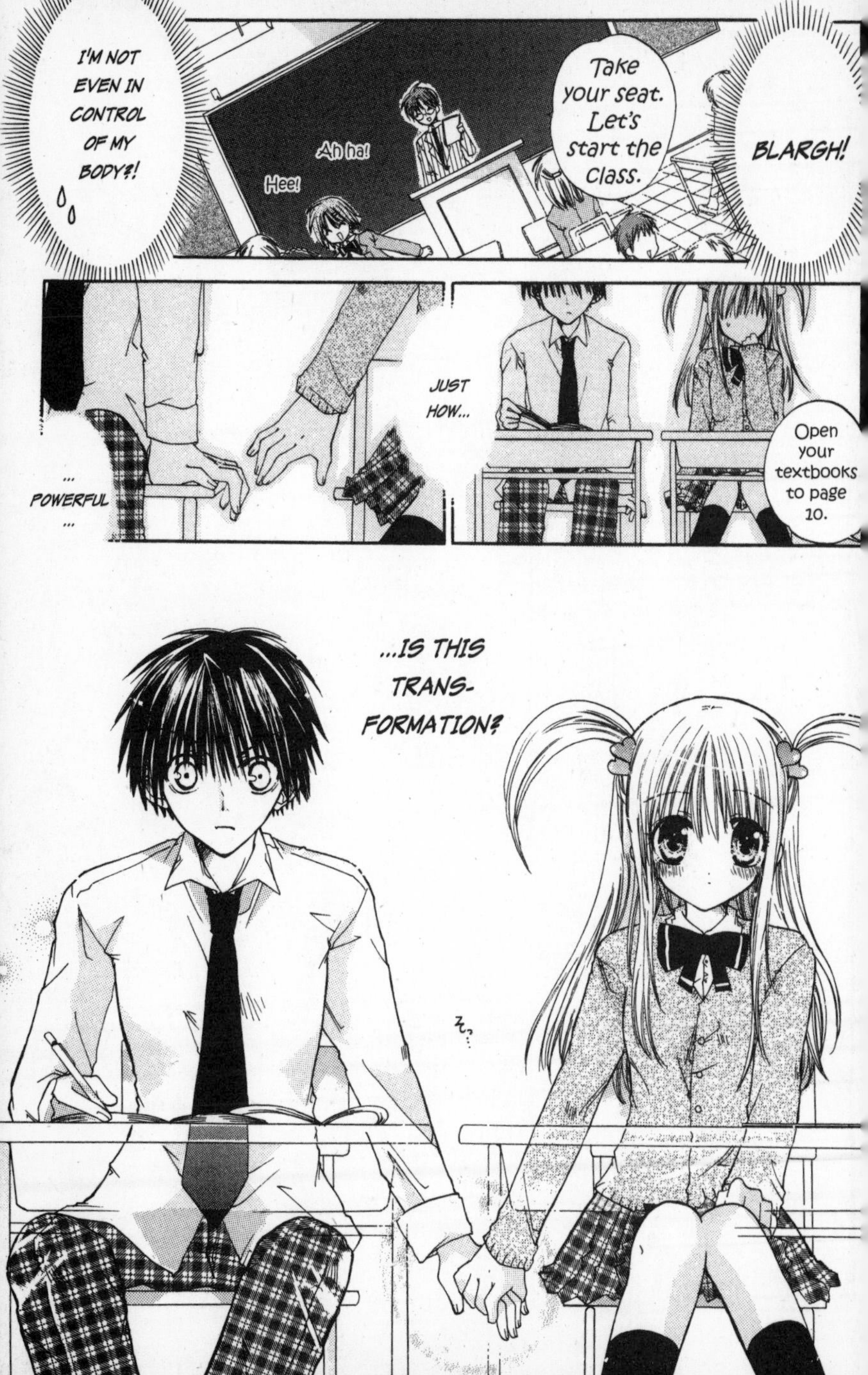
BLARGH!
Take your seat. Let's start the class.
I'M NOT EVEN IN CONTROL OF MY BODY?!
Ah ha!
Hee!
Open your textbooks to page 10.
JUST HOW...
...POWERFUL...
...IS THIS TRANS-FORMATION?

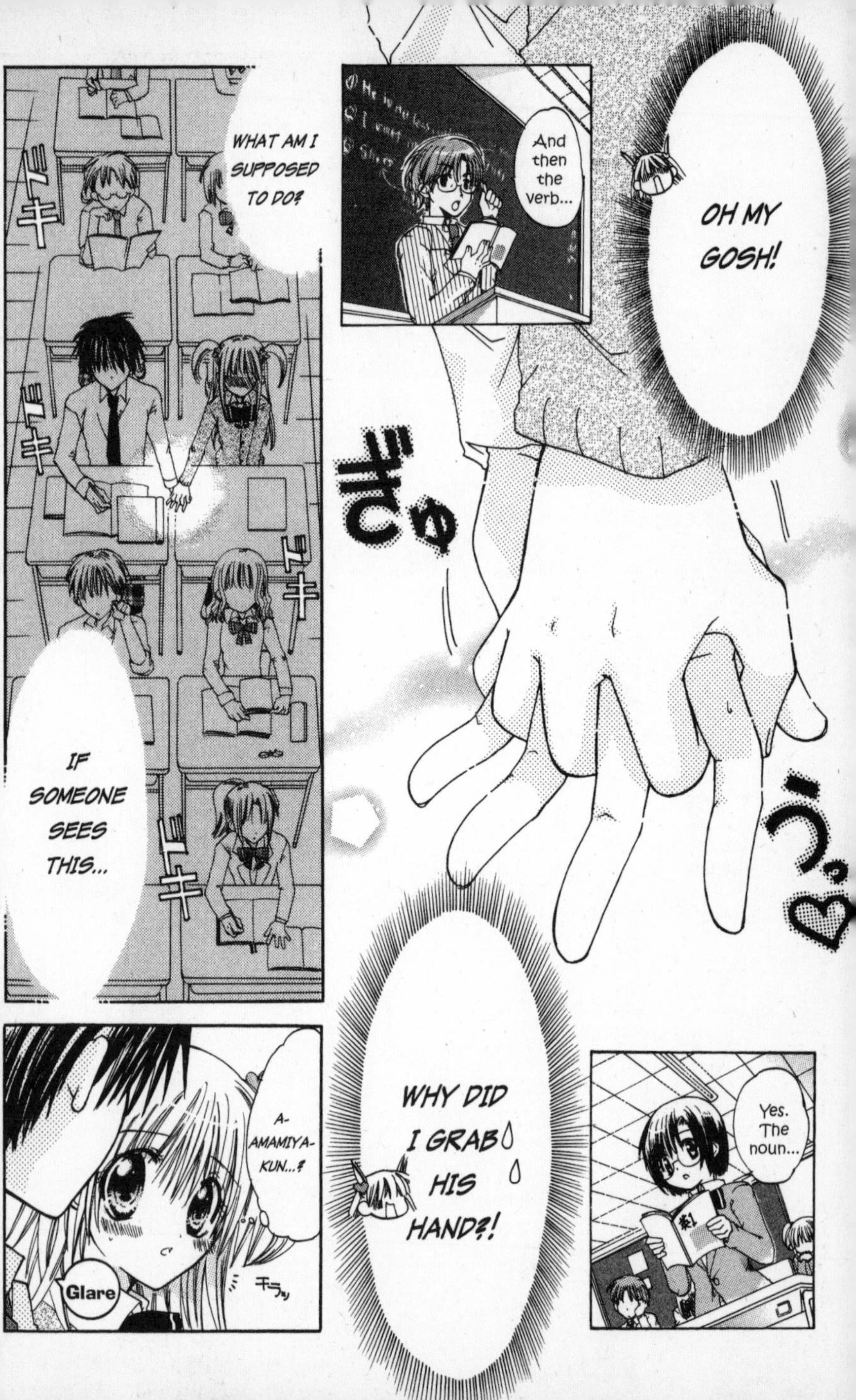
OH MY GOSH!
And then the verb...
WHAT AM I SUPPOSED TO DO?
IF SOMEONE SEES THIS...
Yes. The noun...
WHY DID I GRAB HIS HAND?!
A-AMAMIYA-KUN...?
Glare

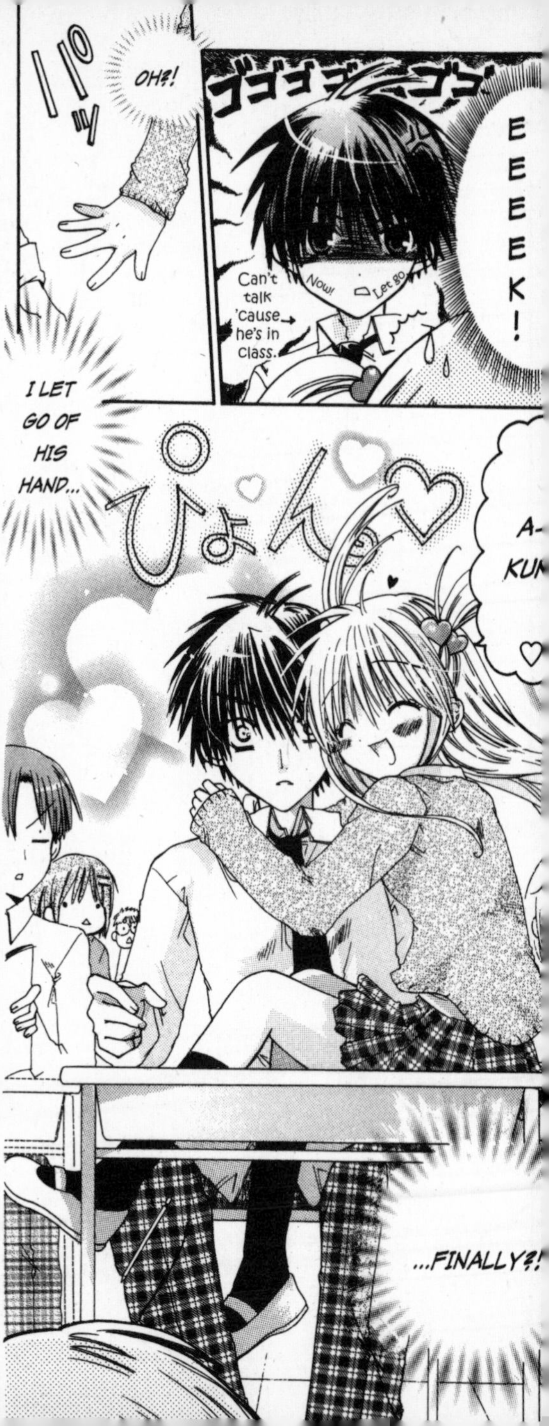
ゴゴゴゴ
EEEEK!
Now! Let go
Can't talk 'cause he's in class.
パッ
OH?!
I LET GO OF HIS HAND...
ぴょん
A-KUN ♡
...FINALLY?!

● Almost Curse ●

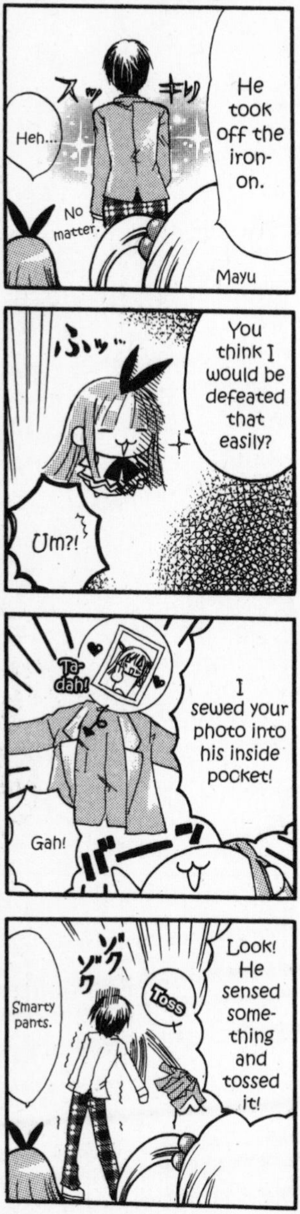
He took off the iron-on.
Heh...
No matter.
Mayu
You think I would be defeated that easily?
Um?!
Ta-dah!
I sewed your photo into his inside pocket!
Gah!
Look! He sensed something and tossed it!
Toss
Smarty pants.

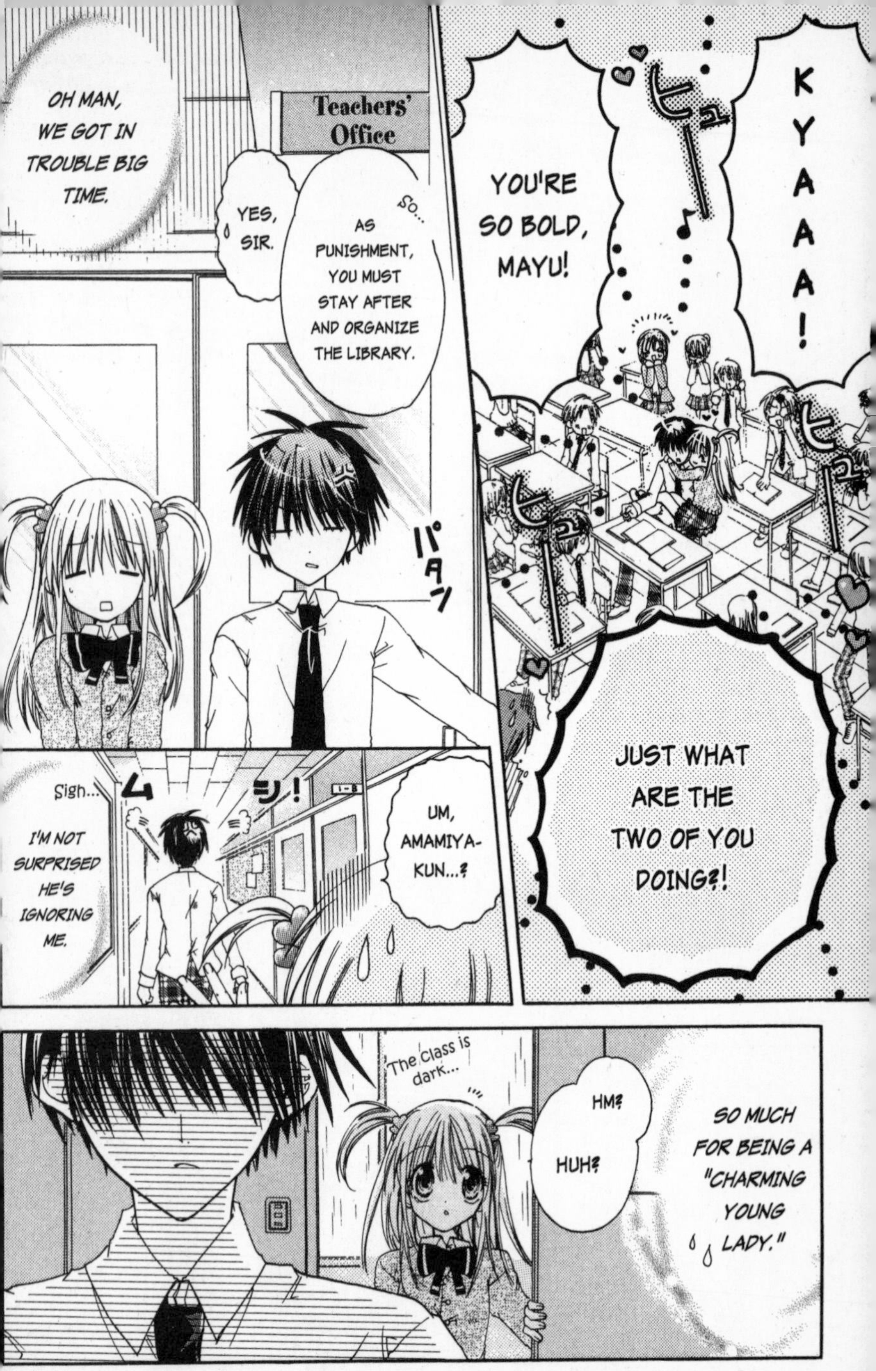
KYAAA!
ヒュー
YOU'RE SO BOLD, MAYU!
ヒュー
JUST WHAT ARE THE TWO OF YOU DOING?!
Teachers' Office
SO...
AS PUNISHMENT, YOU MUST STAY AFTER AND ORGANIZE THE LIBRARY.
YES, SIR.
OH MAN, WE GOT IN TROUBLE BIG TIME.
パタン
UM, AMAMIYA-KUN...?
ムシ!
Sigh...
I'M NOT SURPRISED HE'S IGNORING ME.
SO MUCH FOR BEING A "CHARMING YOUNG LADY."
HM?
HUH?
The class is dark...

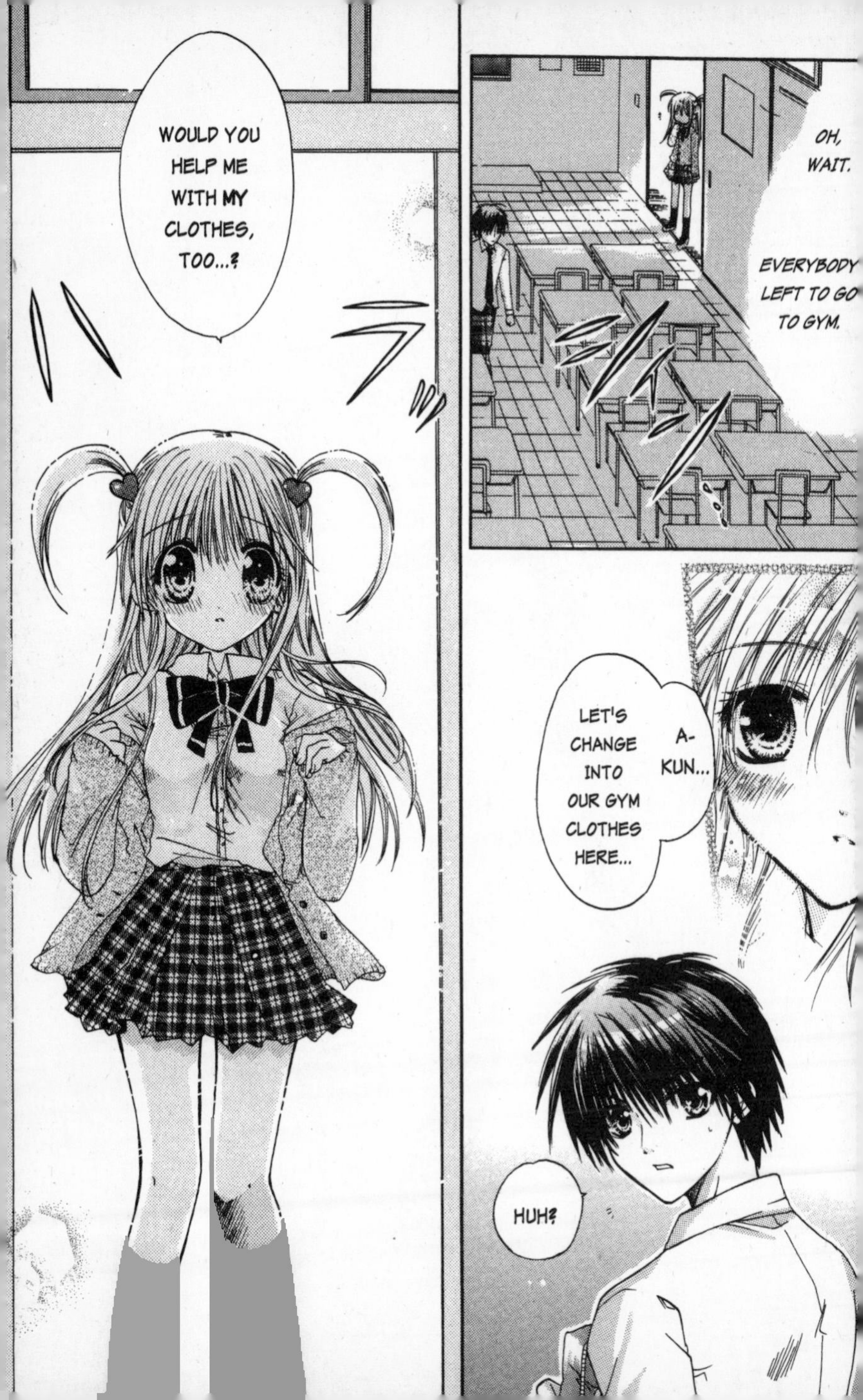
OH, WAIT.
EVERYBODY LEFT TO GO TO GYM.
A-KUN...
LET'S CHANGE INTO OUR GYM CLOTHES HERE...
HUH?
WOULD YOU HELP ME WITH MY CLOTHES, TOO...?

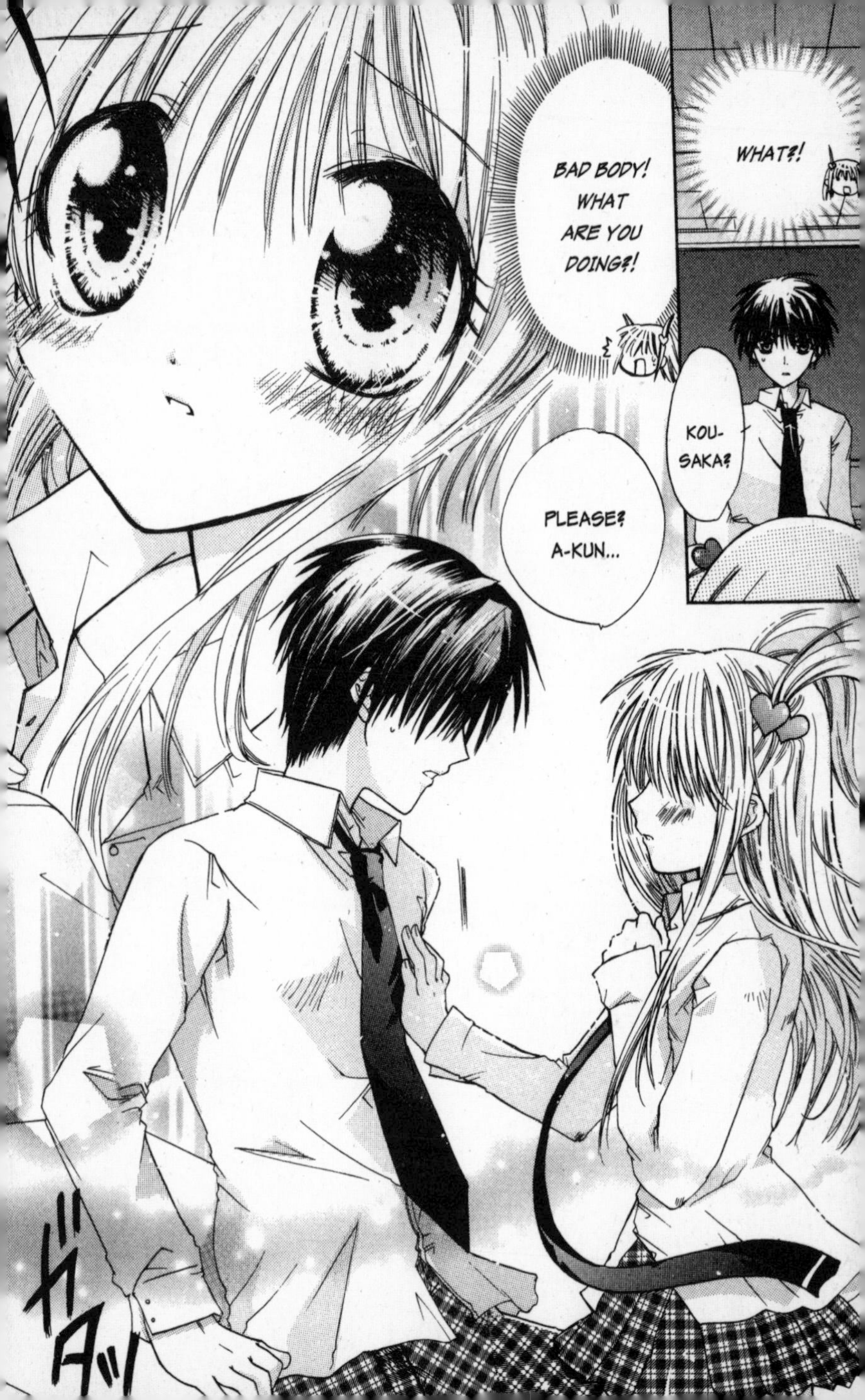
WHAT?!
KOU-SAKA?
BAD BODY! WHAT ARE YOU DOING?!
PLEASE? A-KUN...

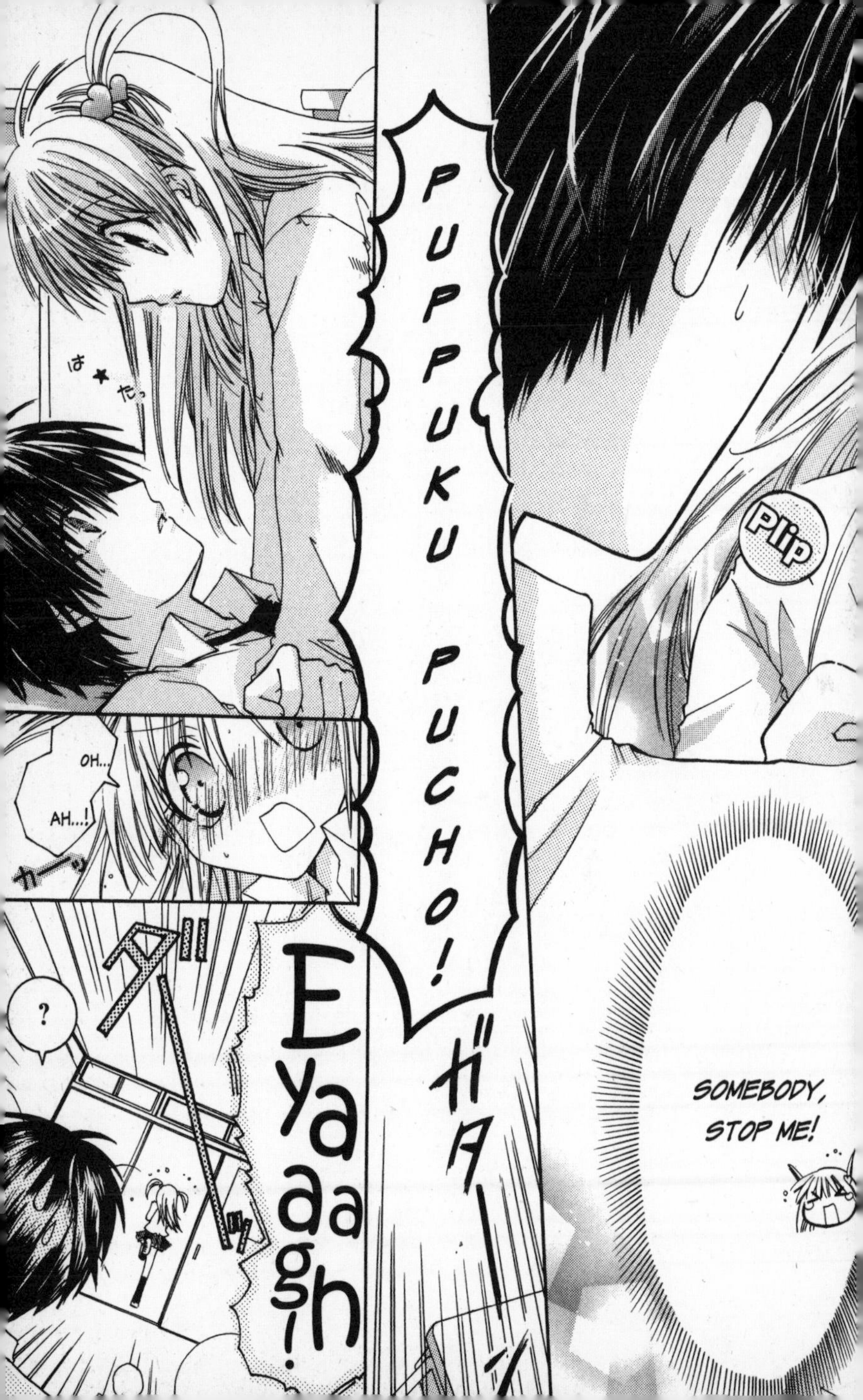
Plip
SOMEBODY, STOP ME!
PUPUPUKU PUPUCHO!
ガァー
は★たっ
OH...
AH...!
?
Eyaaagh!

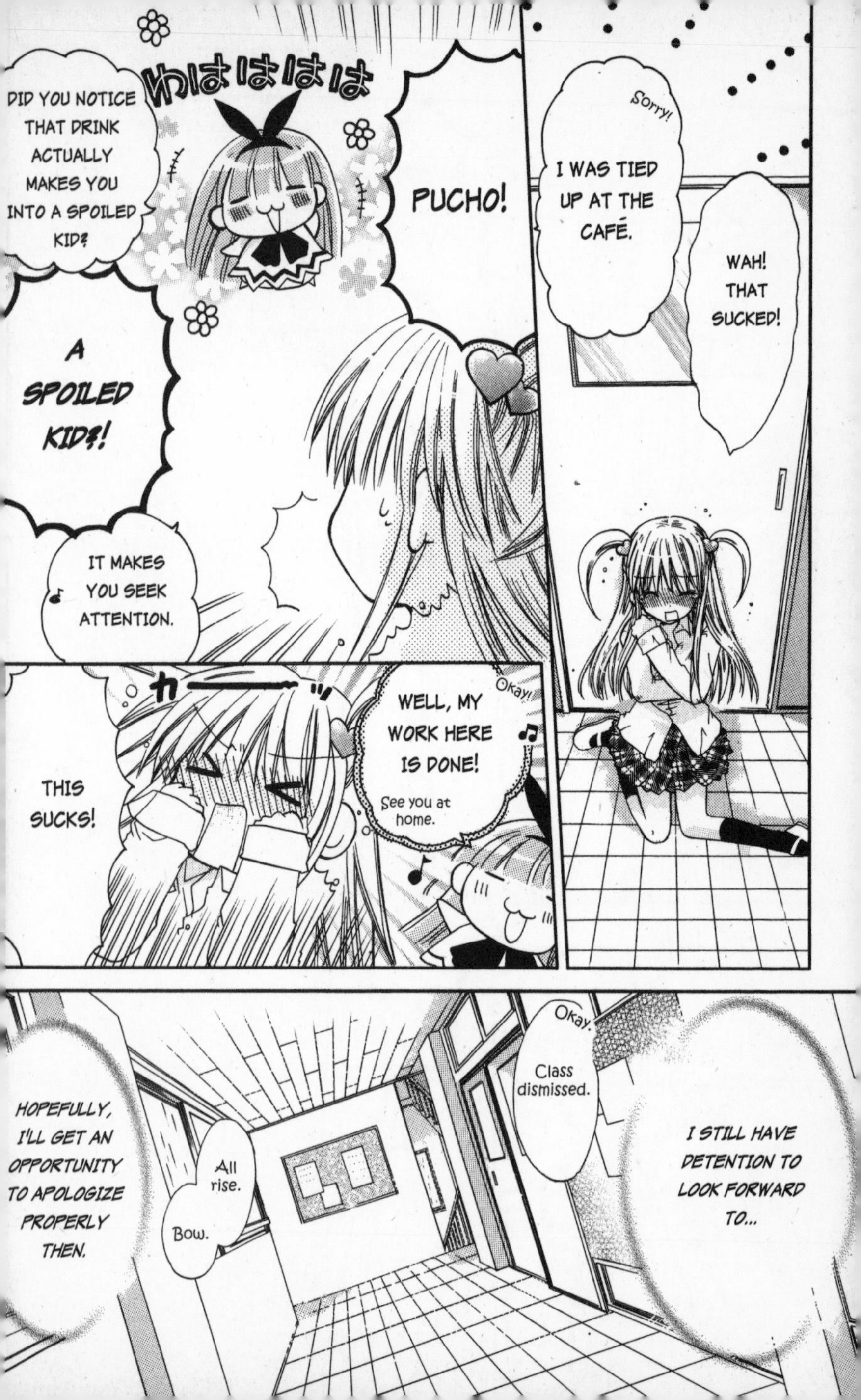
Sorry!
I WAS TIED UP AT THE CAFÉ.
WAH! THAT SUCKED!
PUCHO!
わはははは
DID YOU NOTICE THAT DRINK ACTUALLY MAKES YOU INTO A SPOILED KID?
A SPOILED KID?!
IT MAKES YOU SEEK ATTENTION.
Okay!
WELL, MY WORK HERE IS DONE!
See you at home.
カ――ッ
THIS SUCKS!
Okay.
Class dismissed.
I STILL HAVE DETENTION TO LOOK FORWARD TO...
All rise.
Bow.
HOPEFULLY, I'LL GET AN OPPORTUNITY TO APOLOGIZE PROPERLY THEN.

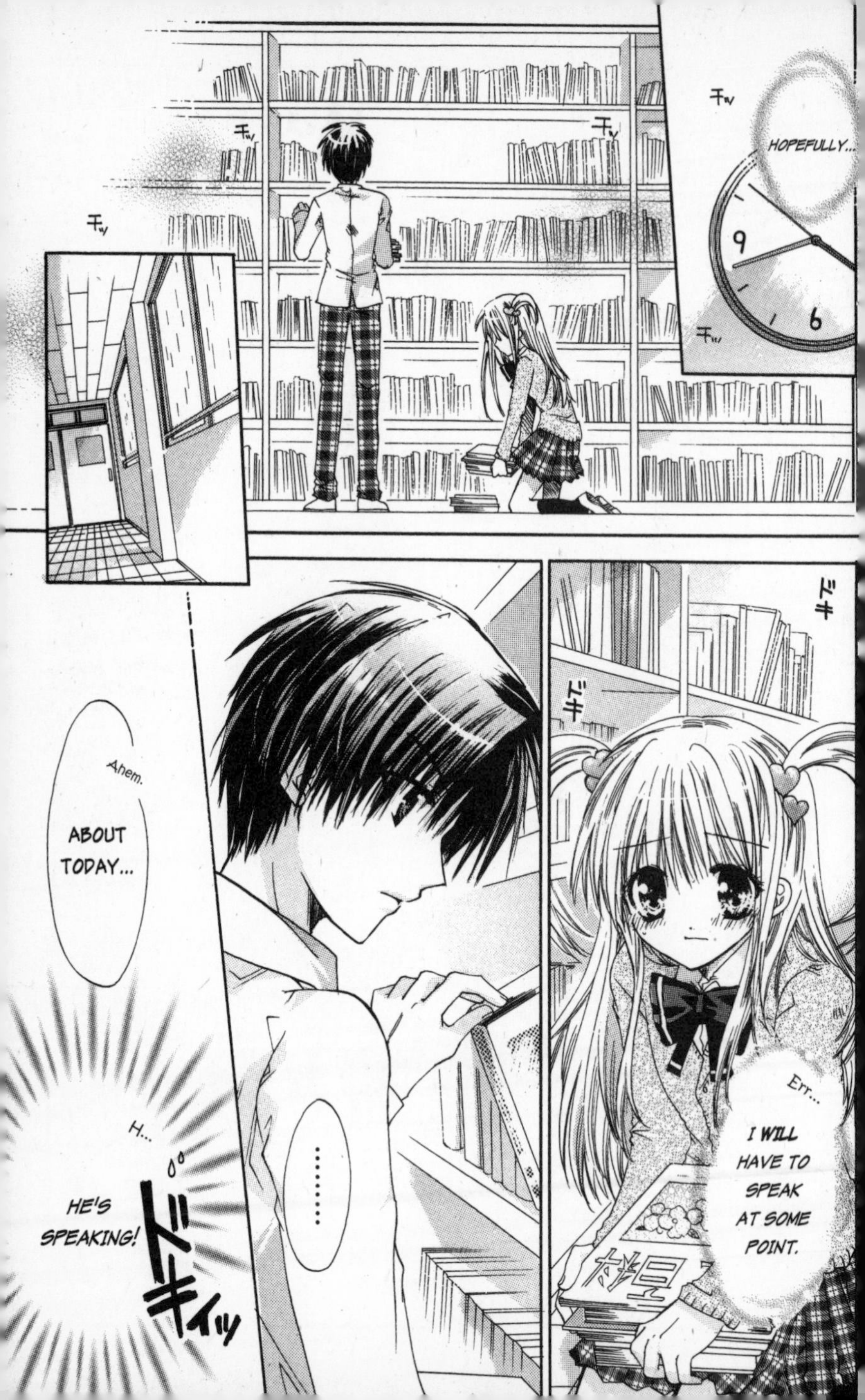

チッ
HOPEFULLY...
チッ
チッ
チッ
チッ
ドキ
ドキ
Err...
I WILL HAVE TO SPEAK AT SOME POINT.
Ahem.
ABOUT TODAY...
......
H...
HE'S SPEAKING!
ドキィッ

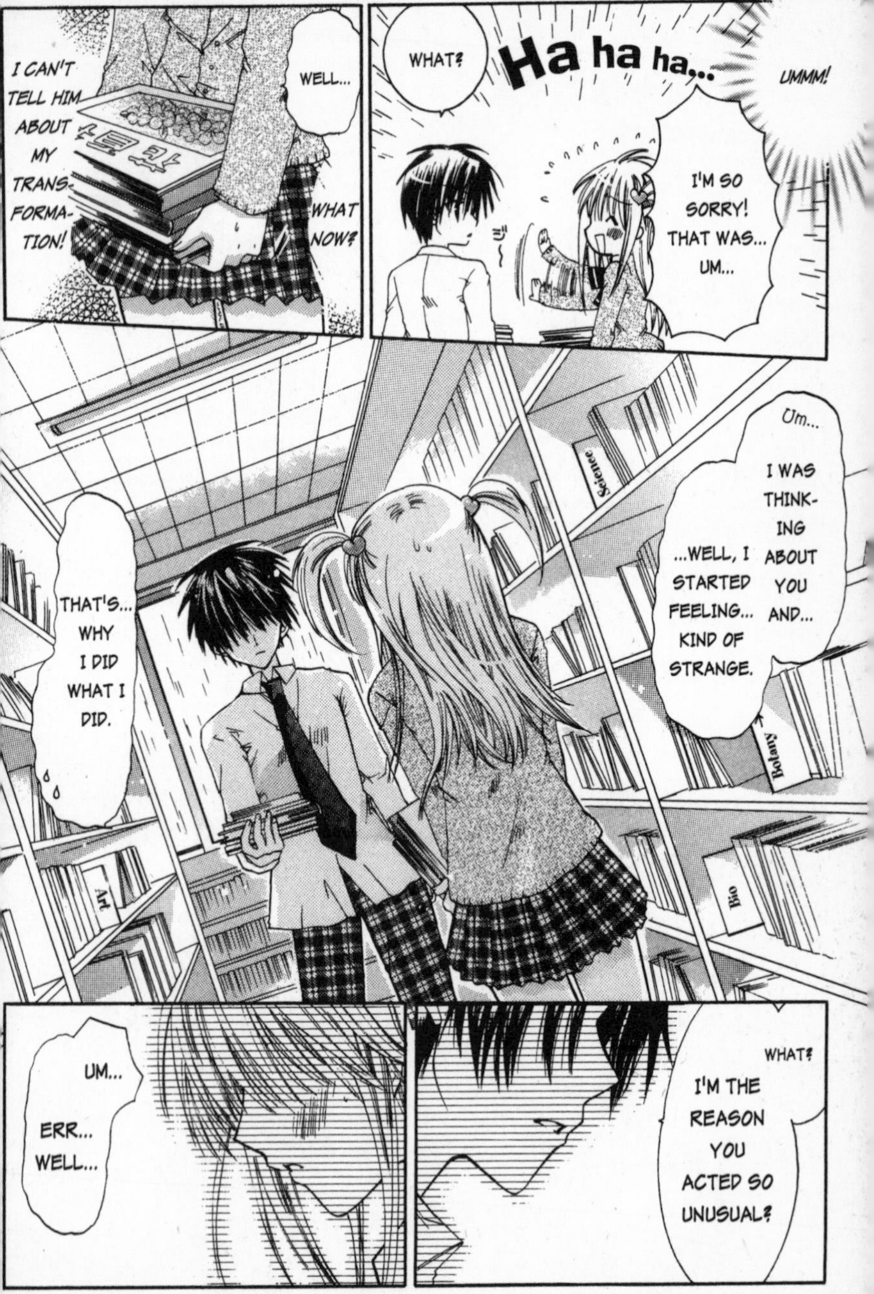
UMMM!
Ha ha ha...
WHAT?
I'M SO SORRY! THAT WAS... UM...
WELL...
WHAT NOW?
I CAN'T TELL HIM ABOUT MY TRANSFORMATION!
Um... I WAS THINKING ABOUT YOU AND...
...WELL, I STARTED FEELING... KIND OF STRANGE.
Science
Botany
Bio
THAT'S... WHY I DID WHAT I DID.
Art
WHAT? I'M THE REASON YOU ACTED SO UNUSUAL?
UM... ERR... WELL...

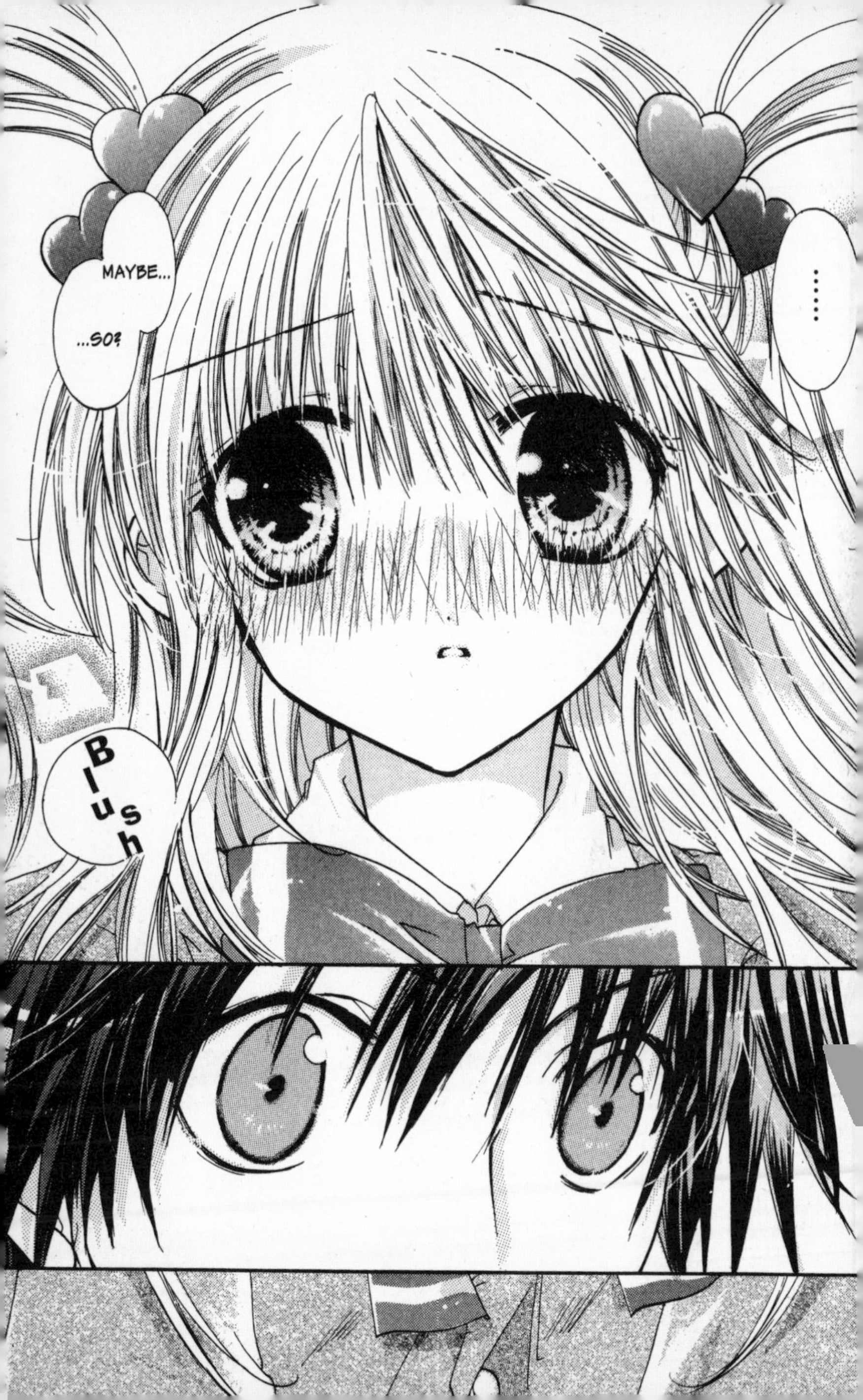
......
MAYBE... ...SO?
Blush

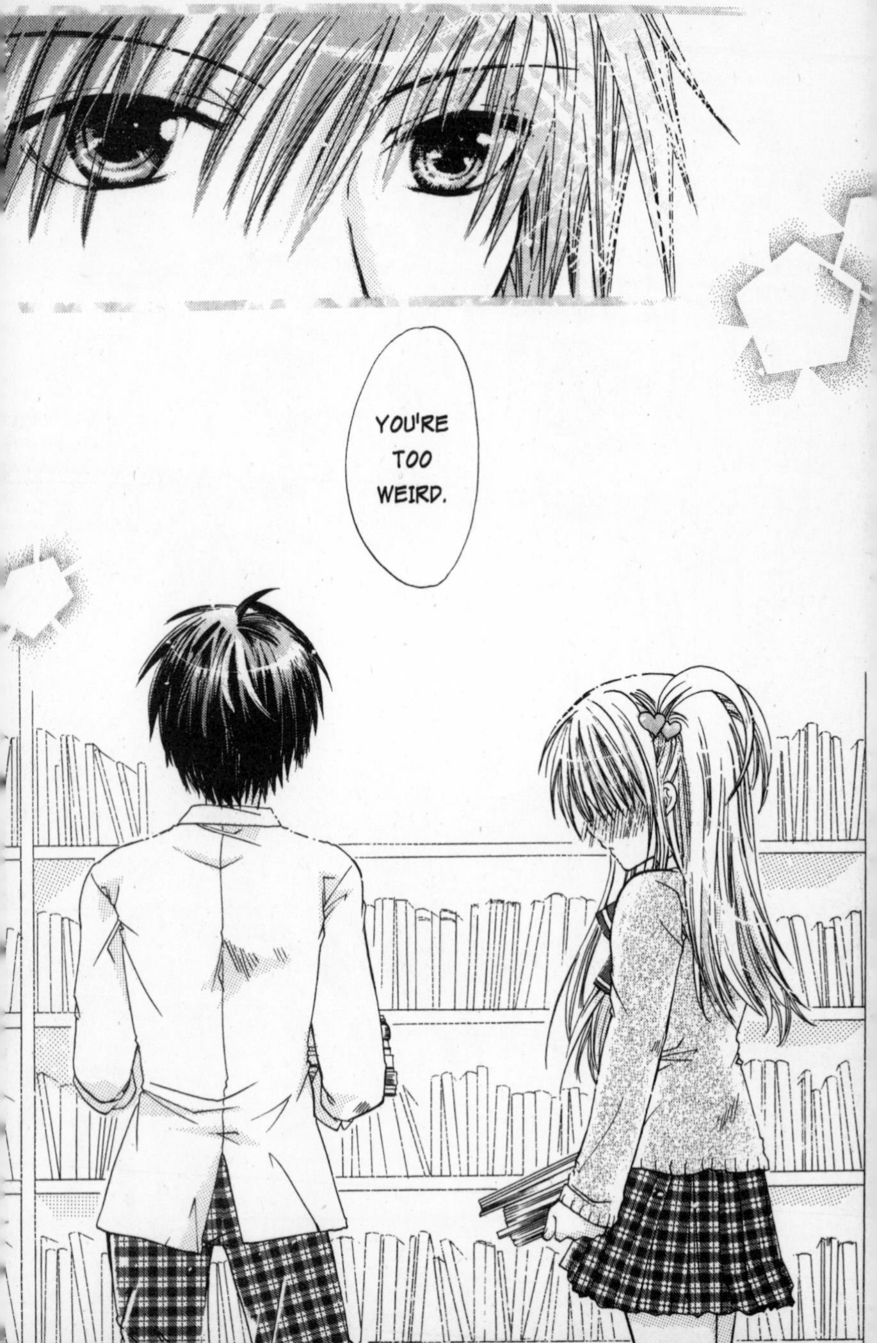
YOU'RE TOO WEIRD.

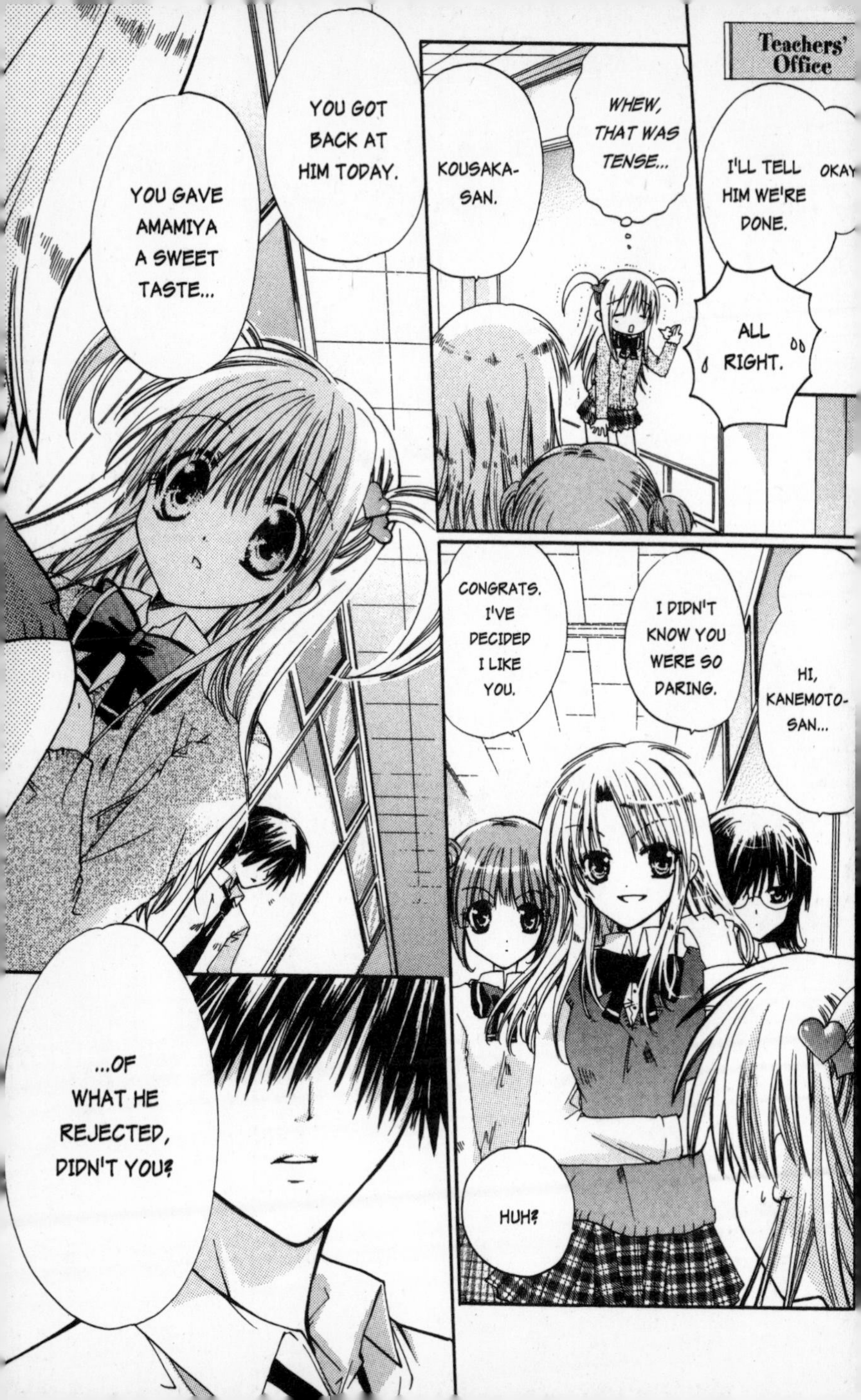
Teachers' Office
OKAY
I'LL TELL HIM WE'RE DONE.
ALL RIGHT.
WHEW, THAT WAS TENSE...
KOUSAKA-SAN.
YOU GOT BACK AT HIM TODAY.
YOU GAVE AMAMIYA A SWEET TASTE...
...OF WHAT HE REJECTED, DIDN'T YOU?
HI, KANEMOTO-SAN...
I DIDN'T KNOW YOU WERE SO DARING.
CONGRATS. I'VE DECIDED I LIKE YOU.
HUH?

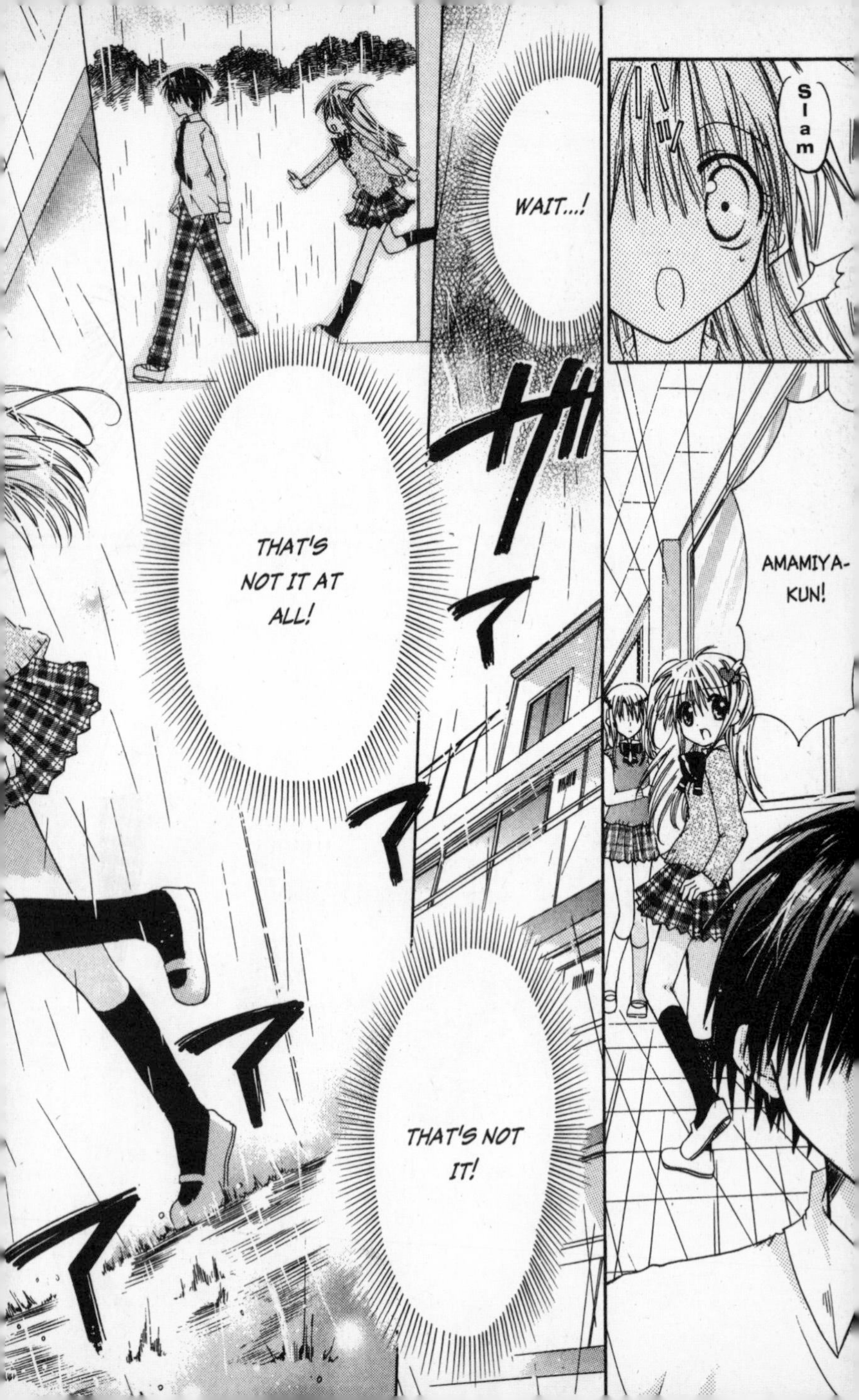
Slam
AMAMIYA-KUN!
WAIT...!
THAT'S NOT IT!
THAT'S NOT IT AT ALL!

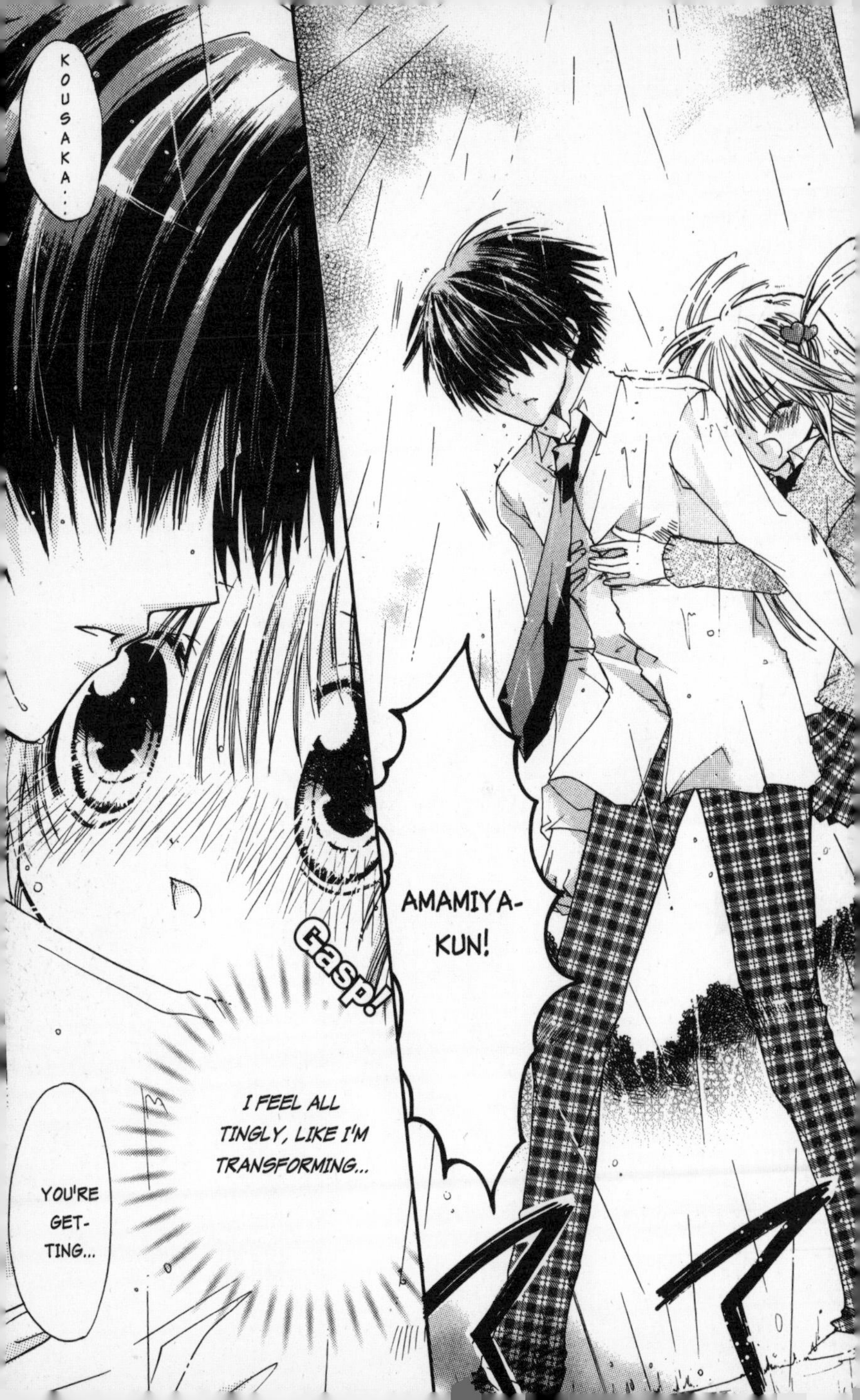
AMAMIYA-KUN!
KOUSAKA...
Gasp!
I FEEL ALL TINGLY, LIKE I'M TRANSFORMING...
YOU'RE GETTING...

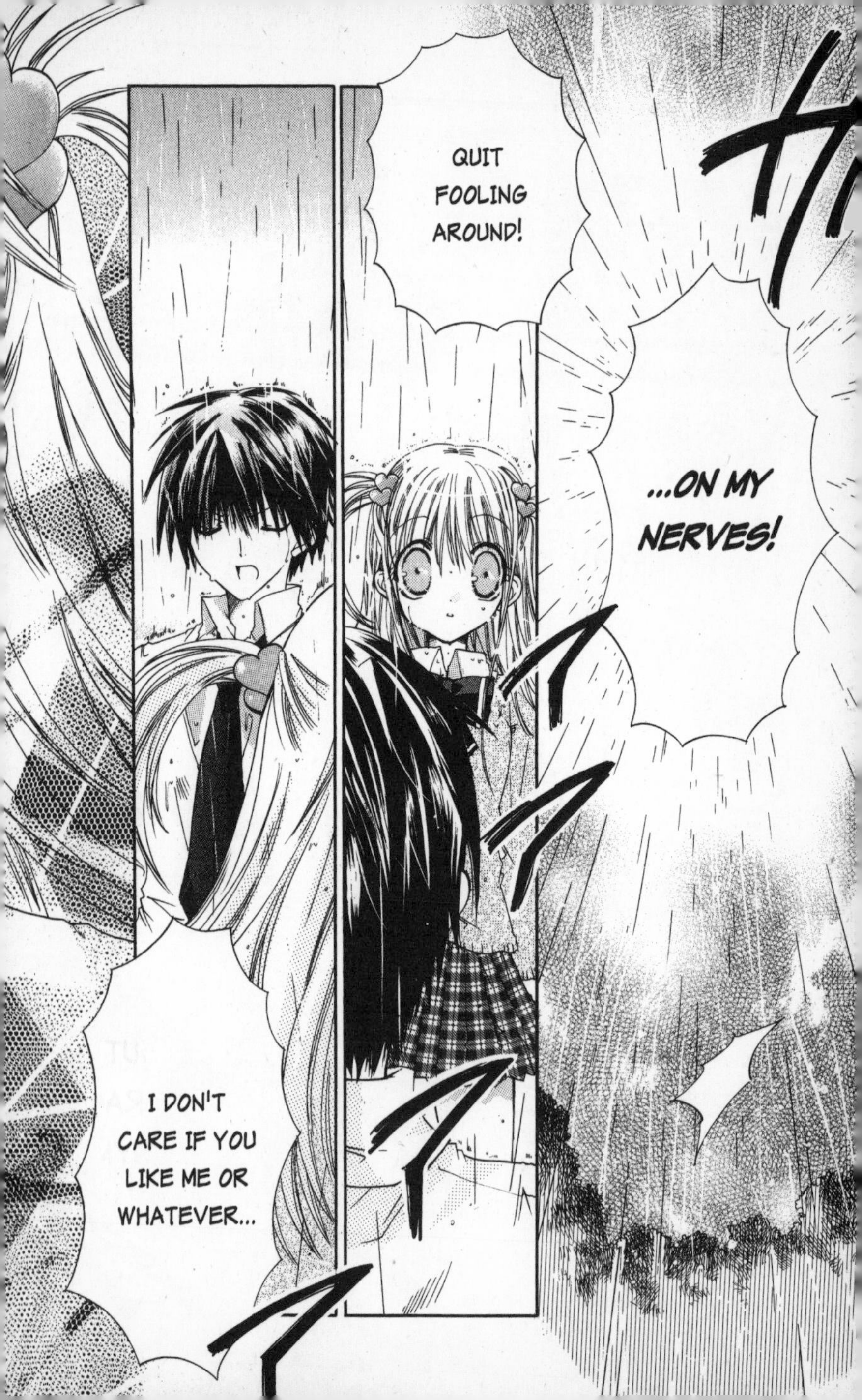
QUIT FOOLING AROUND!
...ON MY NERVES!
I DON'T CARE IF YOU LIKE ME OR WHATEVER...

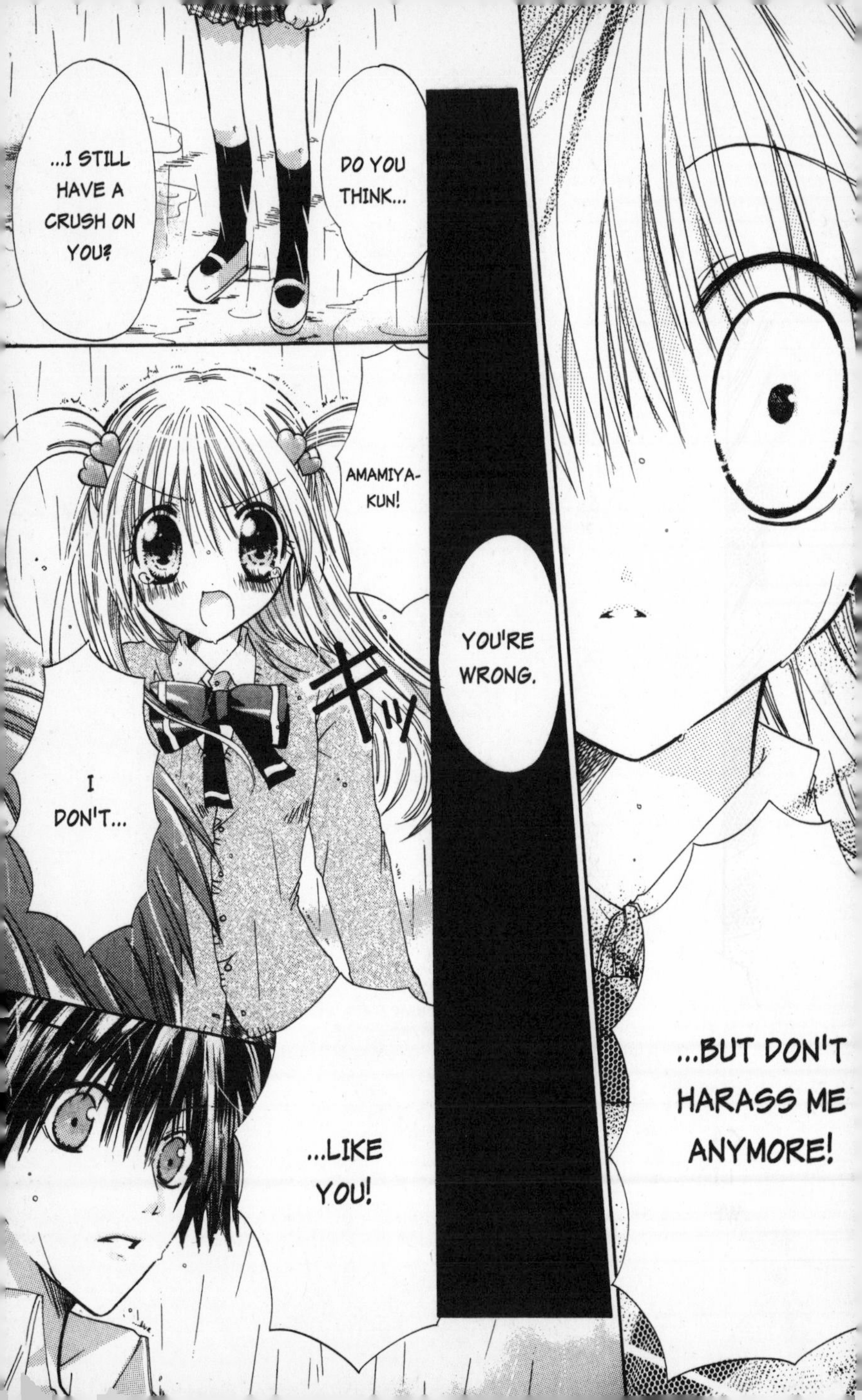
DO YOU THINK...
...I STILL HAVE A CRUSH ON YOU?
YOU'RE WRONG.
AMAMIYA-KUN!
I DON'T...
...LIKE YOU!
...BUT DON'T HARASS ME ANYMORE!

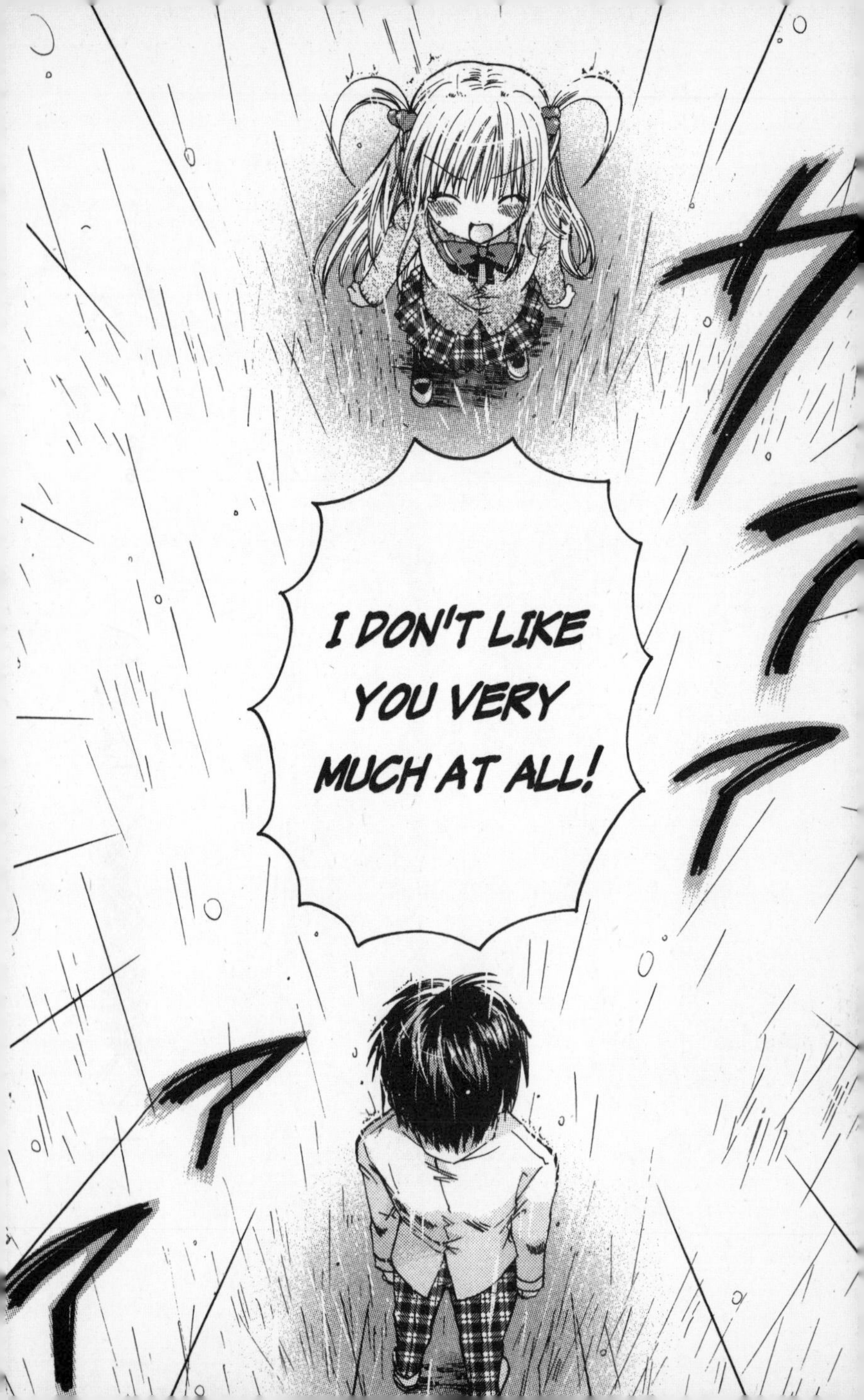
I DON'T LIKE YOU VERY MUCH AT ALL!

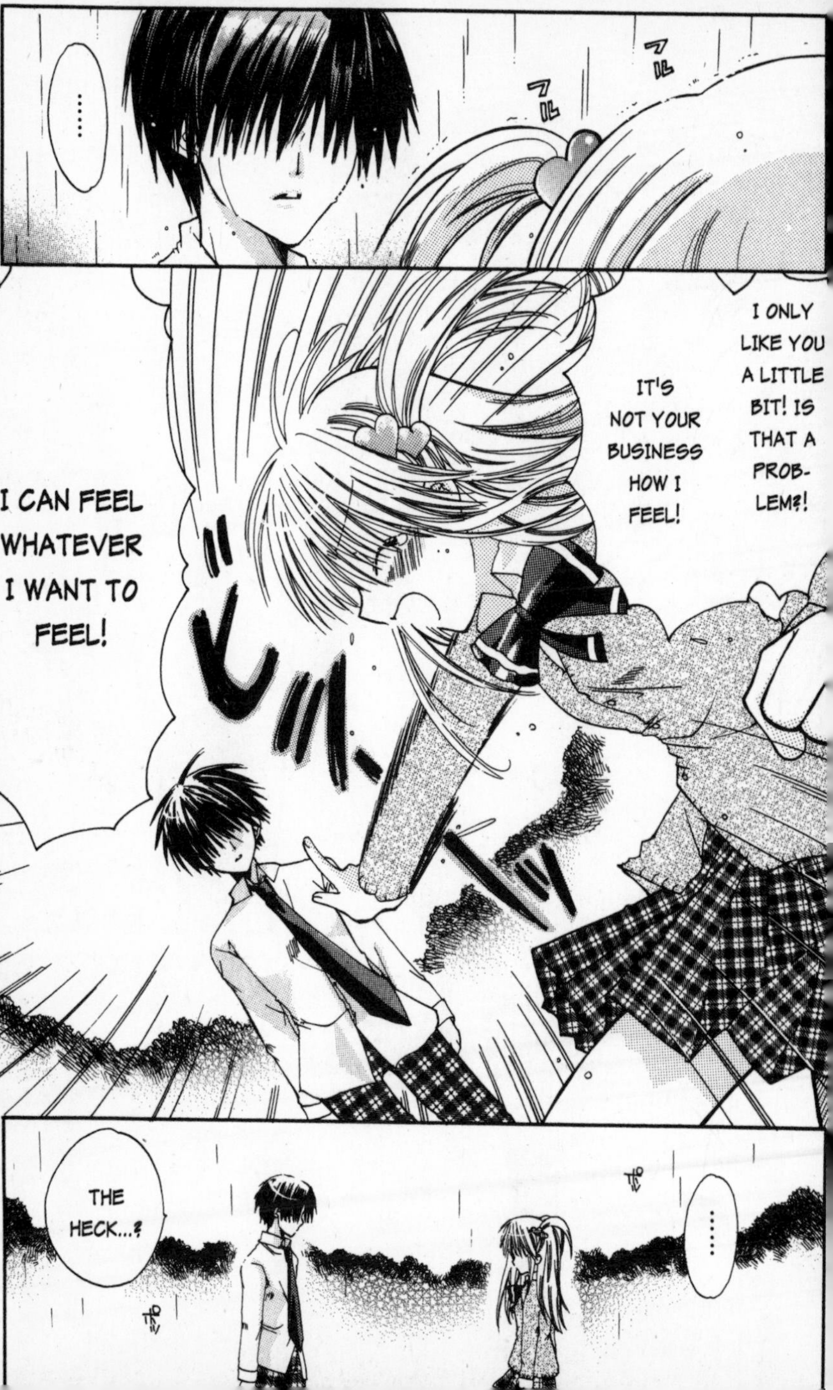
フル
フル
......
I ONLY LIKE YOU A LITTLE BIT! IS THAT A PROB-LEM?!
IT'S NOT YOUR BUSINESS HOW I FEEL!
I CAN FEEL WHATEVER I WANT TO FEEL!
ビシーッ
......
THE HECK...?

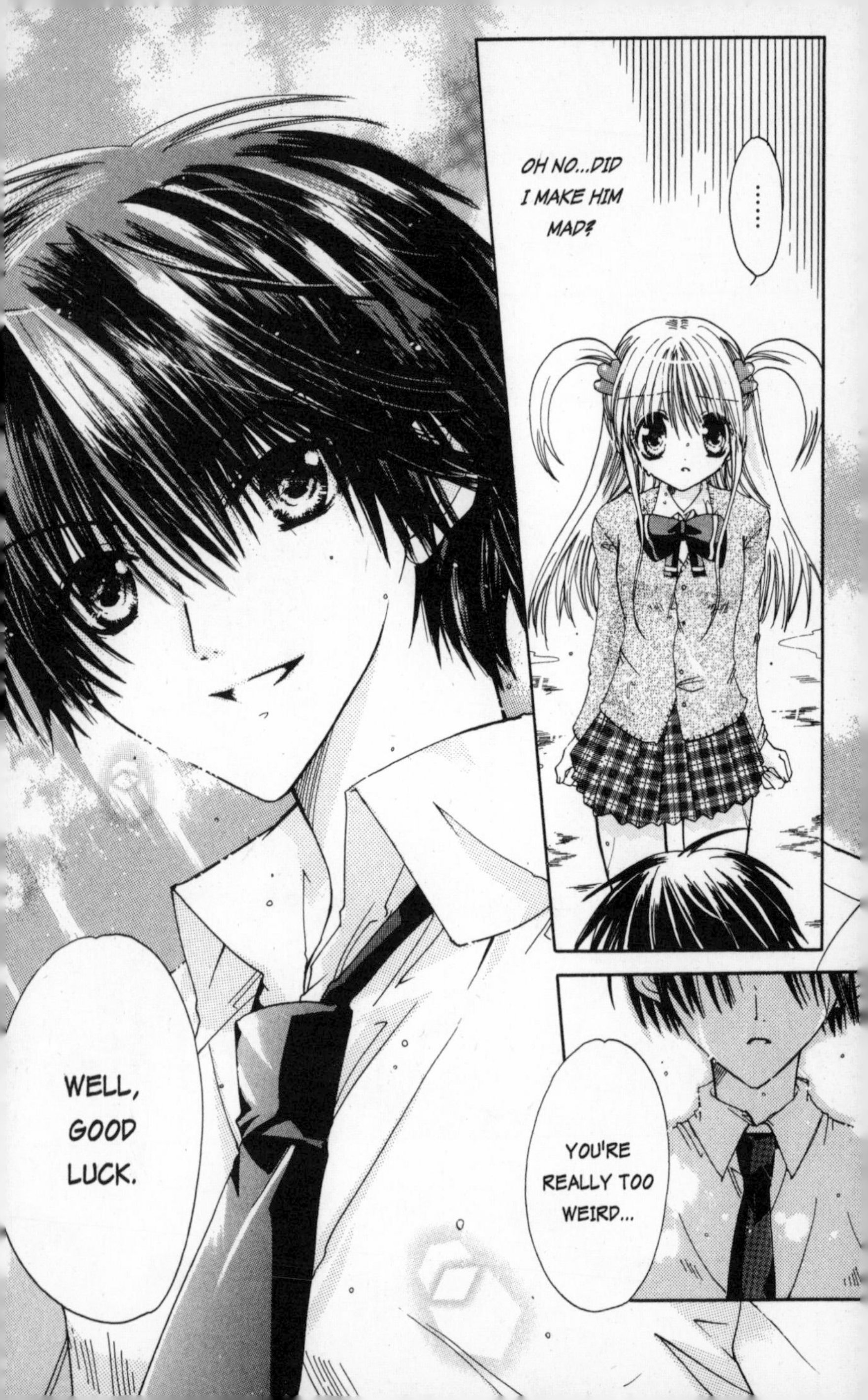
......
OH NO...DID I MAKE HIM MAD?
YOU'RE REALLY TOO WEIRD...
WELL, GOOD LUCK.

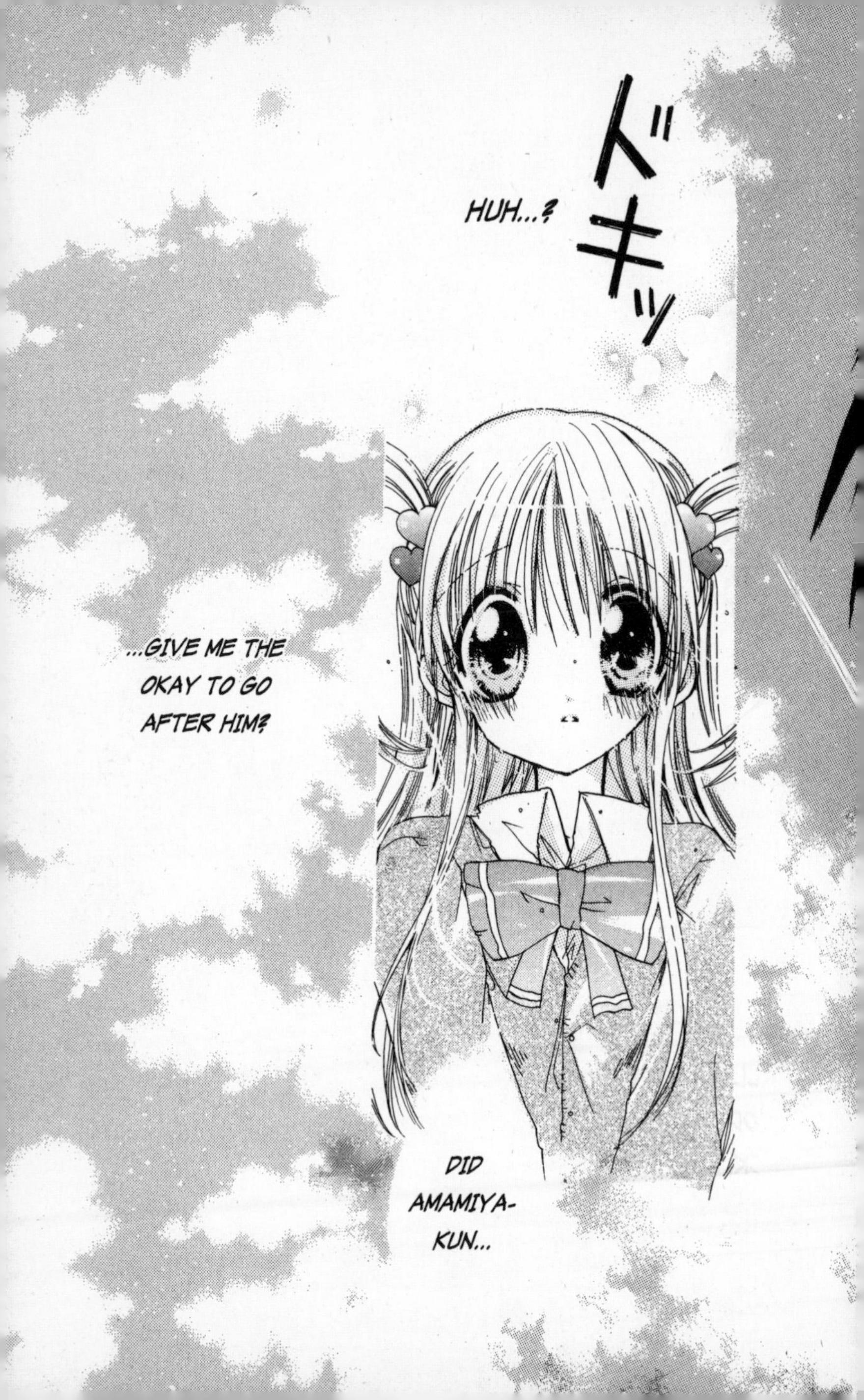
ドキッ
HUH...?
DID AMAMIYA-KUN...
...GIVE ME THE OKAY TO GO AFTER HIM?

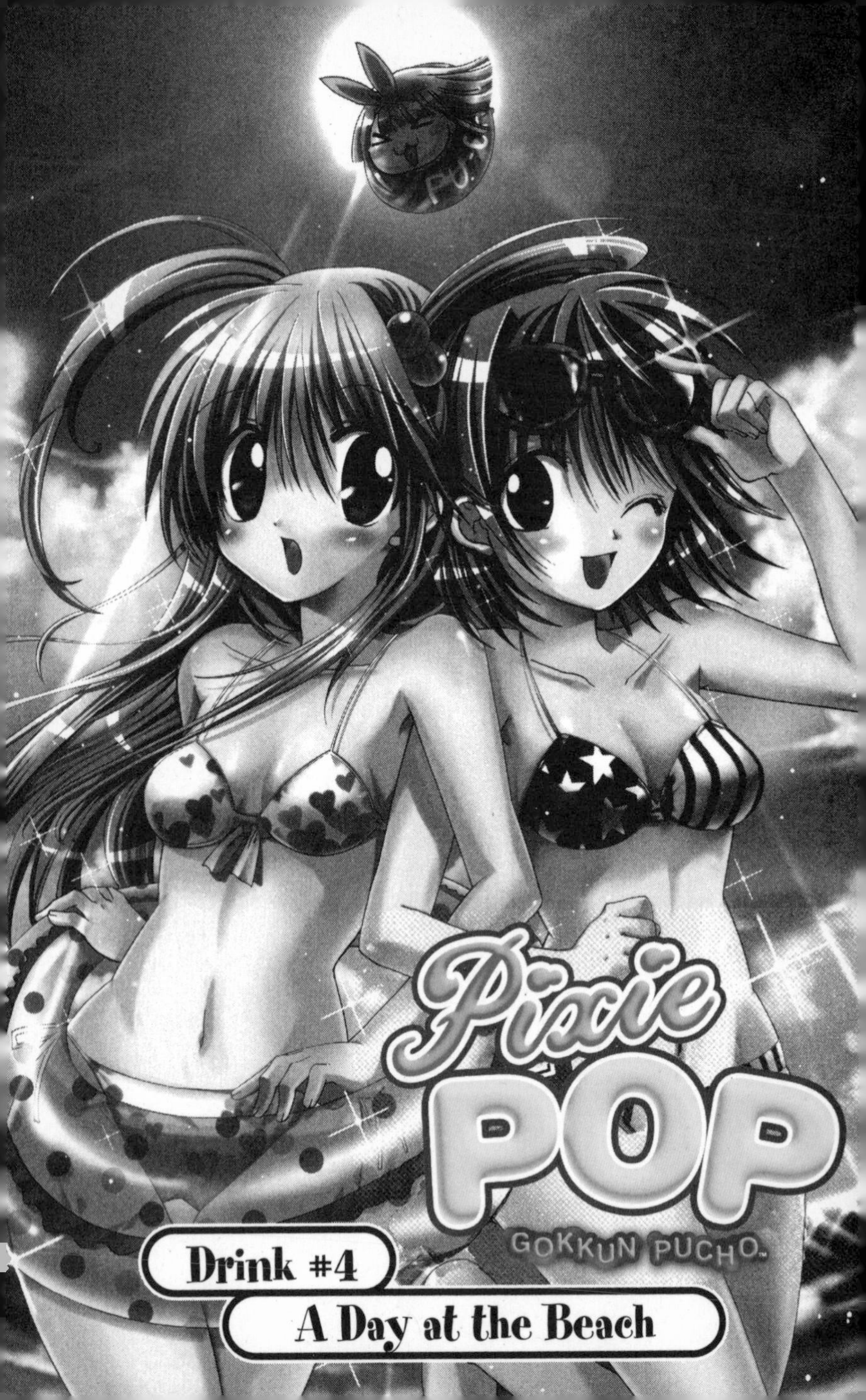
PUCHO
Pixie POP
GOKKUN PUCHO™
Drink #4
A Day at the Beach

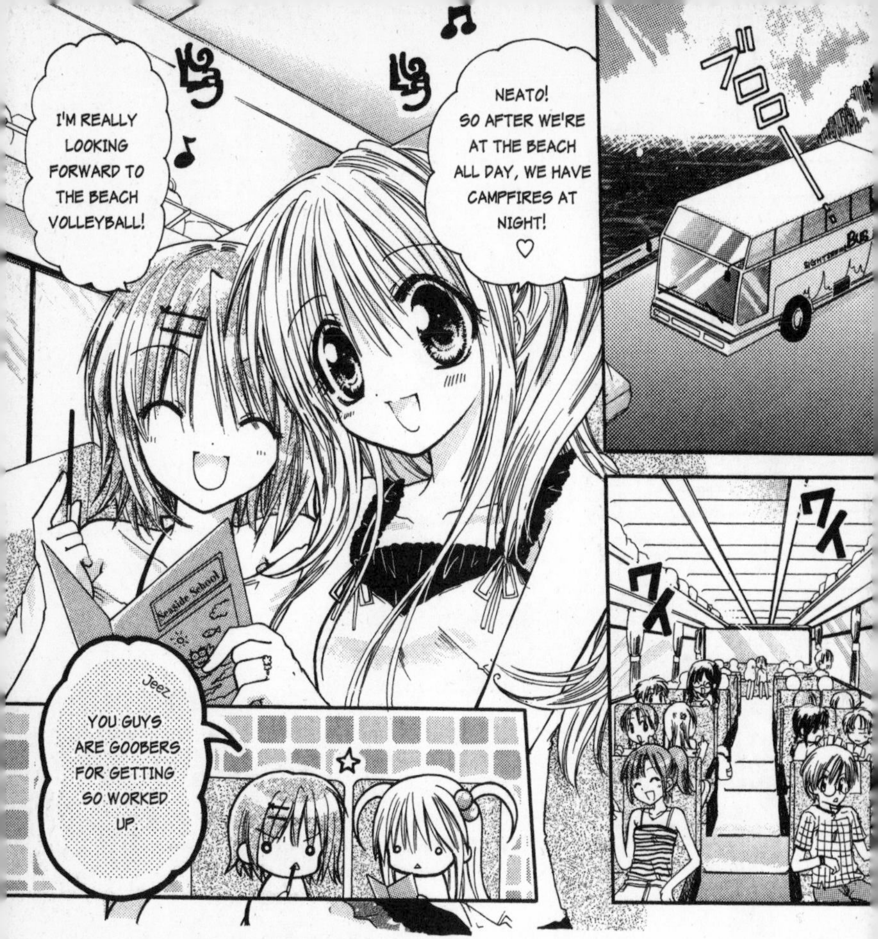
ブロロー
NEATO! SO AFTER WE'RE AT THE BEACH ALL DAY, WE HAVE CAMPFIRES AT NIGHT! ♡
I'M REALLY LOOKING FORWARD TO THE BEACH VOLLEYBALL!
ワイワイ
Jeez. YOU GUYS ARE GOOBERS FOR GETTING SO WORKED UP.

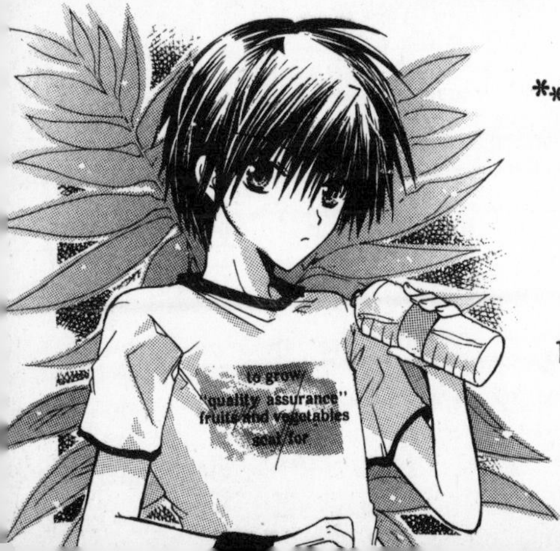
to grow
"quality assurance"
fruits and vegetables

****

♥ Shinya Amamiya ♥

Birthday: December 24th

Sign: Capricorn Bloodtype: AB

Height: 162cm Weight: 50kg

Favorite Drink: Anything fresh and non-sugary

****

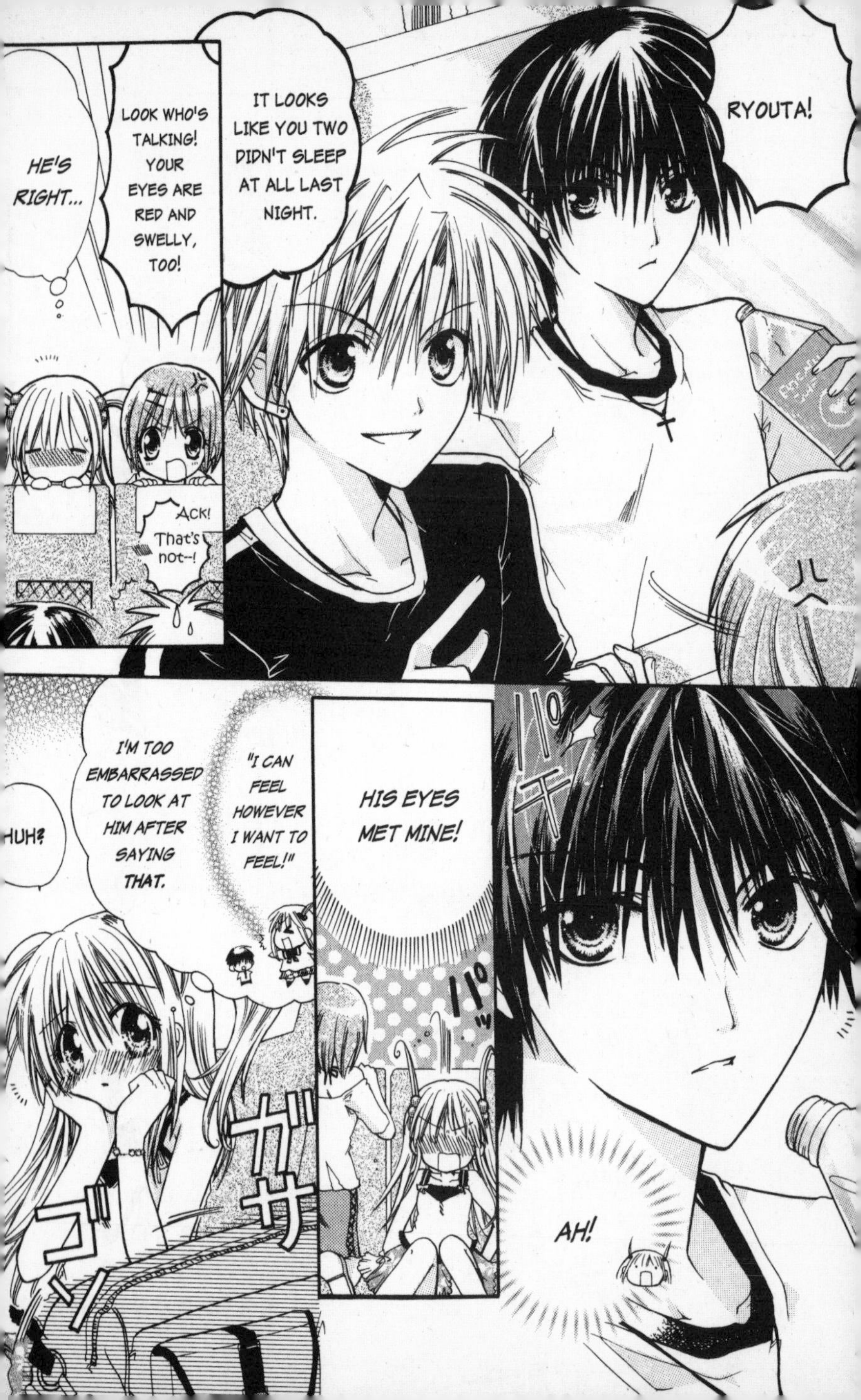
RYOUTA!
IT LOOKS LIKE YOU TWO DIDN'T SLEEP AT ALL LAST NIGHT.
LOOK WHO'S TALKING! YOUR EYES ARE RED AND SWELLY, TOO!
HE'S RIGHT...
Ack! That's not--!
AH!
HIS EYES MET MINE!
"I CAN FEEL HOWEVER I WANT TO FEEL!"
I'M TOO EMBARRASSED TO LOOK AT HIM AFTER SAYING THAT.
HUH?

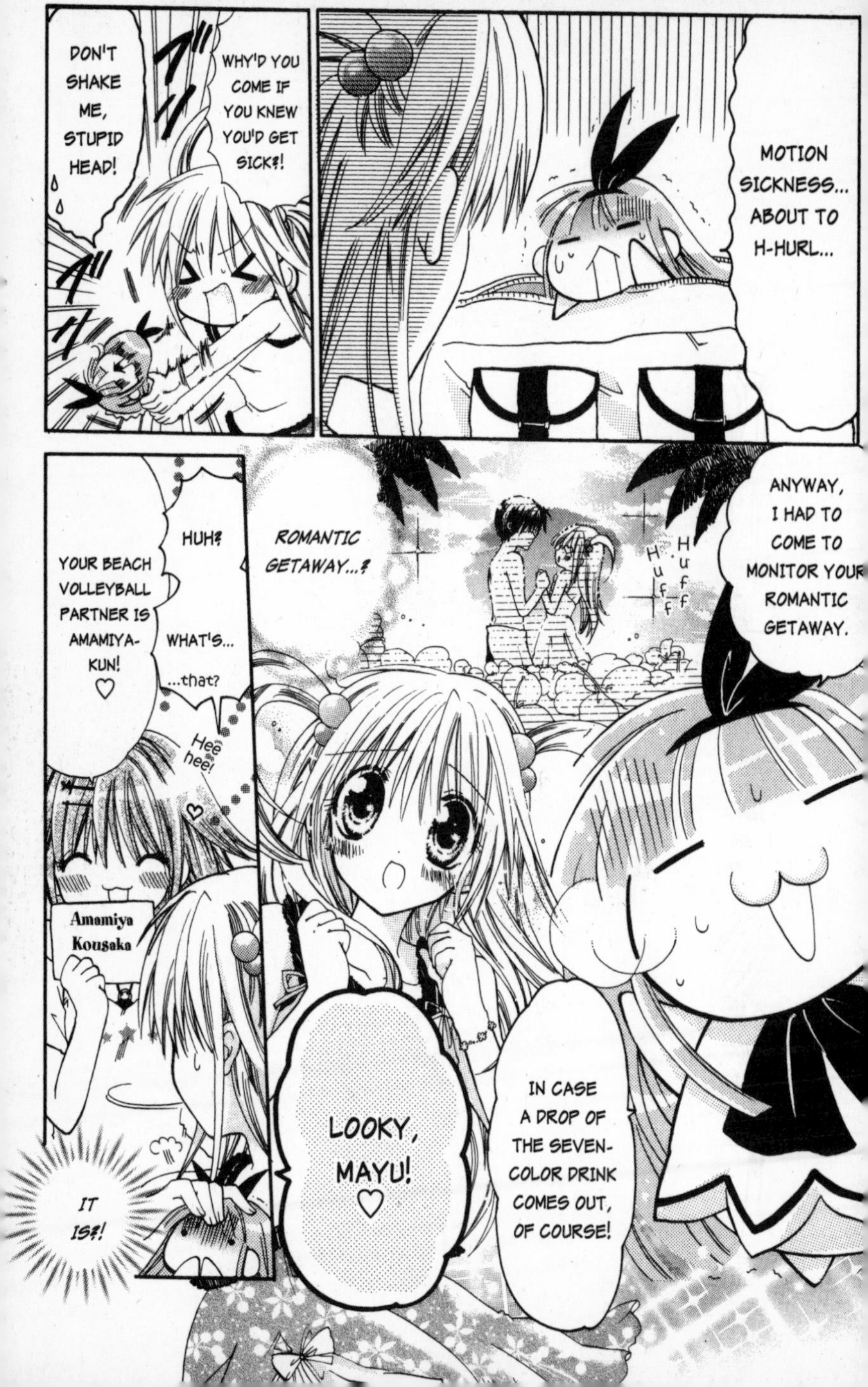
MOTION SICKNESS... ABOUT TO H-HURL...
WHY'D YOU COME IF YOU KNEW YOU'D GET SICK?!
DON'T SHAKE ME, STUPID HEAD!
ANYWAY, I HAD TO COME TO MONITOR YOUR ROMANTIC GETAWAY.
Huff Huff
ROMANTIC GETAWAY...?
IN CASE A DROP OF THE SEVEN-COLOR DRINK COMES OUT, OF COURSE!
LOOKY, MAYU! ♡
HUH?
WHAT'S... ...that?
YOUR BEACH VOLLEYBALL PARTNER IS AMAMIYA-KUN! ♡
Hee hee!
Amamiya Kousaka
IT IS?!

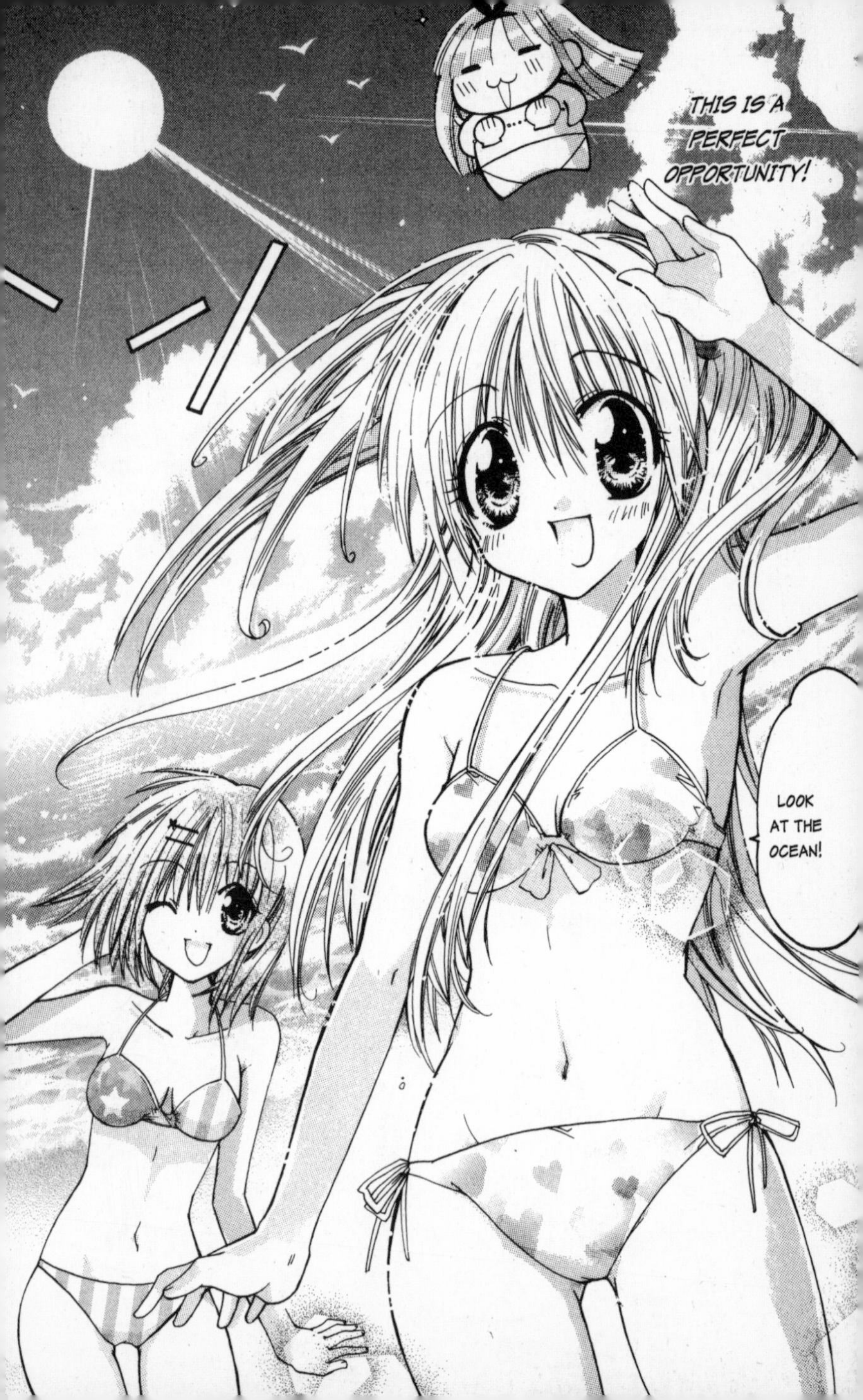
THIS IS A PERFECT OPPORTUNITY!
LOOK AT THE OCEAN!

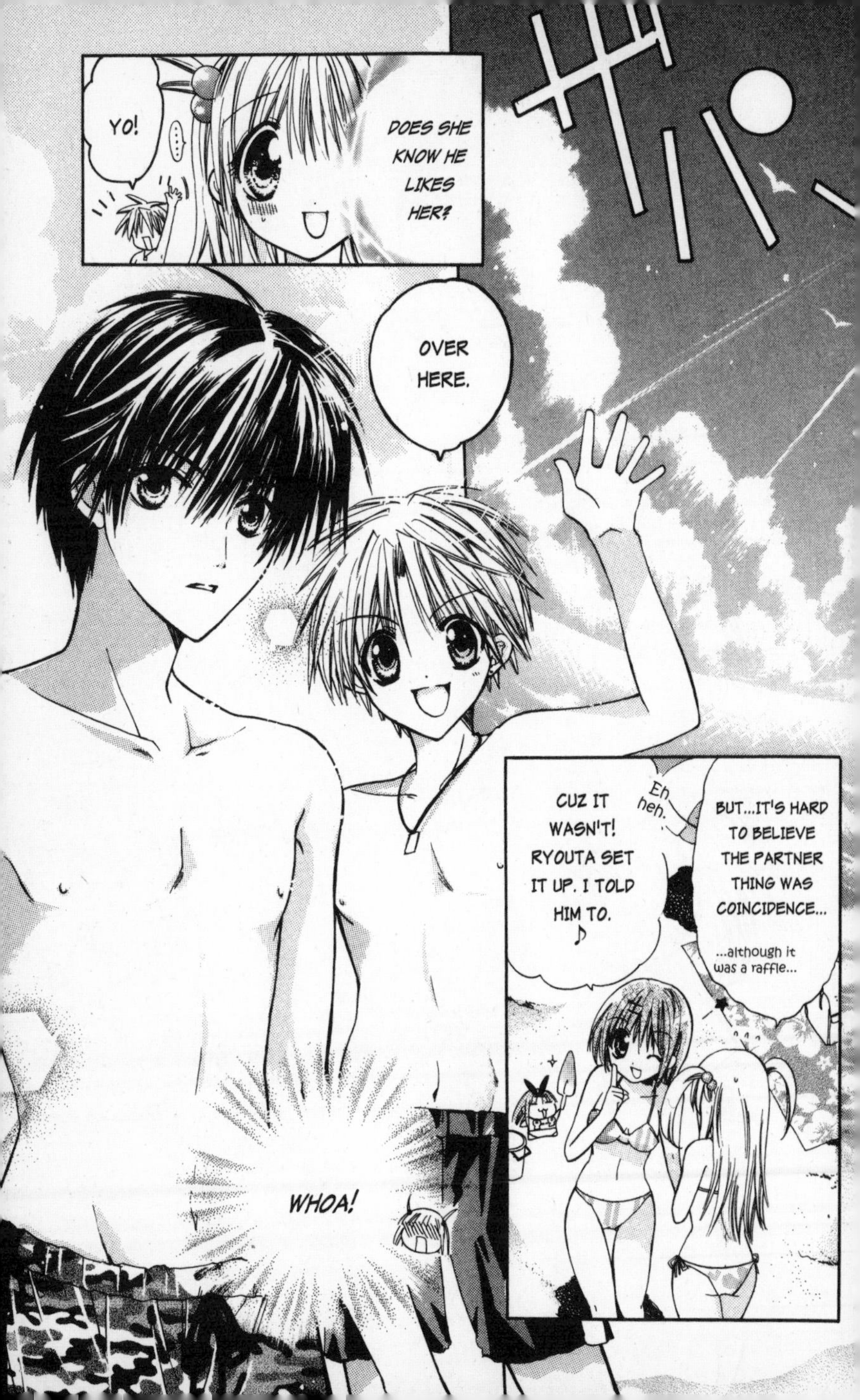
DOES SHE KNOW HE LIKES HER?
...
YO!
OVER HERE.
WHOA!
BUT...IT'S HARD TO BELIEVE THE PARTNER THING WAS COINCIDENCE...
...although it was a raffle...
Eh heh.
CUZ IT WASN'T! RYOUTA SET IT UP. I TOLD HIM TO. ♪

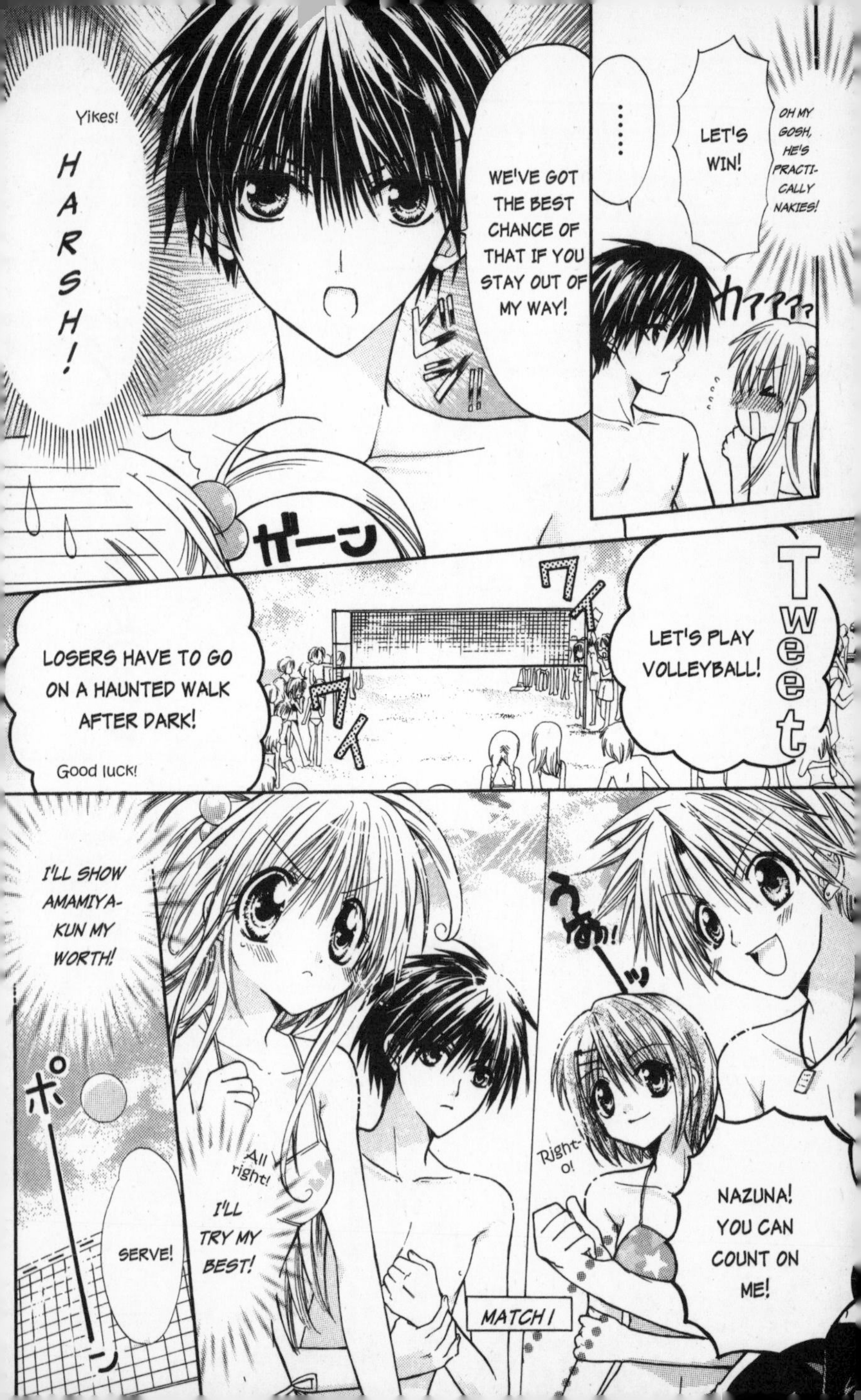
……
LET'S WIN!
OH MY GOSH, HE'S PRACTI-CALLY NAKIES!
WE'VE GOT THE BEST CHANCE OF THAT IF YOU STAY OUT OF MY WAY!
Yikes!
HARSH!
ガーン
Tweet
LET'S PLAY VOLLEYBALL!
ワイ
ワイ
LOSERS HAVE TO GO ON A HAUNTED WALK AFTER DARK!
Good luck!
NAZUNA! YOU CAN COUNT ON ME!
Right-o!
I'LL SHOW AMAMIYA-KUN MY WORTH!
All right!
I'LL TRY MY BEST!
MATCH 1
SERVE!
ポーン

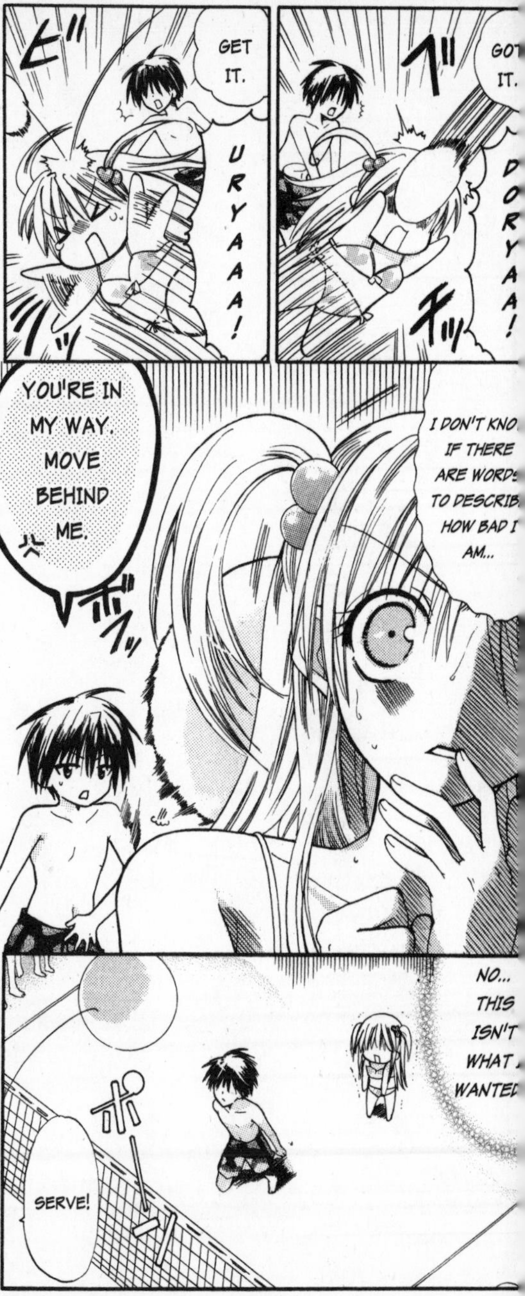
GOT IT.
DORYAA!
GET IT.
URYAAA!
I DON'T KNO IF THERE ARE WORDS TO DESCRIB HOW BAD I AM...
YOU'RE IN MY WAY. MOVE BEHIND ME.
NO... THIS ISN'T WHAT WANTED
SERVE!

● 100 % Innocent ●

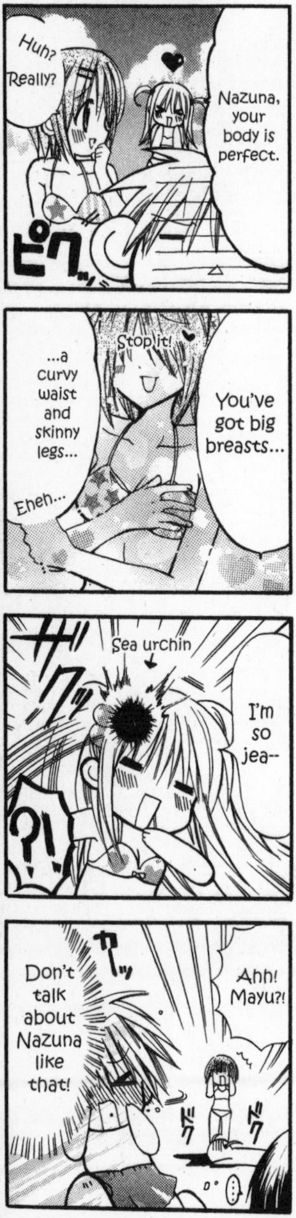
Nazuna, your body is perfect.
Huh? Really?
You've got big breasts...
...a curvy waist and skinny legs...
Stop it!
Eneh...
I'm so jea--
Sea urchin
?!
Ahh! Mayu?!
Don't talk about Nazuna like that!
...

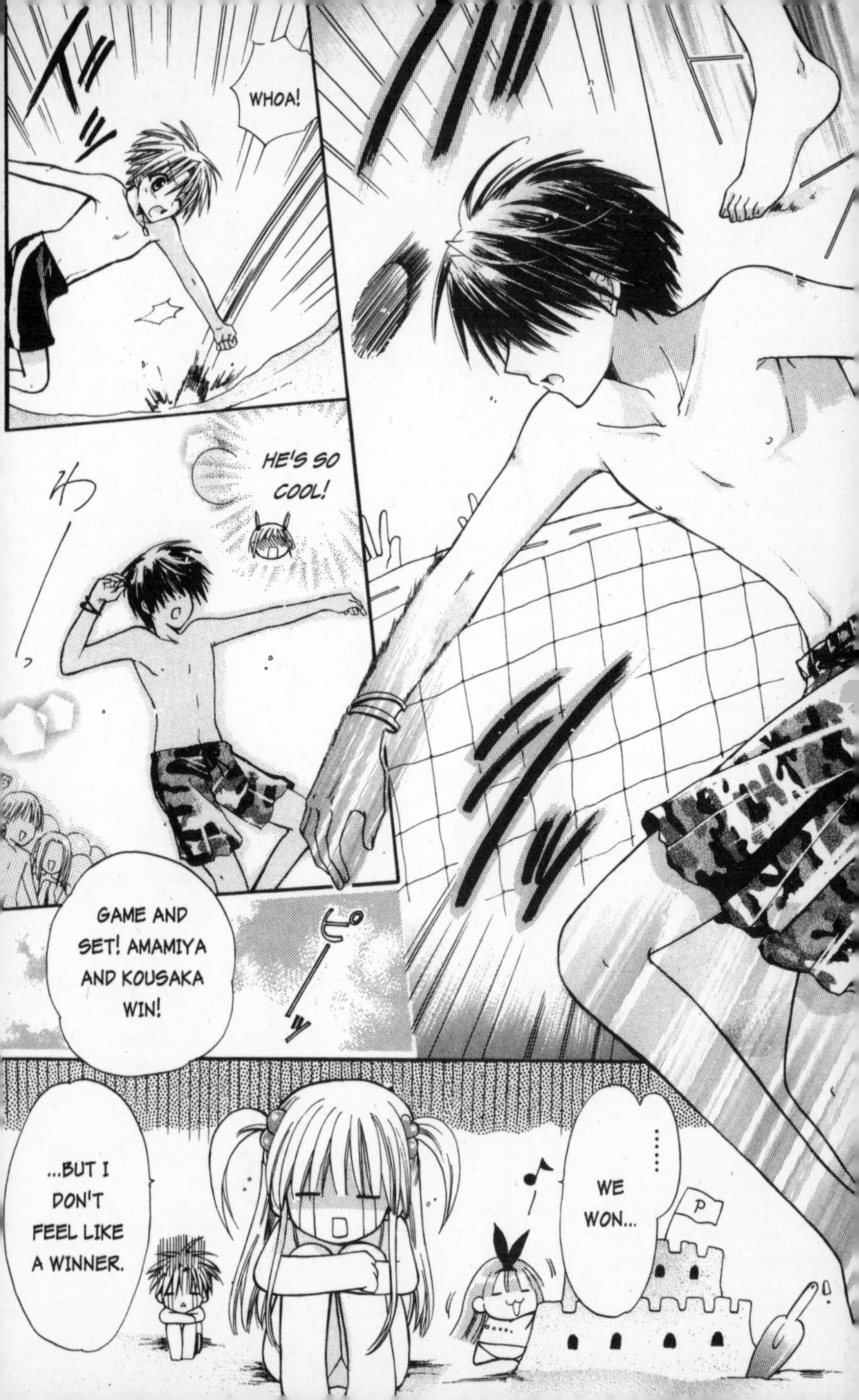
WHOA!
HE'S SO COOL!
GAME AND SET! AMAMIYA AND KOUSAKA WIN!
......
WE WON...
...BUT I DON'T FEEL LIKE A WINNER.

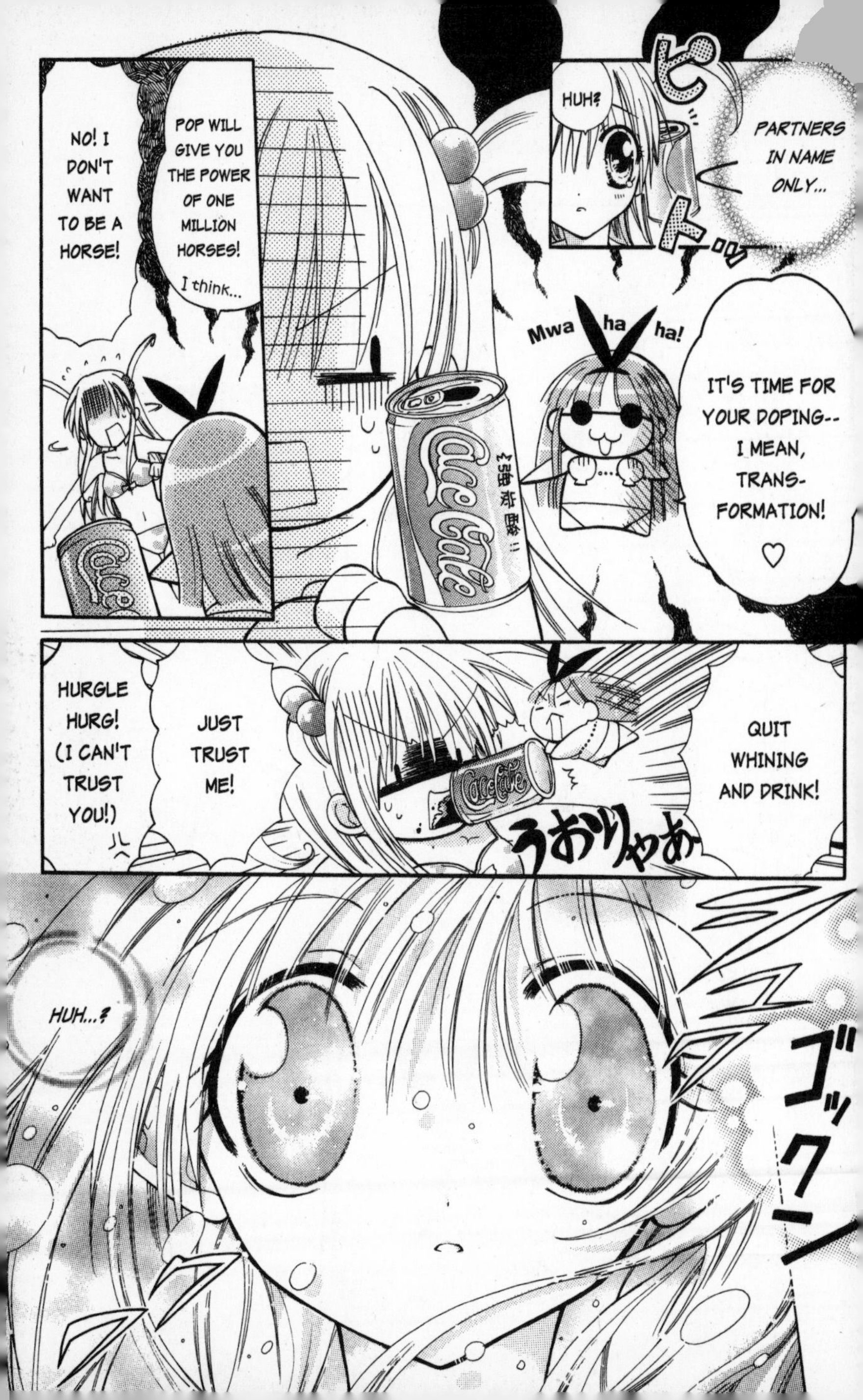
HUH?
PARTNERS IN NAME ONLY...
Mwa ha ha!
IT'S TIME FOR YOUR DOPING-- I MEAN, TRANS-FORMATION! ♡
POP WILL GIVE YOU THE POWER OF ONE MILLION HORSES!
I think...
NO! I DON'T WANT TO BE A HORSE!
QUIT WHINING AND DRINK!
うおりゃあ
JUST TRUST ME!
HURGLE HURG! (I CAN'T TRUST YOU!)
ゴックン
HUH...?

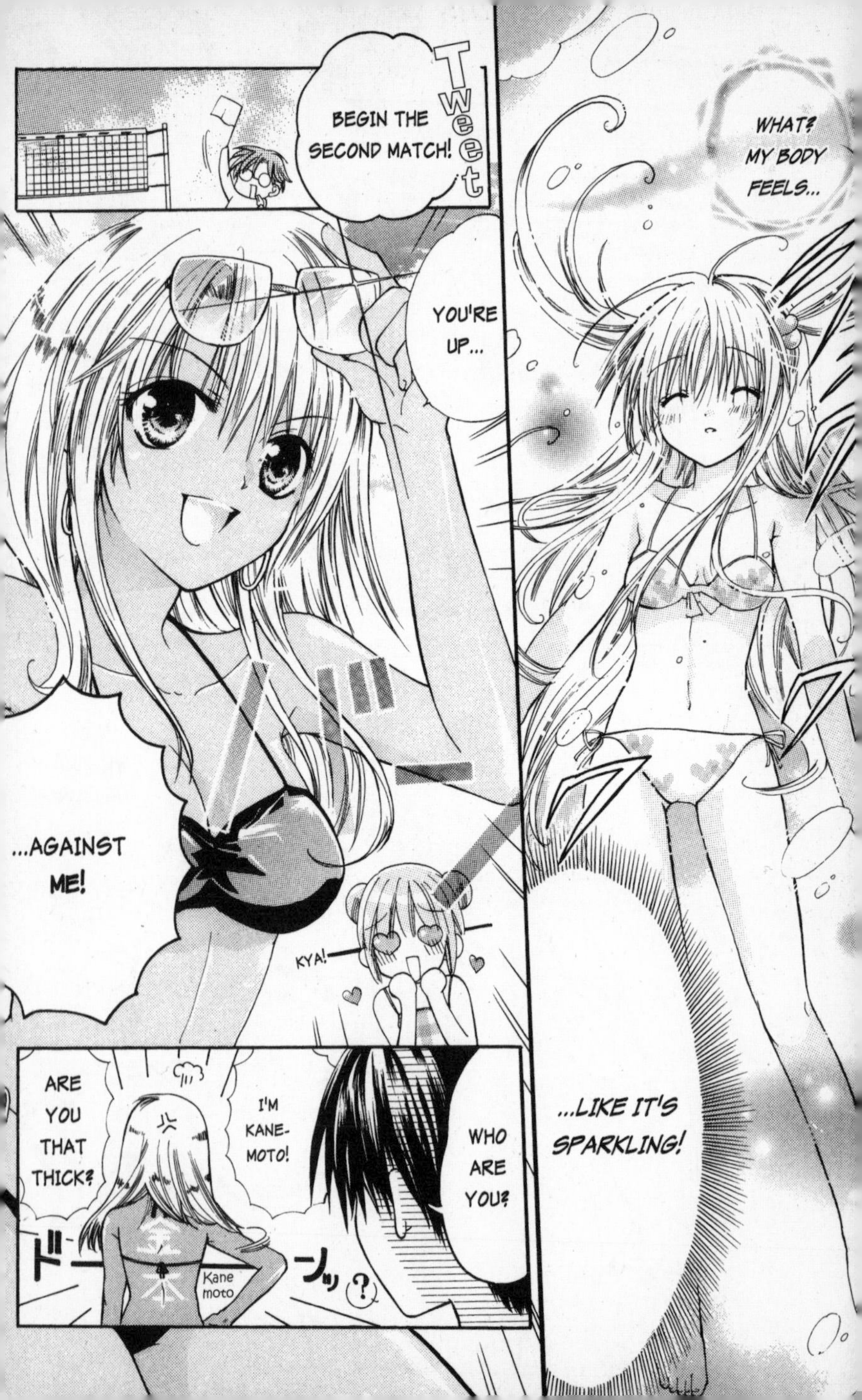
WHAT? MY BODY FEELS...
...LIKE IT'S SPARKLING!
Tweet
BEGIN THE SECOND MATCH!
YOU'RE UP...
...AGAINST ME!
KYA!
WHO ARE YOU?
I'M KANE-MOTO!
ARE YOU THAT THICK?
Kane moto
?

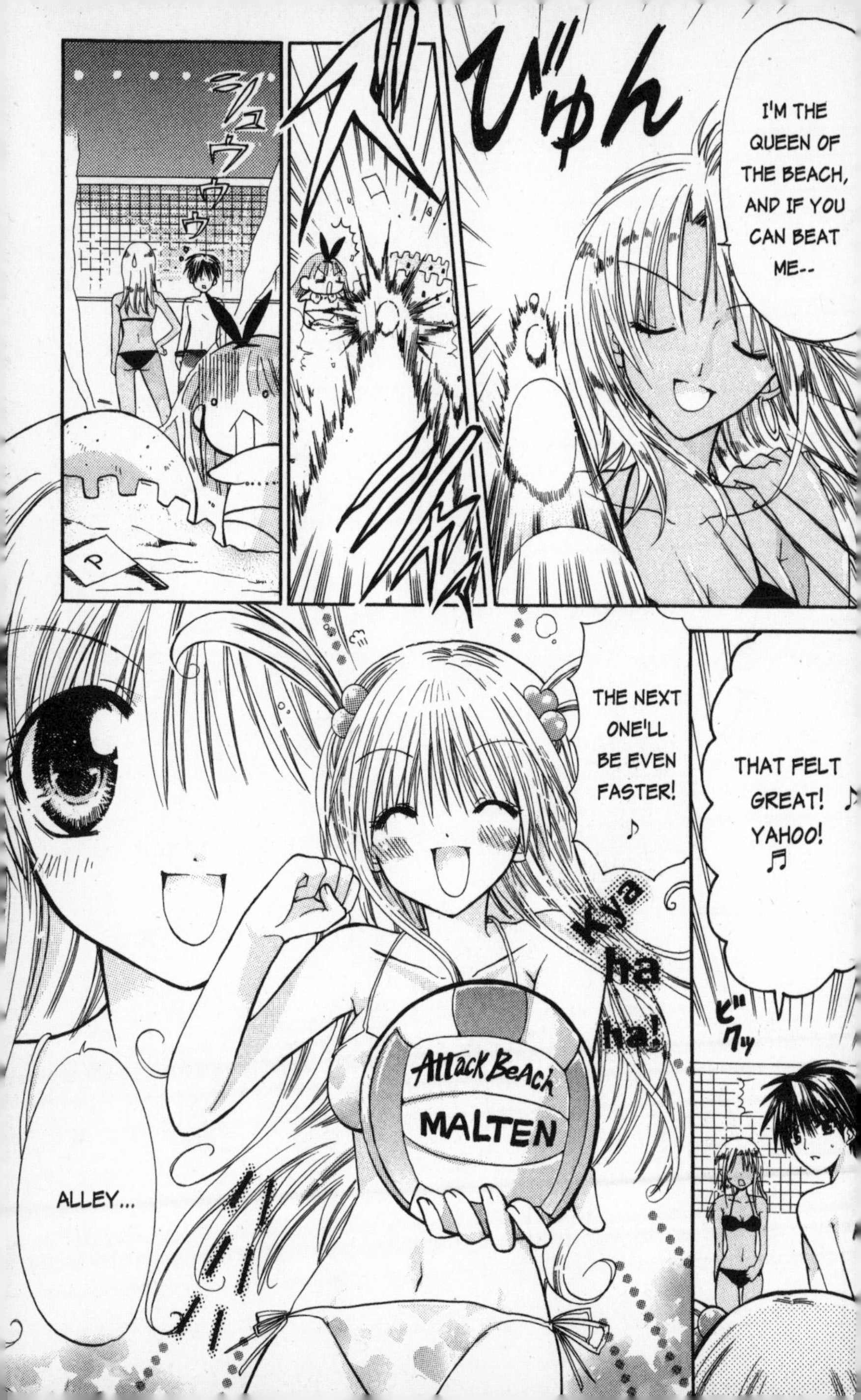
I'M THE QUEEN OF THE BEACH, AND IF YOU CAN BEAT ME--
びゅん
シュウウウウ
THAT FELT GREAT! ♪ YAHOO! ♬
ビクッ
THE NEXT ONE'LL BE EVEN FASTER! ♪
Kya ha ha!
Attack Beach
MALTEN
ALLEY...

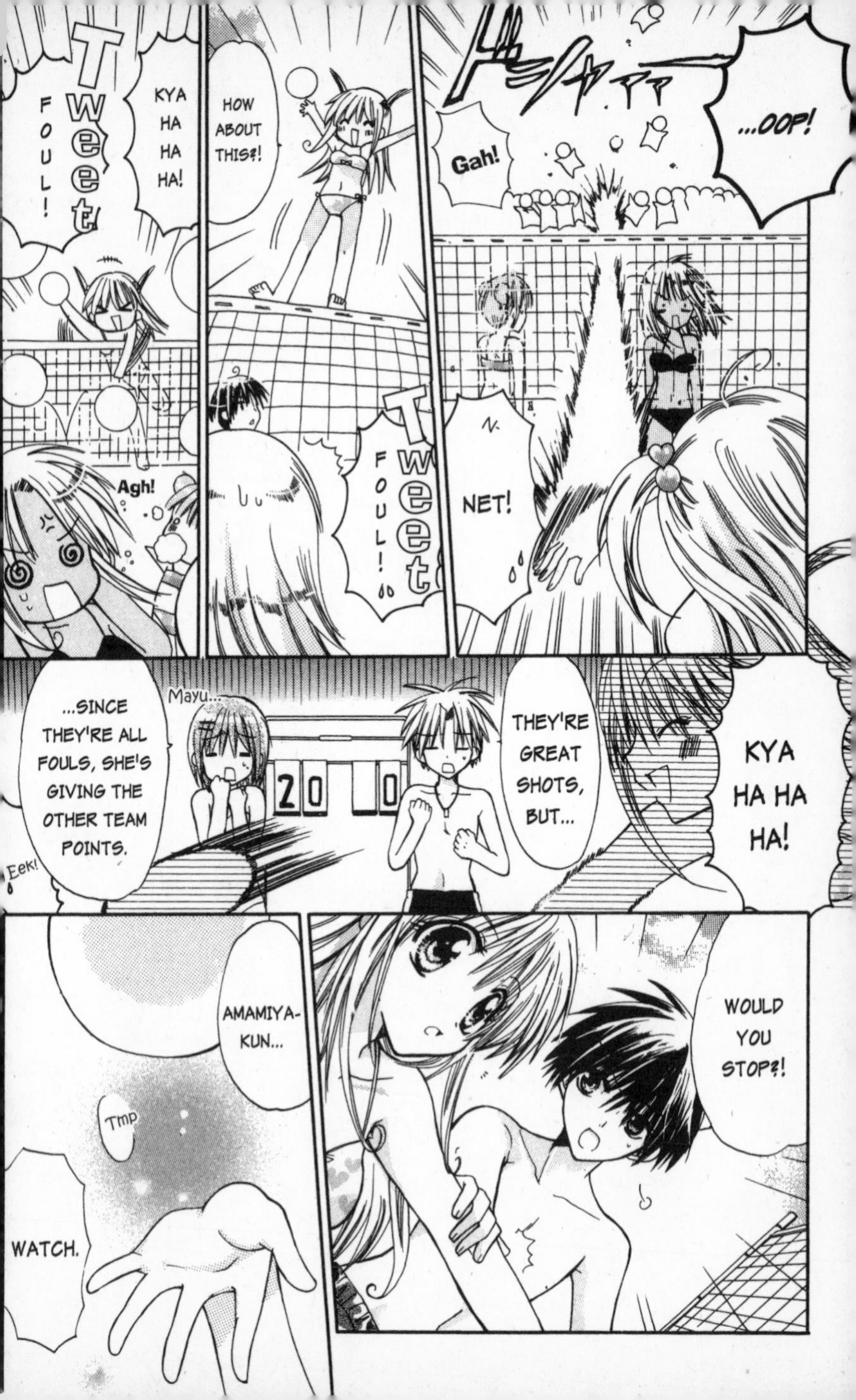
...OOP!
Gah!
N.
NET!
HOW ABOUT THIS?!
Tweet
FOUL!
KYA HA HA HA!
Tweet
FOUL!
Agh!
KYA HA HA HA!
THEY'RE GREAT SHOTS, BUT...
20 0
Mayu...
...SINCE THEY'RE ALL FOULS, SHE'S GIVING THE OTHER TEAM POINTS.
Eek!
WOULD YOU STOP?!
AMAMIYA-KUN...
Tmp
WATCH.

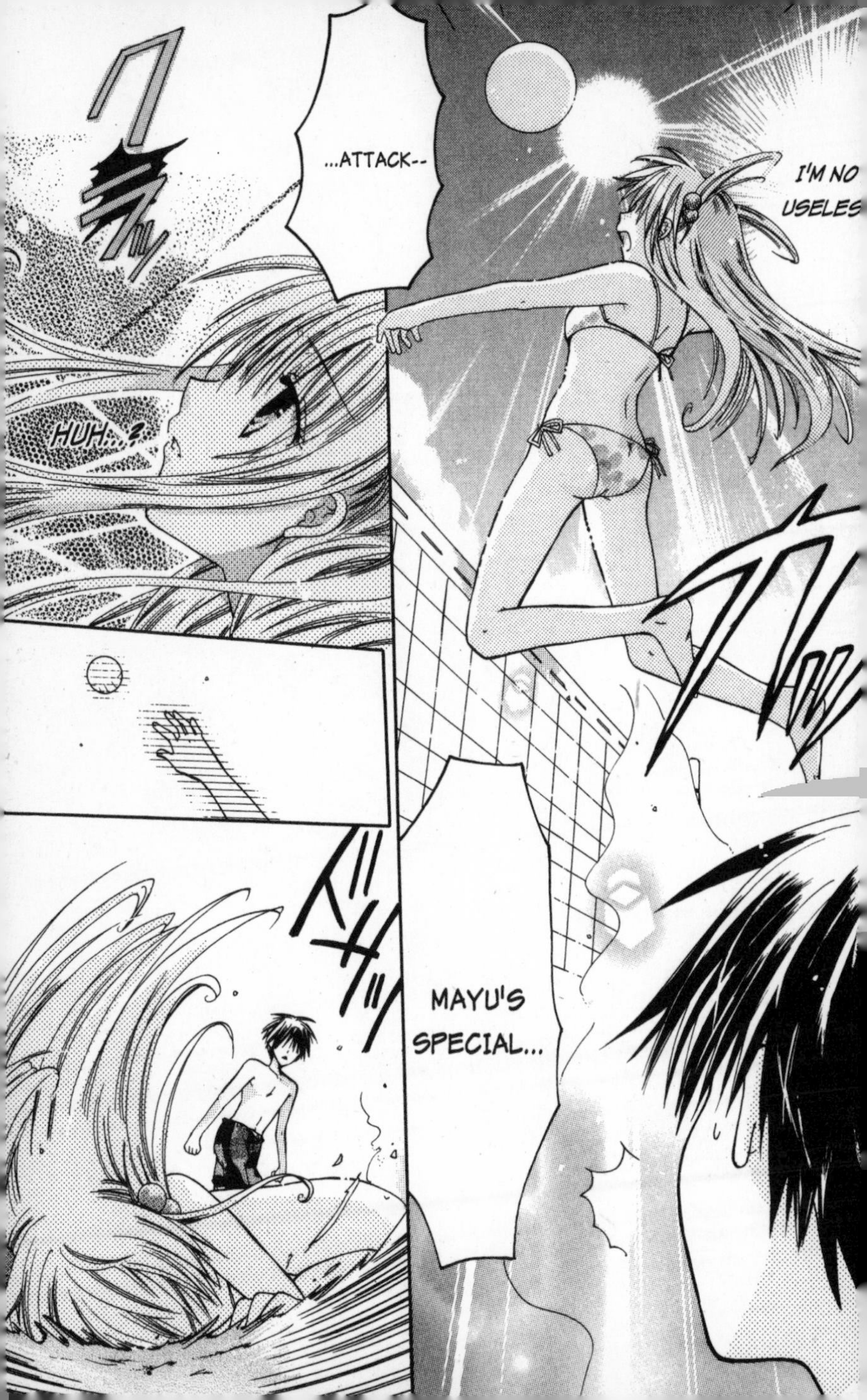

I'M NO
USELES
MAYU'S
SPECIAL...
...ATTACK--
HUH...?

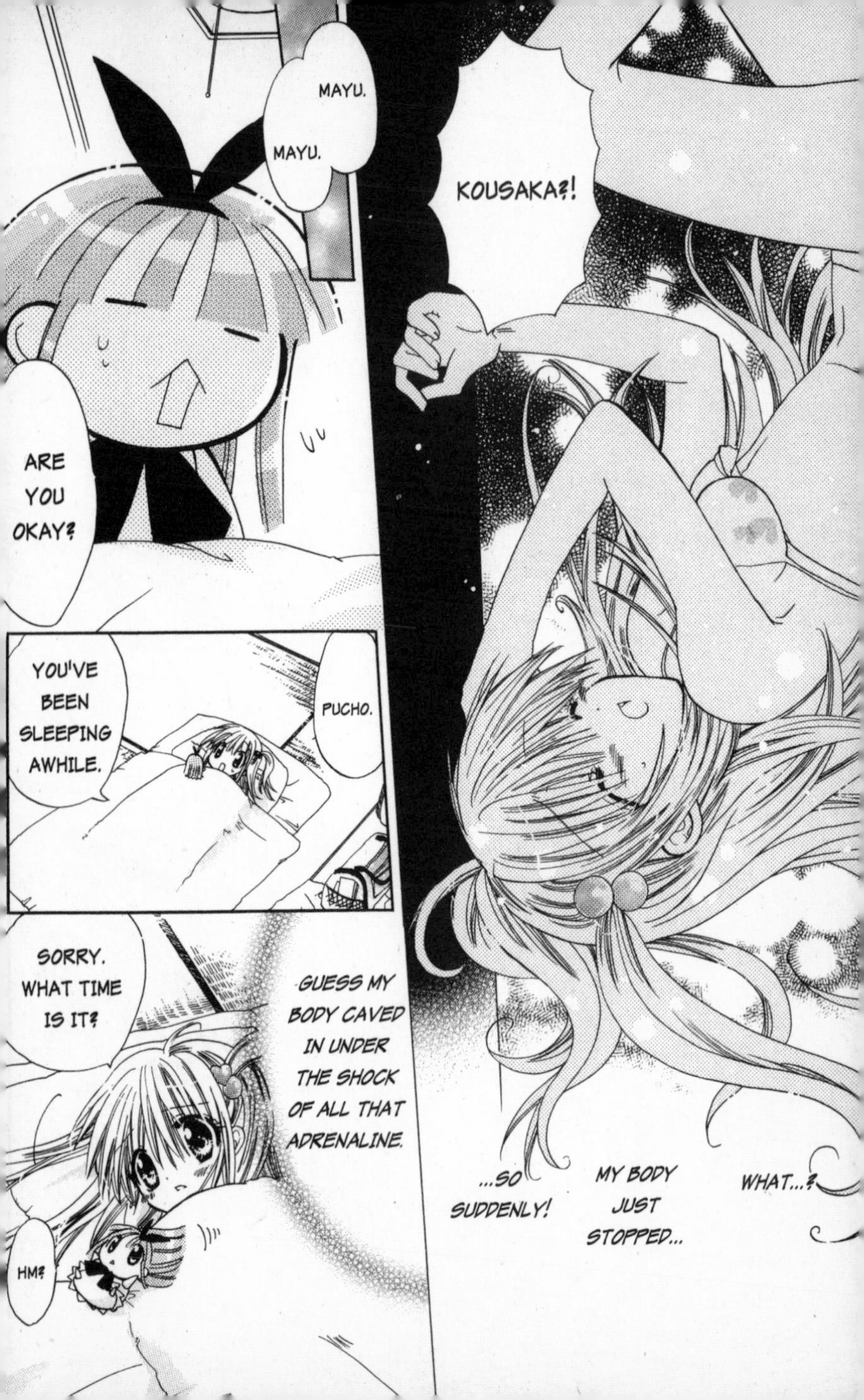
KOUSAKA?!
WHAT...?
MY BODY JUST STOPPED...
...SO SUDDENLY!
MAYU.
MAYU.
ARE YOU OKAY?
PUCHO.
YOU'VE BEEN SLEEPING AWHILE.
GUESS MY BODY CAVED IN UNDER THE SHOCK OF ALL THAT ADRENALINE.
SORRY. WHAT TIME IS IT?
HM?

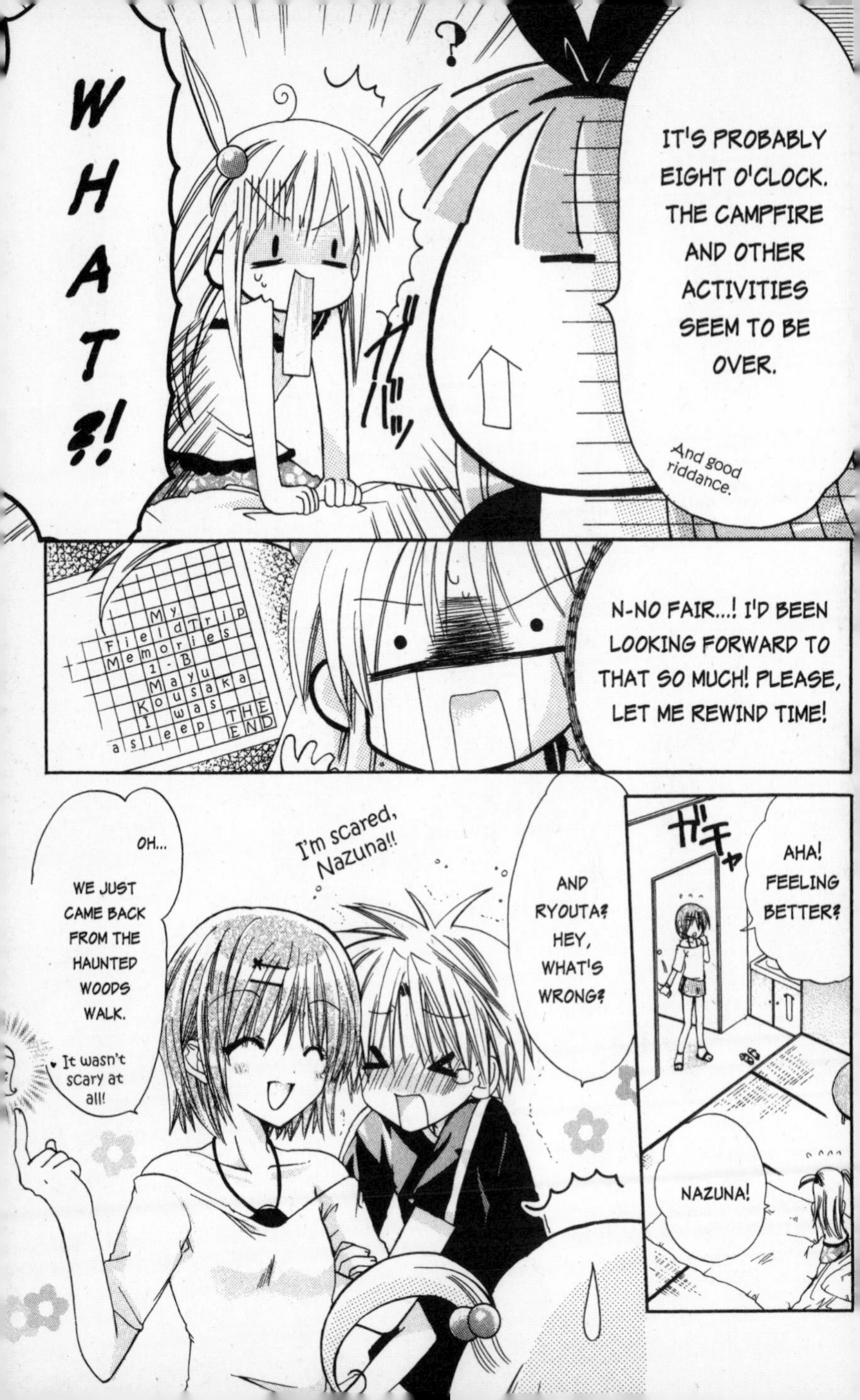
?
IT'S PROBABLY EIGHT O'CLOCK. THE CAMPFIRE AND OTHER ACTIVITIES SEEM TO BE OVER.
And good riddance.
WHAT?!
N-NO FAIR...! I'D BEEN LOOKING FORWARD TO THAT SO MUCH! PLEASE, LET ME REWIND TIME!
My Field Trip Memories
1-B Mayu Kousaka
I was asleep
THE END
ガチャ
AHA! FEELING BETTER?
NAZUNA!
AND RYOUTA? HEY, WHAT'S WRONG?
I'm scared, Nazuna!!
OH... WE JUST CAME BACK FROM THE HAUNTED WOODS WALK.
It wasn't scary at all!

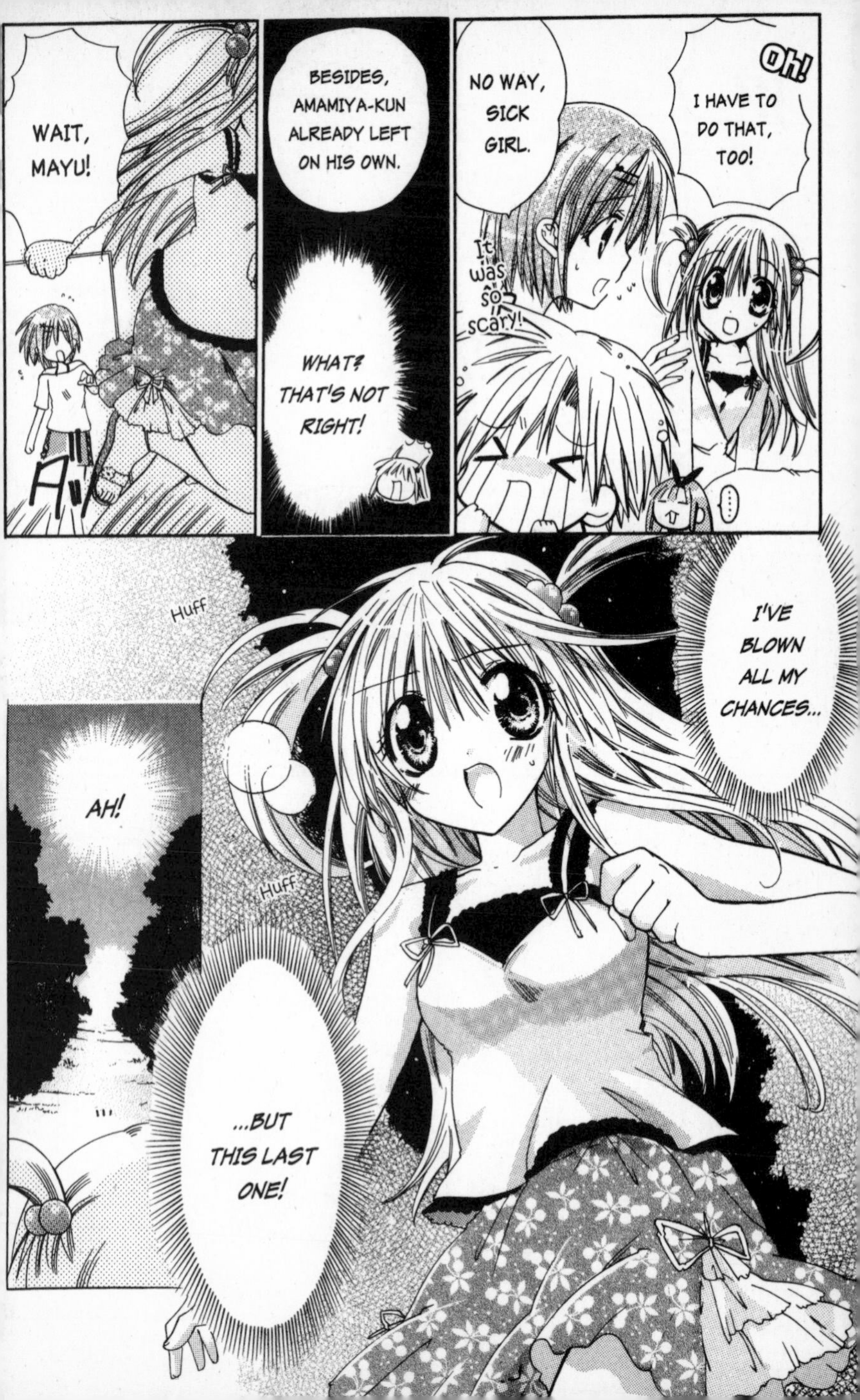
OH!
I HAVE TO DO THAT, TOO!
NO WAY, SICK GIRL.
It was so scary!
...
BESIDES, AMAMIYA-KUN ALREADY LEFT ON HIS OWN.
WHAT? THAT'S NOT RIGHT!
WAIT, MAYU!
I'VE BLOWN ALL MY CHANCES...
Huff
Huff
...BUT THIS LAST ONE!
AH!

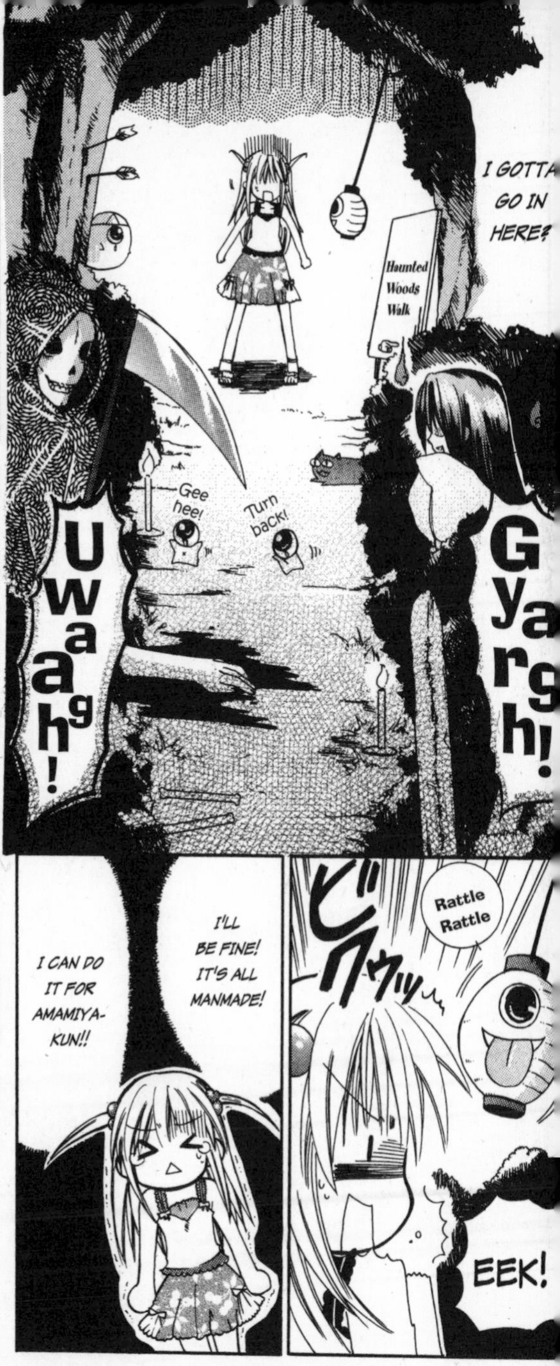
I GOTTA GO IN HERE?
Haunted Woods Walk
Gyargh!
Turn back!
Gee hee!
Uwaagh!
ビクゥッ
Rattle Rattle
EEK!
I'LL BE FINE! IT'S ALL MANMADE!
I CAN DO IT FOR AMAMIYA-KUN!!

I See

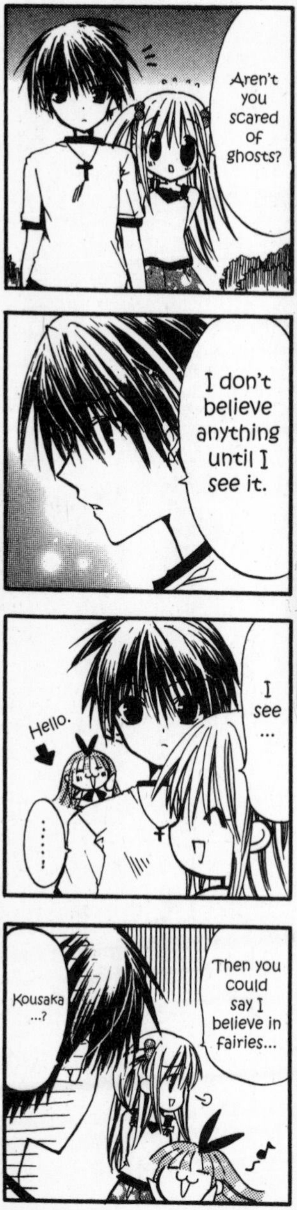
Aren't you scared of ghosts?
I don't believe anything until I see it.
I see ...
Hello.
......!
Then you could say I believe in fairies...
Kousaka ...?

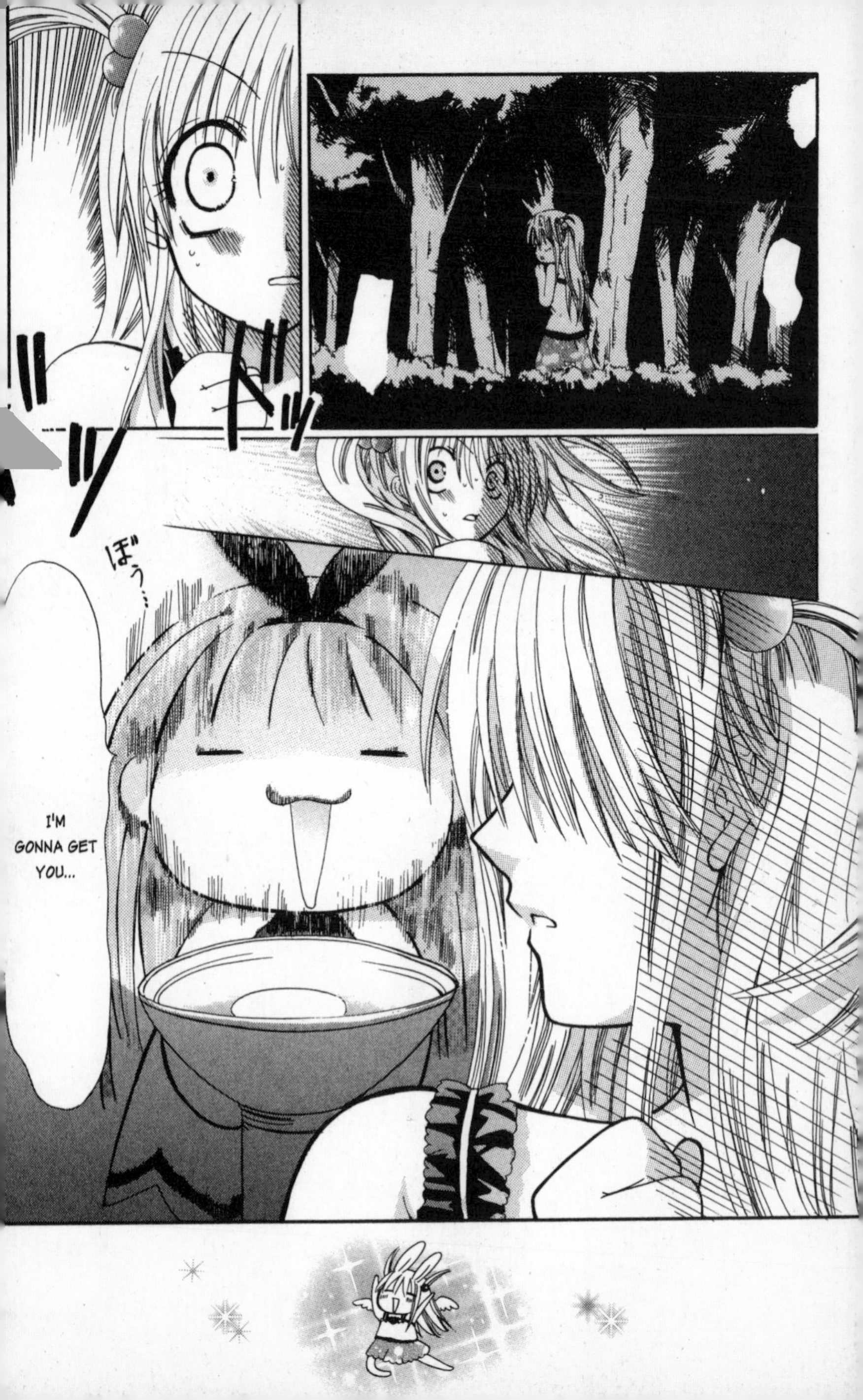

ぼう…
I'M GONNA GET YOU...

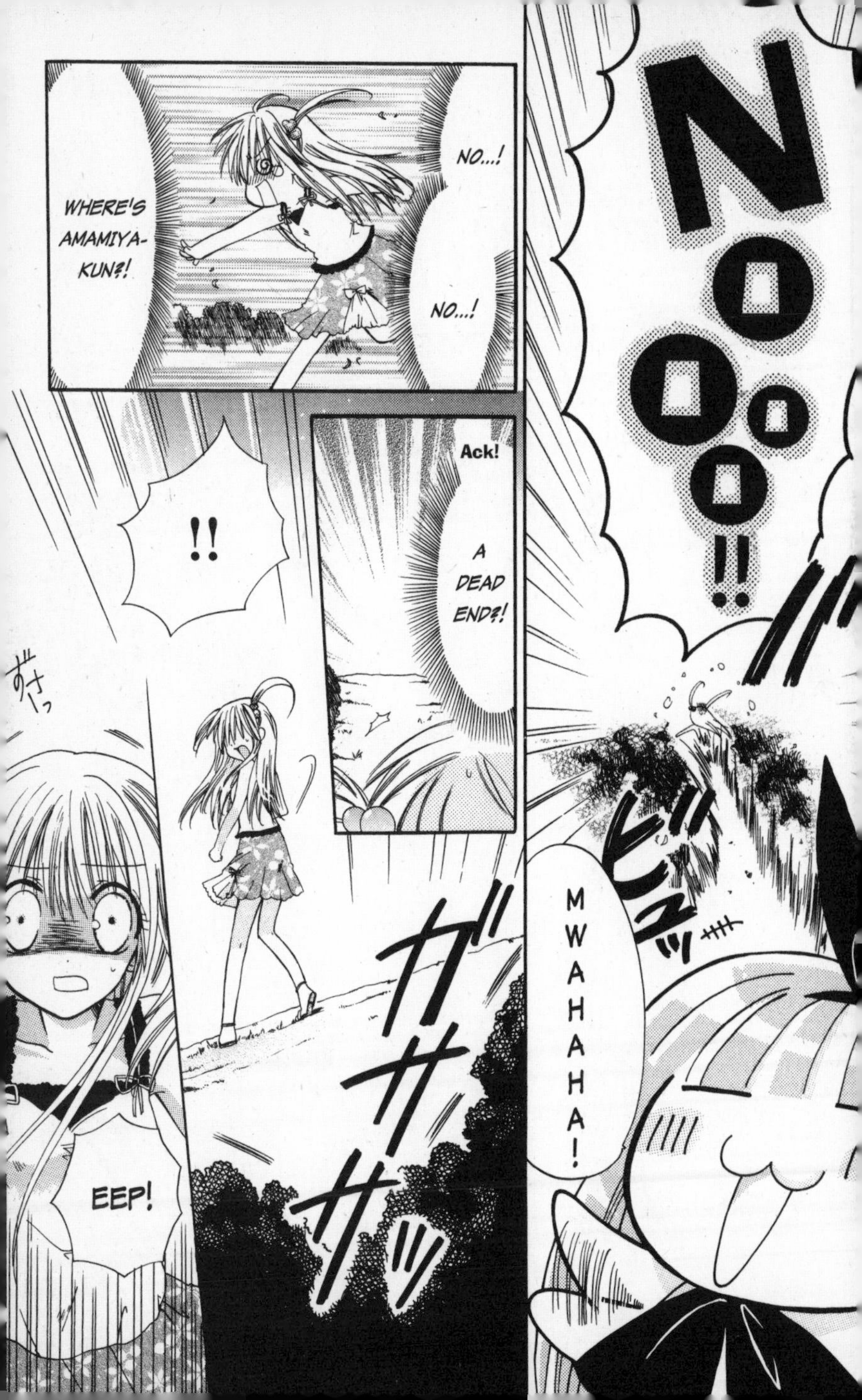
NOOOO!!
MWAHAHAHA!
NO...!
NO...!
WHERE'S AMAMIYA-KUN?!
Ack!
A DEAD END?!
!!
EEP!

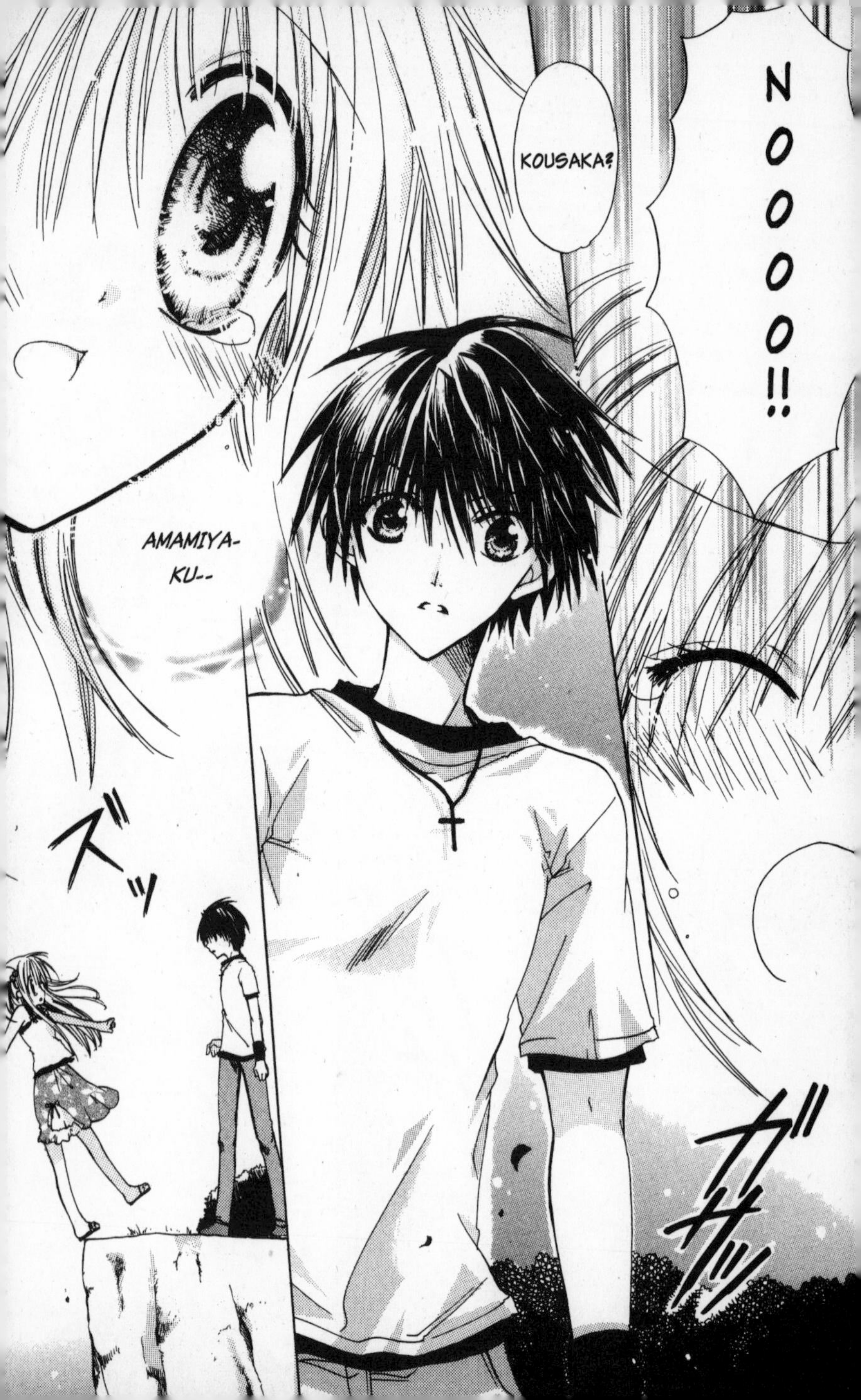
NOOOOO!!
KOUSAKA?
AMAMIYA-KU--
ズッ

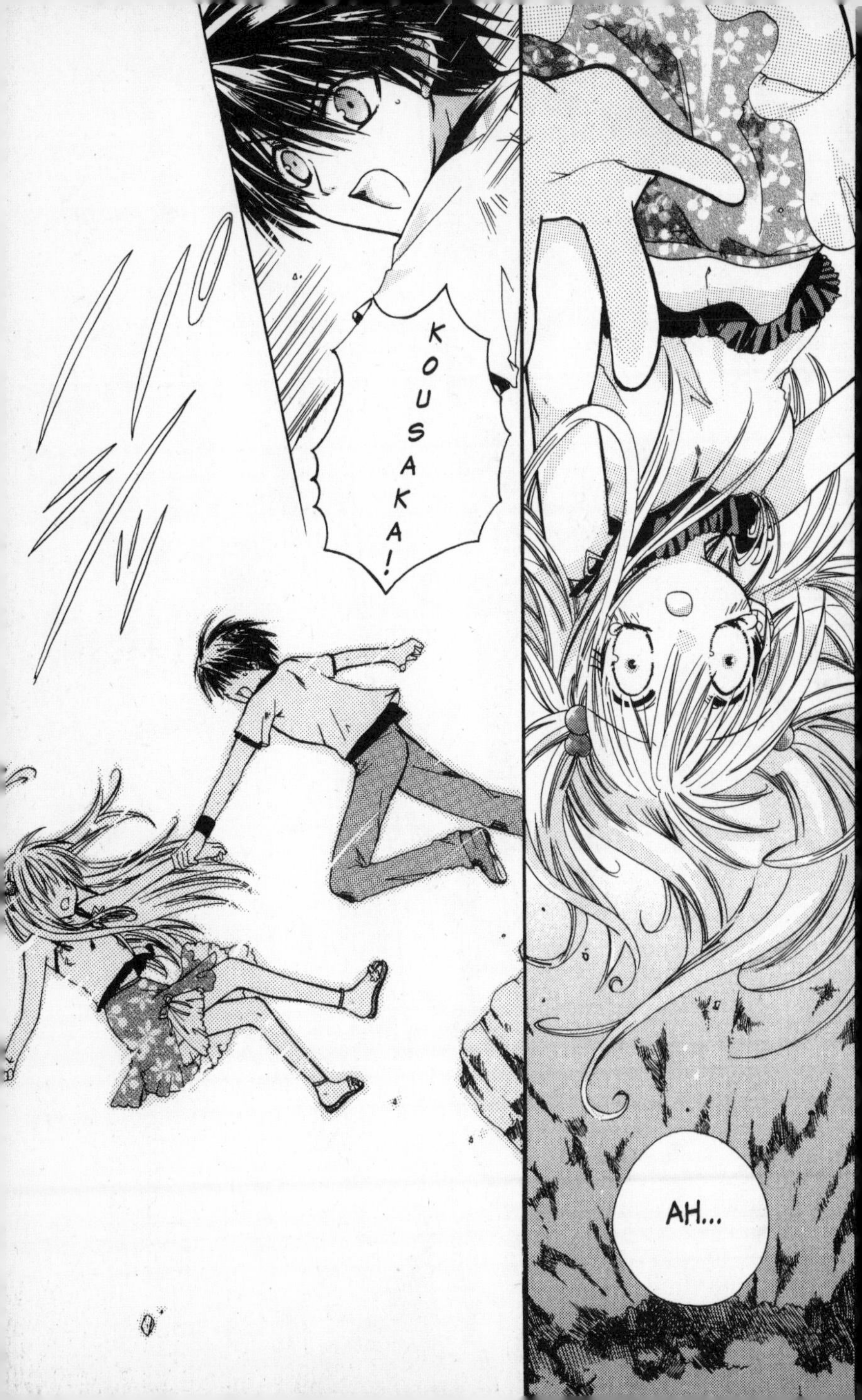
AH...
KOUSAKA!

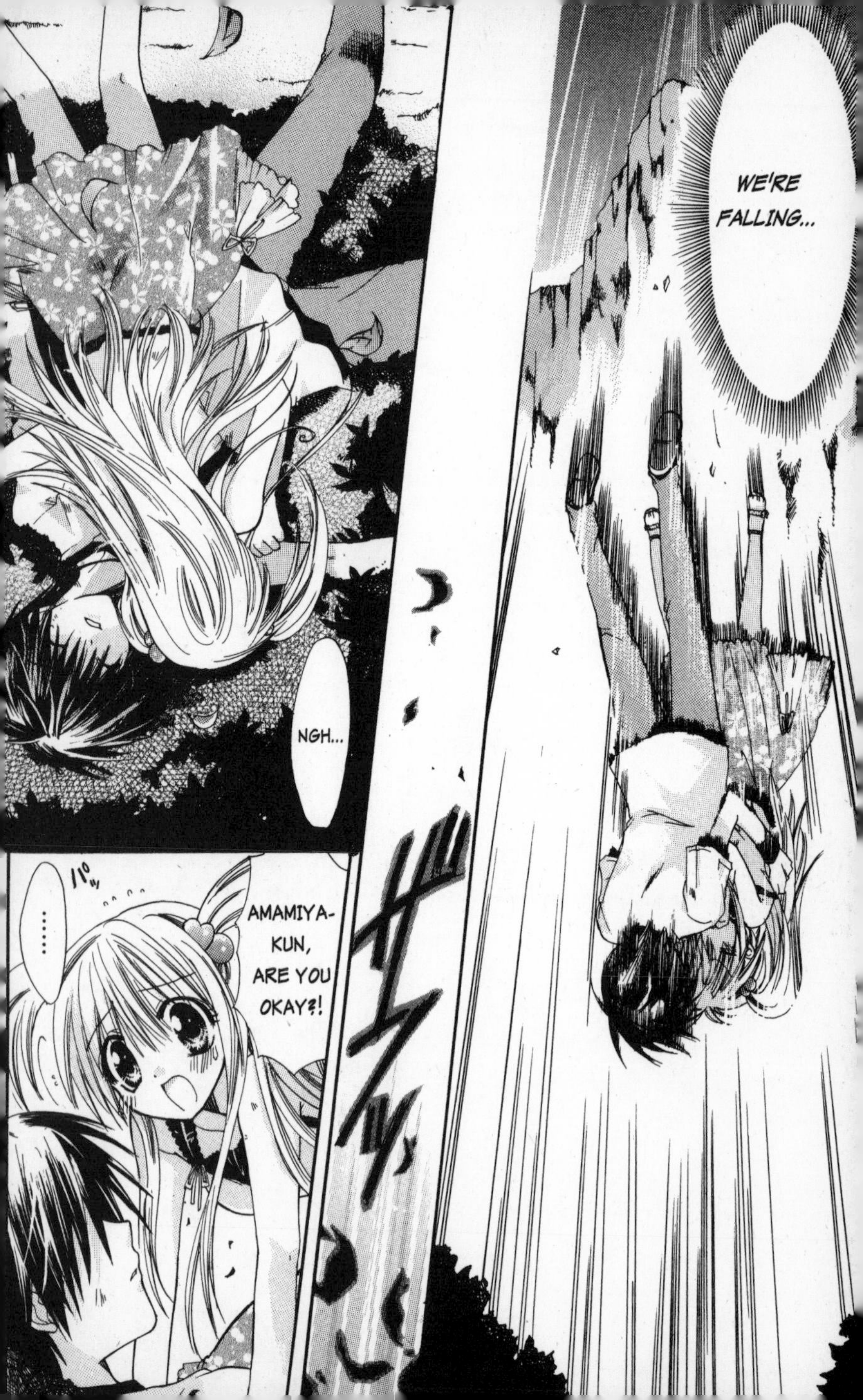
WE'RE FALLING...
NGH...
AMAMIYA-KUN, ARE YOU OKAY?!
......

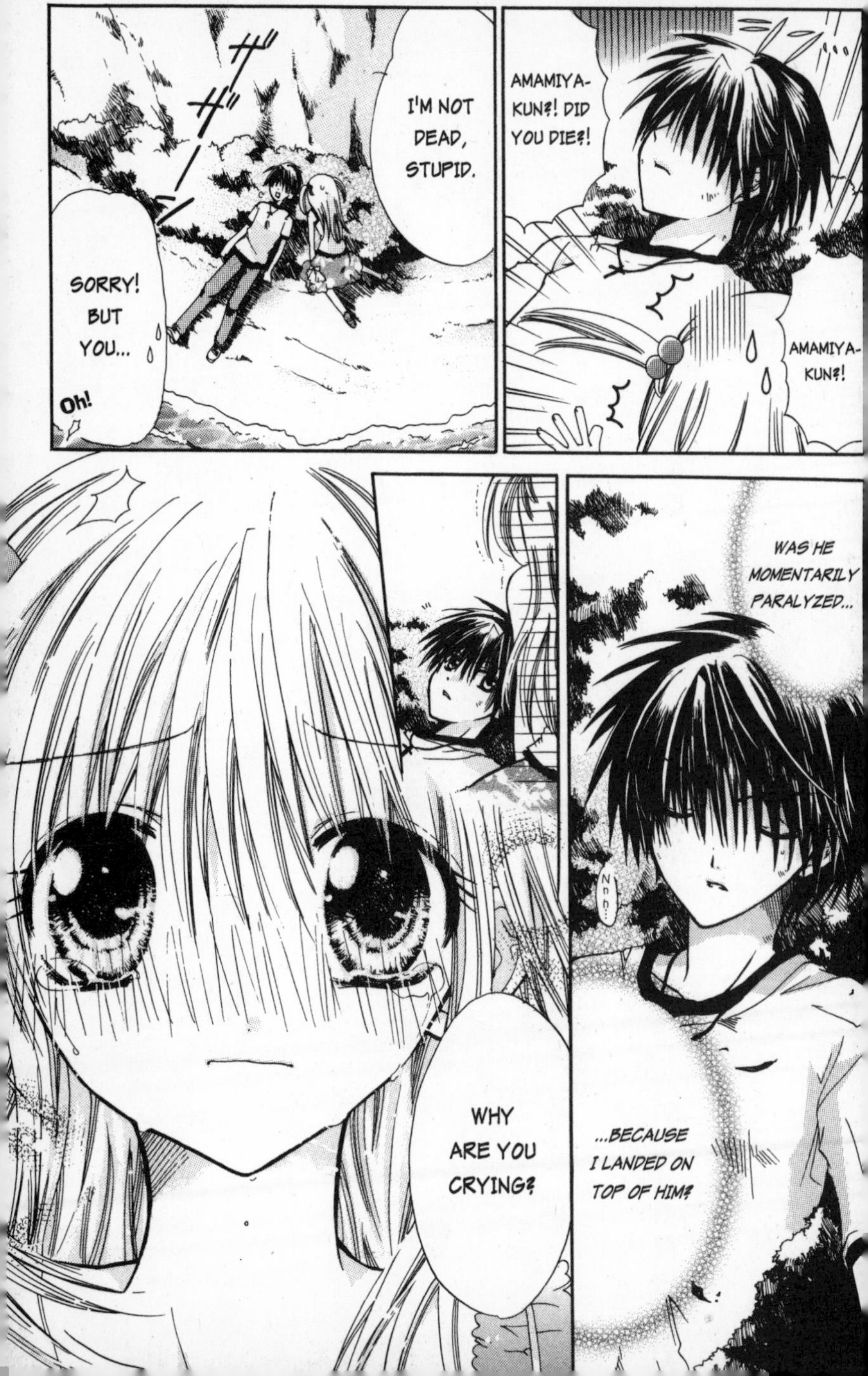
AMAMIYA-KUN?! DID YOU DIE?!
AMAMIYA-KUN?!
I'M NOT DEAD, STUPID.
SORRY! BUT YOU...
Oh!
WAS HE MOMENTARILY PARALYZED...
...BECAUSE I LANDED ON TOP OF HIM?
WHY ARE YOU CRYING?

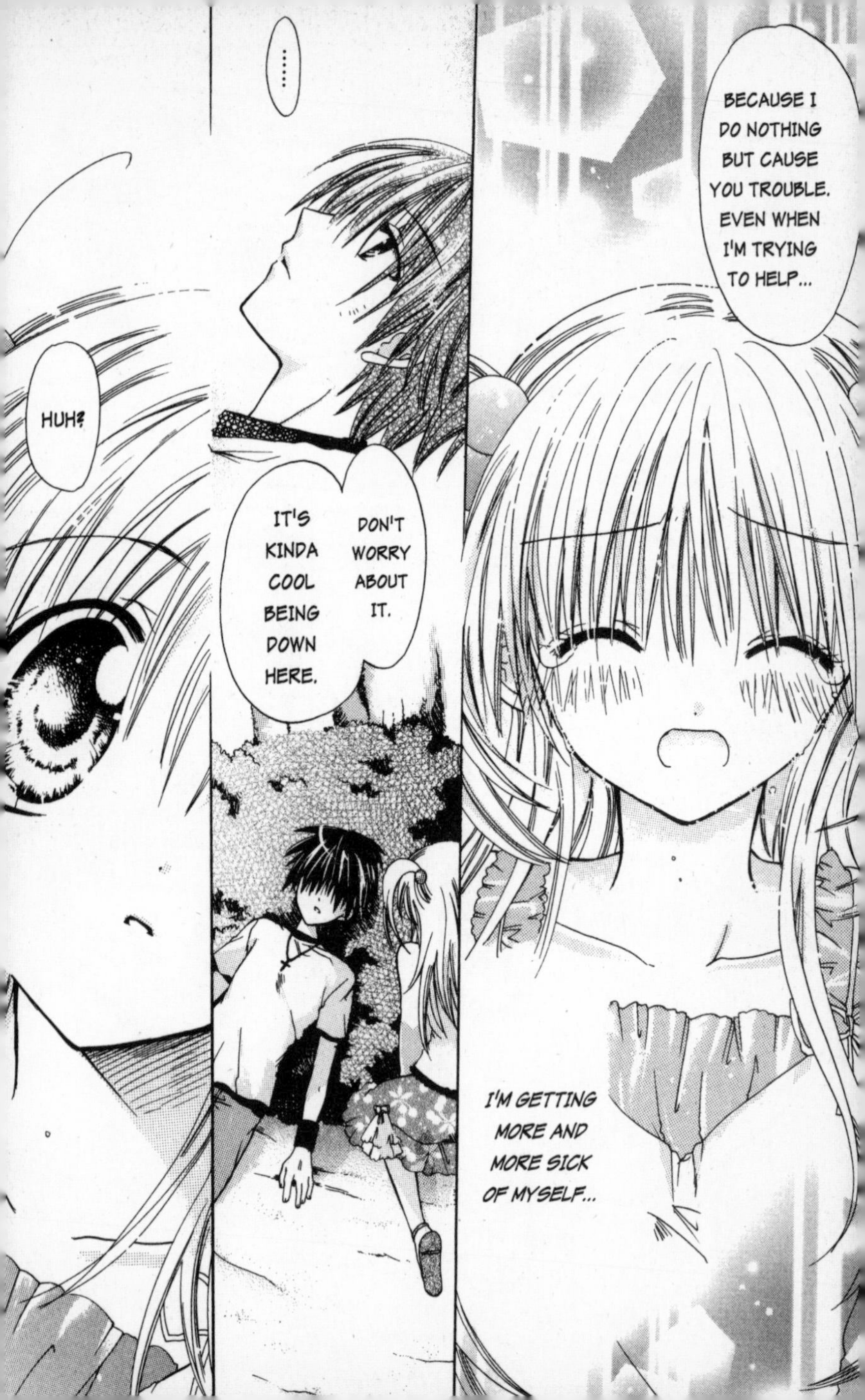
BECAUSE I DO NOTHING BUT CAUSE YOU TROUBLE. EVEN WHEN I'M TRYING TO HELP...
I'M GETTING MORE AND MORE SICK OF MYSELF...
......
DON'T WORRY ABOUT IT.
IT'S KINDA COOL BEING DOWN HERE.
HUH?

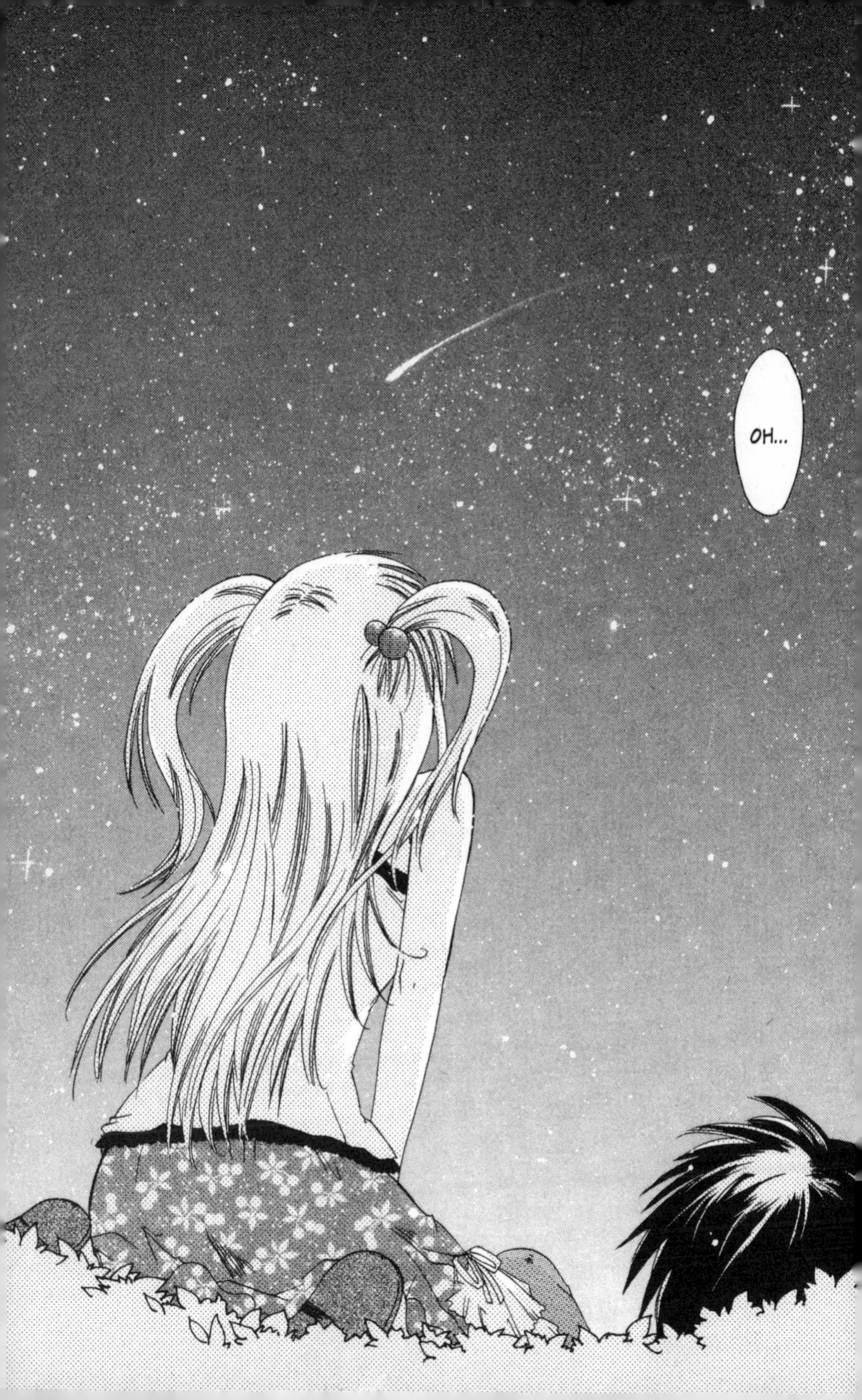
OH...

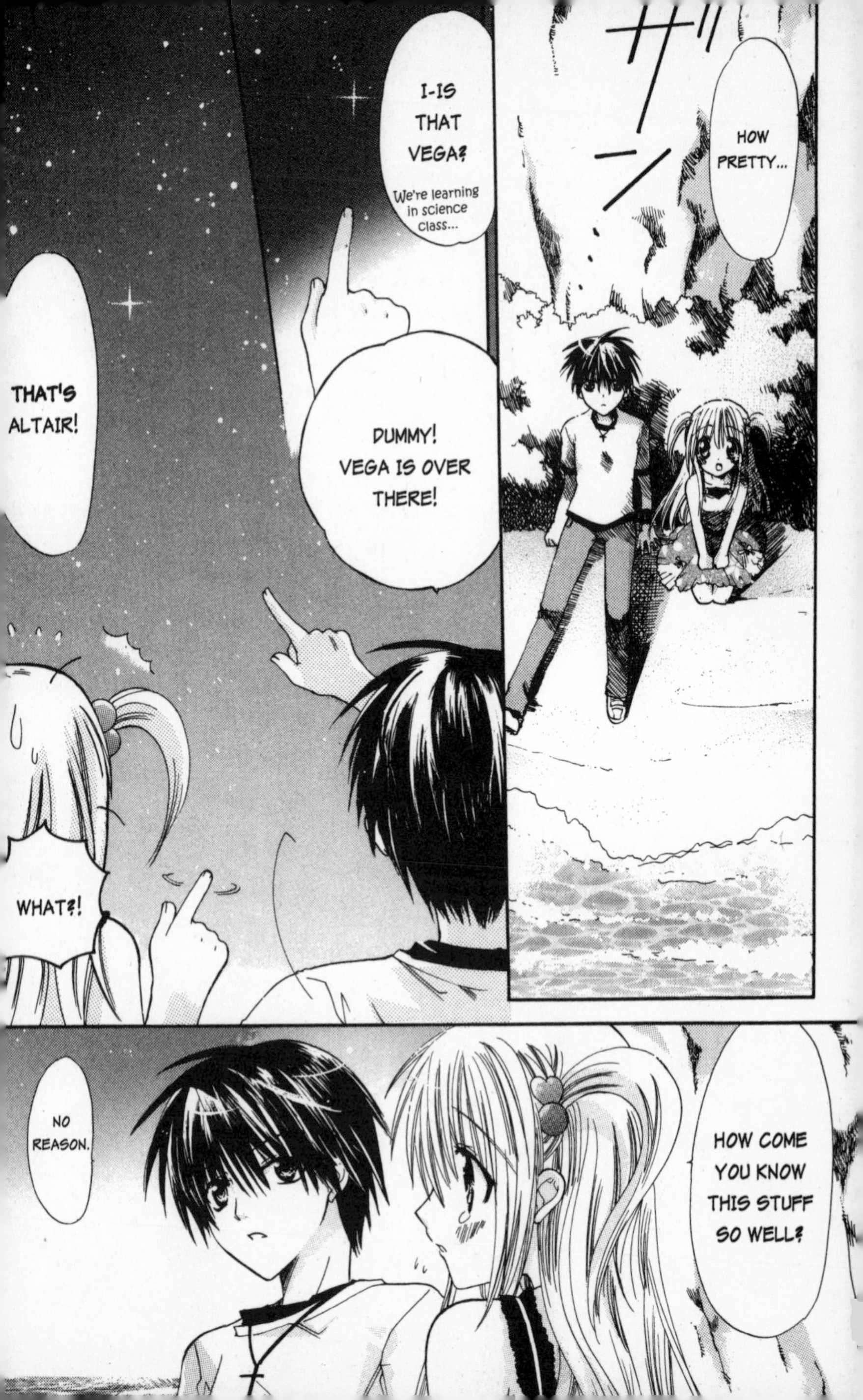
HOW PRETTY...
I-IS THAT VEGA?
We're learning in science class...
DUMMY! VEGA IS OVER THERE!
THAT'S ALTAIR!
WHAT?!
HOW COME YOU KNOW THIS STUFF SO WELL?
NO REASON.

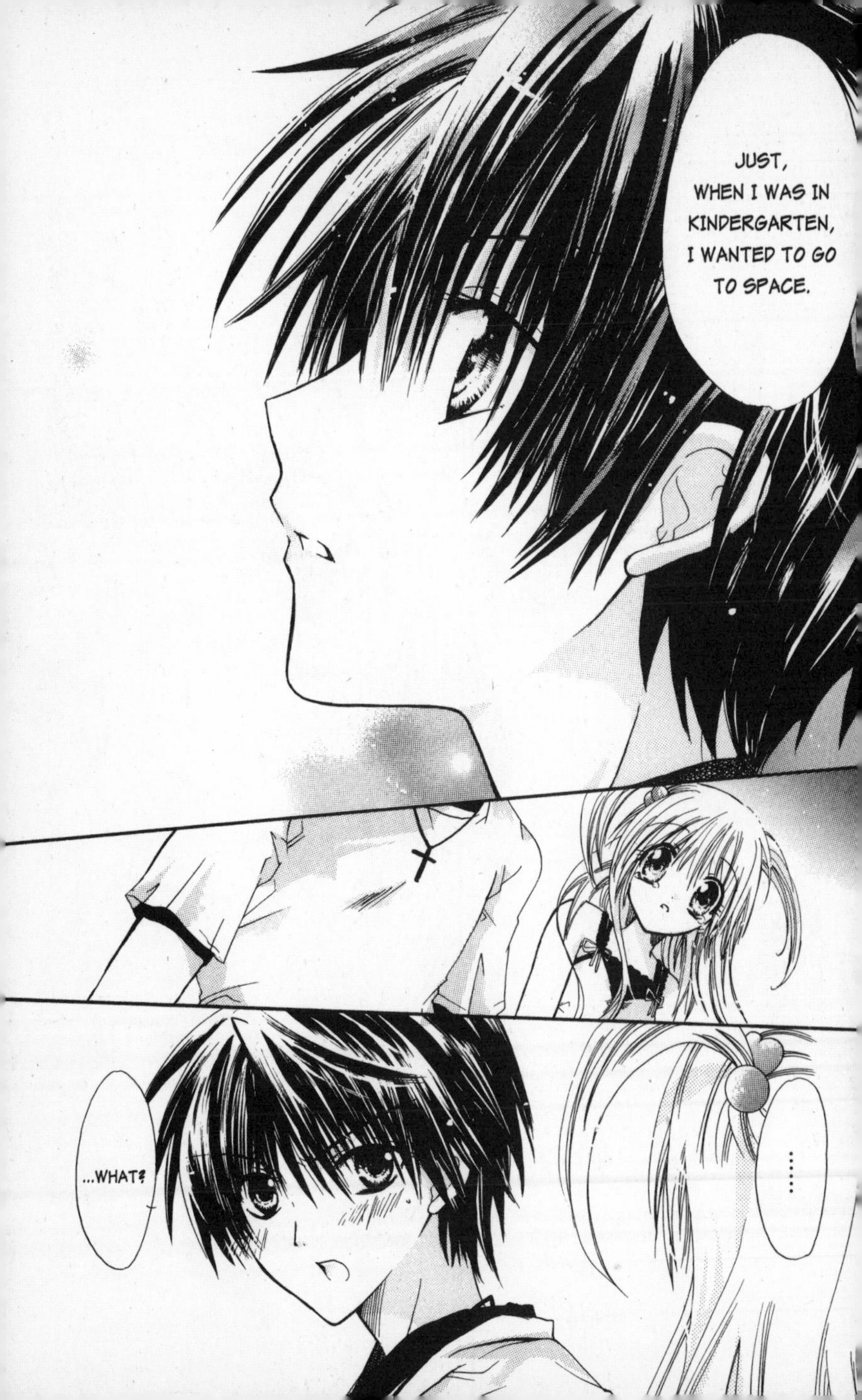
JUST, WHEN I WAS IN KINDERGARTEN, I WANTED TO GO TO SPACE.
......
...WHAT?

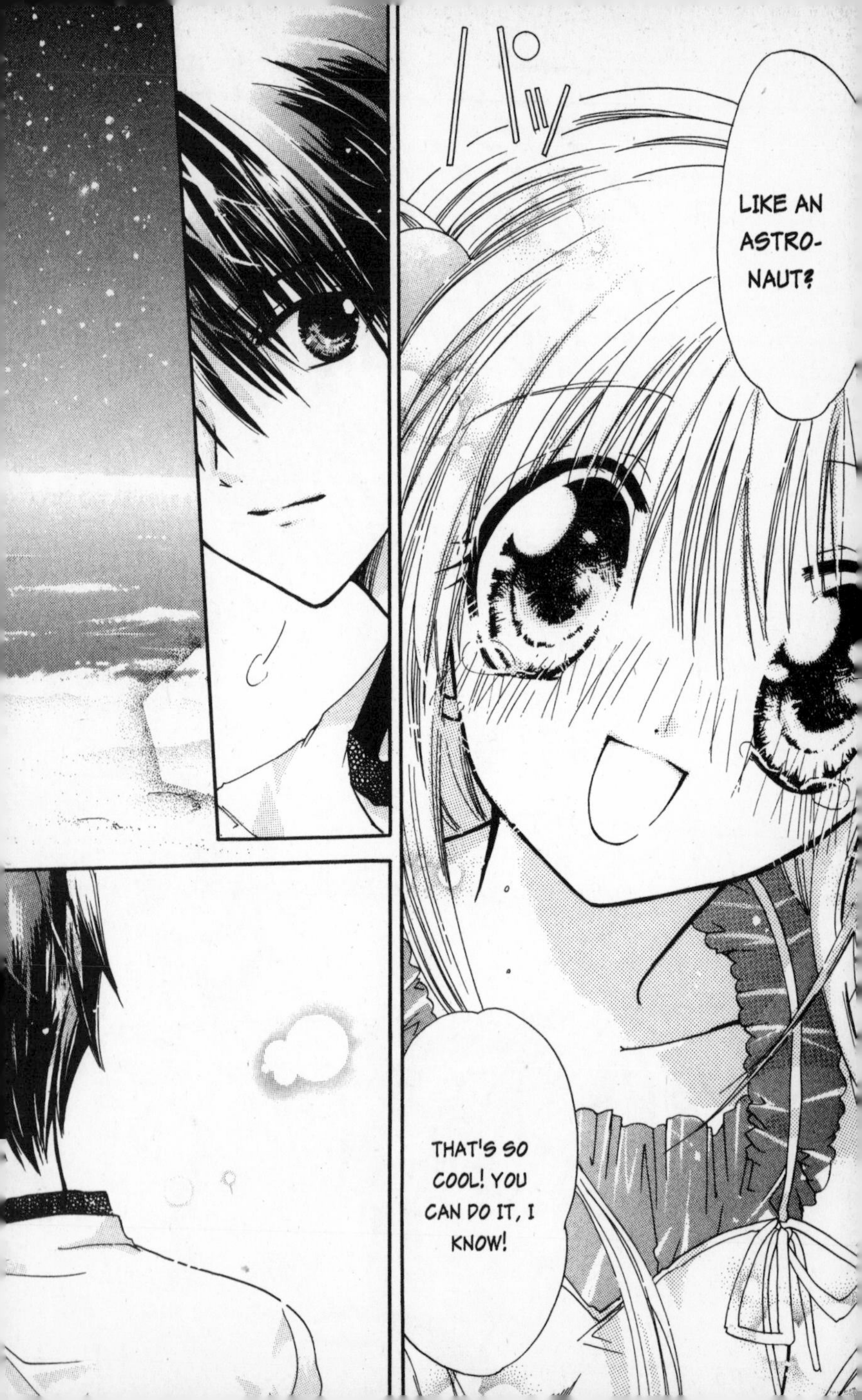
パッ
LIKE AN ASTRO- NAUT?
THAT'S SO COOL! YOU CAN DO IT, I KNOW!

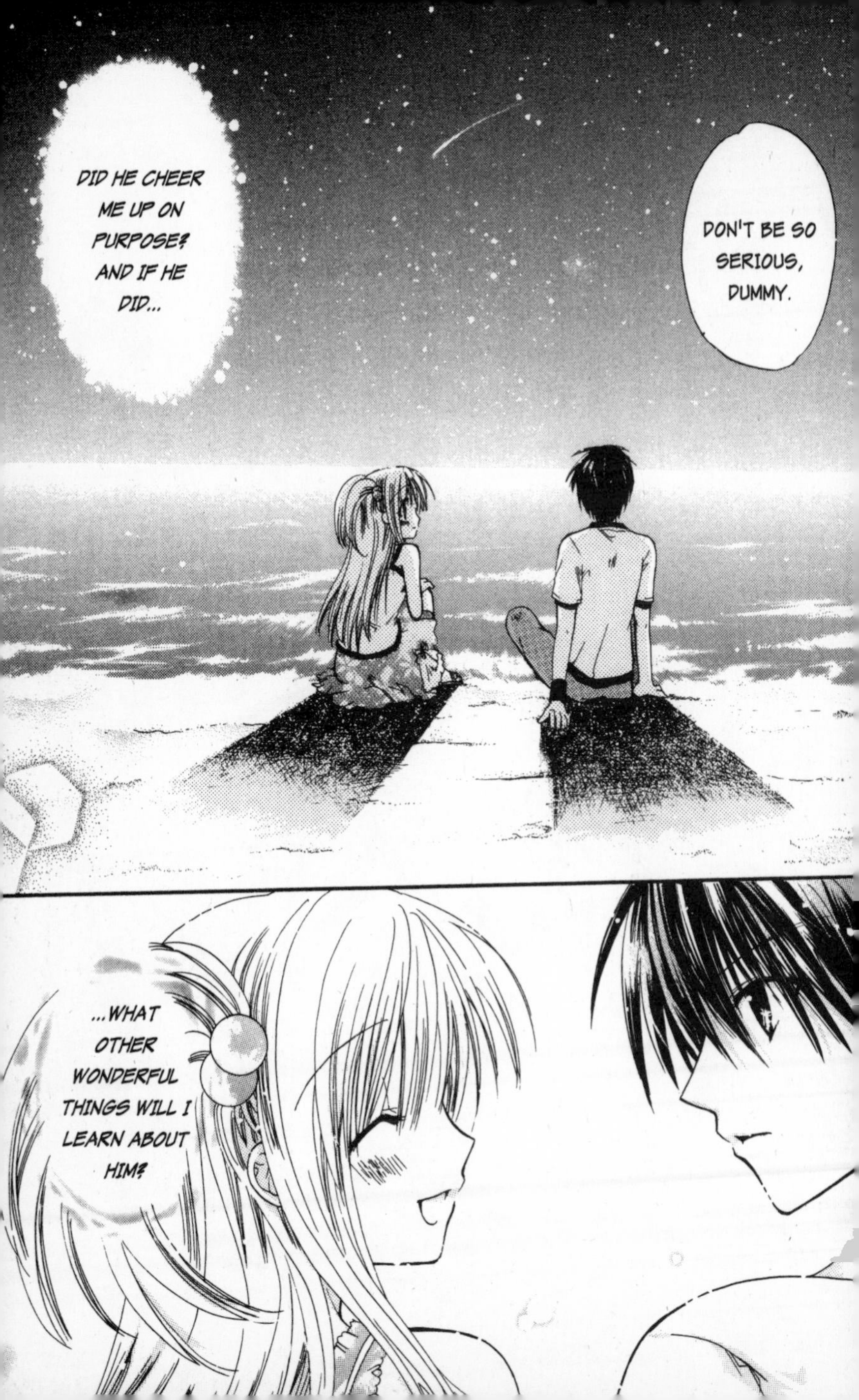
DON'T BE SO SERIOUS, DUMMY.
DID HE CHEER ME UP ON PURPOSE? AND IF HE DID...
...WHAT OTHER WONDERFUL THINGS WILL I LEARN ABOUT HIM?

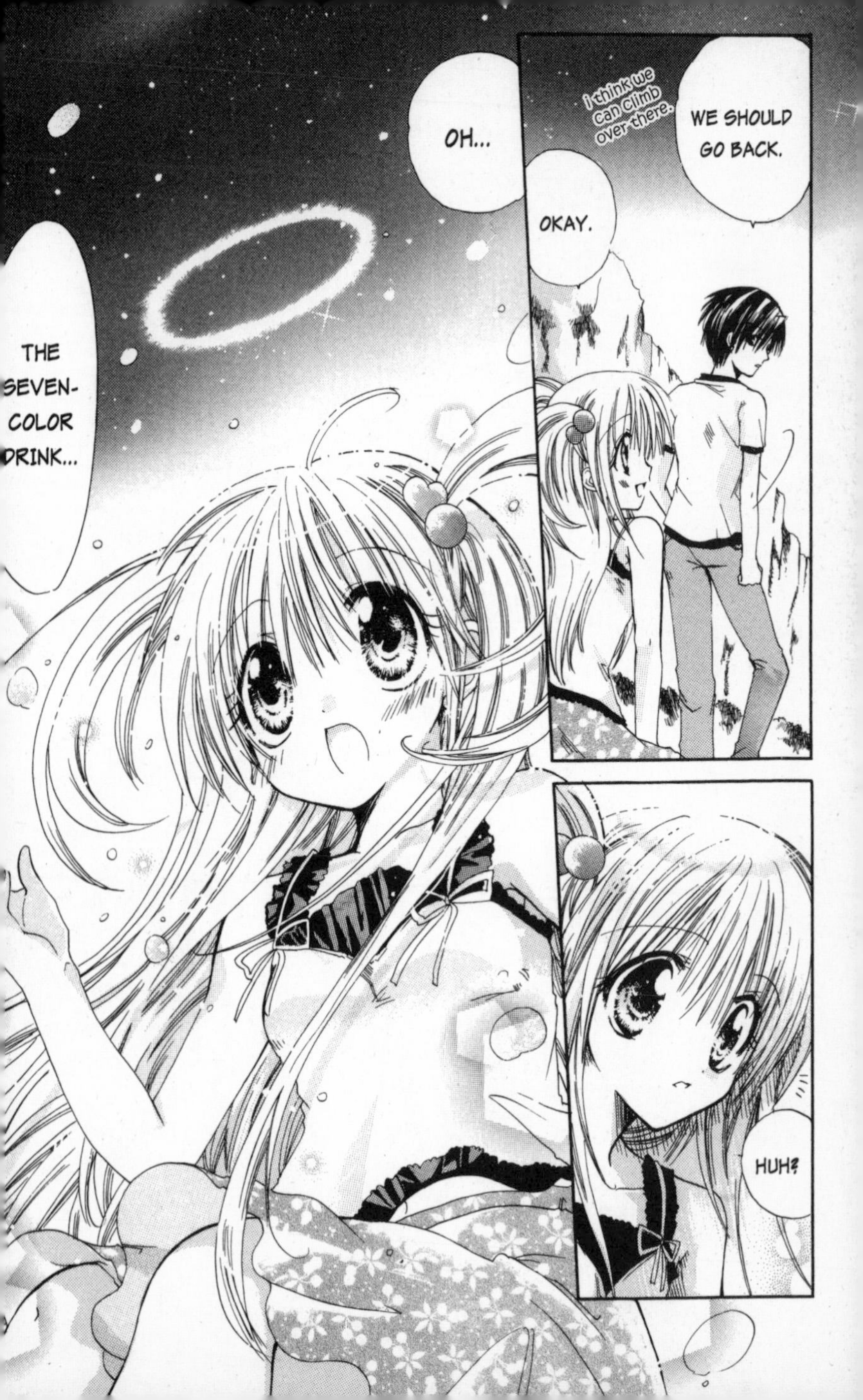
WE SHOULD GO BACK.
i think we can climb over there.
OKAY.
HUH?
OH...
THE SEVEN-COLOR DRINK...

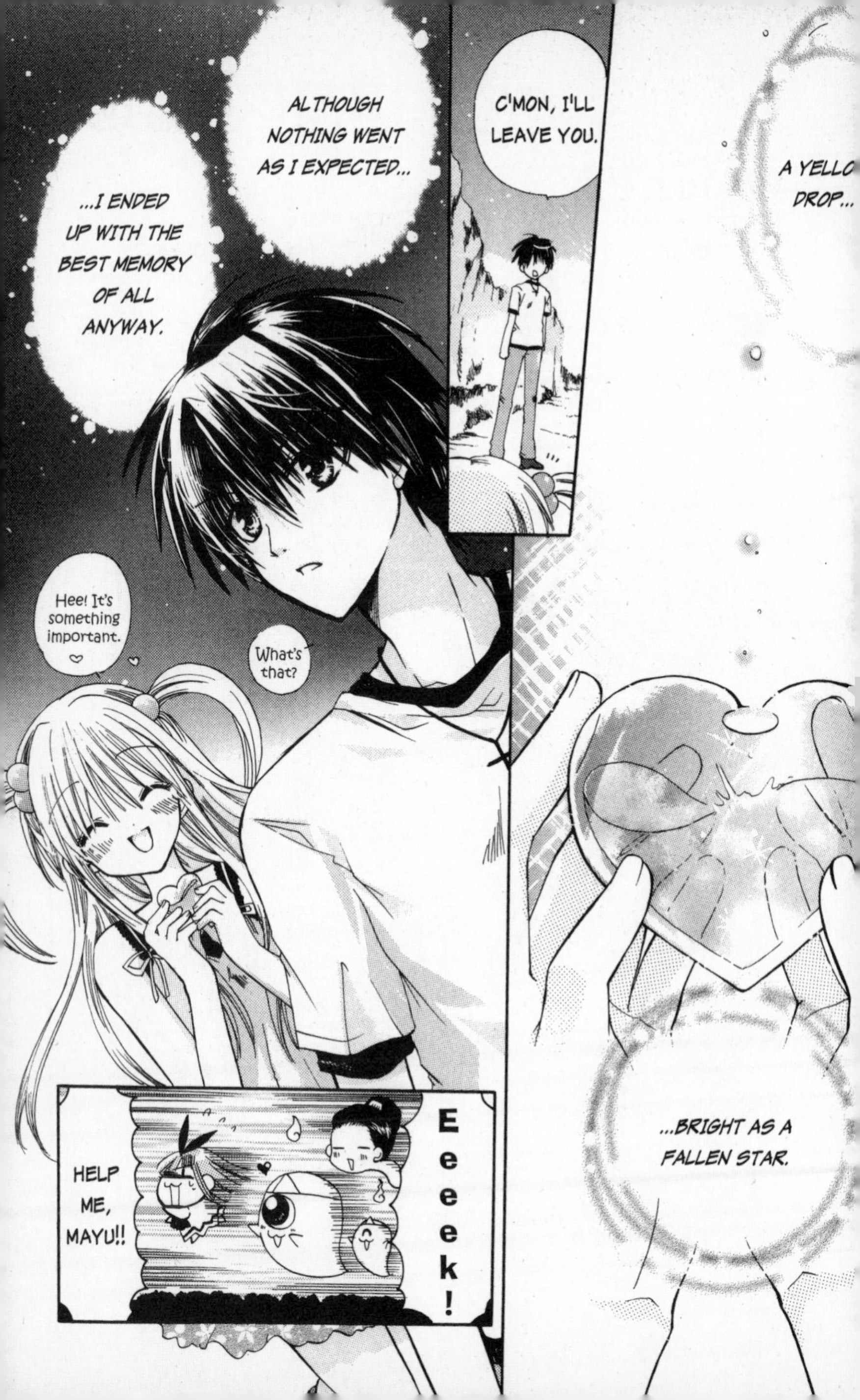

A YELLO
DROP...
...BRIGHT AS A FALLEN STAR.
C'MON, I'LL LEAVE YOU.
ALTHOUGH NOTHING WENT AS I EXPECTED...
...I ENDED UP WITH THE BEST MEMORY OF ALL ANYWAY.
What's that?
Hee! It's something important.
Eeeek!
HELP ME, MAYU!!

GOKKUN! PŪCHO

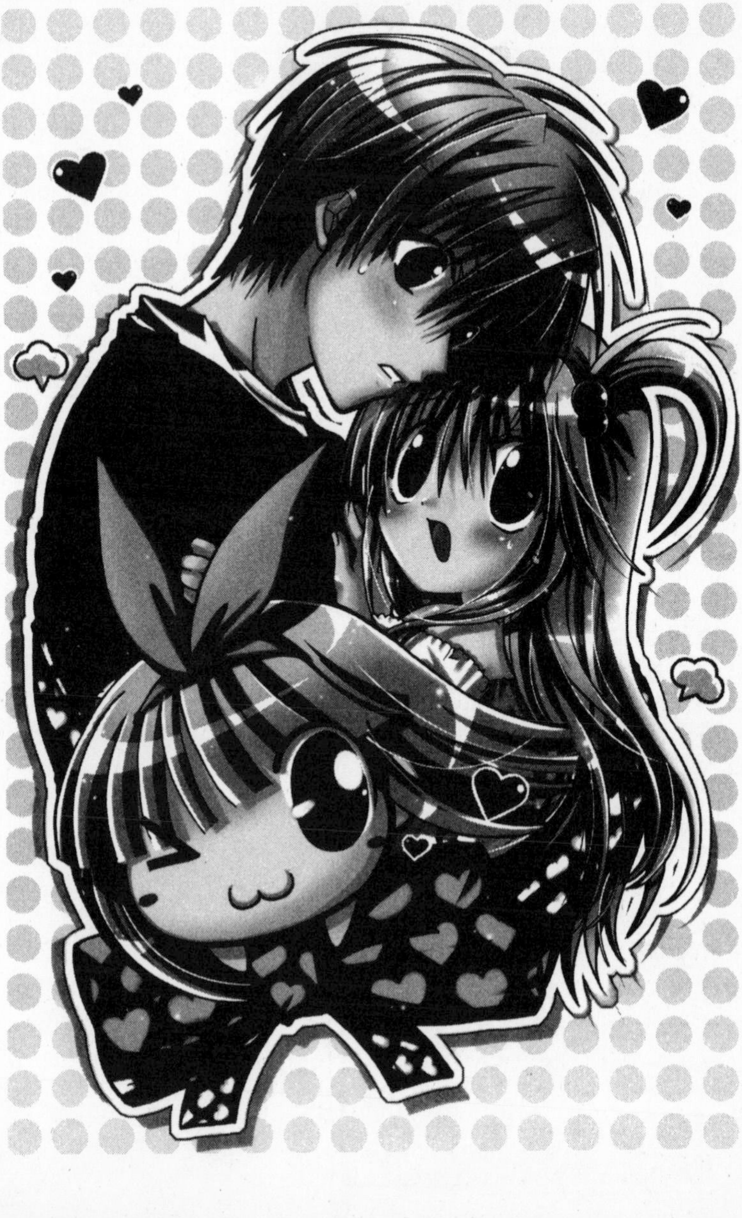

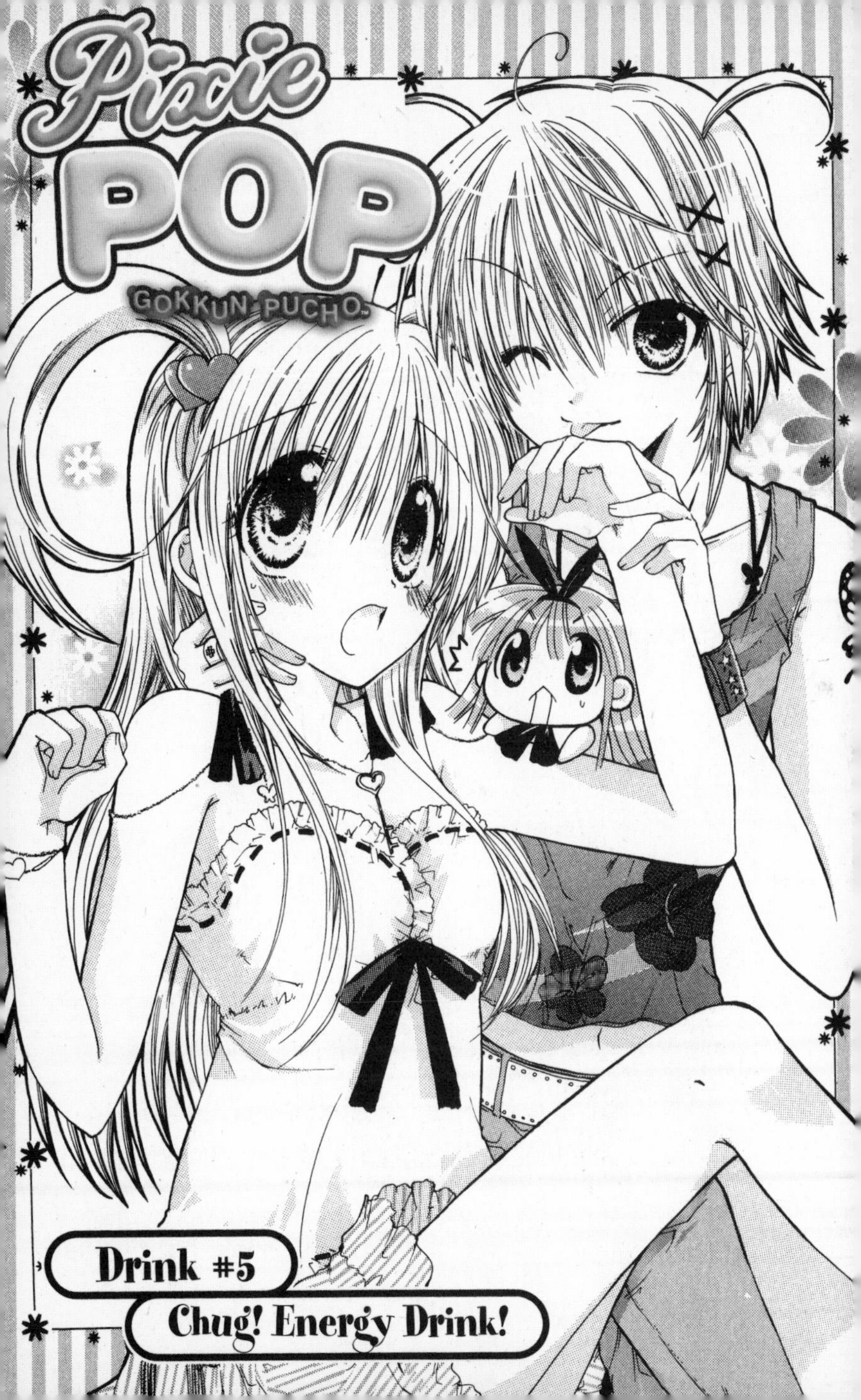

Pixie POP
GOKKUN PUCHO
Drink #5
Chug! Energy Drink!

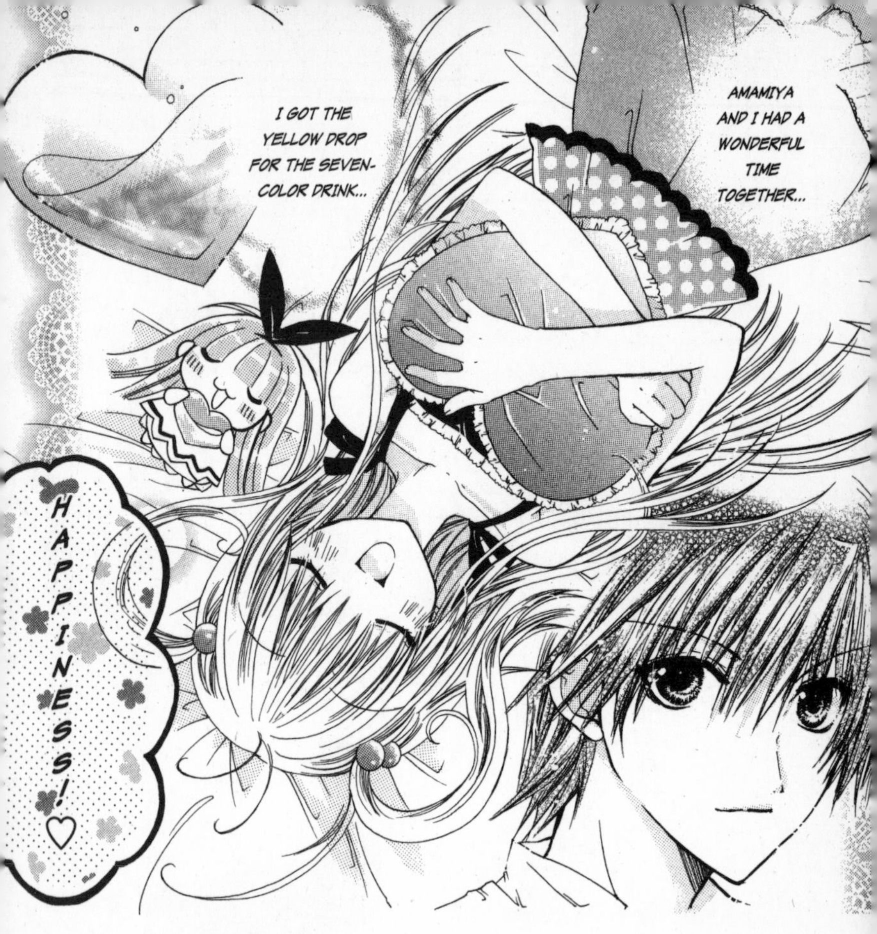
AMAMIYA AND I HAD A WONDERFUL TIME TOGETHER...
I GOT THE YELLOW DROP FOR THE SEVEN-COLOR DRINK...
HAPPINESS!♡

****

♥ Nazuna Hayase ♥

Birthday: June 28th

Sign: Cancer Bloodtype: B

Height: 159cm Weight: 41kg

Favorite Drink: Fruit juice

****

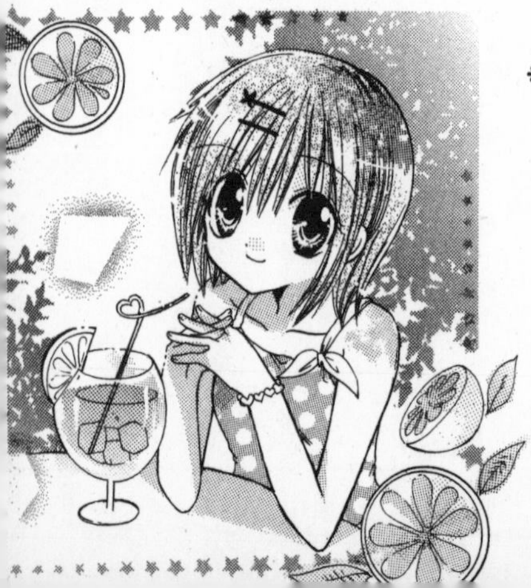

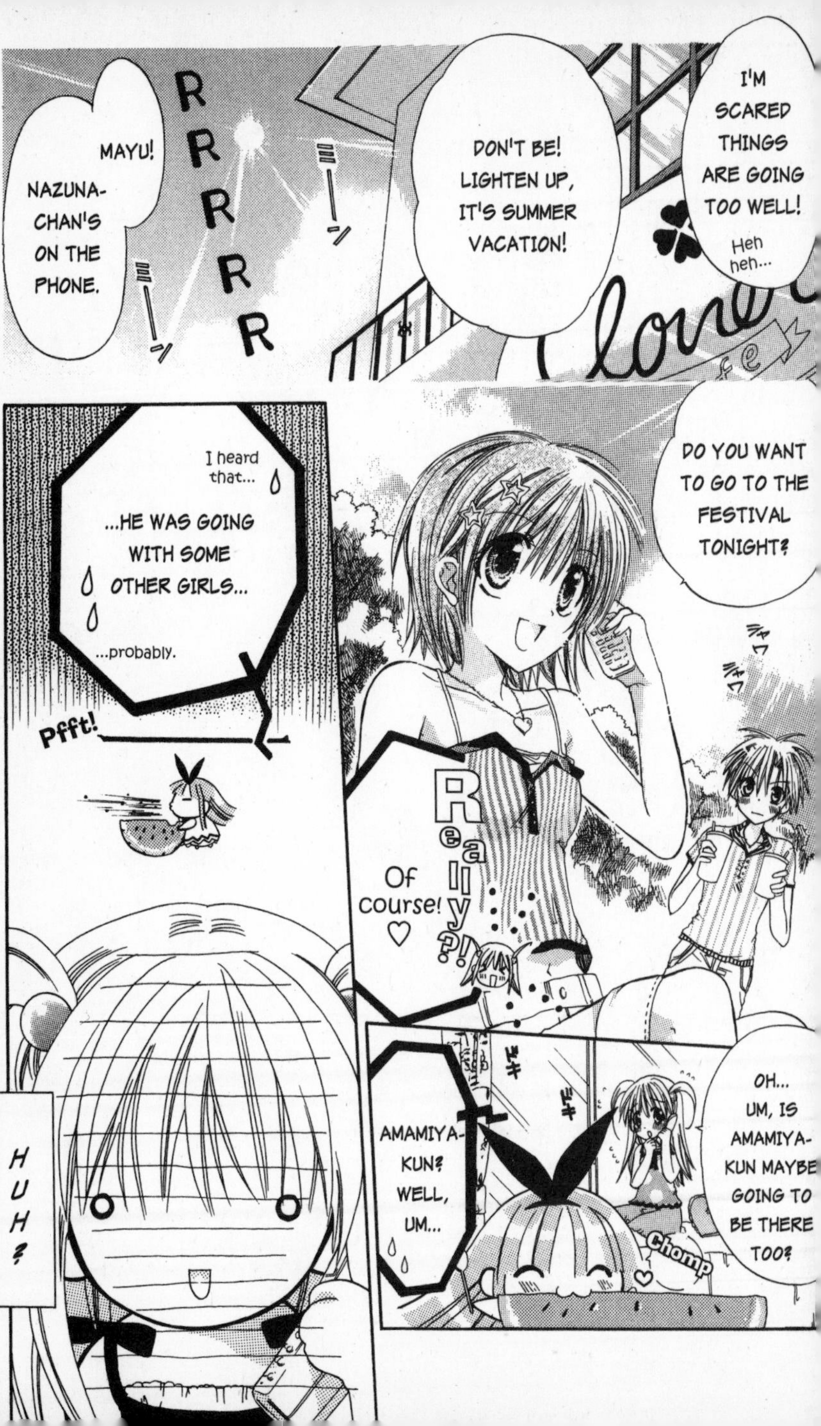
I'M SCARED THINGS ARE GOING TOO WELL!
Heh heh...
DON'T BE! LIGHTEN UP, IT'S SUMMER VACATION!
RRRRR
MAYU! NAZUNA-CHAN'S ON THE PHONE.
DO YOU WANT TO GO TO THE FESTIVAL TONIGHT?
Really?!
Of course! ♡
OH... UM, IS AMAMIYA-KUN MAYBE GOING TO BE THERE TOO?
AMAMIYA-KUN? WELL, UM...
Chomp
I heard that...
...HE WAS GOING WITH SOME OTHER GIRLS...
...probably.
Pfft!
HUH?

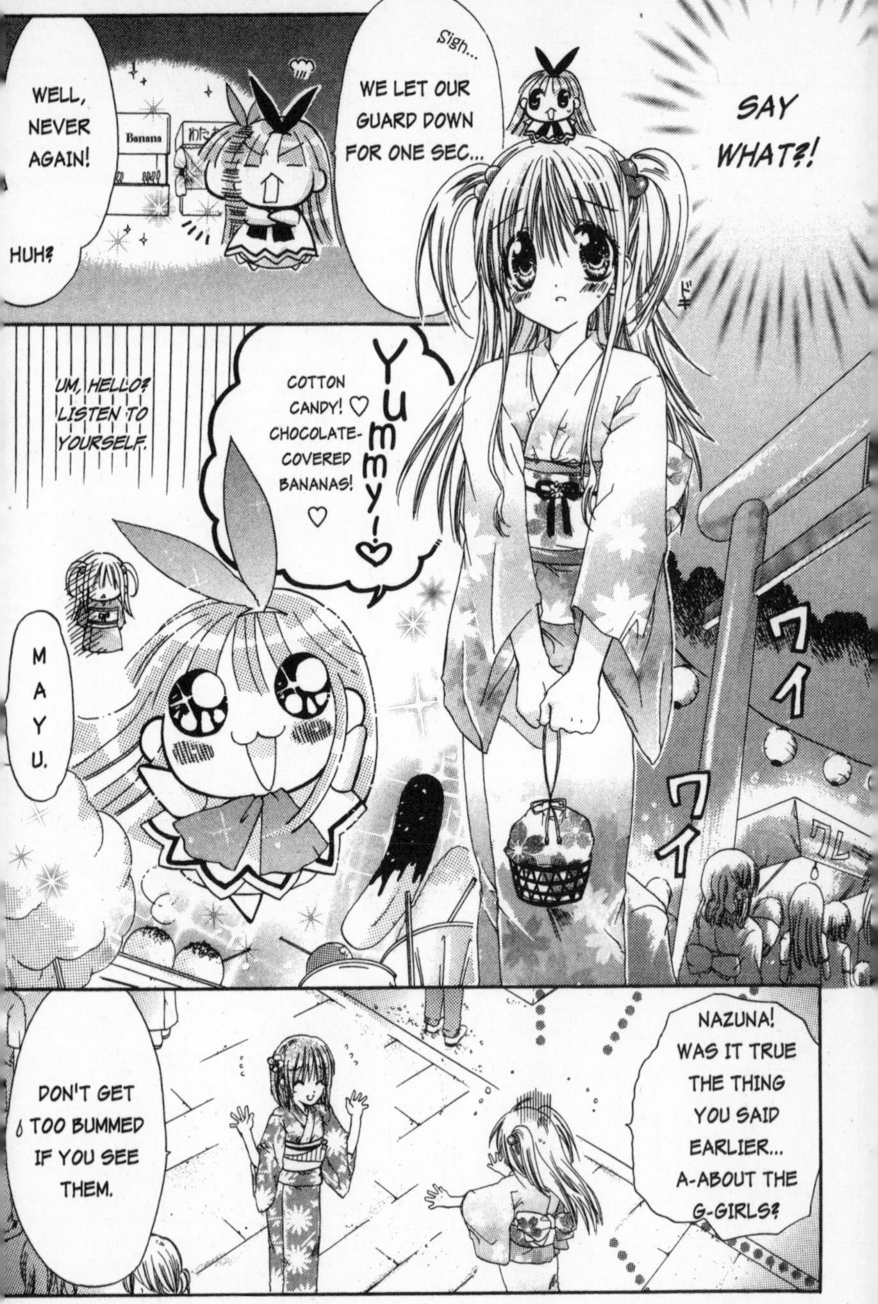
SAY WHAT?!
Sigh...
WE LET OUR GUARD DOWN FOR ONE SEC...
WELL, NEVER AGAIN!
HUH?
ドキ
Yummy!
COTTON CANDY! ♡ CHOCOLATE-COVERED BANANAS! ♡
UM, HELLO? LISTEN TO YOURSELF.
MAYU.
ワイワイ
NAZUNA! WAS IT TRUE THE THING YOU SAID EARLIER... A-ABOUT THE G-GIRLS?
DON'T GET TOO BUMMED IF YOU SEE THEM.

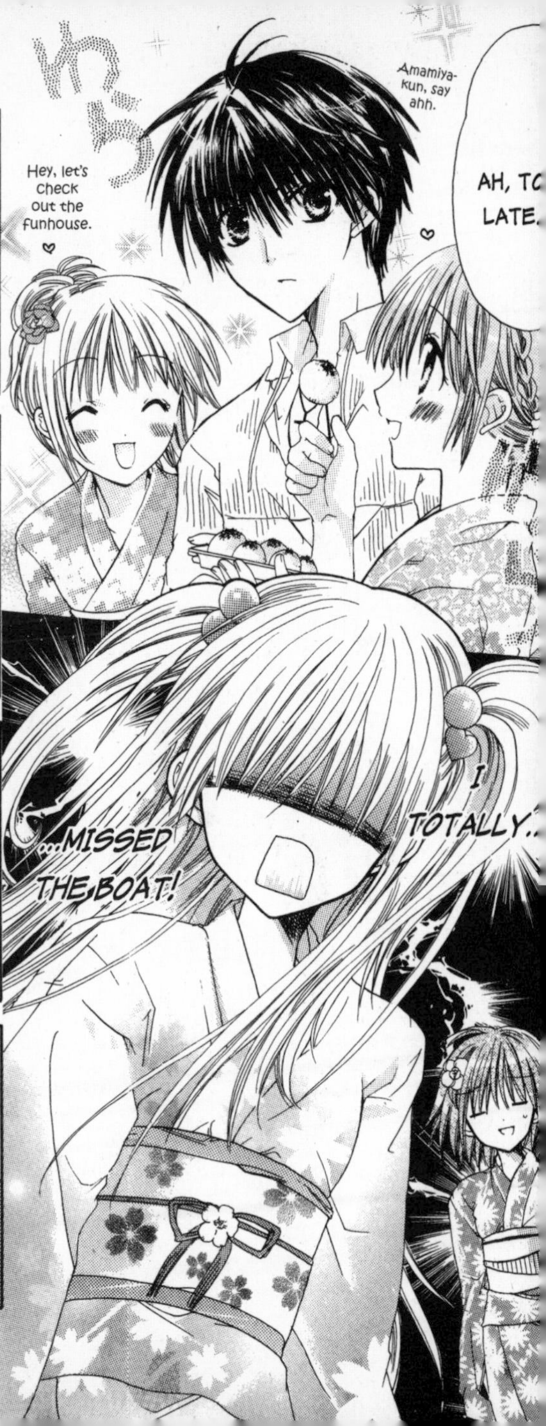

Amamiya-kun, say ahh.
AH, TO LATE.
Hey, let's check out the funhouse.
I TOTALLY...
...MISSED THE BOAT!

● Scar on the Heart ●

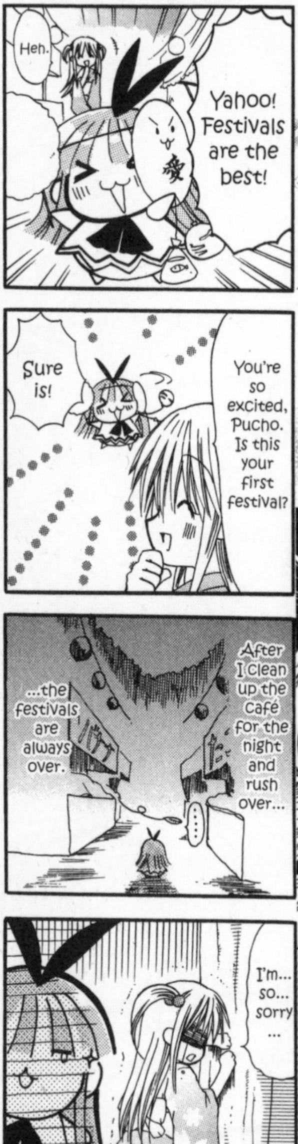

Yahoo! Festivals are the best!
Heh.
You're so excited, Pucho. Is this your first festival?
Sure is!
After I clean up the café for the night and rush over...
...the festivals are always over.
......
I'm... so... sorry...

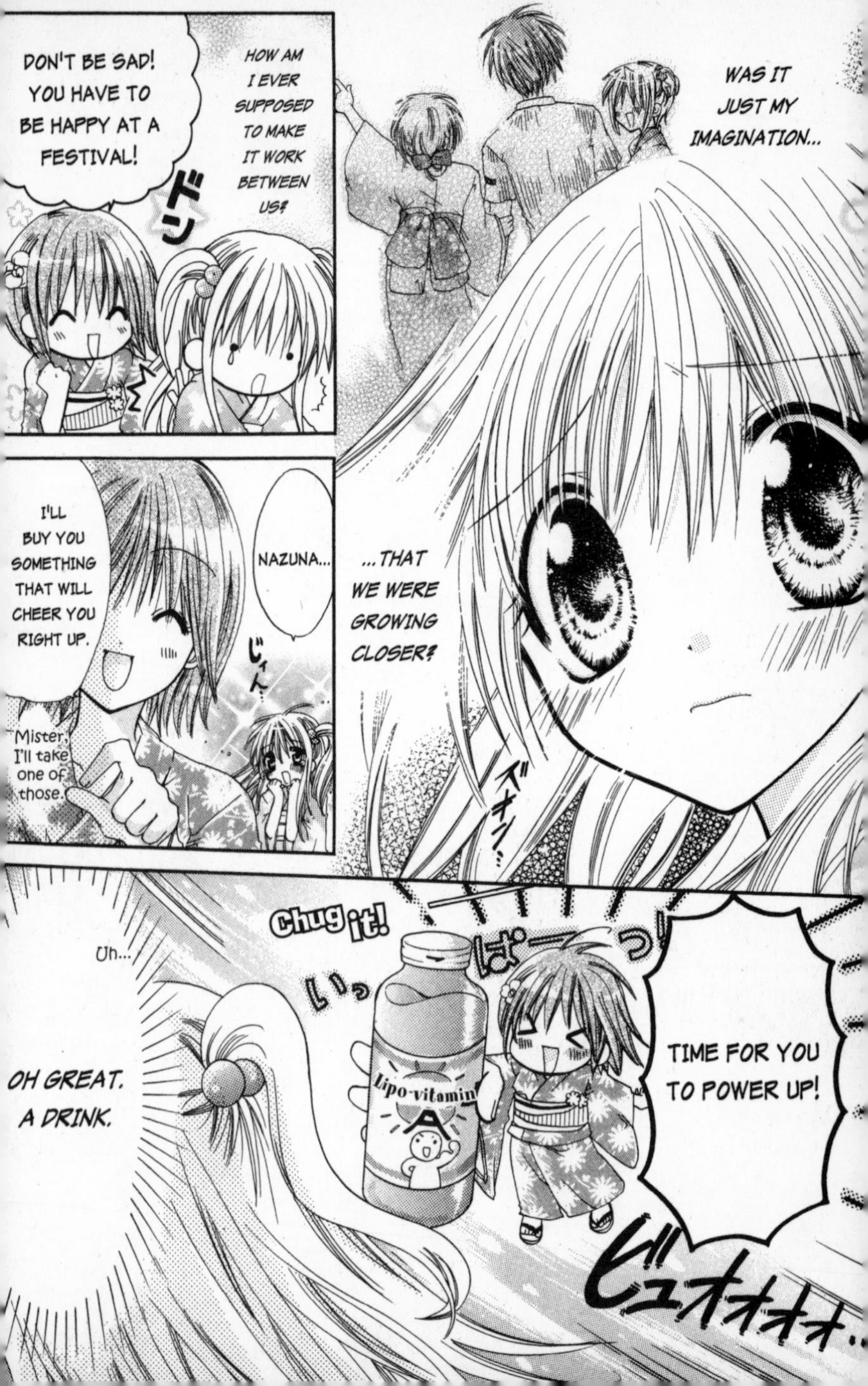
WAS IT JUST MY IMAGINATION...
...THAT WE WERE GROWING CLOSER?
HOW AM I EVER SUPPOSED TO MAKE IT WORK BETWEEN US?
DON'T BE SAD! YOU HAVE TO BE HAPPY AT A FESTIVAL!
ドッ
NAZUNA...
I'LL BUY YOU SOMETHING THAT WILL CHEER YOU RIGHT UP.
Mister, I'll take one of those.
TIME FOR YOU TO POWER UP!
Chug it!
Lipo-vitamin A
Uh...
OH GREAT. A DRINK.

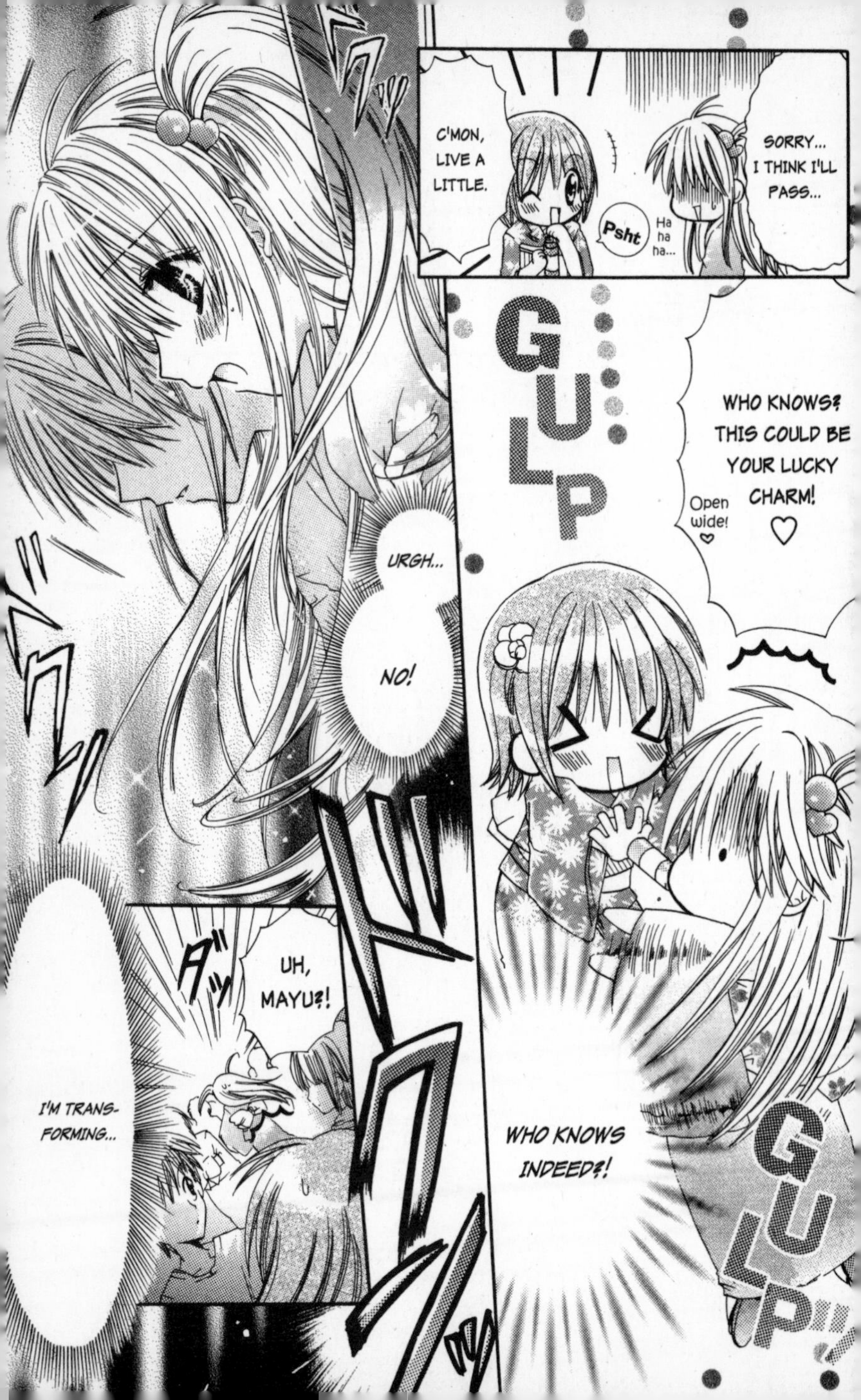
SORRY... I THINK I'LL PASS...
C'MON, LIVE A LITTLE.
Ha ha ha...
Psht
WHO KNOWS? THIS COULD BE YOUR LUCKY CHARM! ♡
Open wide! ♡
GULP
WHO KNOWS INDEED?!
GULP!!
URGH...
NO!
UH, MAYU?!
I'M TRANS-FORMING...

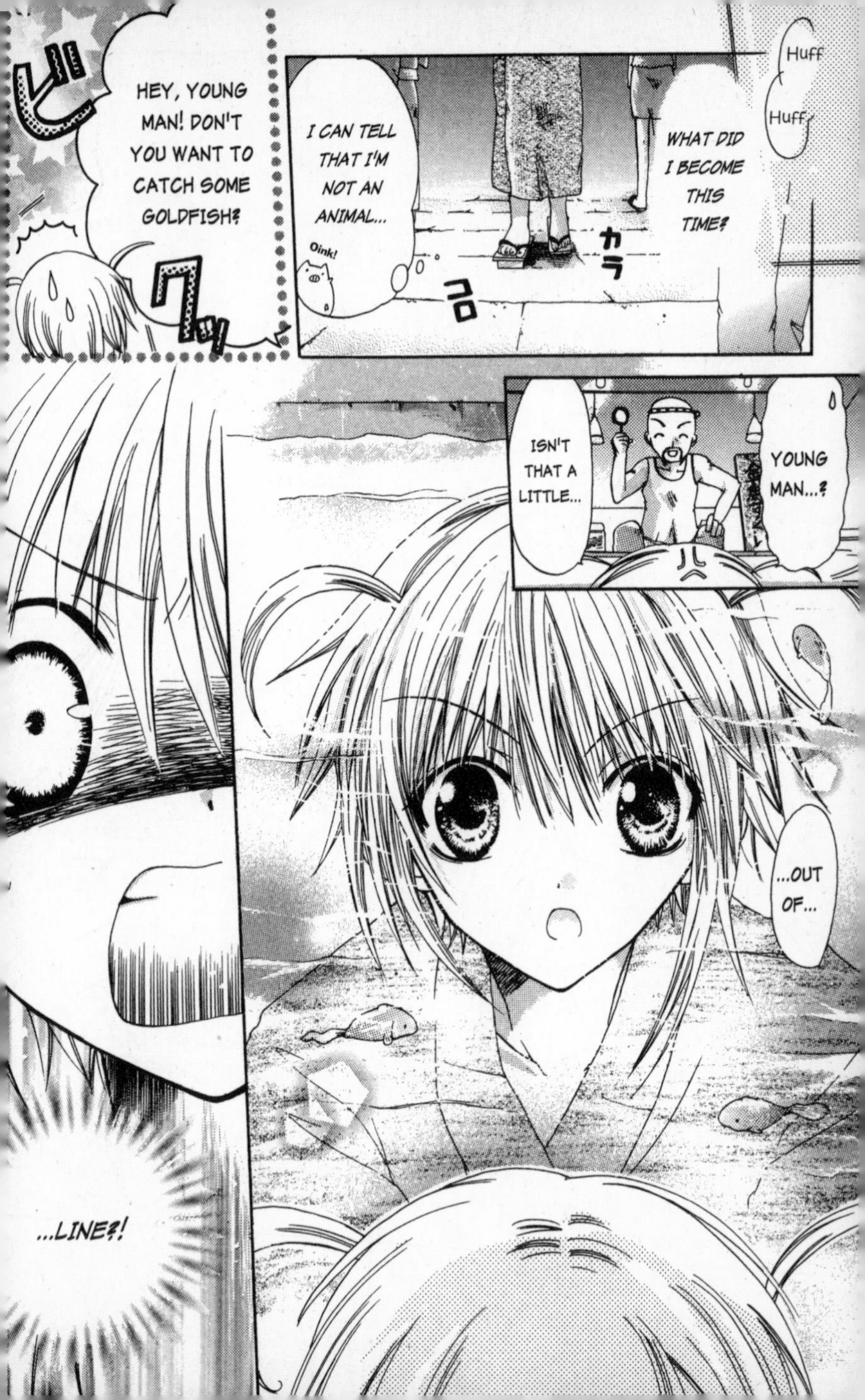
Huff
Huff
WHAT DID I BECOME THIS TIME?
I CAN TELL THAT I'M NOT AN ANIMAL...
Oink!
カラ
コロ
HEY, YOUNG MAN! DON'T YOU WANT TO CATCH SOME GOLDFISH?
YOUNG MAN...?
ISN'T THAT A LITTLE...
...OUT OF...
...LINE?!

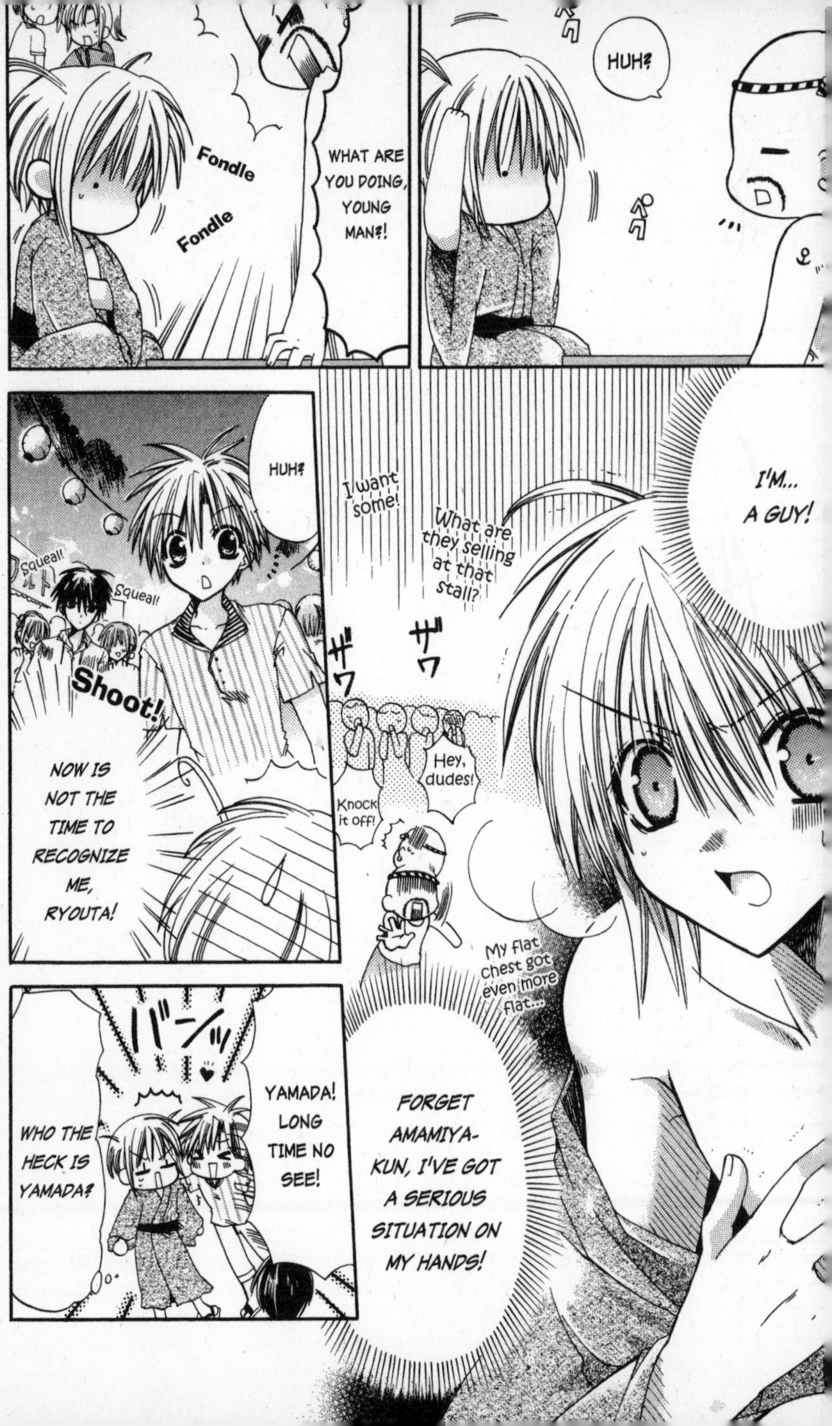
HUH?
...
Fondle
Fondle
WHAT ARE YOU DOING, YOUNG MAN?!
I'M... A GUY!
I want some!
What are they selling at that stall?
ザワ
ザワ
Hey, dudes!
Knock it off!
My flat chest got even more flat...
FORGET AMAMIYA-KUN, I'VE GOT A SERIOUS SITUATION ON MY HANDS!
HUH?
Squeal!
Squeal!
Shoot!
NOW IS NOT THE TIME TO RECOGNIZE ME, RYOUTA!
バンッ
YAMADA! LONG TIME NO SEE!
WHO THE HECK IS YAMADA?

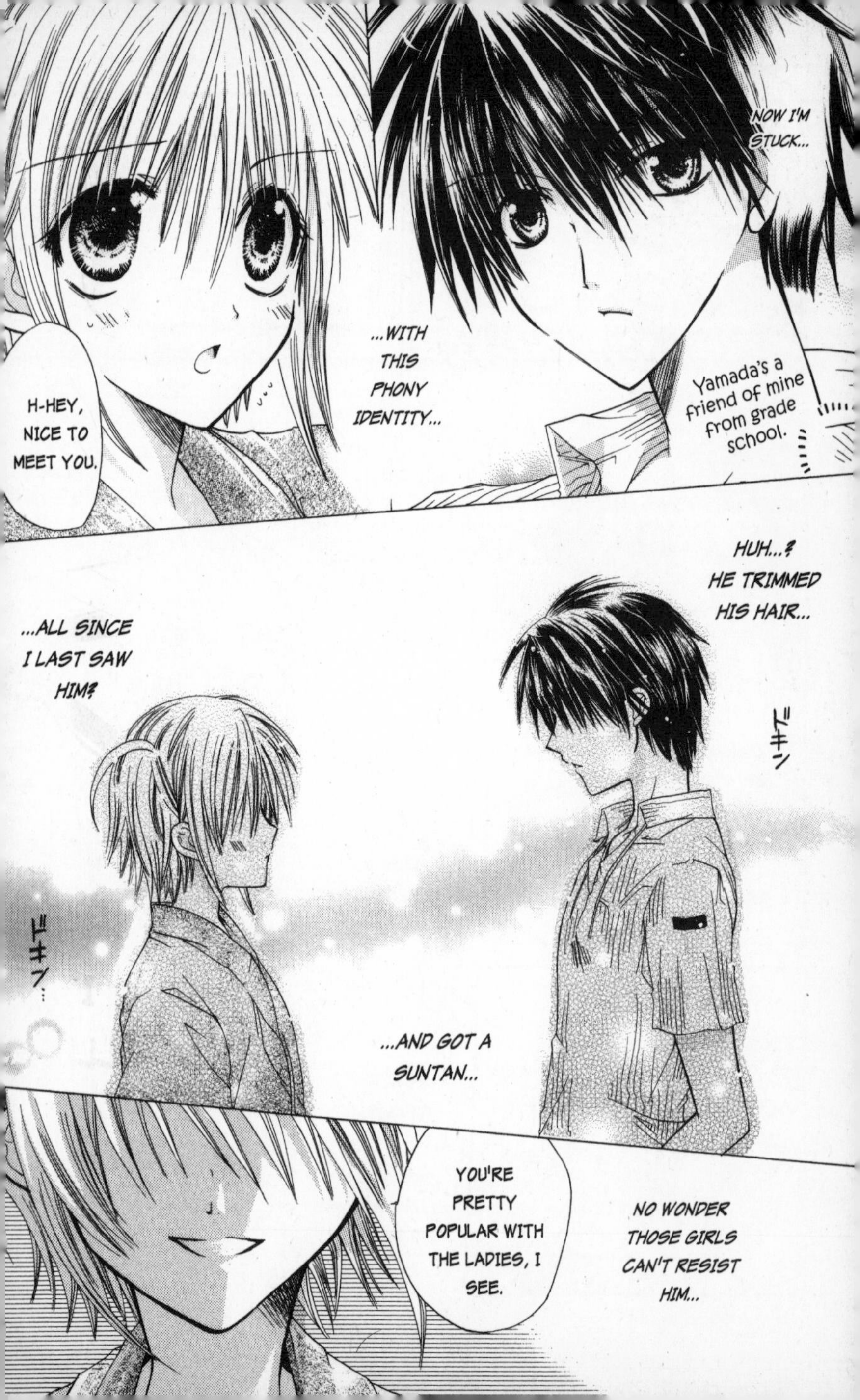
NOW I'M STUCK...
Yamada's a friend of mine from grade school.
...WITH THIS PHONY IDENTITY...
H-HEY, NICE TO MEET YOU.
HUH...? HE TRIMMED HIS HAIR...
ドキッ
...AND GOT A SUNTAN...
...ALL SINCE I LAST SAW HIM?
ドキッ...
NO WONDER THOSE GIRLS CAN'T RESIST HIM...
YOU'RE PRETTY POPULAR WITH THE LADIES, I SEE.

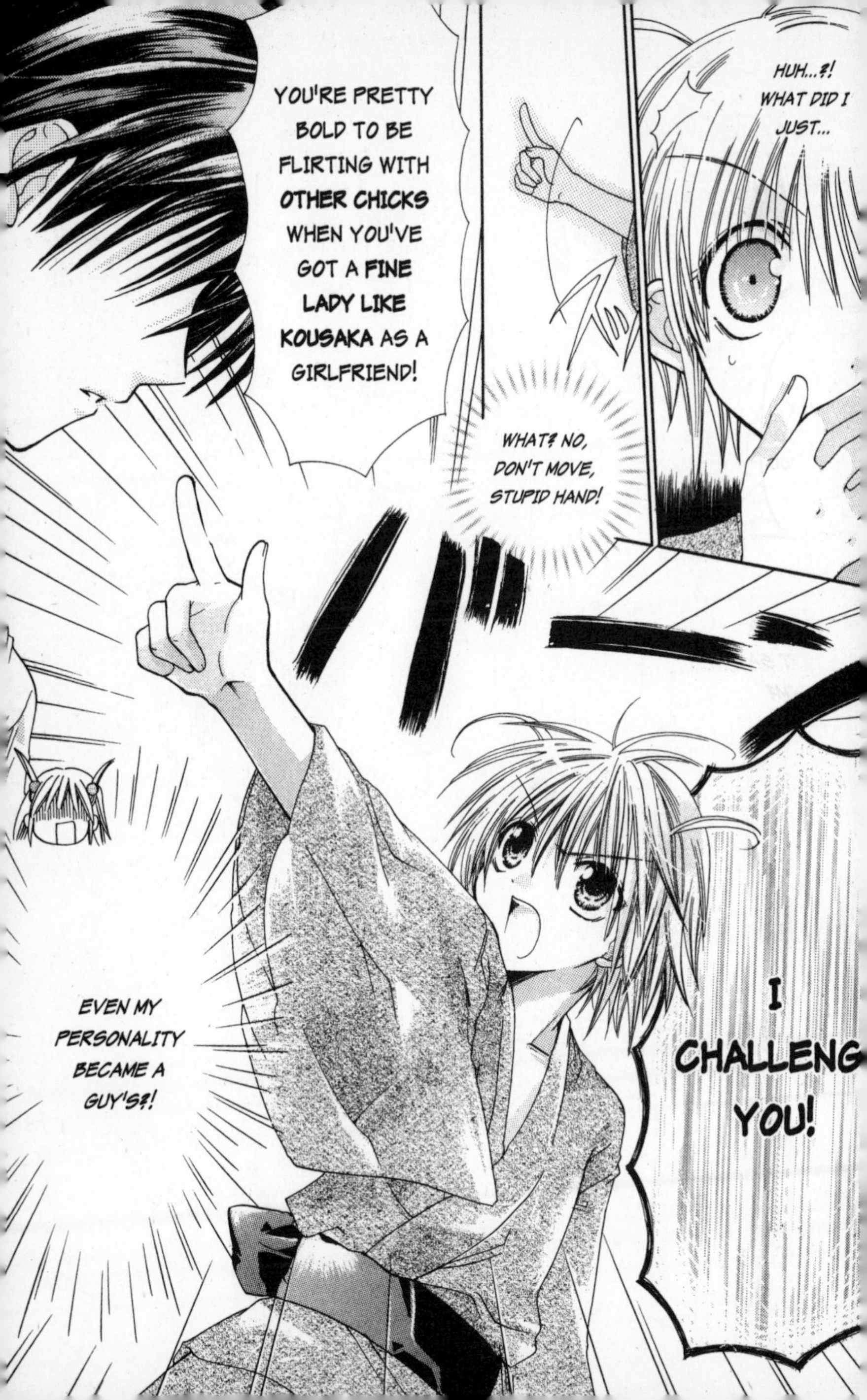
HUH...?! WHAT DID I JUST...
WHAT?! NO, DON'T MOVE, STUPID HAND!
YOU'RE PRETTY BOLD TO BE FLIRTING WITH OTHER CHICKS WHEN YOU'VE GOT A FINE LADY LIKE KOUSAKA AS A GIRLFRIEND!
I CHALLENG YOU!
EVEN MY PERSONALITY BECAME A GUY'S?!

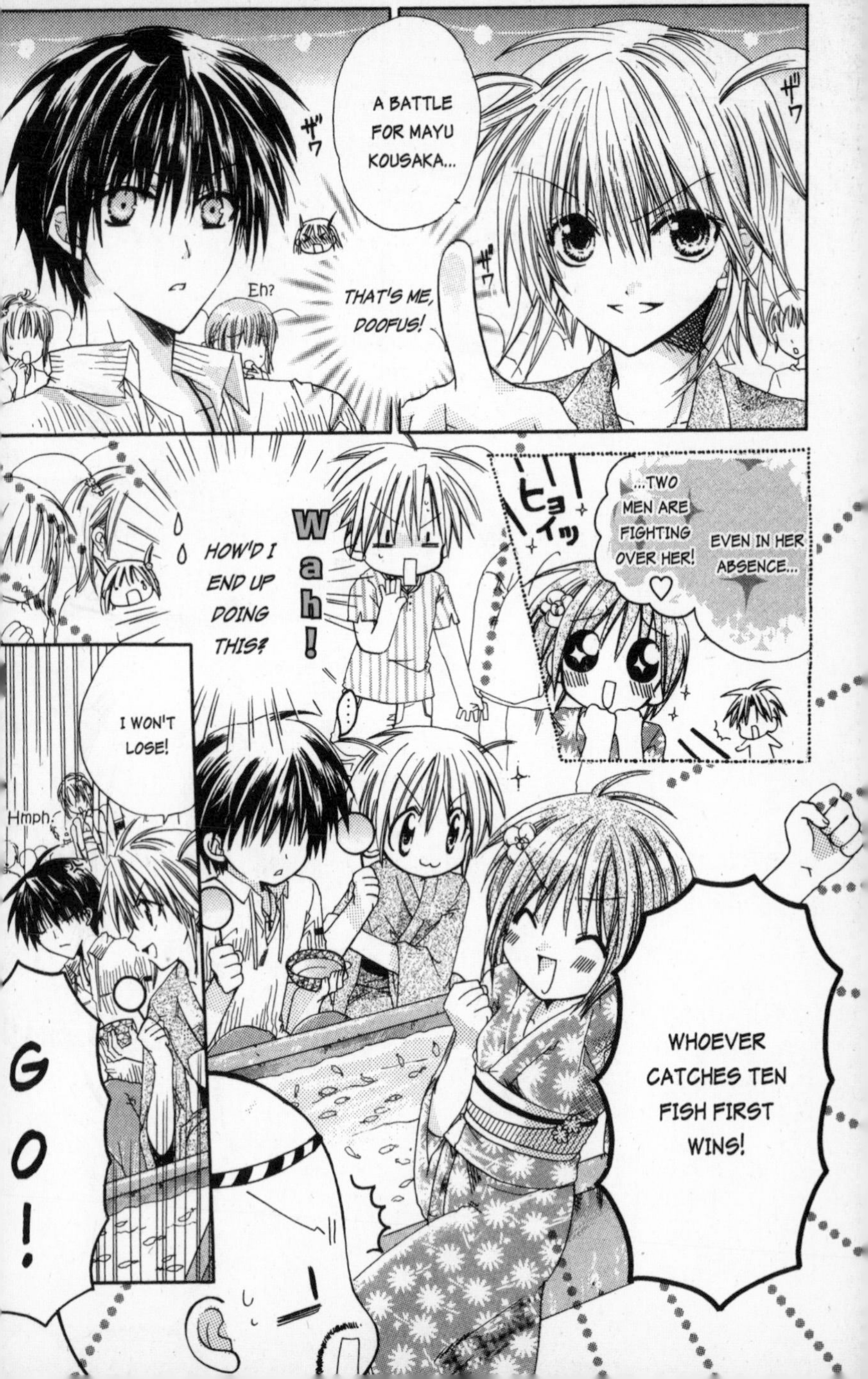
ザワ
ザワ
A BATTLE FOR MAYU KOUSAKA...
ザワ
THAT'S ME, DOOFUS!
ザワ
Eh?
ヒョイッ
EVEN IN HER ABSENCE...
...TWO MEN ARE FIGHTING OVER HER! ♡
Wah!
HOW'D I END UP DOING THIS?
WHOEVER CATCHES TEN FISH FIRST WINS!
I WON'T LOSE!
Hmph.
GO!

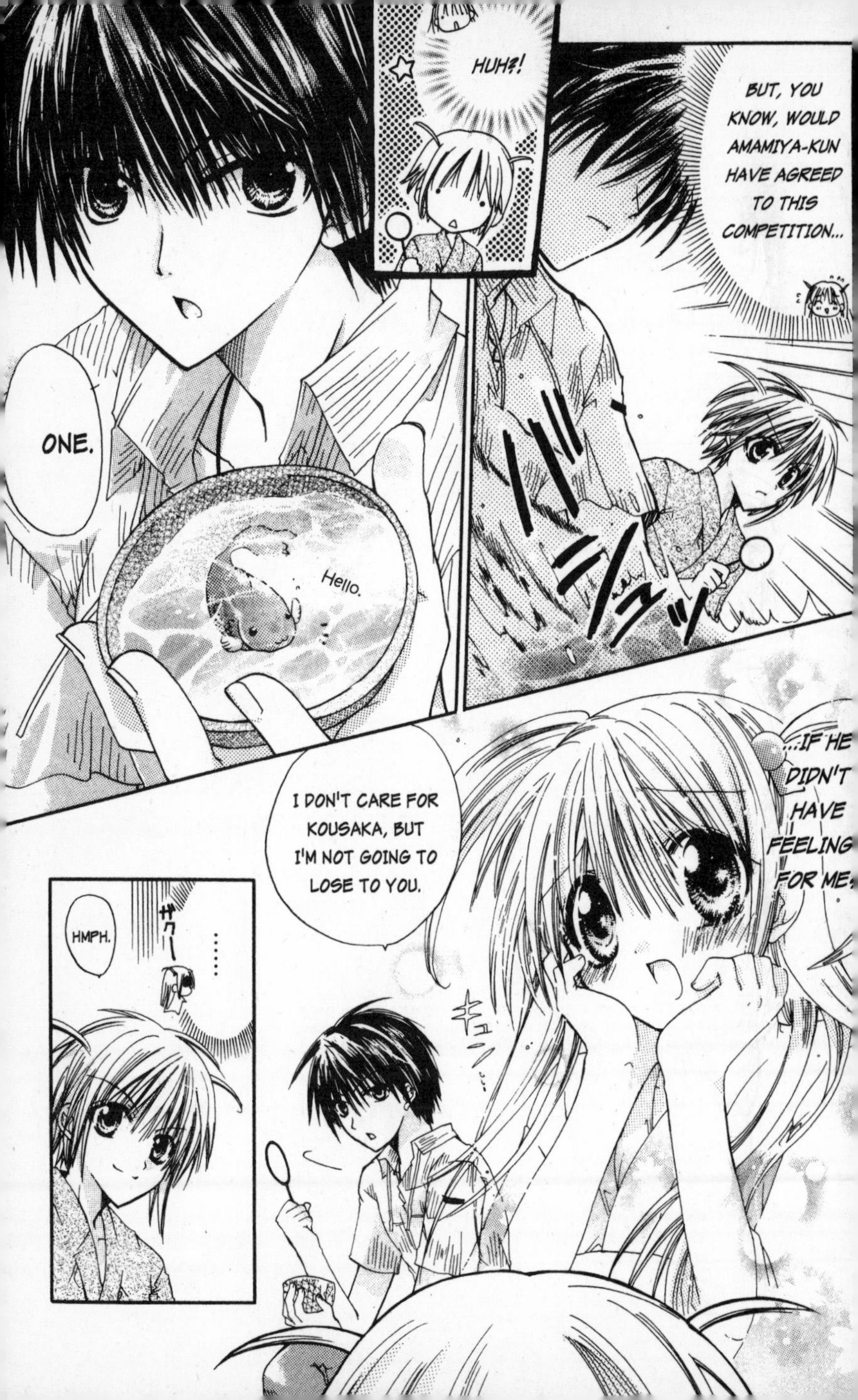
BUT, YOU KNOW, WOULD AMAMIYA-KUN HAVE AGREED TO THIS COMPETITION...
HUH?!
ONE.
Hello.
...IF HE DIDN'T HAVE FEELING FOR ME.
I DON'T CARE FOR KOUSAKA, BUT I'M NOT GOING TO LOSE TO YOU.
HMPH.
......

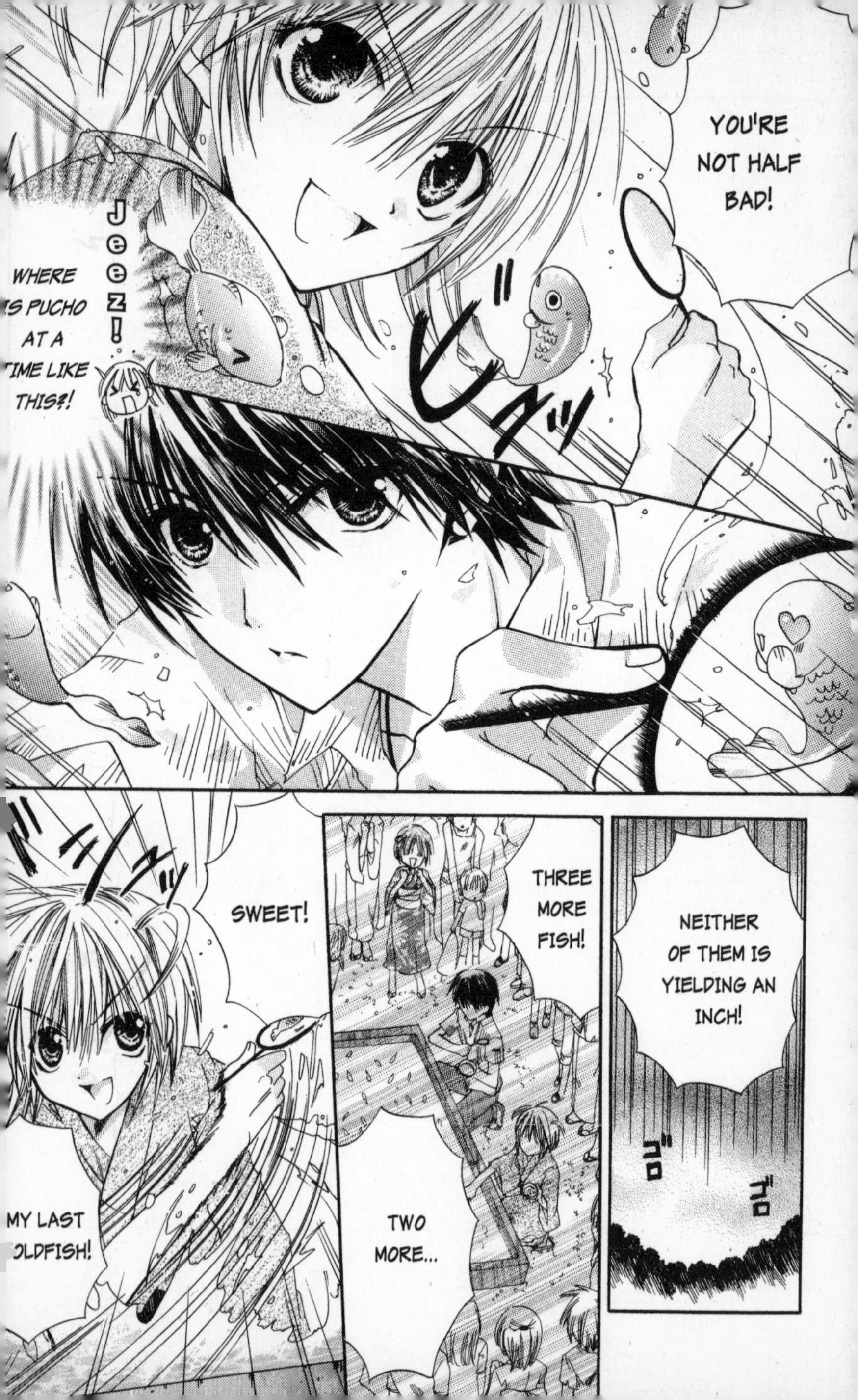
YOU'RE NOT HALF BAD!
Jeez!
WHERE IS PUCHO AT A TIME LIKE THIS?!
NEITHER OF THEM IS YIELDING AN INCH!
ゴロ
ゴロ
THREE MORE FISH!
TWO MORE...
SWEET!
MY LAST GOLDFISH!

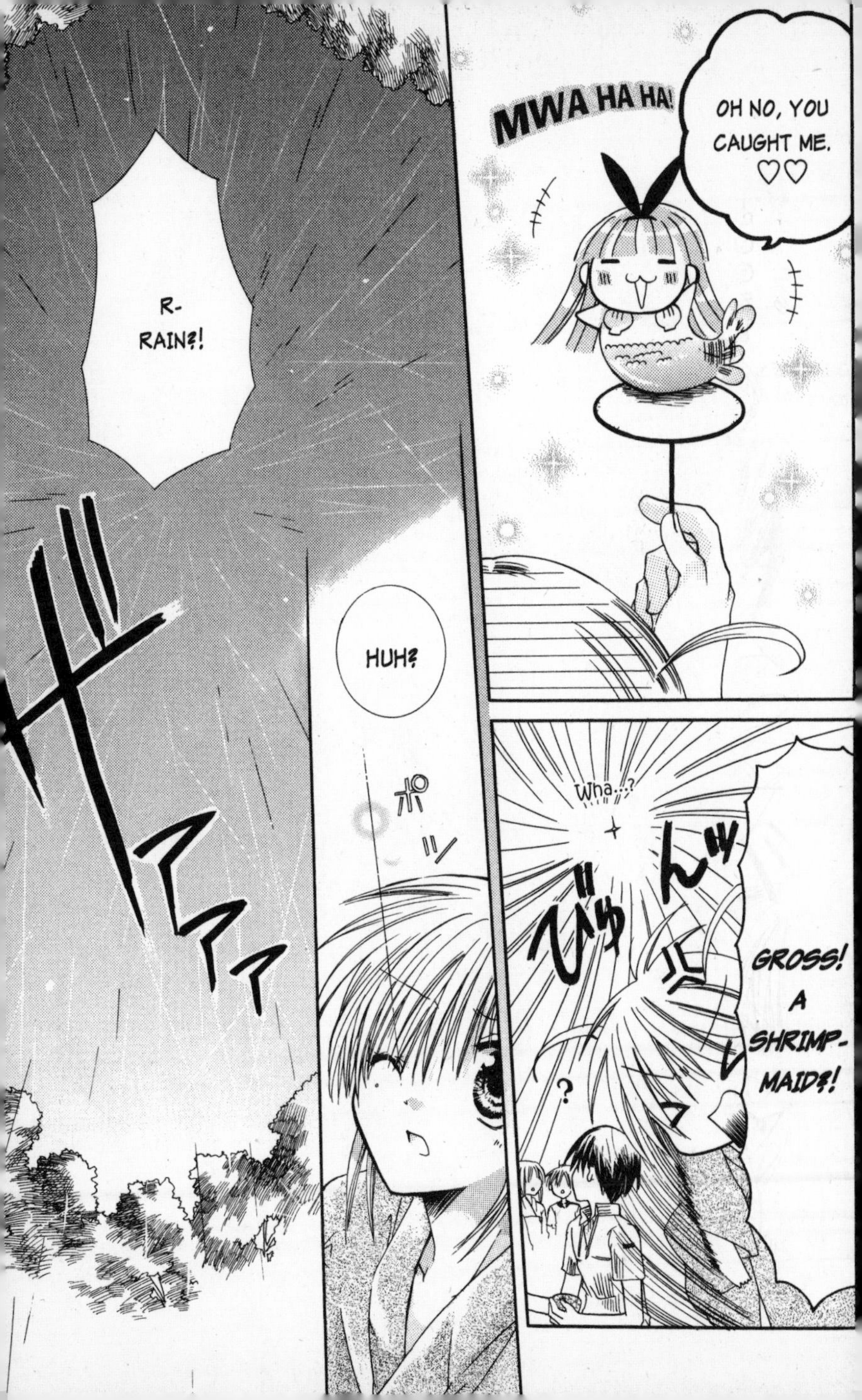
MWA HA HA!
OH NO, YOU CAUGHT ME. ♡♡
Wha...?
GROSS! A SHRIMP-MAID?!
HUH?
R-RAIN?!

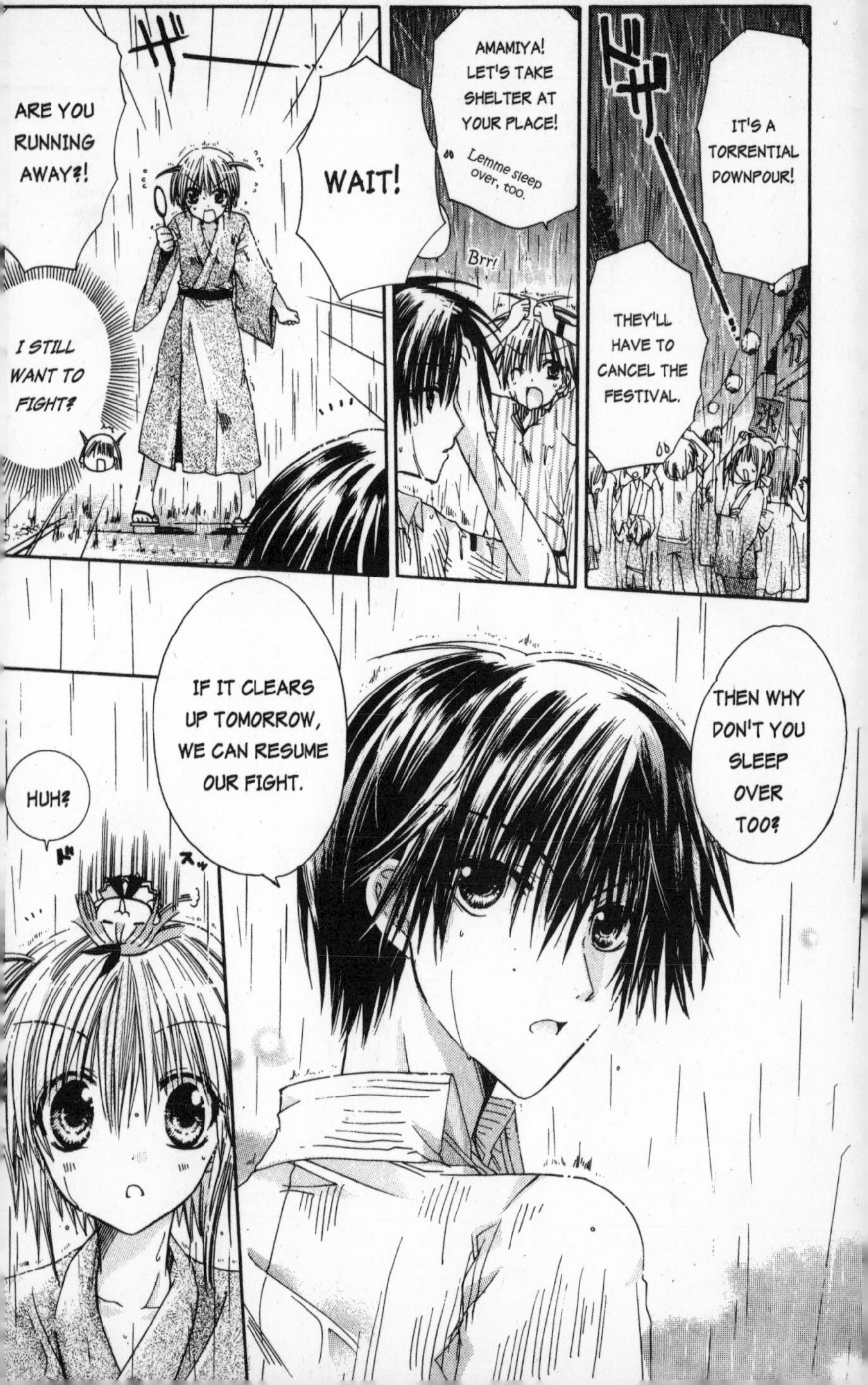
IT'S A TORRENTIAL DOWNPOUR!
THEY'LL HAVE TO CANCEL THE FESTIVAL.
AMAMIYA! LET'S TAKE SHELTER AT YOUR PLACE!
Lemme sleep over, too.
Brr!
WAIT!
ARE YOU RUNNING AWAY?!
I STILL WANT TO FIGHT?
THEN WHY DON'T YOU SLEEP OVER TOO?
IF IT CLEARS UP TOMORROW, WE CAN RESUME OUR FIGHT.
HUH?

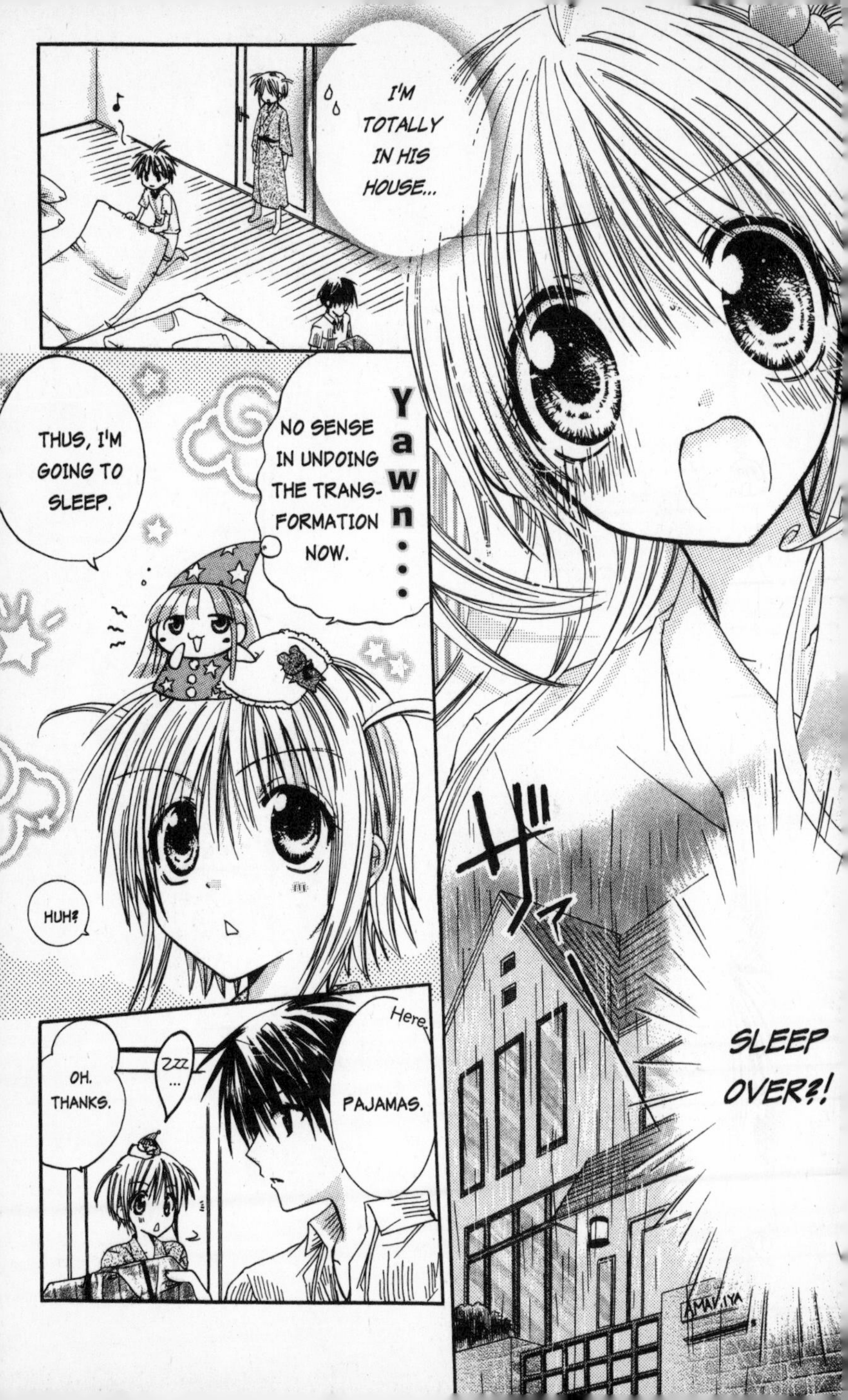
I'M TOTALLY IN HIS HOUSE...
SLEEP OVER?!
NO SENSE IN UNDOING THE TRANS-FORMATION NOW.
Yawn...
THUS, I'M GOING TO SLEEP.
HUH?
Here. PAJAMAS.
ZZZ...
OH. THANKS.

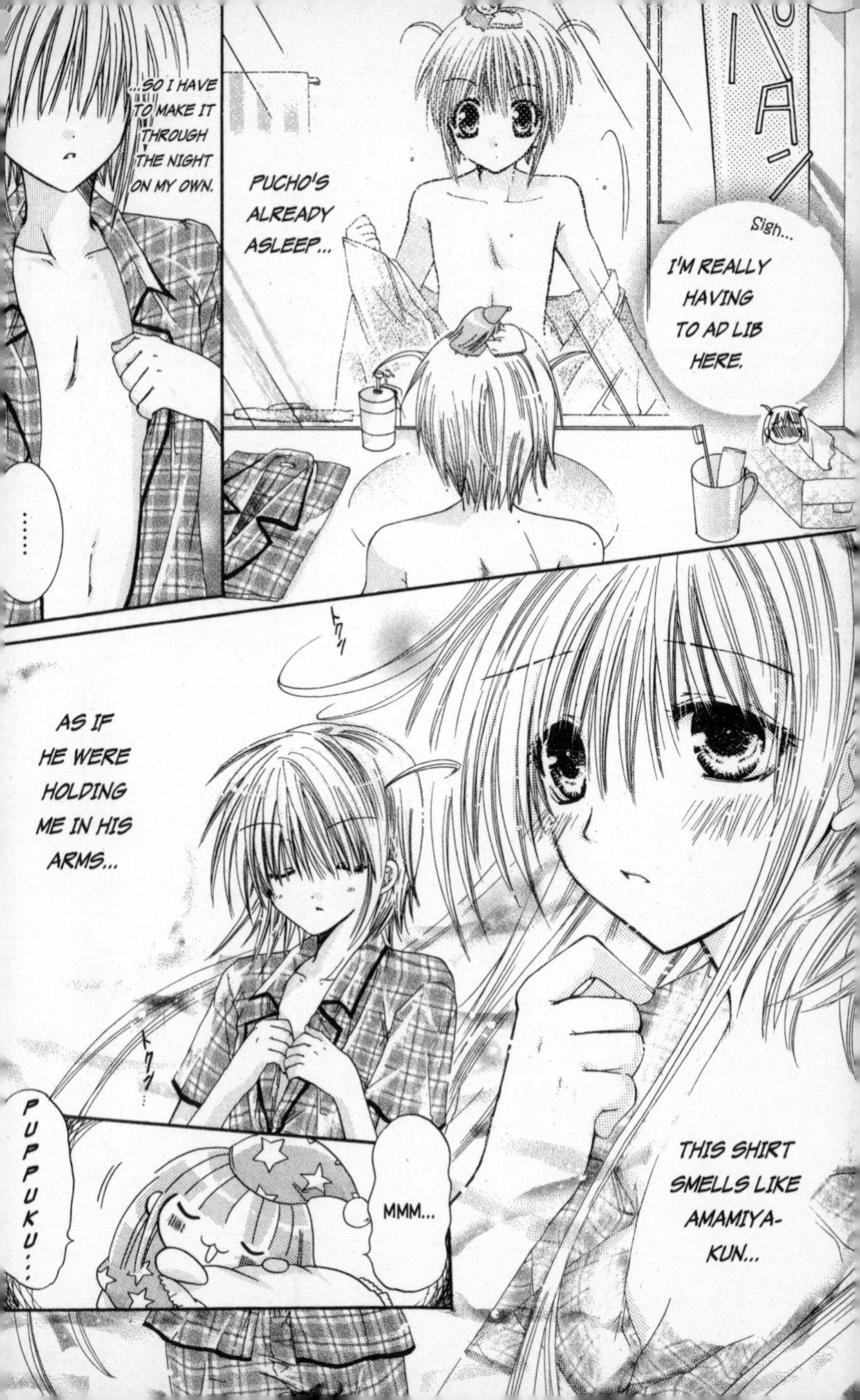

Sigh...
I'M REALLY HAVING TO AD LIB HERE.
PUCHO'S ALREADY ASLEEP...
...SO I HAVE TO MAKE IT THROUGH THE NIGHT ON MY OWN.
......
THIS SHIRT SMELLS LIKE AMAMIYA-KUN...
AS IF HE WERE HOLDING ME IN HIS ARMS...
MMM...
PUPPUKU...

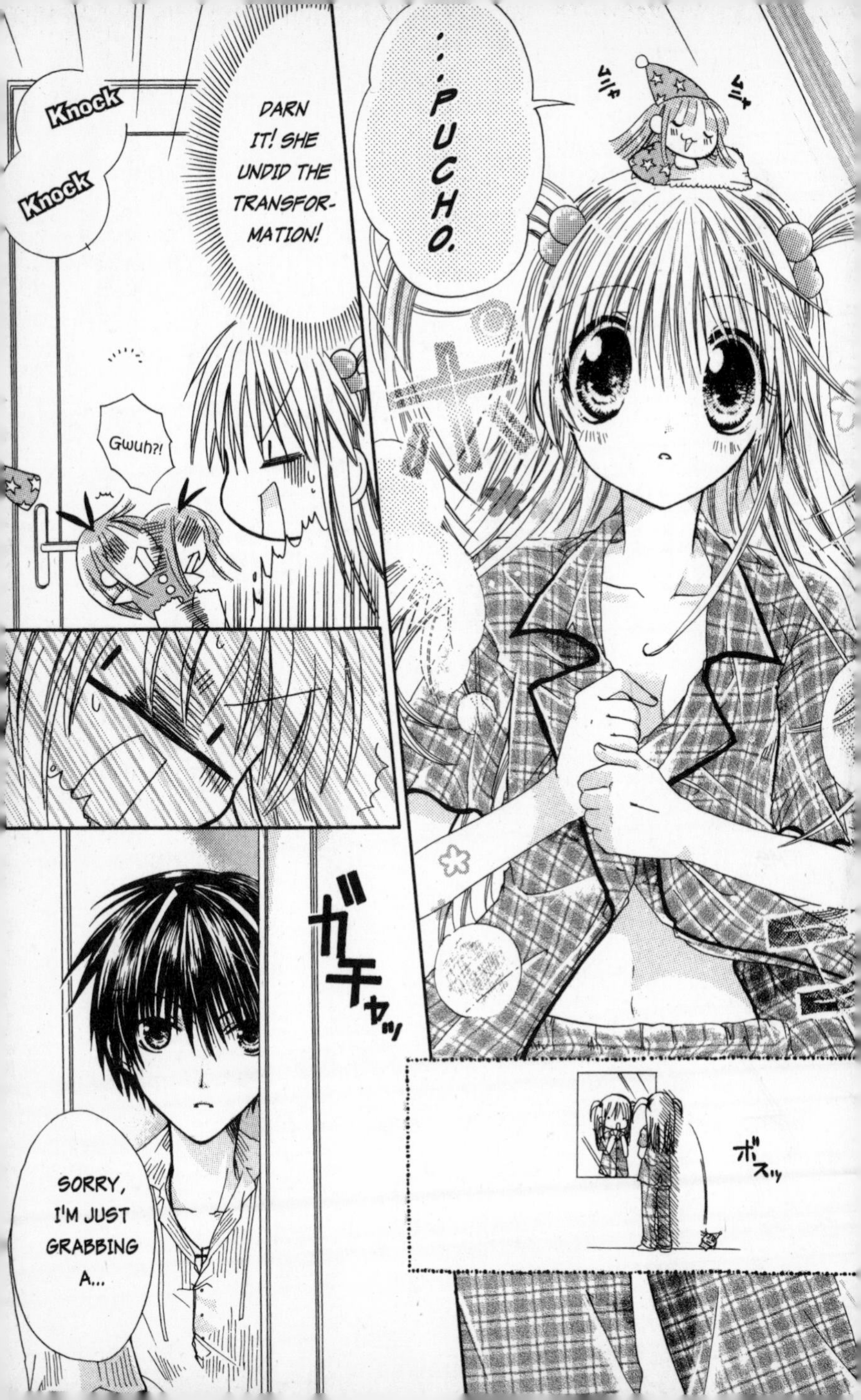
ムニャ
ムニャ
...PUCHO.
DARN IT! SHE UNDID THE TRANSFOR-MATION!
Knock
Knock
Gwuh?!
ガチャッ
SORRY, I'M JUST GRABBING A...
ボスッ

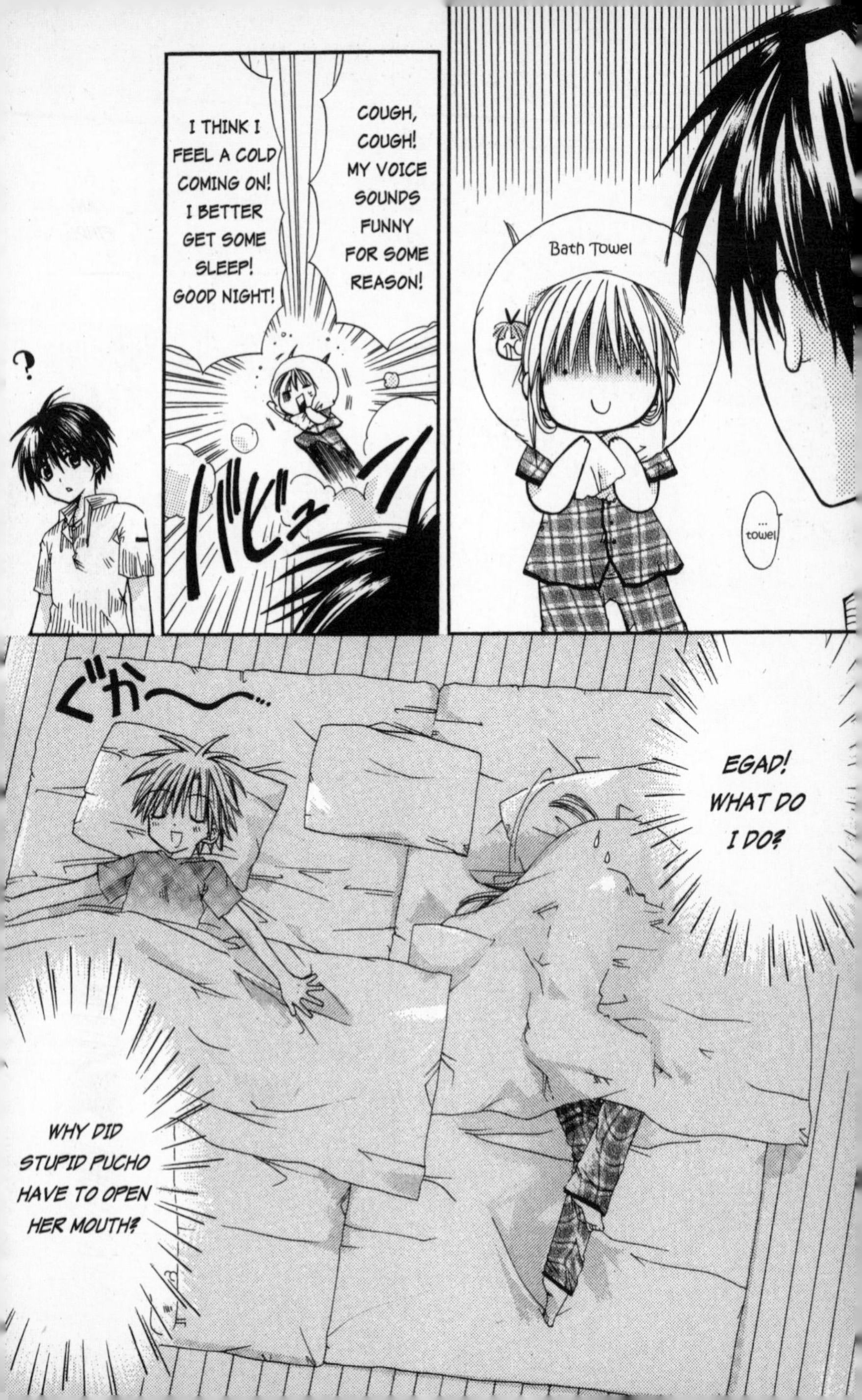
Bath Towel
... towel
COUGH, COUGH! MY VOICE SOUNDS FUNNY FOR SOME REASON!
I THINK I FEEL A COLD COMING ON! I BETTER GET SOME SLEEP! GOOD NIGHT!
バビュ
?
ぐか〜〜…
EGAD! WHAT DO I DO?
WHY DID STUPID PUCHO HAVE TO OPEN HER MOUTH?

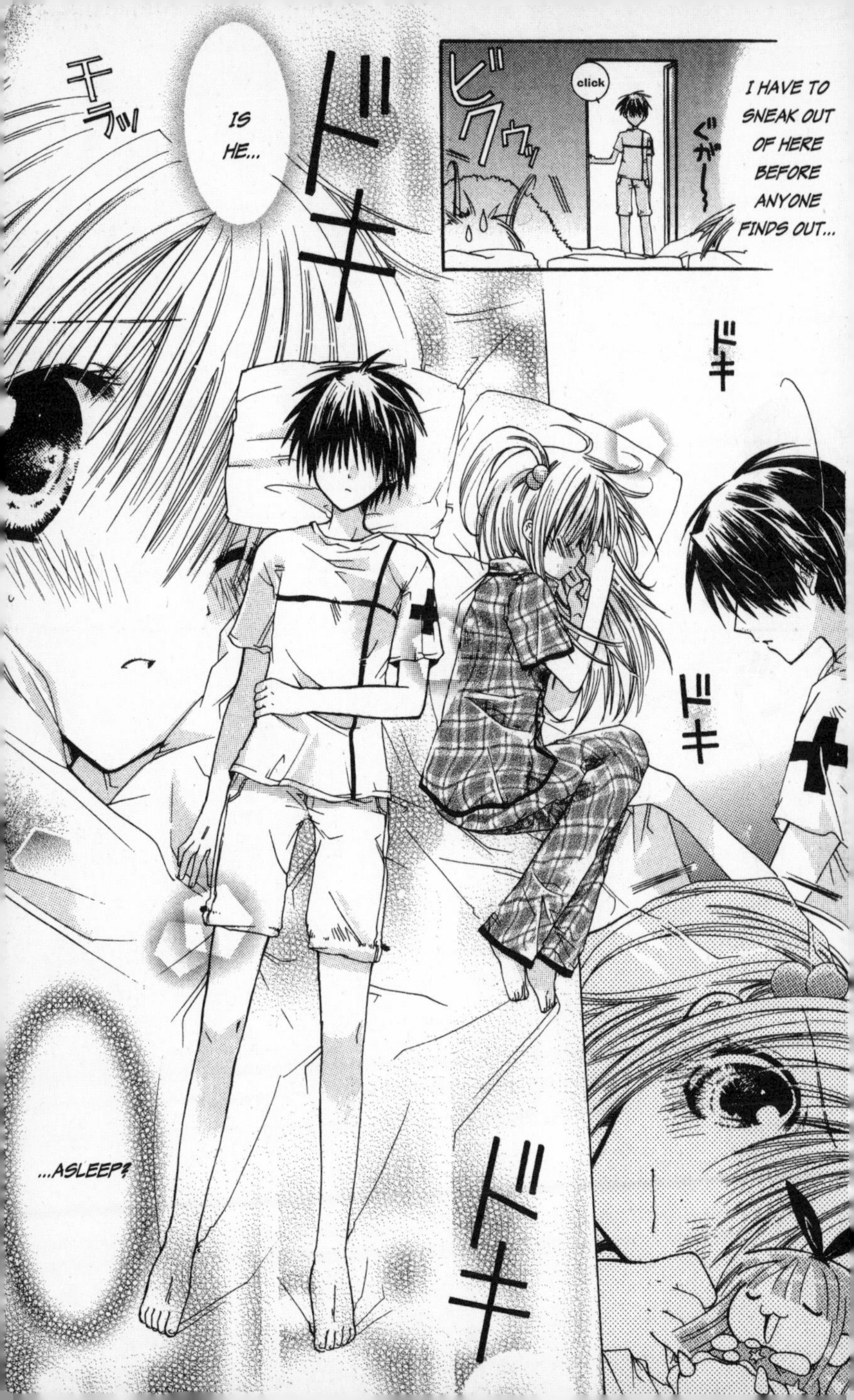

I HAVE TO SNEAK OUT OF HERE BEFORE ANYONE FINDS OUT...
ぐが～～
click
ビクゥッ
チラッ
IS HE...
ドキ
ドキ
ドキ
...ASLEEP?
ドキ

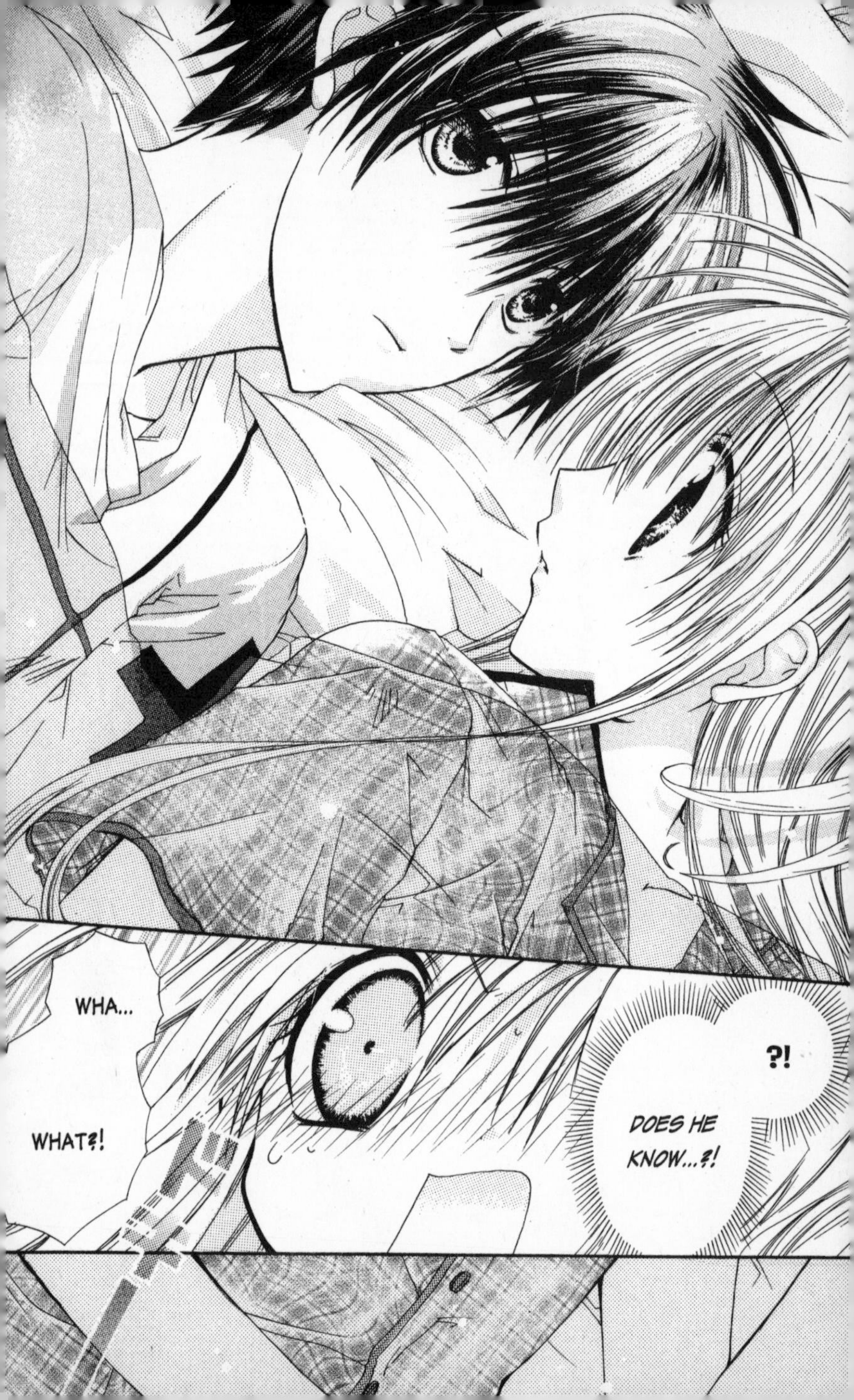
?!
DOES HE KNOW...?!
WHA...
WHAT?!

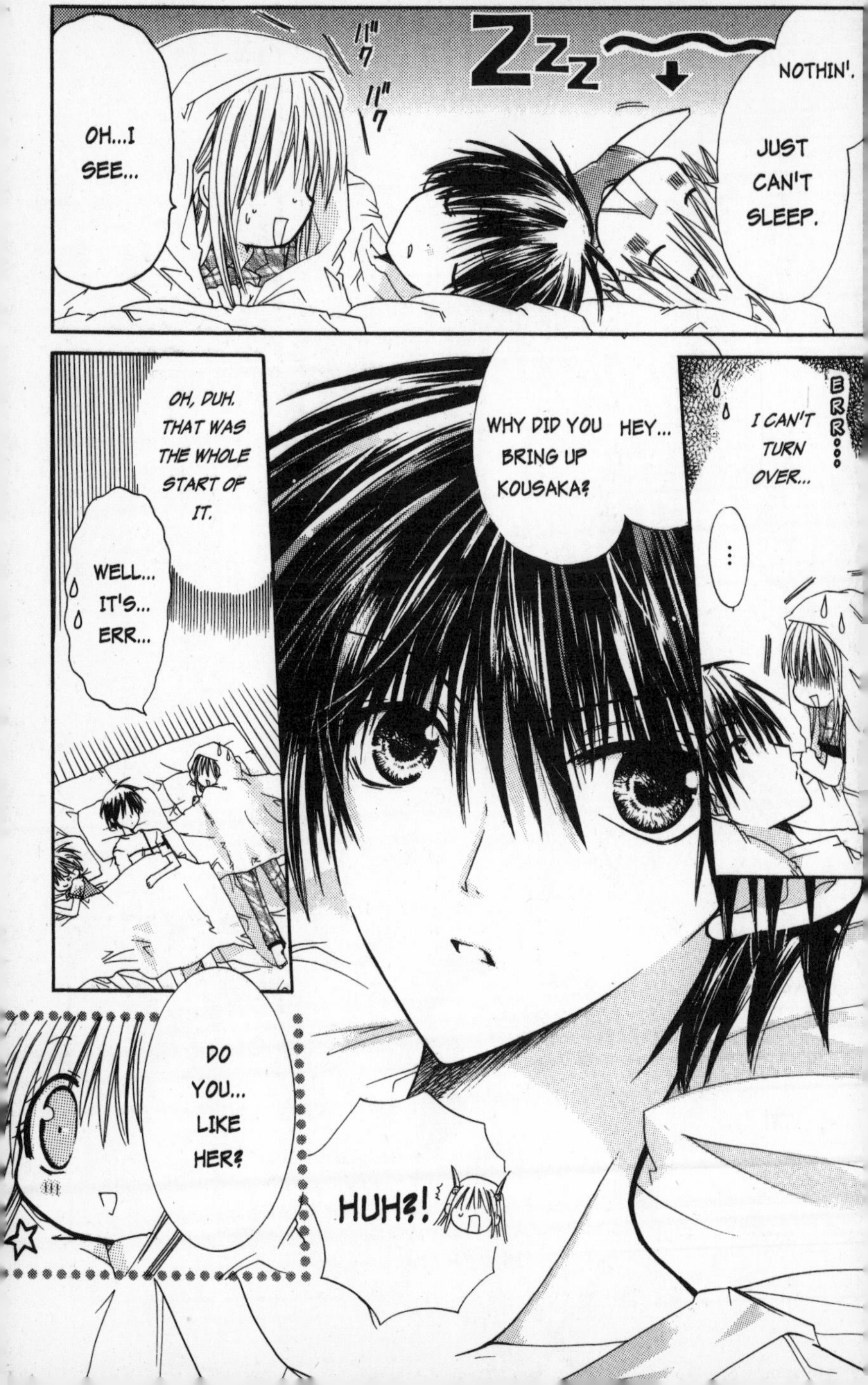

NOTHIN'.
JUST CAN'T SLEEP.
Zzz
バッ
バッ
OH...I SEE...
ERR...
I CAN'T TURN OVER...
...
HEY...
WHY DID YOU BRING UP KOUSAKA?
HUH?!
OH, DUH. THAT WAS THE WHOLE START OF IT.
WELL... IT'S... ERR...
DO YOU... LIKE HER?

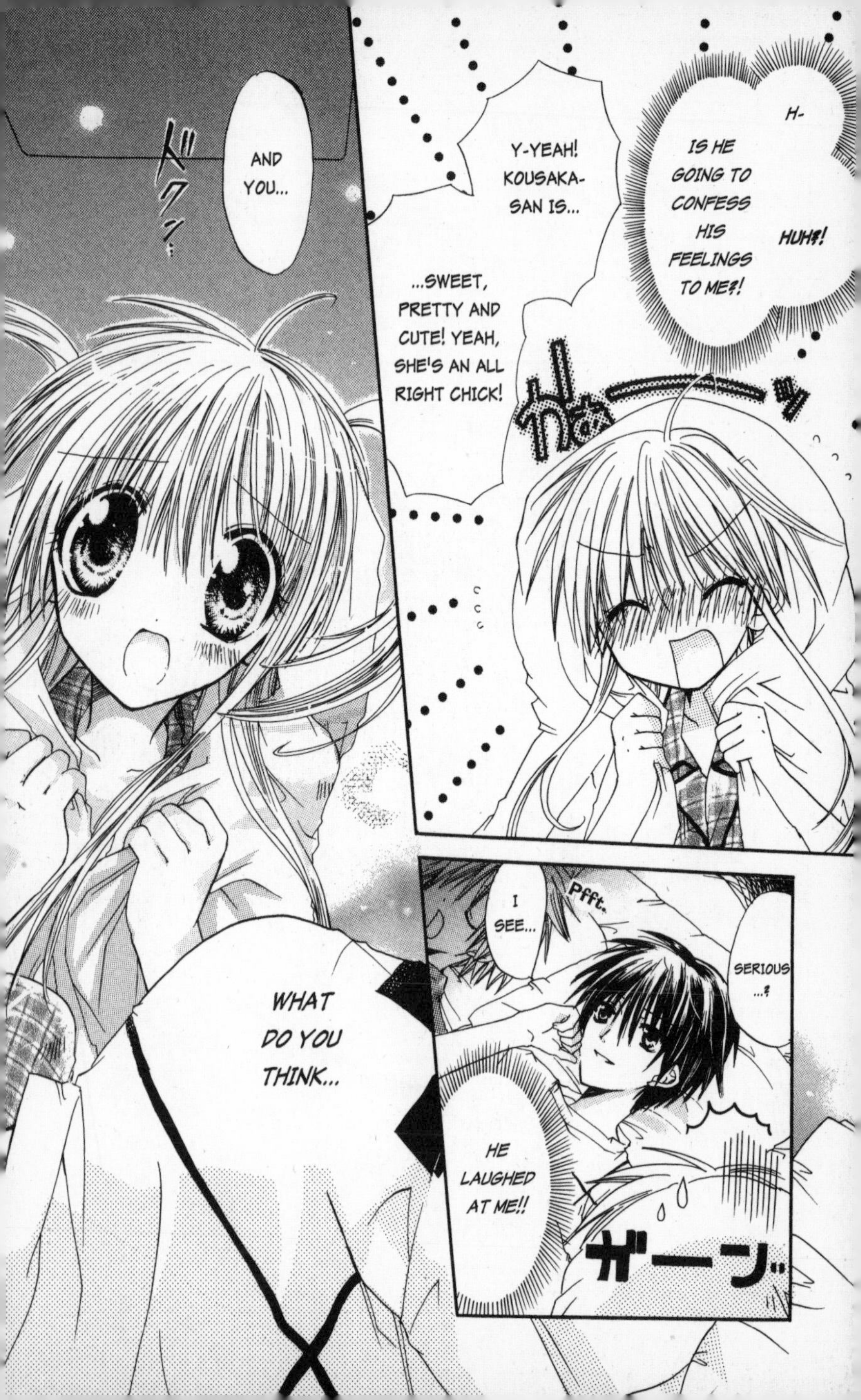
AND YOU...
WHAT DO YOU THINK...
H-
HUH?!
IS HE GOING TO CONFESS HIS FEELINGS TO ME?!
Y-YEAH! KOUSAKA-SAN IS...
...SWEET, PRETTY AND CUTE! YEAH, SHE'S AN ALL RIGHT CHICK!
SERIOUS ...?
I SEE...
Pfft.
HE LAUGHED AT ME!!
ガーン

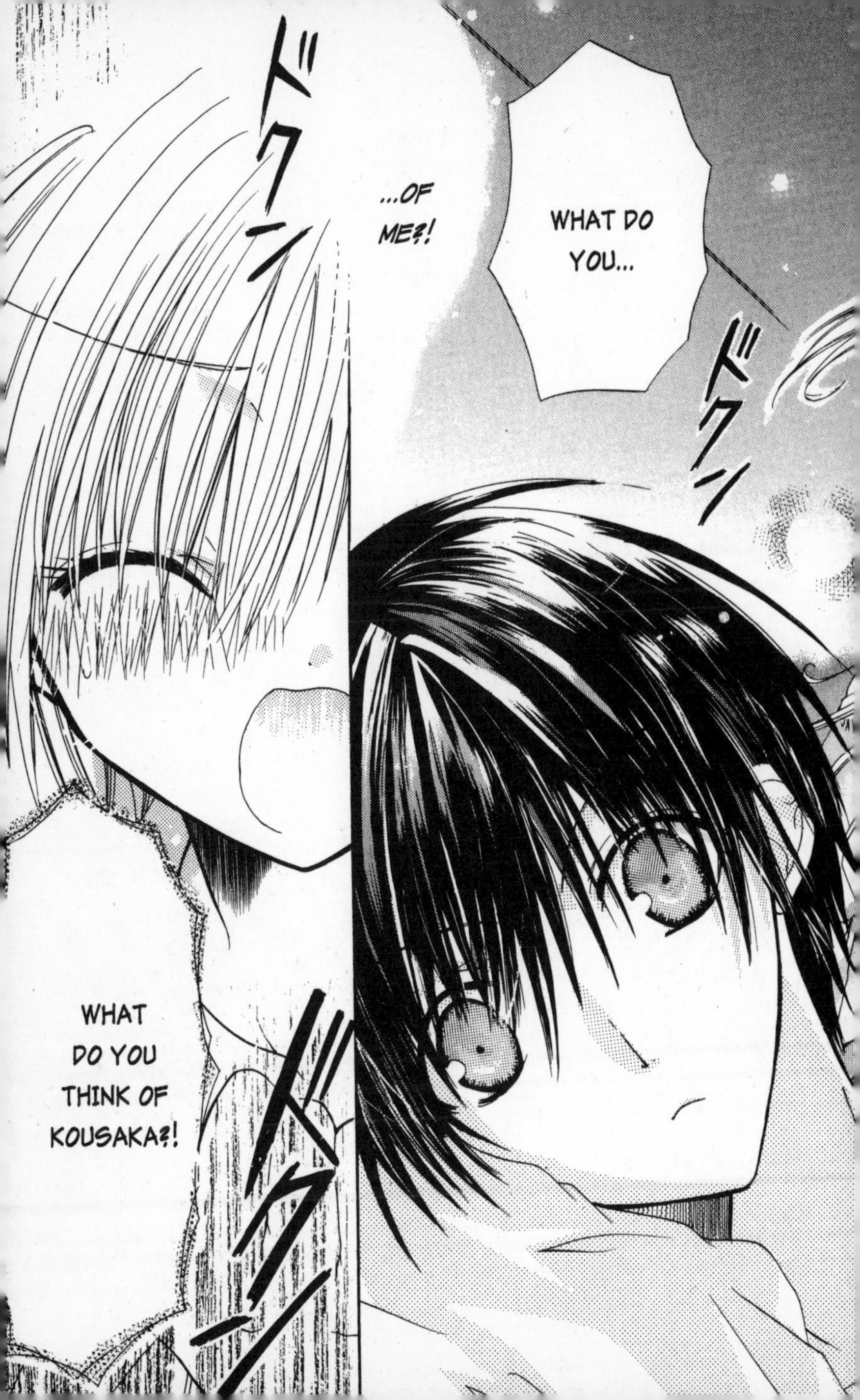
WHAT DO YOU...
ドクン
...OF ME?!
ドクン
WHAT DO YOU THINK OF KOUSAKA?!
ドクン

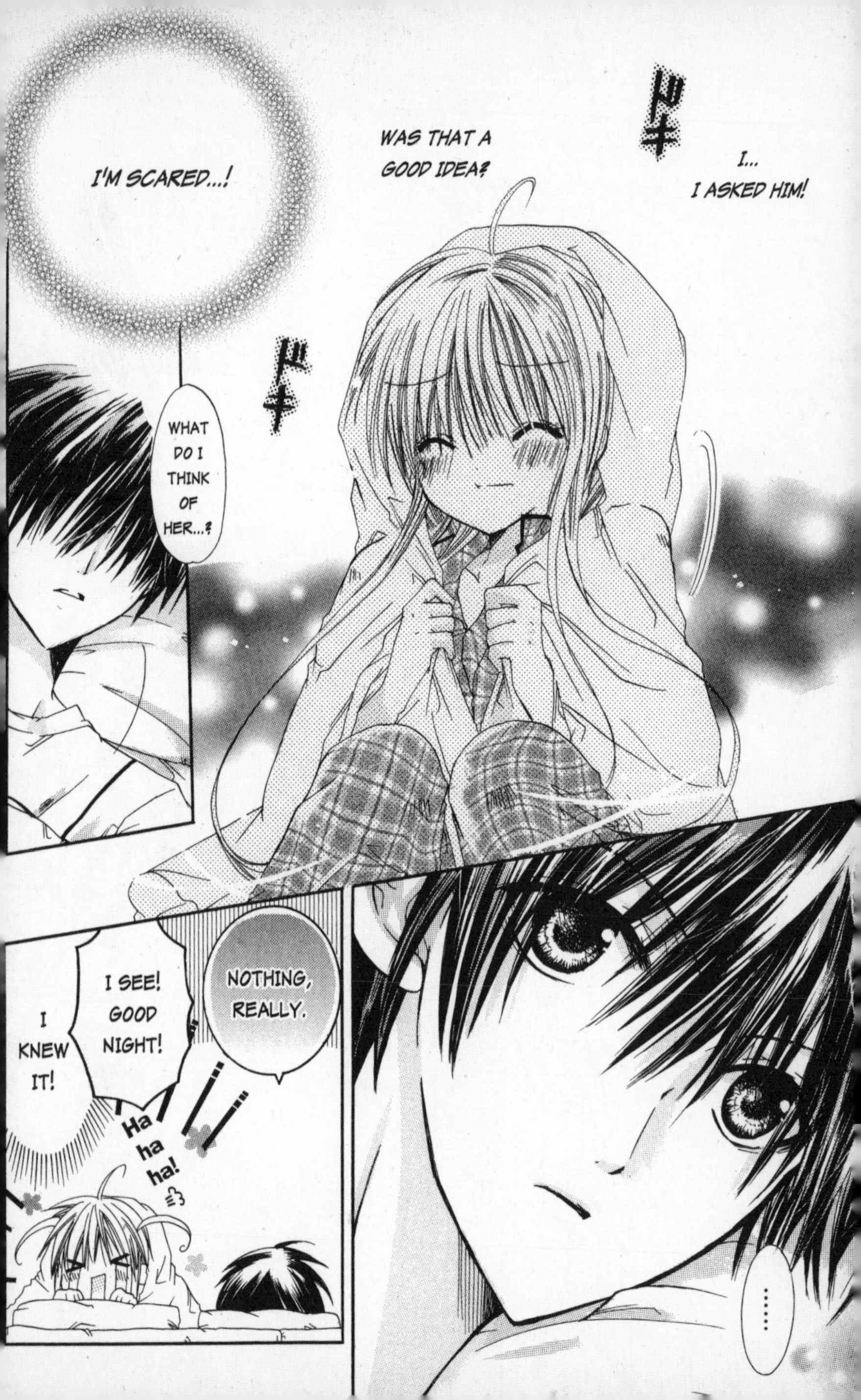

I...
I ASKED HIM!
ドキ
WAS THAT A GOOD IDEA?
ドキ
I'M SCARED...!
WHAT DO I THINK OF HER...?
......
NOTHING, REALLY.
I SEE! GOOD NIGHT!
I KNEW IT!
Ha ha ha!

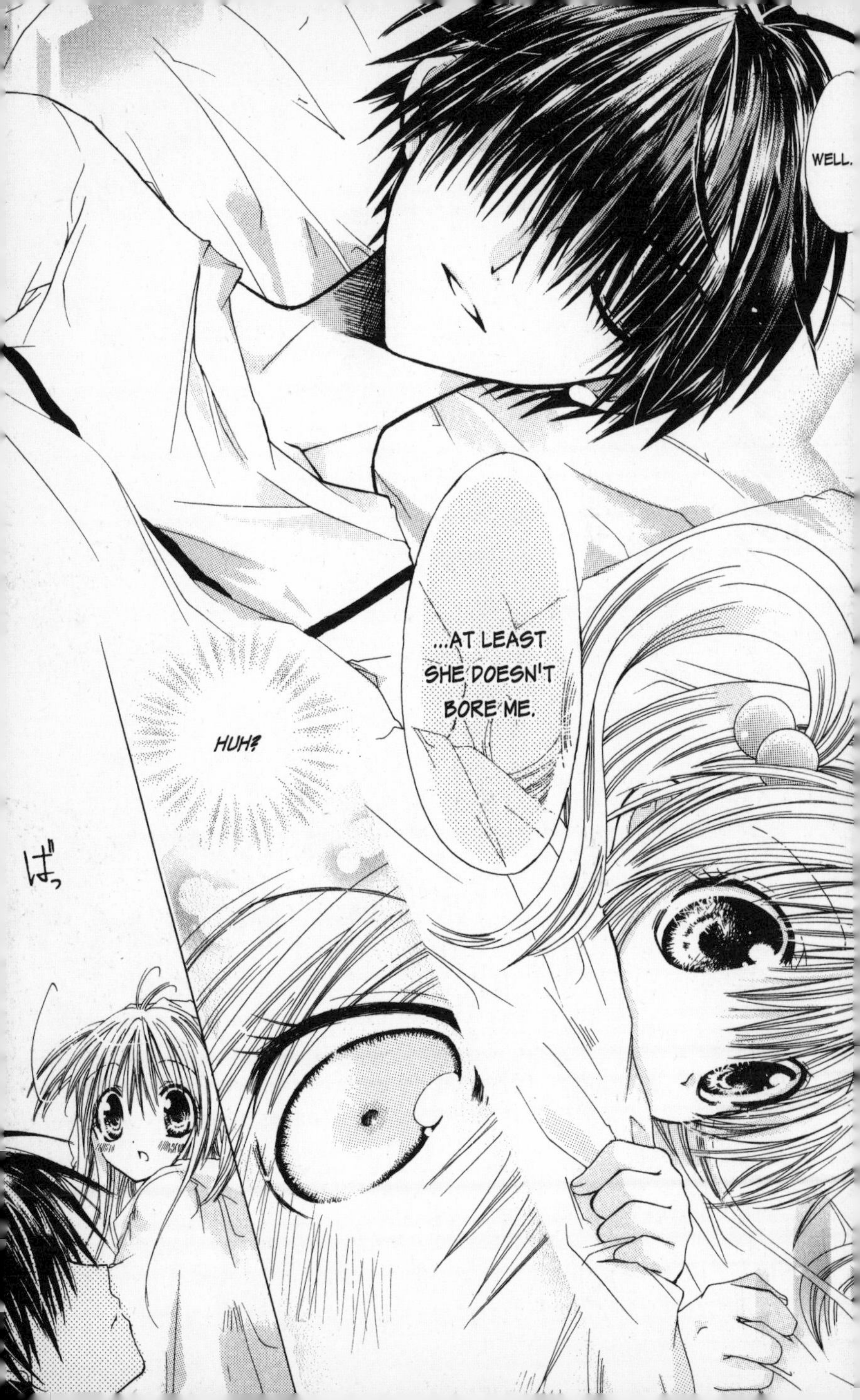
WELL.
...AT LEAST SHE DOESN'T BORE ME.
HUH?
ばっ

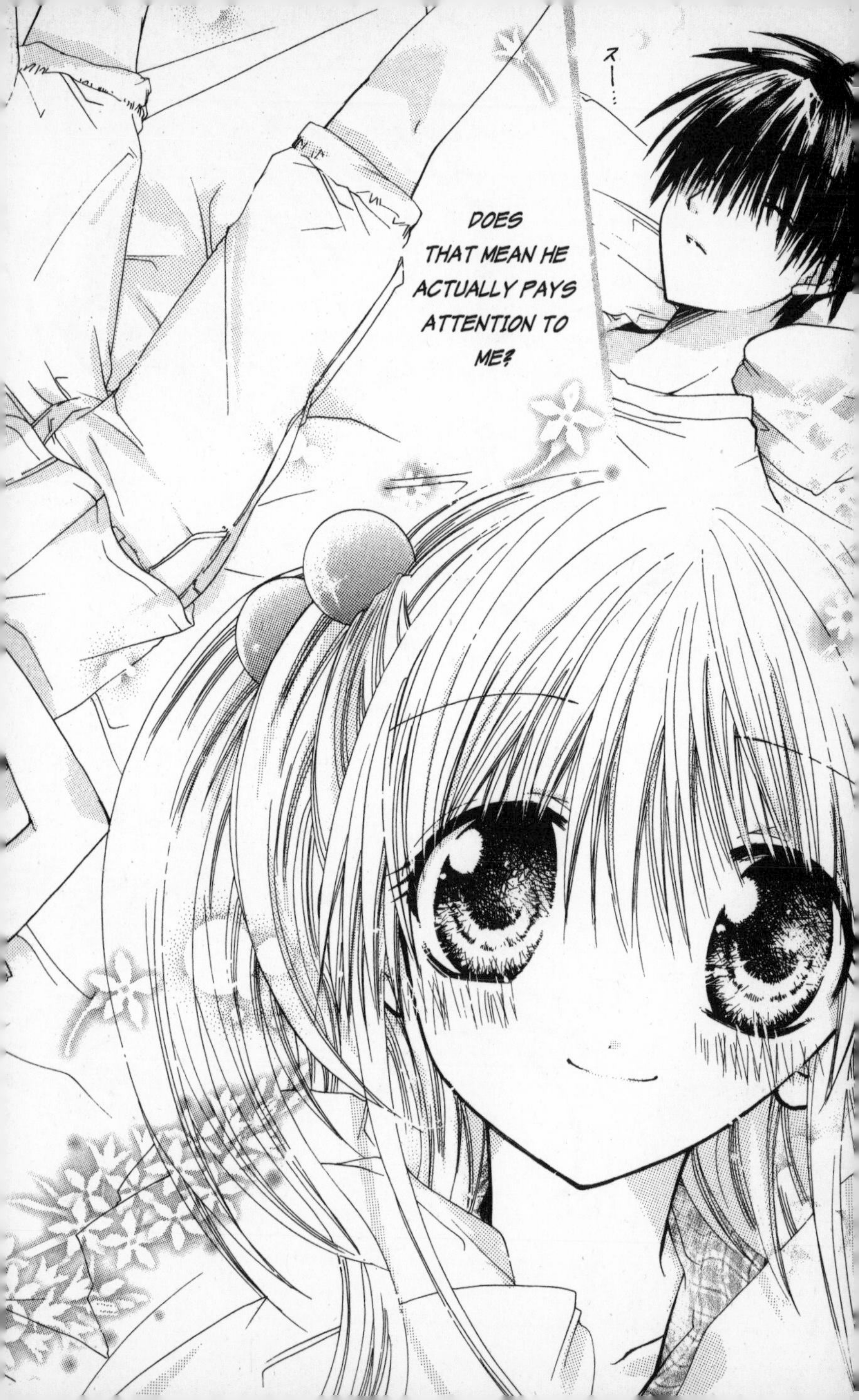
スー…
DOES THAT MEAN HE ACTUALLY PAYS ATTENTION TO ME?

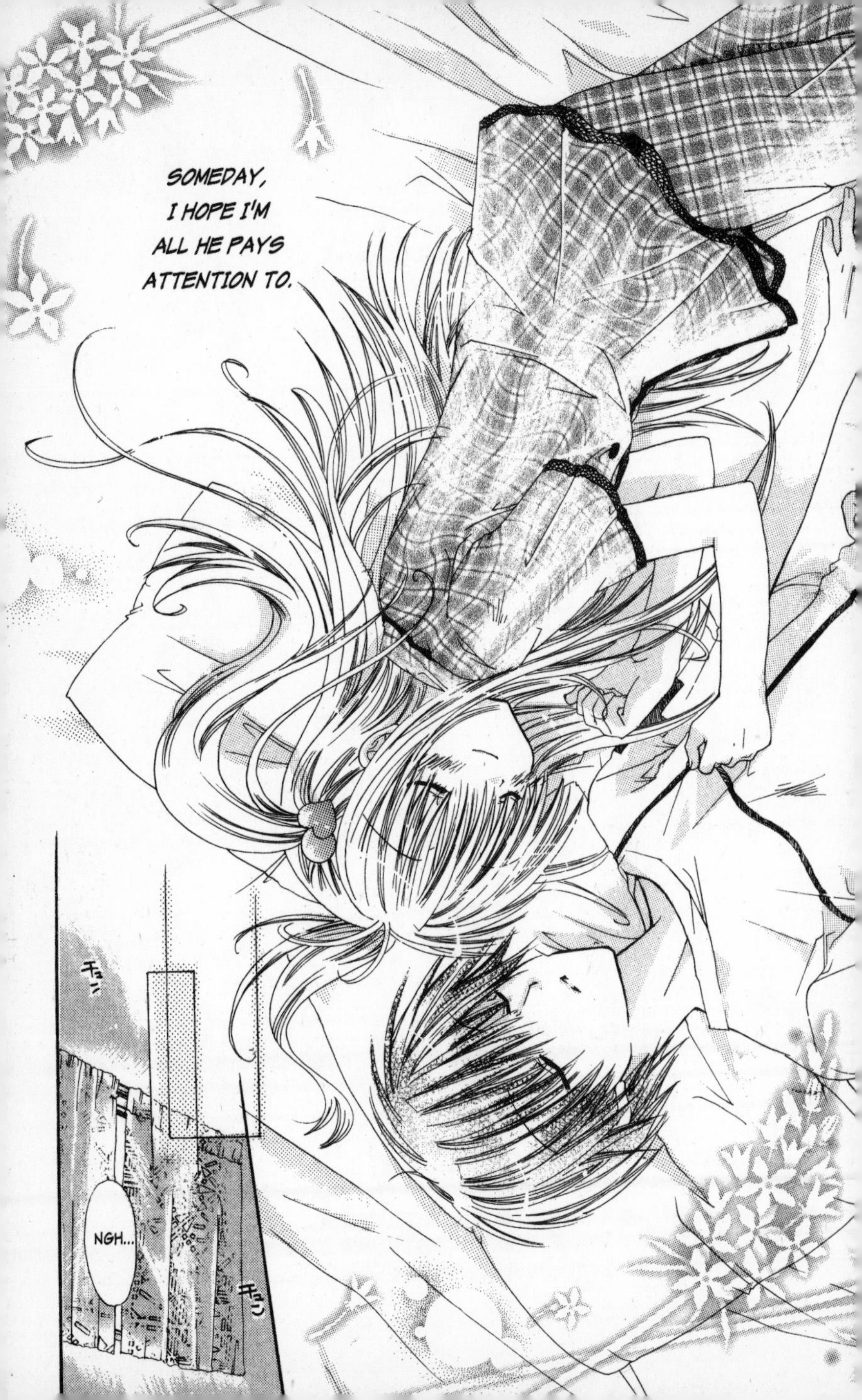
SOMEDAY, I HOPE I'M ALL HE PAYS ATTENTION TO.
NGH...

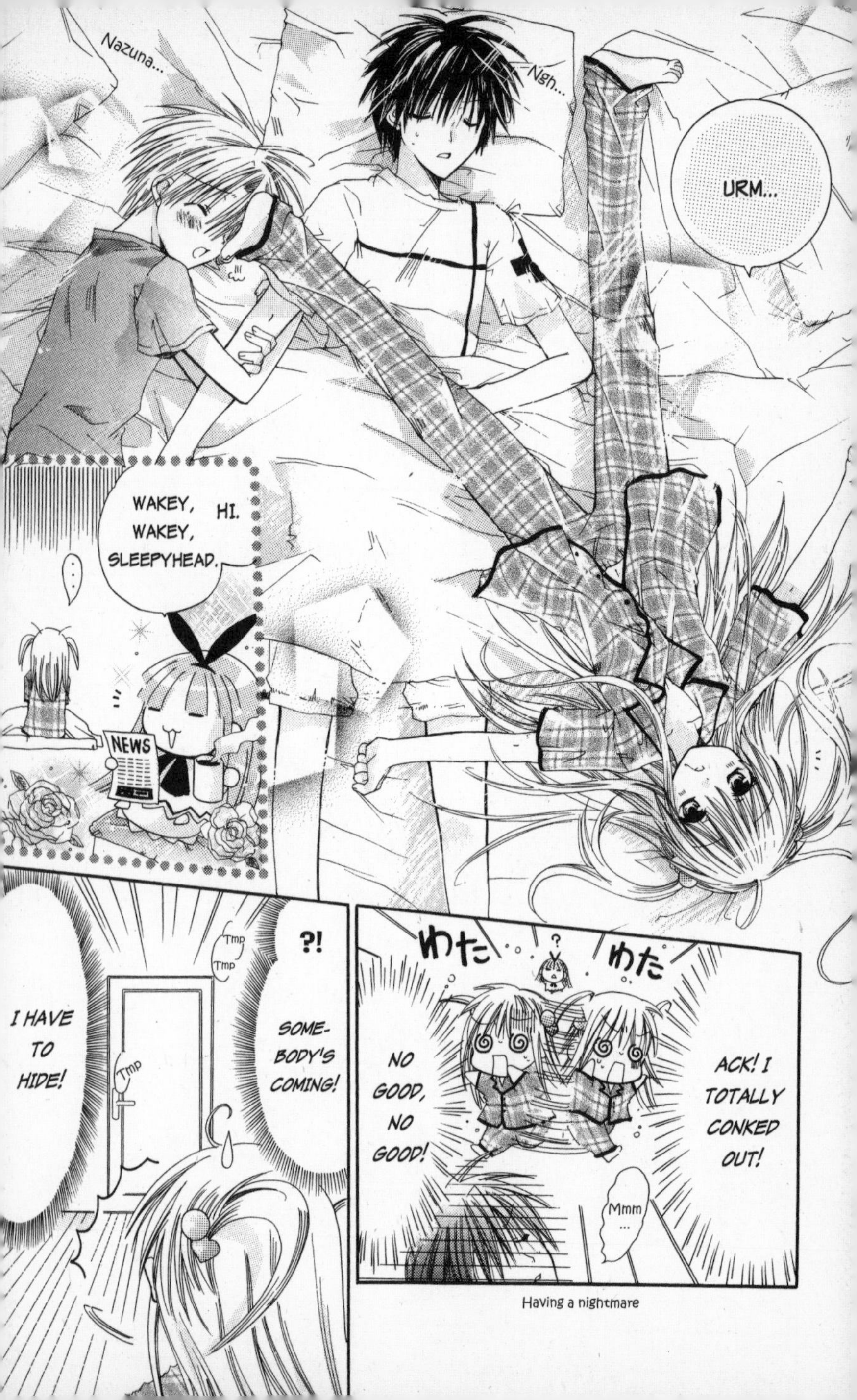
Ngh...
Nazuna...
URM...
HI.
WAKEY, WAKEY, SLEEPYHEAD.
...
NEWS
わた
わた
?
ACK! I TOTALLY CONKED OUT!
NO GOOD, NO GOOD!
Mmm...
?!
Tmp
Tmp
SOME-BODY'S COMING!
Tmp
I HAVE TO HIDE!
Having a nightmare

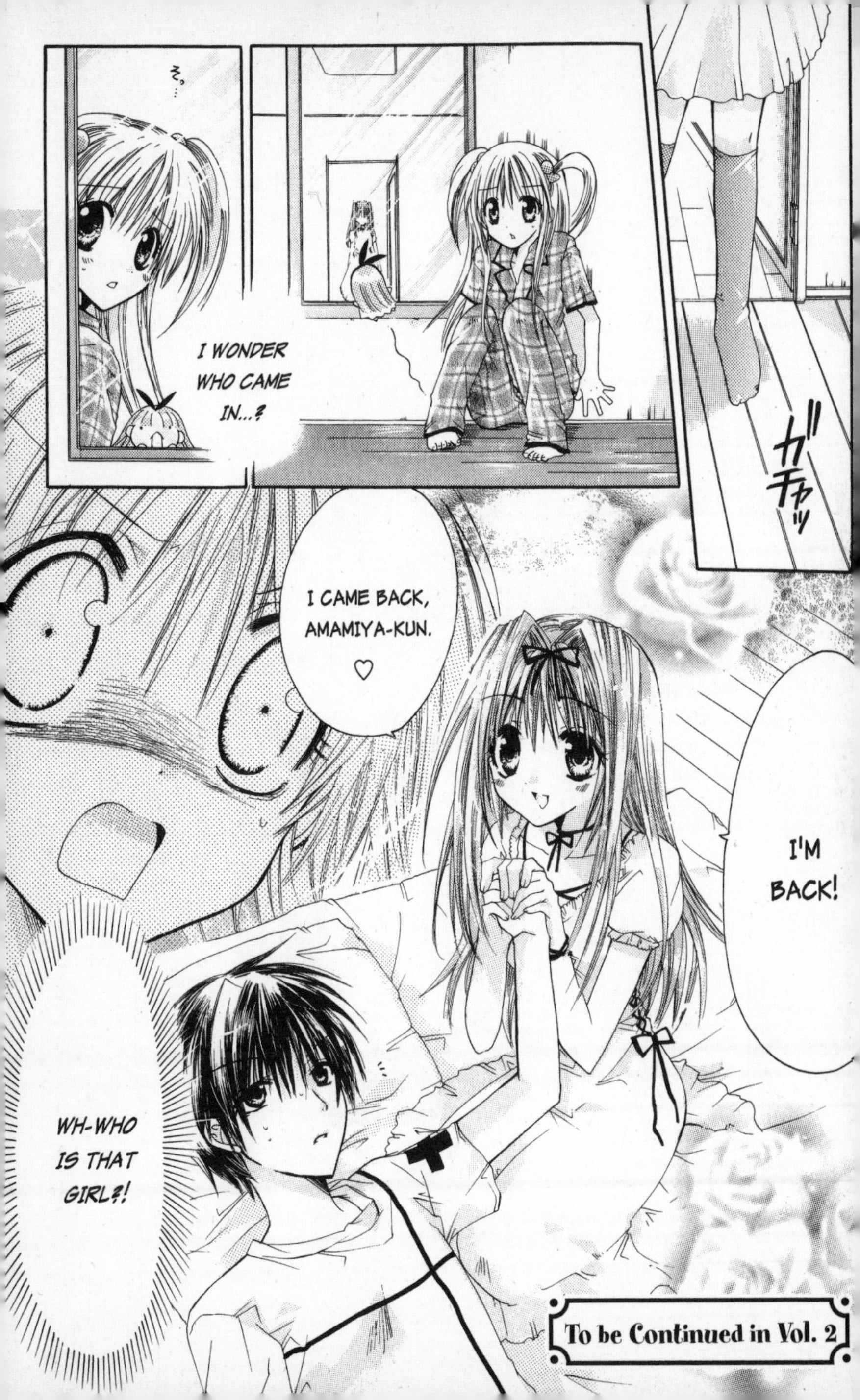
ガチャッ
そっ…
I WONDER WHO CAME IN...?
I'M BACK!
I CAME BACK, AMAMIYA-KUN. ♡
WH-WHO IS THAT GIRL?!
To be Continued in Vol. 2

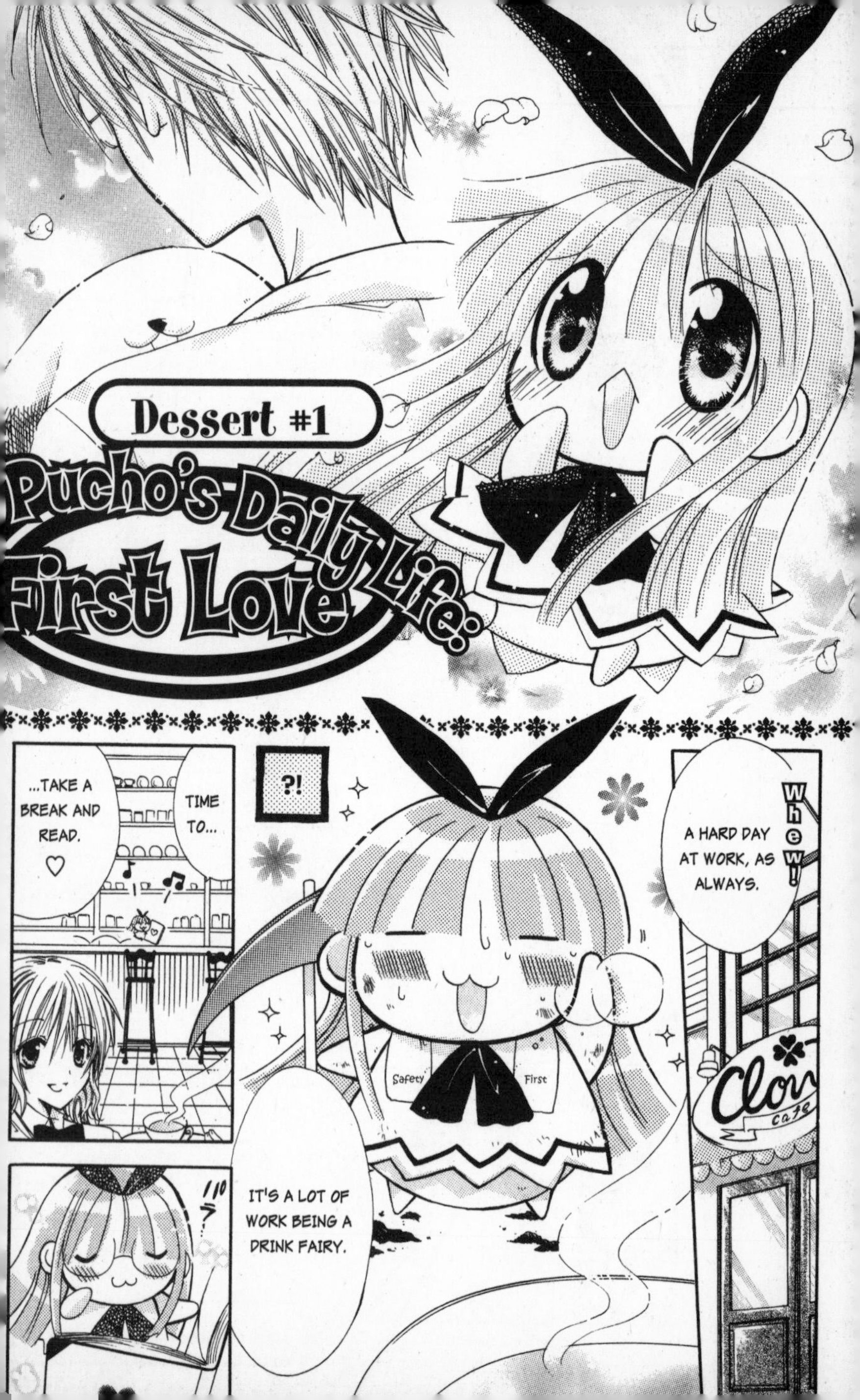

Dessert #1
Pucho's Daily Life: First Love
Whew!
A HARD DAY AT WORK, AS ALWAYS.
?!
IT'S A LOT OF WORK BEING A DRINK FAIRY.
Safety First
TIME TO...
...TAKE A BREAK AND READ. ♡

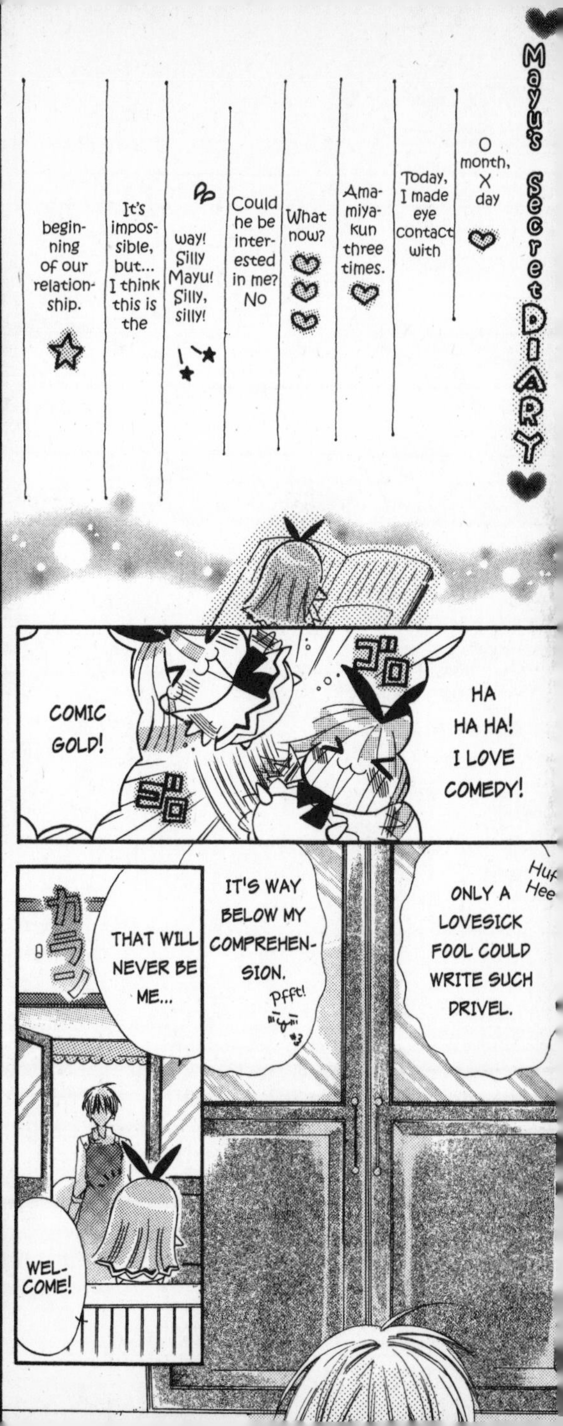
Mayu's Secret DIARY
O month, X day
Today, I made eye contact with
Amamiya-kun three times.
What now?
Could he be interested in me? No
way! Silly Mayu! Silly, silly!
It's impossible, but... I think this is the
beginning of our relationship.
HA HA HA! I LOVE COMEDY!
ゴロ
COMIC GOLD!
ゴロ
ONLY A LOVESICK FOOL COULD WRITE SUCH DRIVEL.
Huf Hee
IT'S WAY BELOW MY COMPREHENSION.
Pfft!
THAT WILL NEVER BE ME...
カラン
WEL-COME!

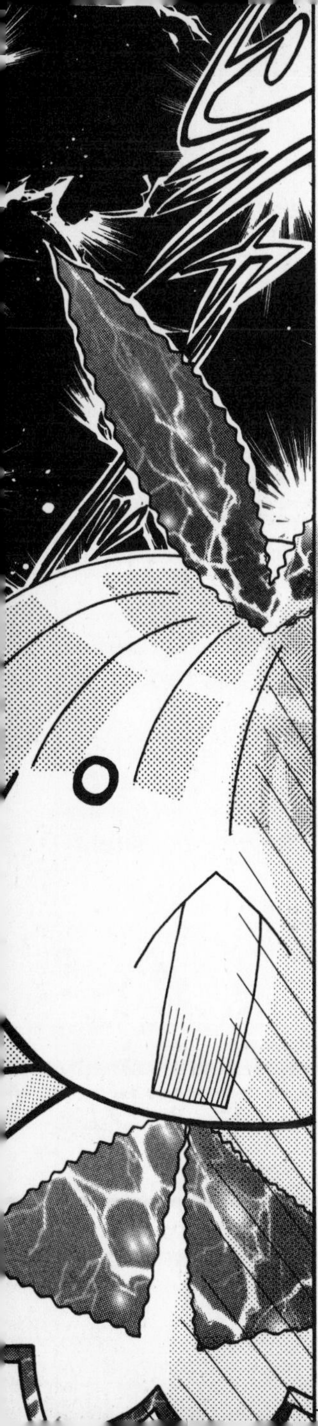

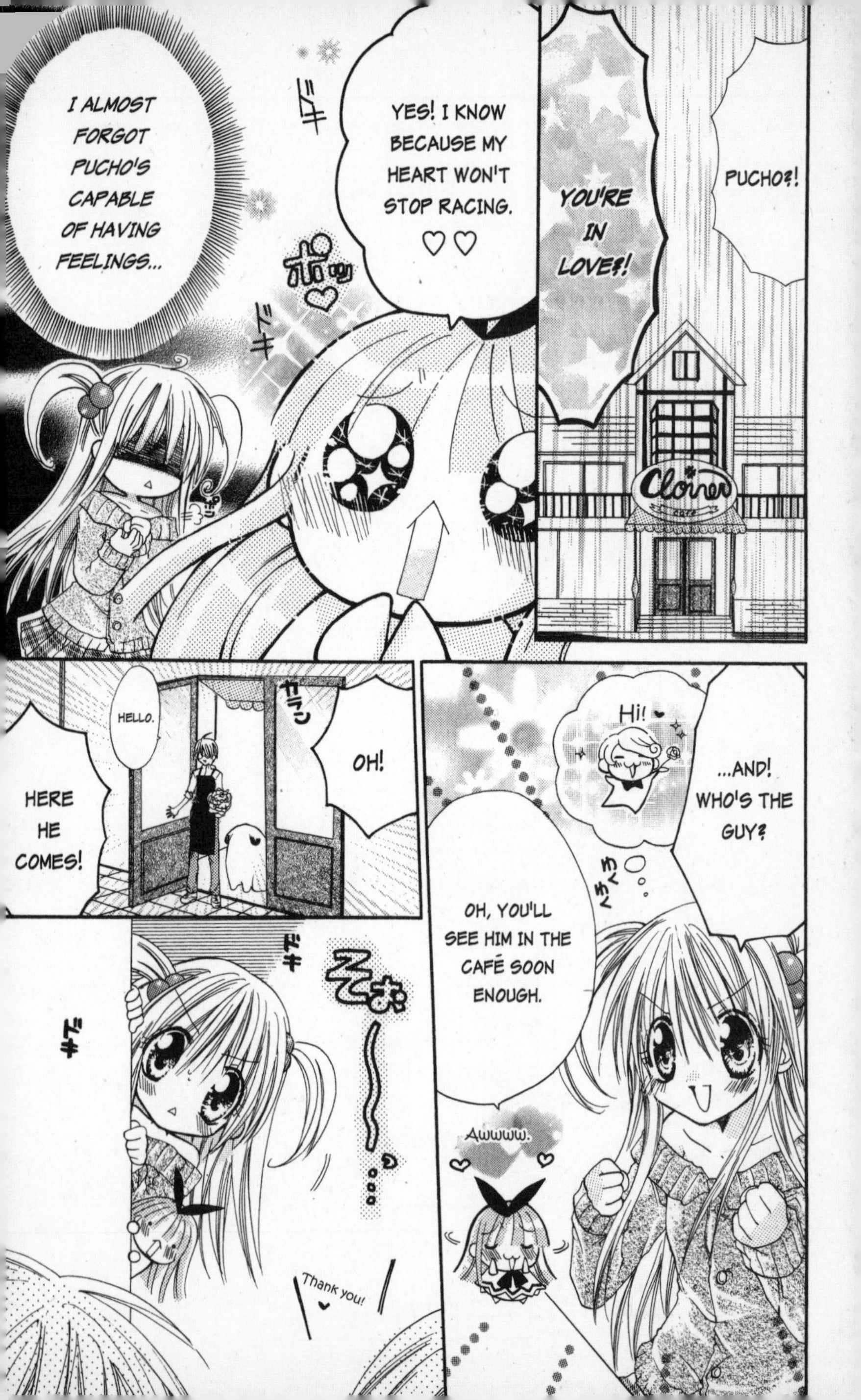
PUCHO?!
YOU'RE IN LOVE?!
YES! I KNOW BECAUSE MY HEART WON'T STOP RACING. ♡♡
I ALMOST FORGOT PUCHO'S CAPABLE OF HAVING FEELINGS...
...AND! WHO'S THE GUY?
Hi!
OH, YOU'LL SEE HIM IN THE CAFÉ SOON ENOUGH.
Awwww.
OH!
HELLO.
HERE HE COMES!
Thank you!

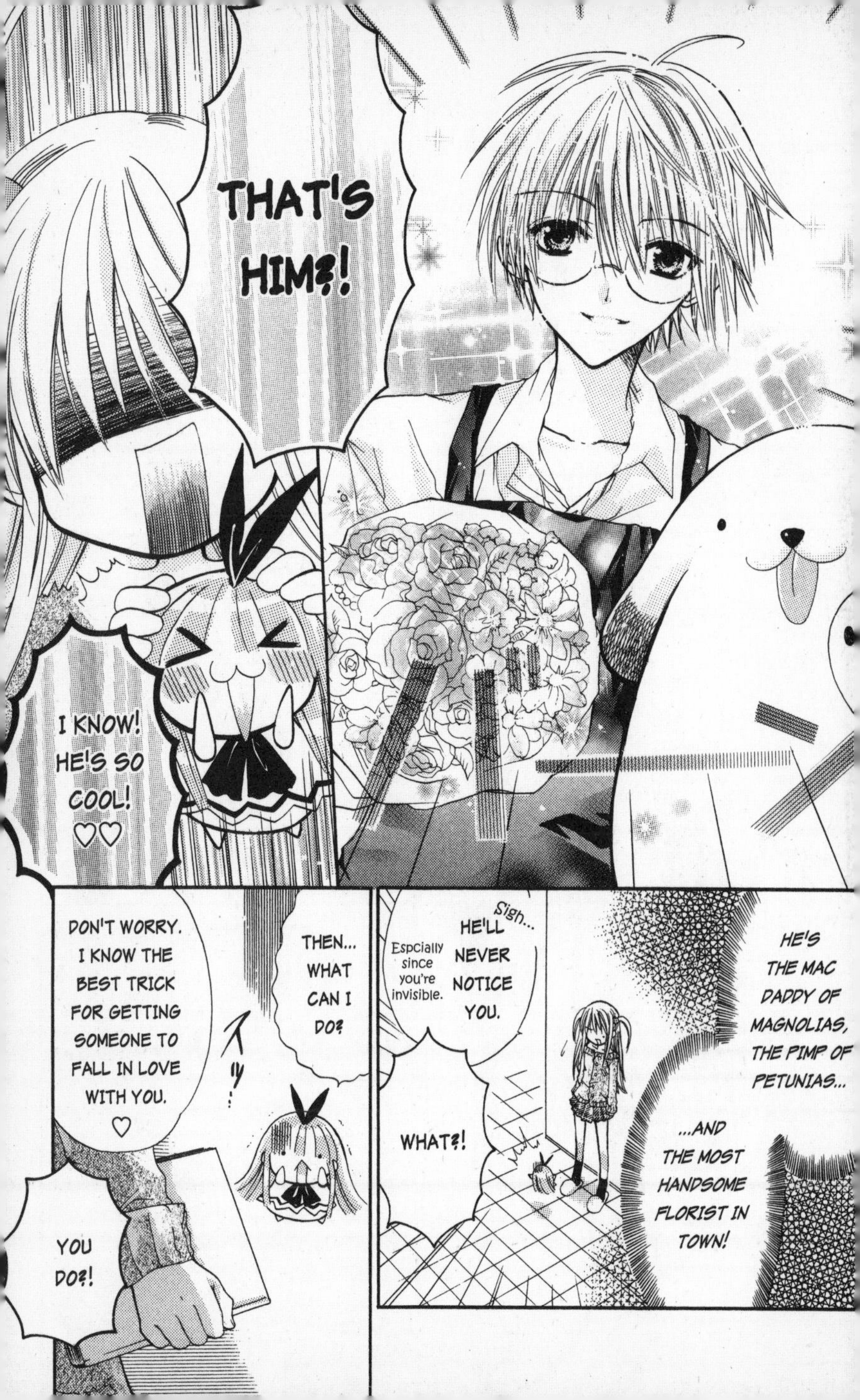
THAT'S HIM?!
I KNOW! HE'S SO COOL! ♡♡
HE'S THE MAC DADDY OF MAGNOLIAS, THE PIMP OF PETUNIAS...
...AND THE MOST HANDSOME FLORIST IN TOWN!
Sigh...
HE'LL NEVER NOTICE YOU.
Espcially since you're invisible.
WHAT?!
THEN... WHAT CAN I DO?
DON'T WORRY. I KNOW THE BEST TRICK FOR GETTING SOMEONE TO FALL IN LOVE WITH YOU. ♡
YOU DO?!

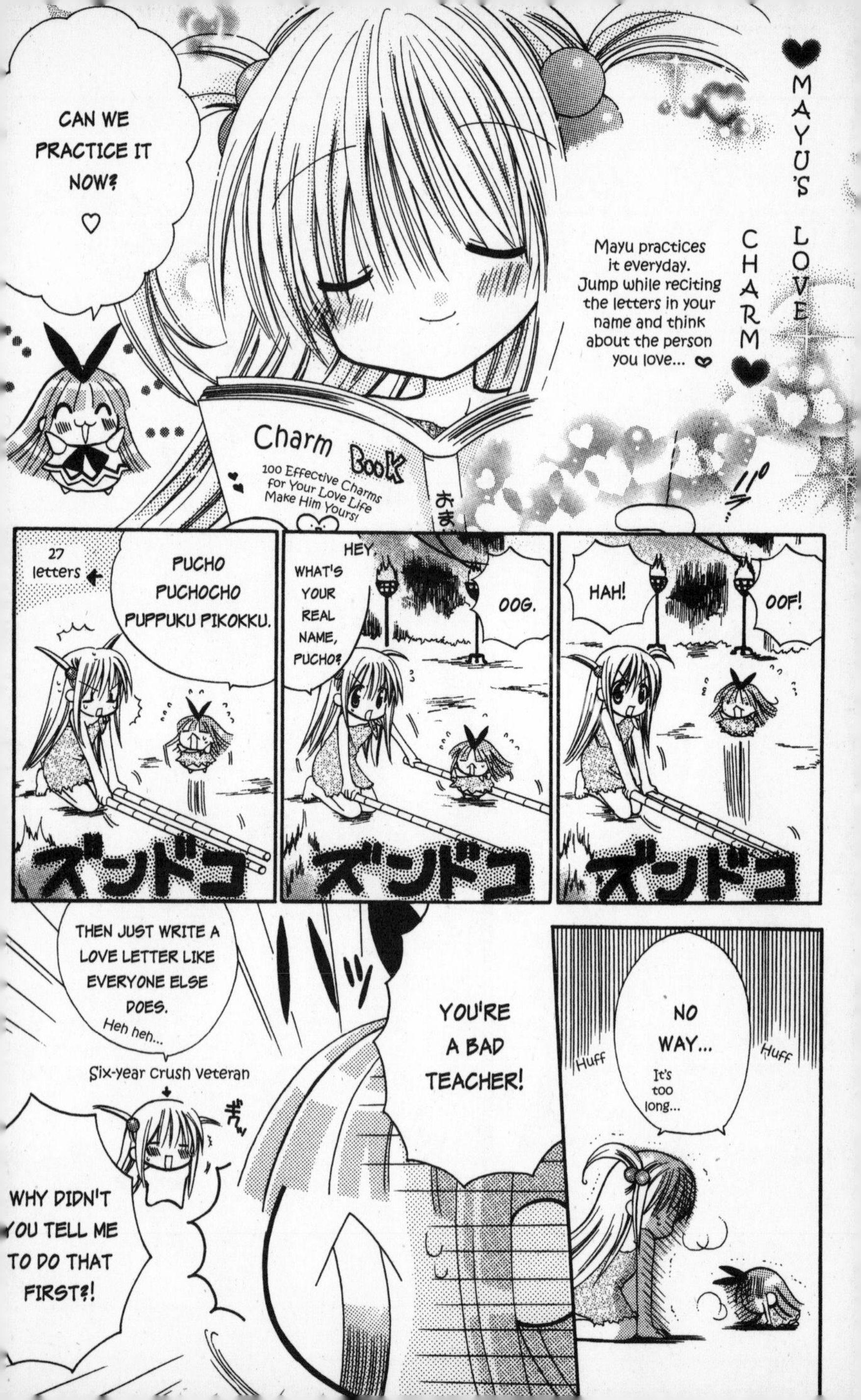

♥ MAYU'S LOVE CHARM ♥
Mayu practices it everyday. Jump while reciting the letters in your name and think about the person you love...
パ
Charm Book
100 Effective Charms for Your Love Life Make Him Yours!
CAN WE PRACTICE IT NOW? ♡
OOF!
HAH!
ズンドコ
OOG.
HEY, WHAT'S YOUR REAL NAME, PUCHO?
ズンドコ
PUCHO PUCHOCHO PUPPUKU PIKOKKU.
27 letters
ズンドコ
Huff
NO WAY...
It's too long...
Huff
THEN JUST WRITE A LOVE LETTER LIKE EVERYONE ELSE DOES.
Heh heh...
Six-year crush veteran
WHY DIDN'T YOU TELL ME TO DO THAT FIRST?!
YOU'RE A BAD TEACHER!

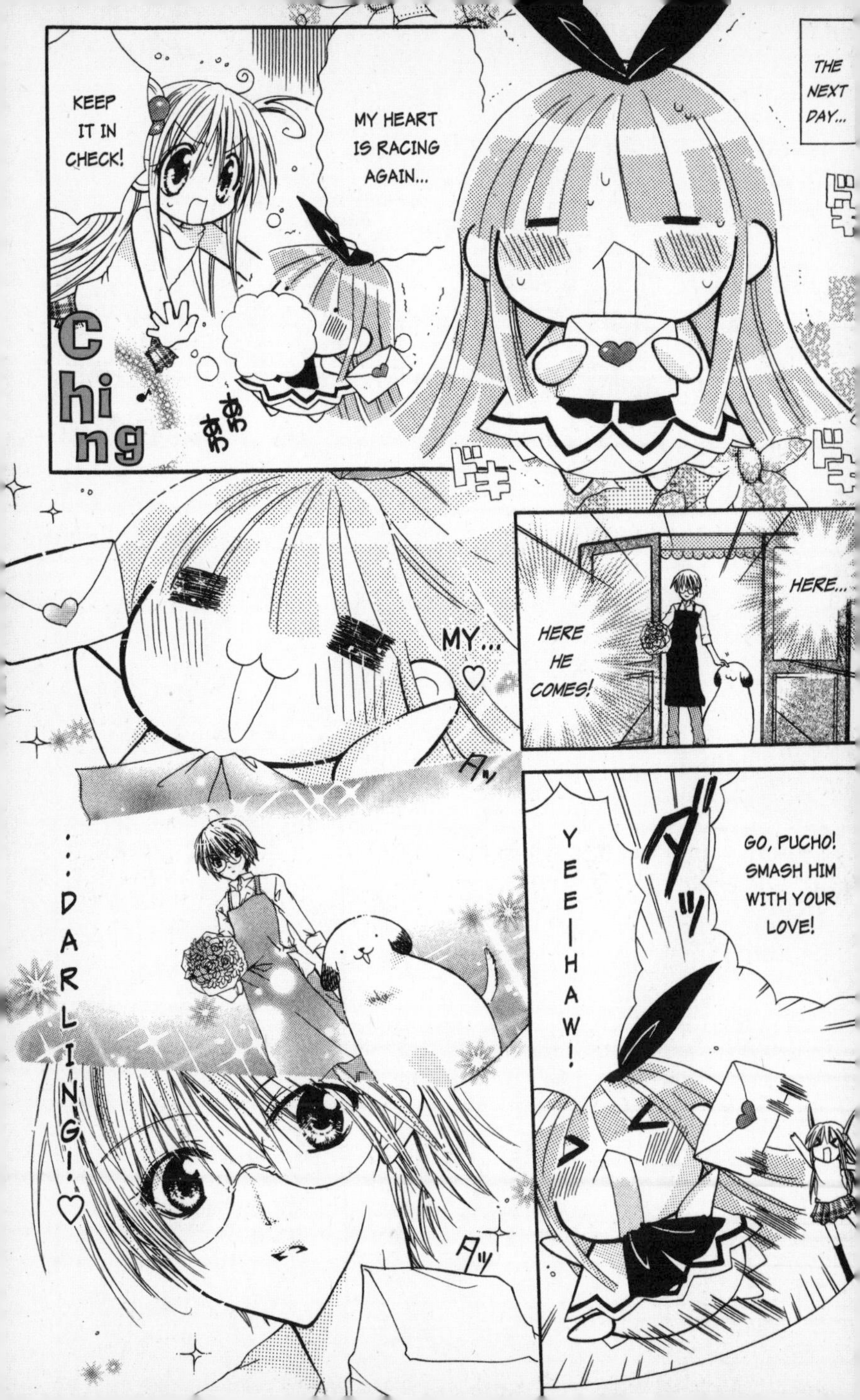
THE NEXT DAY...
ドキ
ドキ
ドキ
MY HEART IS RACING AGAIN...
KEEP IT IN CHECK!
あわあわ
Ching
HERE...
HERE HE COMES!
MY... ♡
タッ
GO, PUCHO! SMASH HIM WITH YOUR LOVE!
ダッ
YEEIHAW!
...DARLING!♡
タッ

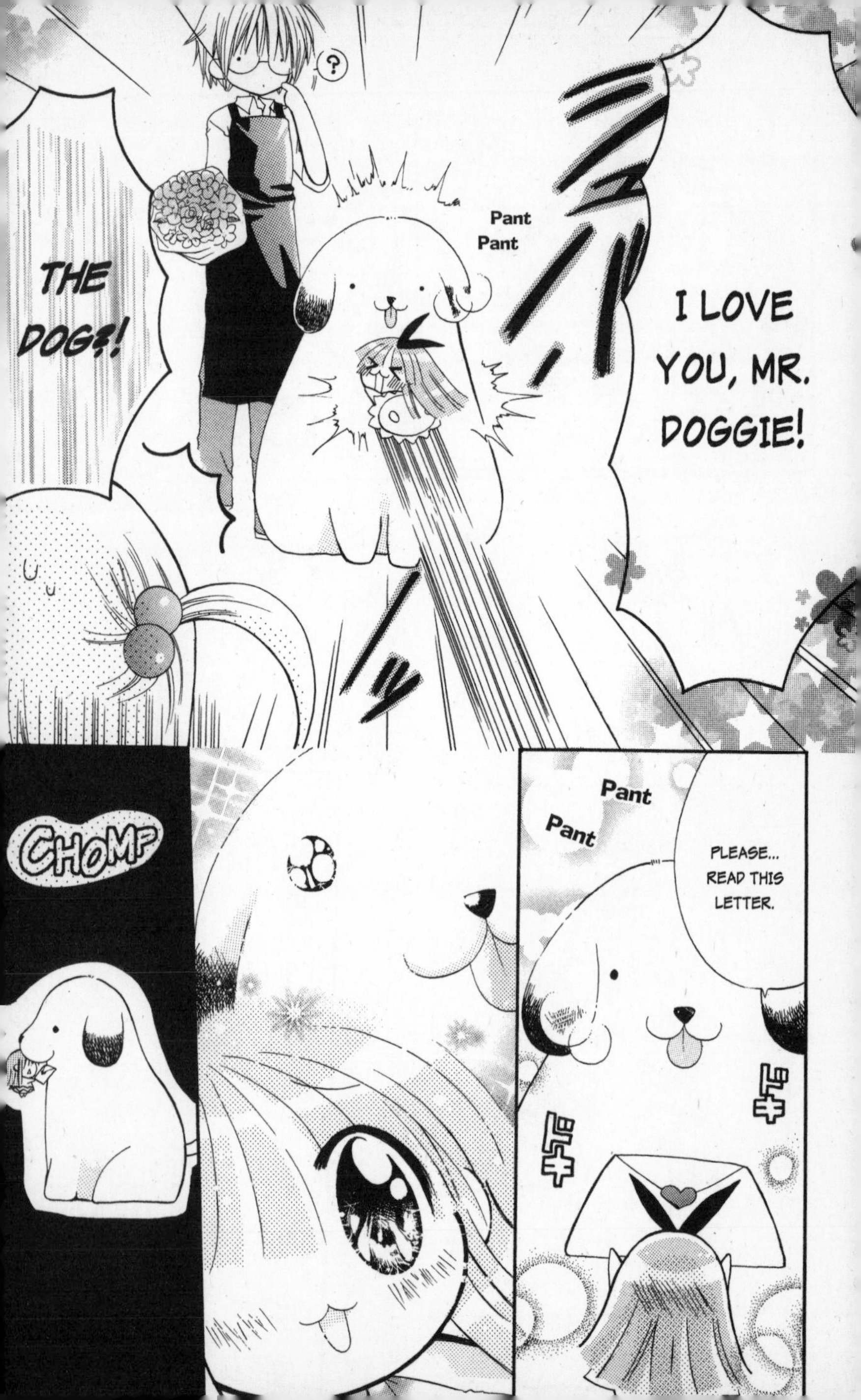
I LOVE YOU, MR. DOGGIE!
Pant
Pant
?
THE DOG?!
Pant
Pant
PLEASE... READ THIS LETTER.
ドキ
ドキ
CHOMP

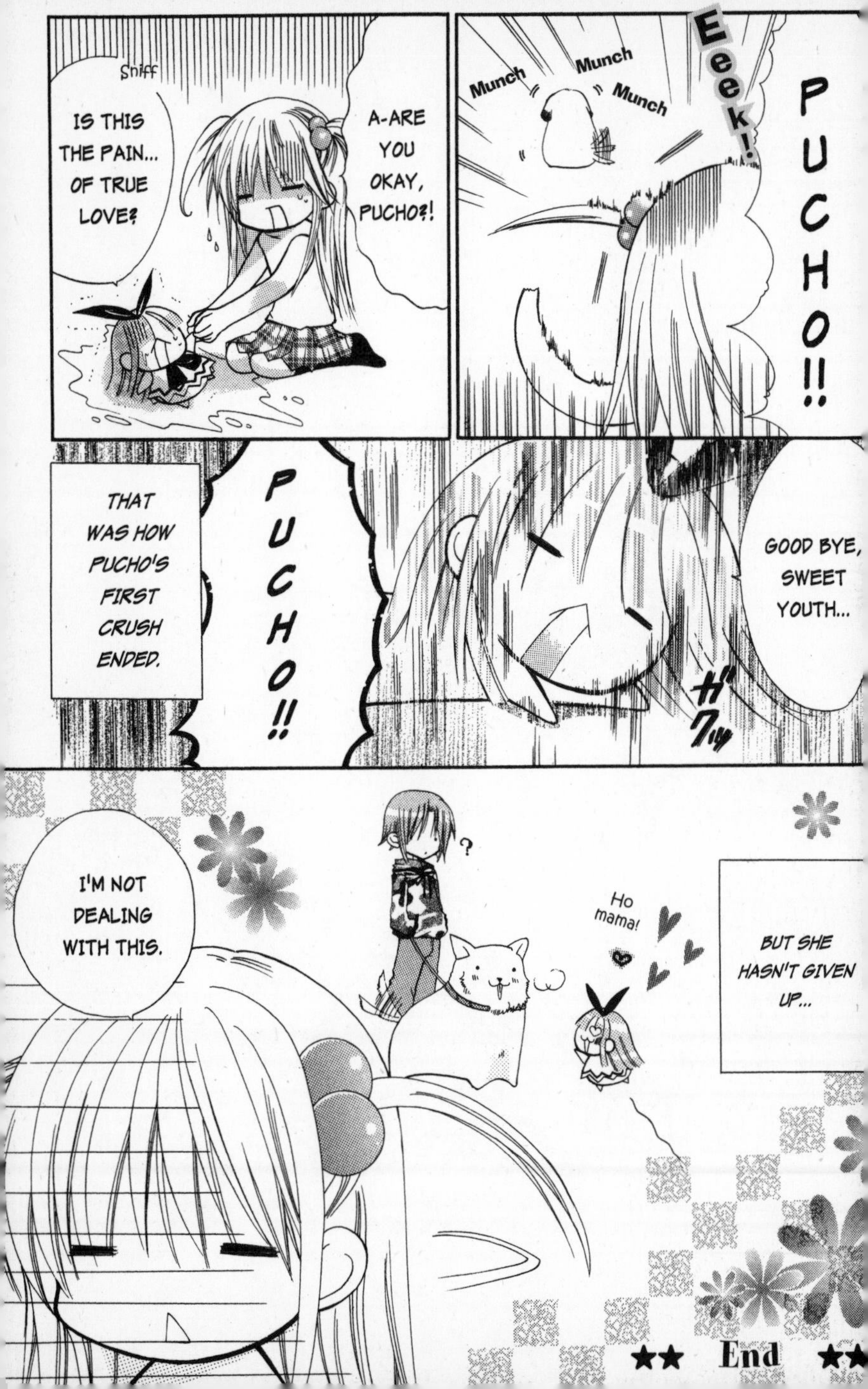
Munch
Munch
Munch
Eeek!
PUCHO!!
A-ARE YOU OKAY, PUCHO?!
Sniff
IS THIS THE PAIN... OF TRUE LOVE?
GOOD BYE, SWEET YOUTH...
ガブッ
PUCHO!!
THAT WAS HOW PUCHO'S FIRST CRUSH ENDED.
BUT SHE HASN'T GIVEN UP...
Ho mama!
?
I'M NOT DEALING WITH THIS.
★★ End ★★

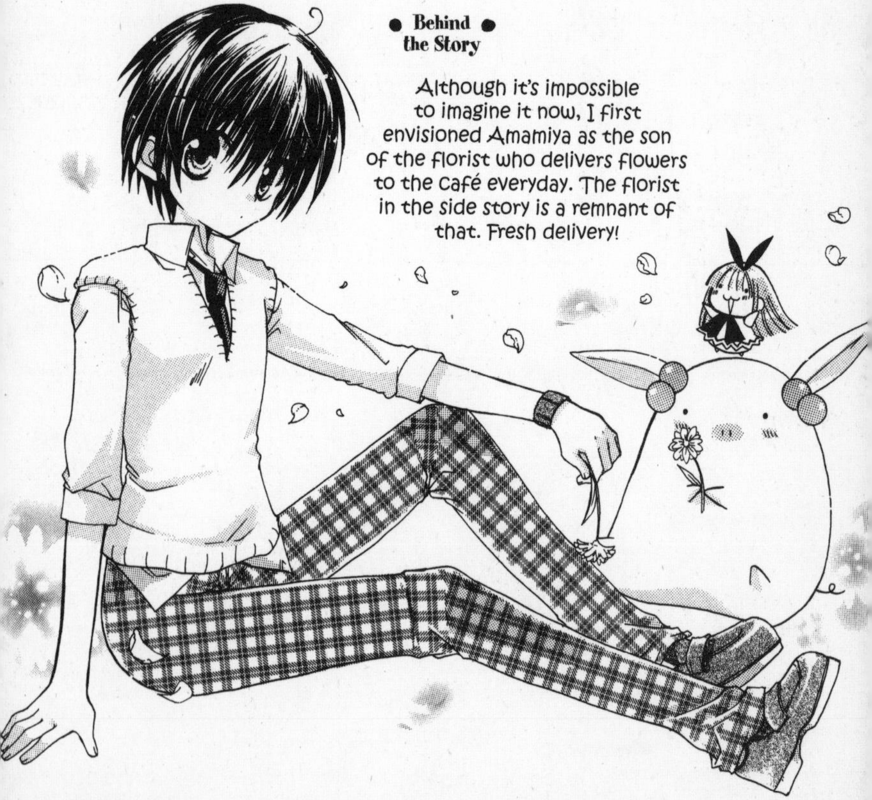
Behind the Story
Although it's impossible to imagine it now, I first envisioned Amamiya as the son of the florist who delivers flowers to the café everyday. The florist in the side story is a remnant of that. Fresh delivery!

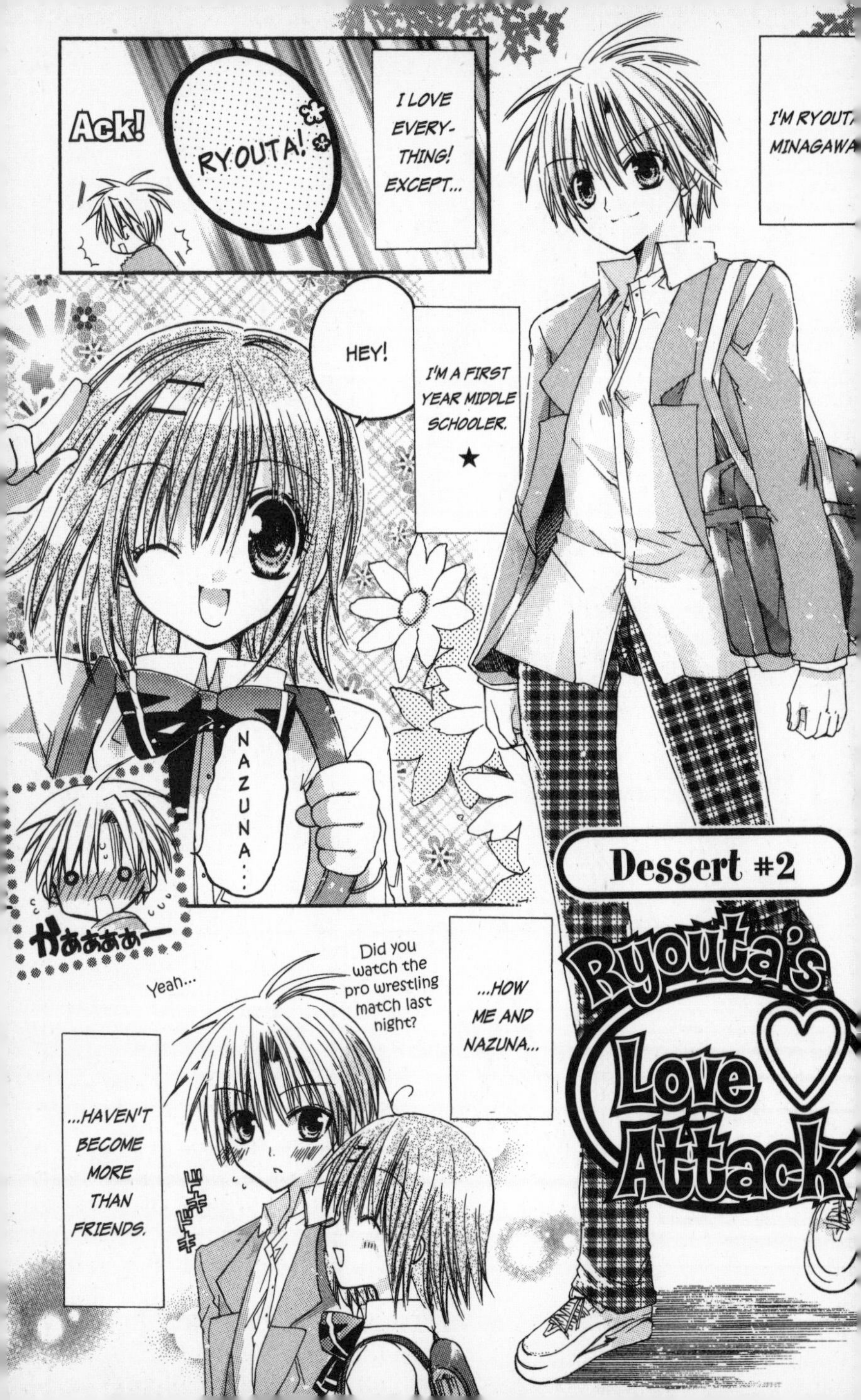

I'M RYOUT
MINAGAWA
I'M A FIRST YEAR MIDDLE SCHOOLER. ★
I LOVE EVERY-THING! EXCEPT...
RYOUTA!
Ack!
HEY!
NAZUNA...
かあああああー
Dessert #2
Ryouta's ♡ Love Attack
...HOW ME AND NAZUNA...
Did you watch the pro wrestling match last night?
Yeah...
...HAVEN'T BECOME MORE THAN FRIENDS.
ドキドキ

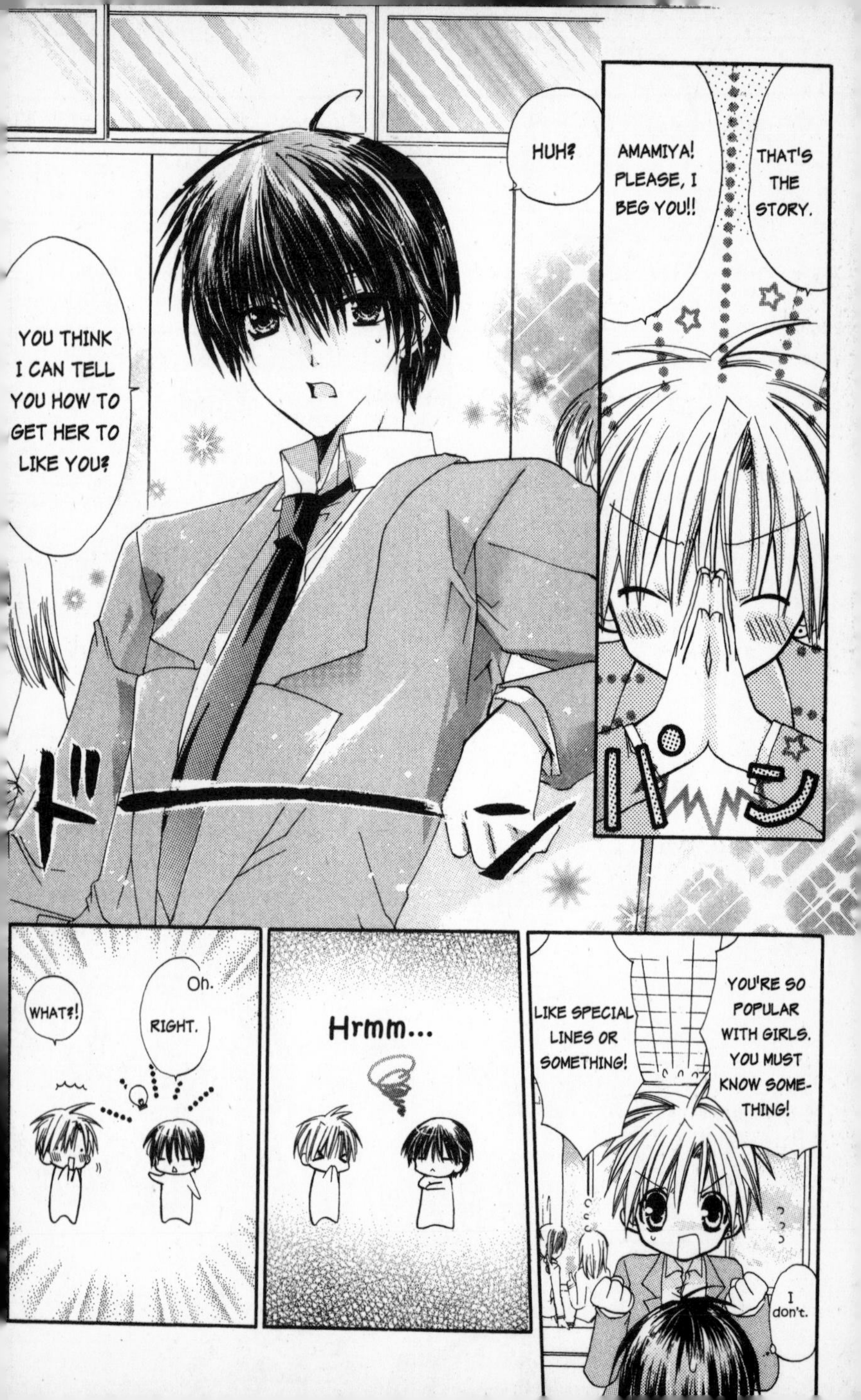
THAT'S THE STORY.
AMAMIYA! PLEASE, I BEG YOU!!
パン
HUH?
YOU THINK I CAN TELL YOU HOW TO GET HER TO LIKE YOU?
ドー
YOU'RE SO POPULAR WITH GIRLS. YOU MUST KNOW SOME-THING!
LIKE SPECIAL LINES OR SOMETHING!
I don't.
Hrmm...
Oh. RIGHT.
WHAT?!

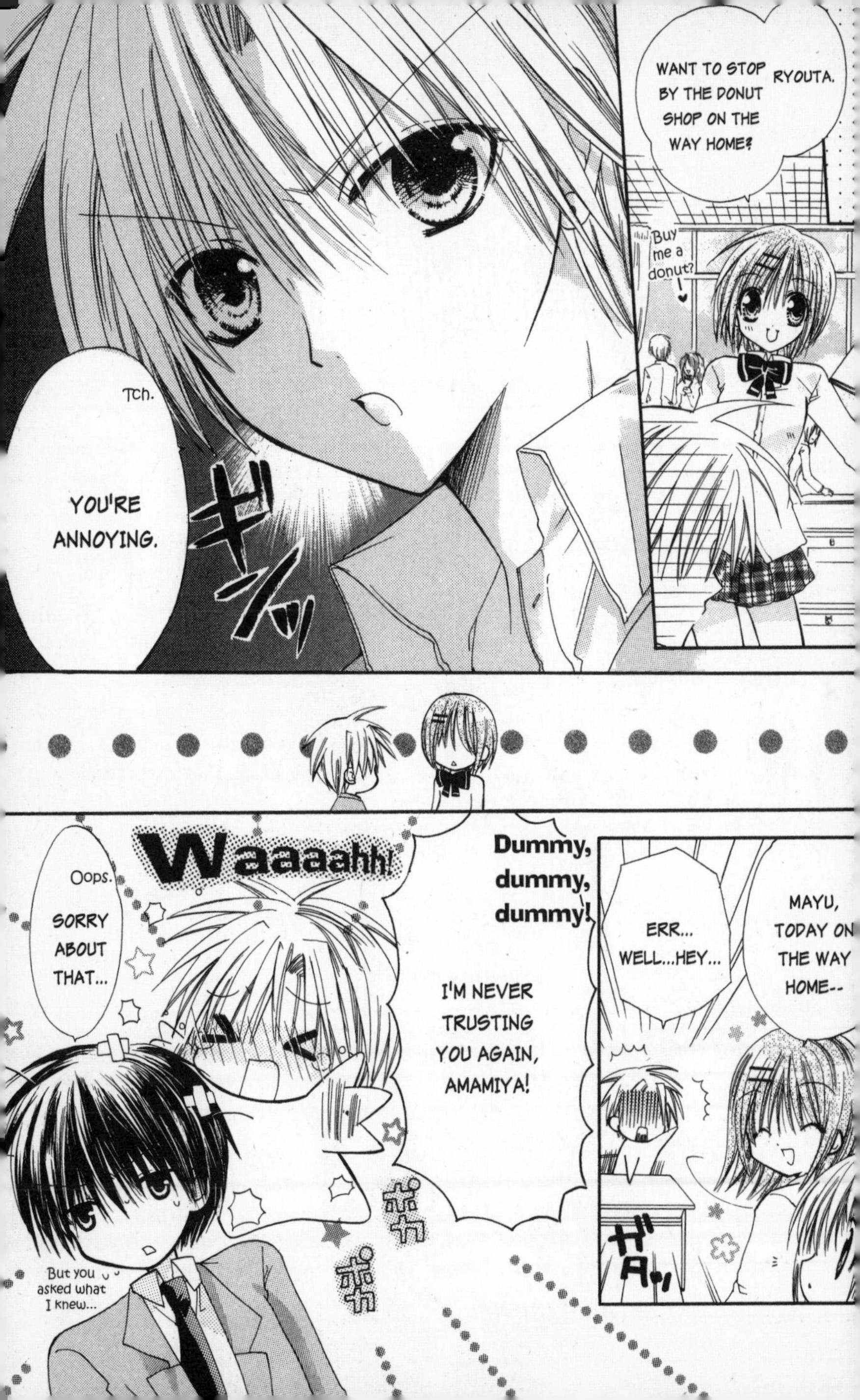
RYOUTA.
WANT TO STOP BY THE DONUT SHOP ON THE WAY HOME?
Buy me a donut? ♥
Tch.
YOU'RE ANNOYING.
MAYU, TODAY ON THE WAY HOME--
ERR... WELL...HEY...
Dummy, dummy, dummy!
Waaaaahh!
I'M NEVER TRUSTING YOU AGAIN, AMAMIYA!
Oops.
SORRY ABOUT THAT...
But you asked what I knew...

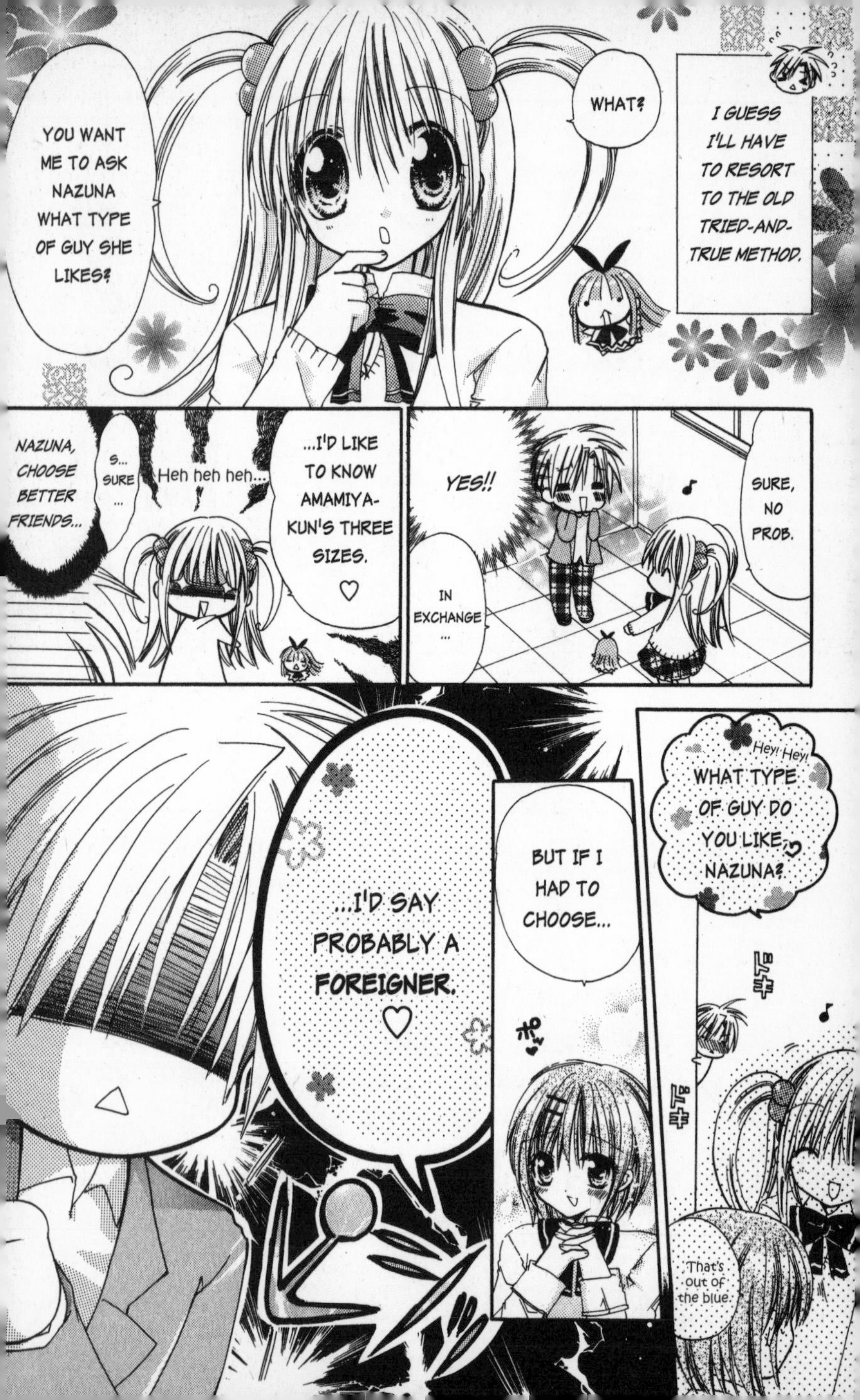
I GUESS I'LL HAVE TO RESORT TO THE OLD TRIED-AND-TRUE METHOD.
WHAT?
YOU WANT ME TO ASK NAZUNA WHAT TYPE OF GUY SHE LIKES?
SURE, NO PROB.
YES!!
IN EXCHANGE...
...I'D LIKE TO KNOW AMAMIYA-KUN'S THREE SIZES. ♡
Heh heh heh...
S... SURE...
NAZUNA, CHOOSE BETTER FRIENDS...
Hey! Hey!
WHAT TYPE OF GUY DO YOU LIKE, NAZUNA? ♡
ドキ
ドキ
That's out of the blue.
BUT IF I HAD TO CHOOSE...
ポッ
...I'D SAY PROBABLY A FOREIGNER. ♡

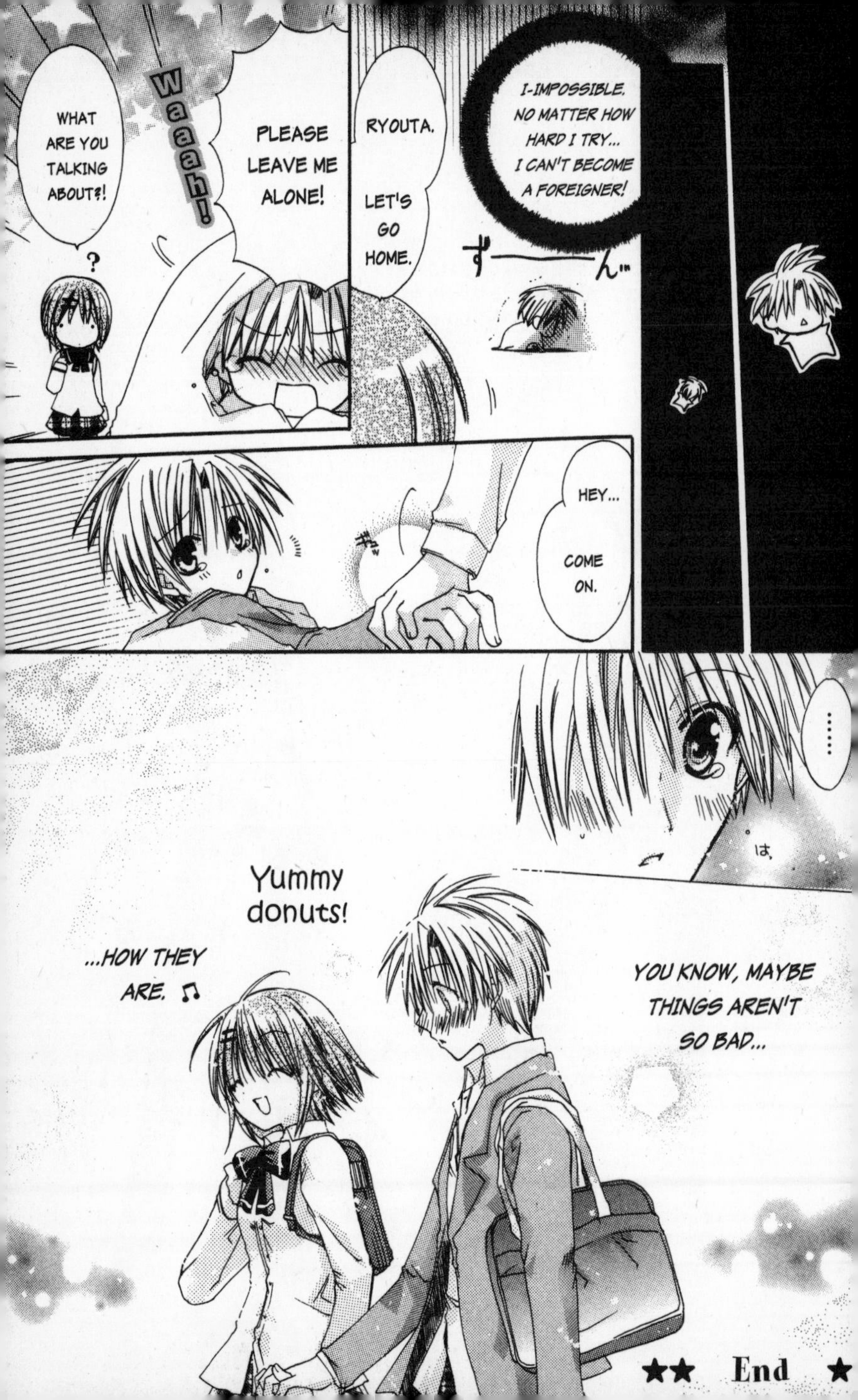
I-IMPOSSIBLE. NO MATTER HOW HARD I TRY... I CAN'T BECOME A FOREIGNER!
ずーーーん
RYOUTA.
LET'S GO HOME.
PLEASE LEAVE ME ALONE!
Waaah!
WHAT ARE YOU TALKING ABOUT?!
?
HEY...
COME ON.
......
は
YOU KNOW, MAYBE THINGS AREN'T SO BAD...
Yummy donuts!
...HOW THEY ARE. ♫
★★ End ★

Cafe Clover

Thank you so much for reading all the way through. Did you enjoy it? If you're the kind of reader that gets excited along with the characters, then you're my favorite kind of reader! It was a lot of fun for me to draw the bonus stories. ♪ Please give me your feedback. 'Til volume 2! ♥ Bow... ♪

2004 XX Ema Toyama

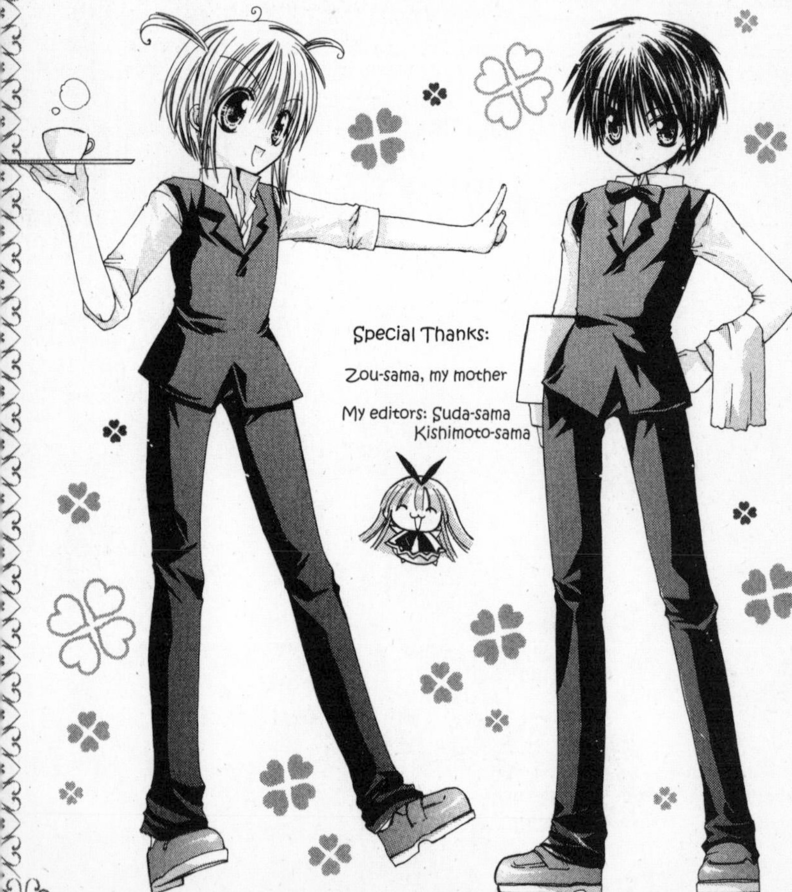

Special Thanks:

Zou-sama, my mother

My editors: Suda-sama
Kishimoto-sama

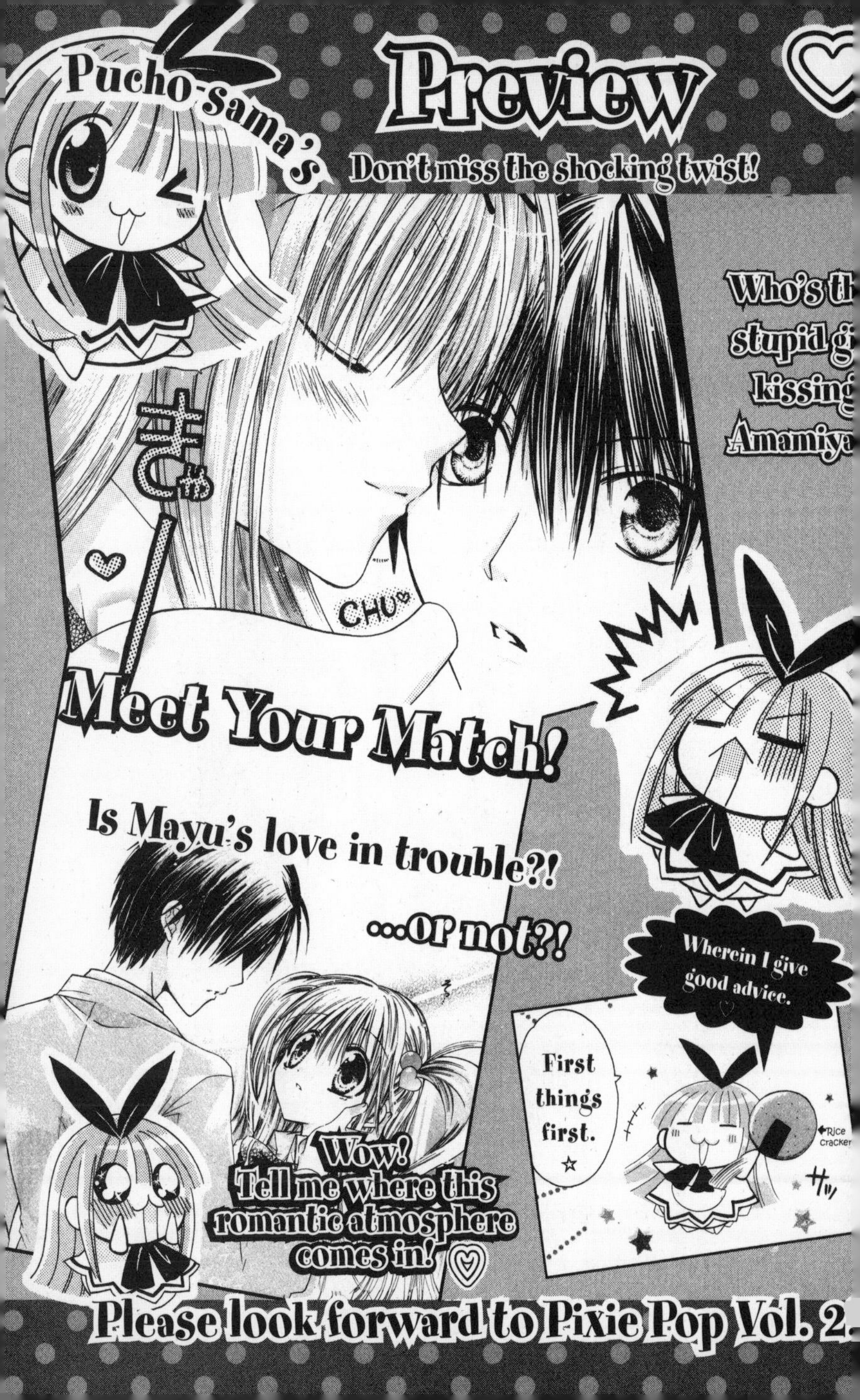
Pucho-Sama's
Preview
Don't miss the shocking twist!
Who's th
stupid g
kissing
Amamiya
CHU
Meet Your Match!
Is Mayu's love in trouble?!
...or not?!
Wherein I give good advice.
First things first.
Rice cracker
Wow! Tell me where this romantic atmosphere comes in!
Please look forward to Pixie Pop Vol. 2.

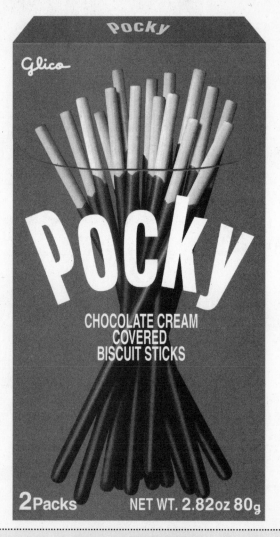

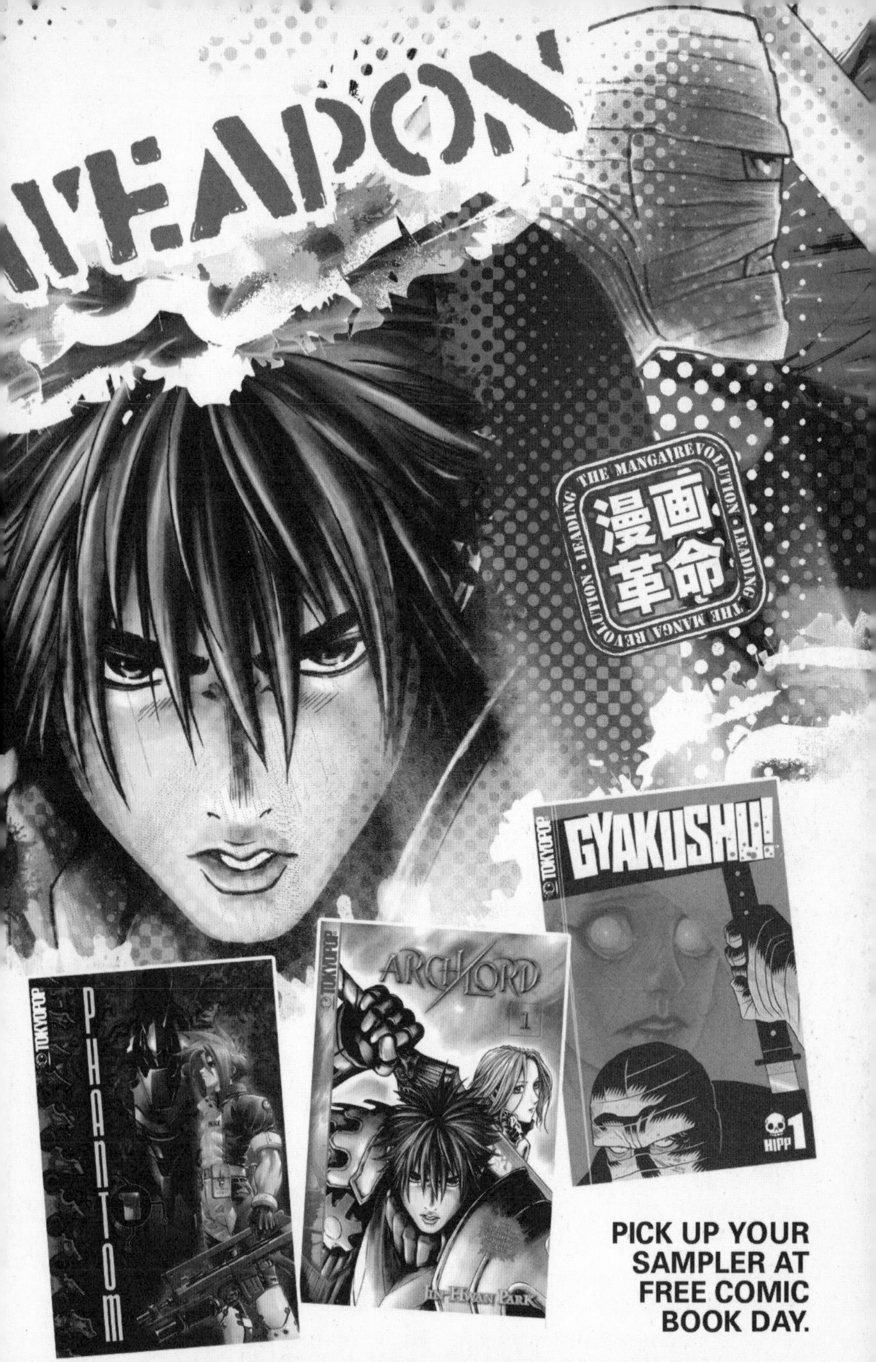
LEADING THE MANGA REVOLUTION
漫画革命
TOKYOPOP
GYAKUSHU!
HIPP 1
TOKYOPOP
ARCHLORD
1
JIN-HWAN PARK
TOKYOPOP
PHANTOM
PICK UP YOUR SAMPLER AT FREE COMIC BOOK DAY.

STOP!

This is the back of the book.
You wouldn't want to spoil a great ending!

This book is printed "manga-style," in the authentic Japanese right-to-left format. Since none of the artwork has been flipped or altered, readers get to experience the story just as the creator intended. You've been asking for it, so TOKYOPOP® delivered: authentic, hot-off-the-press, and far more fun!

DIRECTIONS

If this is your first time reading manga-style, here's a quick guide to help you understand how it works.

It's easy... just start in the top right panel and follow the numbers. Have fun, and look for more 100% authentic manga from TOKYOPOP®!